D1738246

CONTEXTUALIZING SECESSION

Contextualizing Secession

Normative Studies in Comparative Perspective

Edited by

Bruno Coppieters and Richard Sakwa

OXFORD
UNIVERSITY PRESS

OXFORD
UNIVERSITY PRESS

Great Clarendon Street, Oxford OX2 6DP

Oxford University Press is a department of the University of Oxford.
It furthers the University's objective of excellence in research, scholarship,
and education by publishing worldwide in

Oxford New York

Auckland Bangkok Buenos Aires Cape Town Chennai
Dar es Salaam Delhi Hong Kong Istanbul Karachi Kolkata
Kuala Lumpur Madrid Melbourne Mexico City Mumbai Nairobi
São Paulo Shanghai Taipei Tokyo Toronto

Oxford is a registered trade mark of Oxford University Press
in the UK and in certain other countries

Published in the United States
by Oxford University Press Inc., New York

British Library Cataloguing in Publication Data

Data available

Library of Congress Cataloging in Publication Data

Data available

ISBN 0–19–925871–6

1 3 5 7 9 10 8 6 4 2

Typeset by Newgen Imaging Systems (P) Ltd., Chennai, India
Printed in Great Britain
on acid-free paper by
Biddles Ltd., Guildford and King's Lynn

Acknowledgements

The contributions to this volume were first discussed at a conference that took place in Leuven on 5 and 6 May 2000, but since then they have been thoroughly revised and updated. We would like to thank Frank Delmartino from the Institute for European Policy of the Katholieke Universiteit Leuven, who co-organized the Leuven conference with the Department of Political Science of the Vrije Universiteit Brussel (VUB). Michel Huysseune also provided invaluable help in preparing the conference, and we are most grateful to him for support and helpful criticism throughout the time this project has been taking shape. The Flemish Community provided financial support for a research programme on secession, which made our book project possible. Additional financial resources were provided by VUB. Our sincerest gratitude goes to Veronica Kelly, who has patiently taken care of all the language corrections and who throughout has helped ensure clarity of expression and presentation. Thanks are also due to Tom Chandler for the final copy editing. The book has greatly benefited from the constructive criticism of two anonymous reviewers, whom we thank for their efforts. Finally, we would like to extend our gratitude to Dominic Byatt and Alison Heard at Oxford University Press for their encouragement.

B.C., R.S.

Contents

Notes on Contributors

Bruno Coppieters is Associate Professor and Head of the Department of Political Science of the Vrije Universiteit Brussel. Recent publications include: *Federalism and Conflict in the Caucasus* (London, Royal Institute of International Affairs, 2001), and as a co-editor with Nick Fotion, *Moral Constraints on War: Principles and Cases* (Lanham, Md., Lexington Books, 2002).

Raymond Detrez is Professor of Eastern European and Modern Greek History at the University of Ghent. He has published books and articles on Balkan history, minorities policy, and nationalism in south-eastern Europe. His recent publications include *Historical Dictionary of the Republic of Bulgaria* (Metuchen, NJ, and London, The Scarecrow Press Inc., 1997), and *Kosovo: De uitgestelde oorlog* (Antwerp, Hadewych, 1998).

Michel Huysseune is a senior researcher at the Department of Political Science at the Vrije Universiteit Brussel. He has published numerous articles on the political, social, and cultural aspects of intellectual discourse. He is preparing a book on the intellectual and academic debates provoked by the emergence of the Lega Nord in Italy. On this subject he has published 'Putnam interpreteren vanuit een Italiaanse context', *Tijdschrift voor Sociologie*, 20:3–4 (1999), and 'Masculinity and Secessionism in Italy: an Assessment', *Nations and Nationalism*, 6:4 (2000).

Richard Kearney is Professor of Philosophy at University College Dublin and Boston College. He is author of several books on political thought and European philosophy, including *Reimagining Ireland* (Dublin, Wolfhound Press, 2001), *On Stories* (London and New York, Routledge, 2001), and *Postnationalist Ireland* (London and New York, Routledge, 1997). He was involved in several presentations to the Commission on Northern Ireland, including papers on joint sovereignty and the British–Irish Council.

Gunter Lauwers is a teaching assistant in the Department of Political Science at the Vrije Universiteit Brussel. He is preparing a doctoral dissertation on the emergence of ethno-terrorism in Corsica. Recent publications include (with Stefaan Smis), 'New Dimensions of the Right to Self-Determination: A Study of the International Response to the Kosovo Crisis', *Nationalism and Ethnic Politics*, 6:2 (2000).

Ronald Rudin is Professor of History at Concordia University in Montreal, Quebec, Canada. His fields of research are the history of Quebec, the history of Ireland, the social and political implications of historical writing, and commemoration and historical memory. His recent publications include, *Making History in Twentieth-Century Quebec* (Toronto, University of Toronto Press, 1997), and 'On Difference and National Identity in Quebec Historical Writing', *Canadian Historical Review*, 80 (1999).

Richard Sakwa is Professor of Russian and European Politics at the University of Kent at Canterbury. His recent publications include *Russian Politics and Society* (London and New York, Routledge, 1993; 2nd edn. 1996; 3rd edn. 2002), *Postcommunism* (Buckingham, Open University Press, 1999), *The Rise and Fall of the Soviet Union, 1917–1991* (London and New York, Routledge, 1999), and *Contemporary Europe* (Basingstoke and London, Macmillan, 2000) (co-edited with Anne Stevens). His current research interests focus on problems of democratic development and the state in Russia, the nature of post-communism, and the global challenges facing the former communist countries.

Xiaokun Song is a researcher at the Department for Political Science, Vrije Universiteit Brussel. She is preparing a Ph.D. on the transformation of national identity in Taiwan. Her recent publications include 'Confederalism: A Review of Recent Literature', in Bruno Coppieters, David Darchiashvili, and Natella Akaba (eds.), *Federal Practice: Exploring Alternatives for Georgia and Abkhazia* (Brussels, VUB University Press, 2000), and 'Thinking Federal: the Relevance of Federalism to China', *Regional and Federal Studies*, 10:3.

Nathalie Tocci is a Ph.D. candidate at the London School of Economics and a research fellow at the Centre for European Policy Studies. Her recent publications include 'Power or Policy: A Comparative Study of the Cohesion of Italian Coalition Governments in the First and Second Republics', *Journal of Modern Italian Studies*, 5:1 (2000), and with Michael Emerson and Sergiu Celac, 'A Stability Pact for the Caucasus' (Brussels, CEPS Publications, May 2000), published electronically at the address http://www.ceps.be/

Alexei Zverev is a graduate of the Moscow Foreign Languages Institute and has completed a Masters programme in European Politics, Cultures, and Society at the Vrije Universiteit Brussel. His recent publications include 'The Value of the Tatarstan Experience for Georgia and Abkhazia', in Bruno Coppieters, David Darchiashvili, and Natella Akaba (eds.), *Federal Practice: Exploring Alternatives for Georgia and Abkhazia* (Brussels, VUB University Press, 2000). He co-edited (with Bruno Coppieters and Dmitri Trenin) *Commonwealth and Independence in Post-Soviet Eurasia* (London, Frank Cass, 1998).

1

Introduction

Bruno Coppieters

In the world today there are roughly 190 sovereign states. This number has increased significantly since the beginning of the twentieth century, when only some fifty or so had been acknowledged. The number rose to seventy-five before World War II, and by 1979 there were over 150. Many of the new-comers in the second half of the last century were former colonies.[1] The number of independent states increased fourfold over the twentieth century, and it may grow considerably in the coming decades. Several potential states are already at various stages of secession in Asia and Europe, particularly in the Caucasus and the Balkans. On what basis should some of these putative states join the community of nations, and others not? What guiding principles should be used in designing constitutional rules for secession, or institutional alternatives to independence? Can democracy, federalism, and minority rights help in finding the right balance between the principle of national self-determination and the right of states to territorial integrity? These questions and others are addressed in this book, which deals with the fate of Abkhazia, Chechnya, Corsica, Cyprus, Italy, Northern Ireland, Tatarstan, Quebec, Taiwan, Bosnia and Herzegovina, Kosovo, and Montenegro—which are the scene of only a few of the secessionist crises being played out in the world today. We have chosen these as case studies not because they are repre-sentative—this would be impossible, since each individual example of a seces-sionist movement is unique—but because they illustrate some of the broader theoretical and normative problems we wish to discuss.

The problems raised by secession have led to an intensive theoret-ical debate on its normative aspects.[2] The themes addressed in these

---

[1] James Crawford, *The Creation of States in International Law* (Oxford, Clarendon Press, 1979), 3; Alan James, 'The Practice of Sovereign Statehood in Contemporary International Society', in Robert Jackson (ed.), *Sovereignty at the Millennium* (Oxford, Blackwell, 1999), 42.

[2] e.g. Lee C. Buchheit, *Secession: The Legitimacy of Self-Determination* (New Haven, Yale University Press, 1978); Harry Beran, 'A Liberal Theory of Secession', *Political Studies* 32 (1984), 21–31; Allen Buchanan, *Secession. The Morality of Political Divorce from Fort Sumter to Lithuania and Quebec* (Boulder, Colo., San Francisco, and Oxford, Westview Press, 1991); Margaret Moore (ed.), *National Self-Determination and Secession* (Oxford, Oxford University Press, 1998); Percy B. Lehning (ed.), *Theories of Secession* (London, Routledge, 1998).

discussions are diverse. The legitimizing value of the principle of national self-determination and the circumstances in which a unilateral right to secession may be justified constitutes one topic of discussion. The meaning of 'self' in defining this principle is addressed in the literature on the ethnic and civic dimensions of state- and nation-building.[3] The sovereignty debate—a third issue in normative studies on secession—deals with the significance of the core characteristics of statehood and their transformation in a globalizing world.

The exploration of these three themes is divided into specific traditions of normative analysis, yet they all remain closely interrelated. The moral conditions for the exercise of the right to secession, the definition of self in the principle of self-determination and the debate about whether sovereignty is and will remain the cornerstone of the international order are common concerns of authors dealing with secession. While these three themes are most prominent in the literature on the ethics of secession, others have been excluded. The most important of these issues is the legitimacy of the use of force in achieving independent statehood. The just war tradition, which deals with the moral justification for and constraints on warfare, remains remarkably isolated from mainstream secessionist studies. Despite the fact that so many secessionist conflicts turn violent, and despite the fact that similar moral arguments are found in debates on the legitimacy of secession and in those on the justification of the use of force, the ethics of secession and the ethics of war are entirely separate fields of research—a compartmentalization that has impeded the fruitful interchange of ideas between the two ethical traditions. This book aims to link the two forms of ethical thinking: a fourth theme that will be explored here is thus the relevance of just war theory to normative discussions on secession.

A further characteristic of normative studies on secession is the preponderance of deductive reasoning. Authors discuss the relevance, meaning, and relative weight of particular principles that are used in making a judgement

---

[3] On the ethnic/civic distinction see Nicholas Xenos, 'Civic Nationalism: Oxymoron?', in *Critical Review* 10:2 (1996), 213–31; Bernard Yack, 'The Myth of a Civic Nation', in Ronald Beiner (ed.), *Theorizing Nationalism* (New York, State University of New York Press, 1999), 103–18; Kai Nielsen, 'Cultural Nationalism, Neither Ethnic nor Civic', in ibid. 119–30; Rogers Brubaker, 'Myths and Misconceptions in the Study of Nationalism', in Moore, *National Self-Determination and Secession*, 233–65; Michel Seymour, Jocelyne Couture, and Kai Nielsen, 'Introduction: Questioning the Ethnic/Civic Dichotomy', in Jocelyne Couture, Kai Nielsen, and Michel Seymour (eds.), *Rethinking Nationalism* (Calgary, University of Calgary Press, 1996), 1–61; Dominique Schnapper, 'Beyond the Opposition: Civic Nation versus Ethnic Nation', in ibid. 219–34; David Brown, *Contemporary Nationalism: Civic, Ethnocultural and Multicultural Politics* (London and New York, Routledge, 2000); Rogers Brubaker, 'The Manichean Myth: Rethinking the Distinction between "Civic" and "Ethnic" Nationalism', in Hanspeter Kriesi, Klaus Armingeon, Hannes Siegrist, and Andreas Wimmer (eds.), *Nation and National Identity. The European Experience in Perspective* (Zurich, Verlag Rüegger, 1999), 55–71.

on secession. This particular style and method of political philosophy has made the strongest imprint on current discussions, even though scholars from disciplines other than philosophy have been involved. Developments in applied ethics and the relevance for normative analysis of disciplines such as history, comparative federalism, and security studies have been insufficiently brought to the fore.

The present volume is based on an alternative path of research, which tries to overcome the two problems of compartmentalization and abstract deduction. This approach is based on contextualizing the debate on secession. Each contribution explores the various normative aspects of one particular case. In the light of these empirical studies, the authors examine the strengths and weaknesses of the different normative approaches currently to be found in the literature on secession. A contextualization of the principles necessarily shifts the focus of research from political philosophy to history, international law, and the social sciences, without, however, neglecting the relevance of philosophical discussions.

This broadening of the field of research through contextualization affects the analysis of conflict dynamics in individual cases and the assessment of the feasibility of alternatives to independence. These two subjects are central to this volume. The grievances voiced by secessionists include political oppression (which may vary from the denial of representation or participation in state structures to threats of genocide), past injustices, and economic or cultural discrimination. The contributions here examine the extent to which such grievances are valid in a particular case, and what remedies may lead to their resolution. The potential for reform of the state is one of the main elements in any assessment of the feasibility of alternatives to the last resort solution—independence—for those seeking a change in their status.

The extent to which a contextualized approach may open up new avenues of research for secession studies has to be examined for each of the four themes outlined above. The conditions under which unilateral secession may be considered legitimate is the main theme in normative secession studies. It also attracts the most attention in the present introduction. It will be shown here that a contextualized approach requires, among other things, a more differentiated approach to the concept of secession itself. A distinction will therefore be made between the meanings of the terms 'secession', 'secessionist movement', and 'secessionist process'. This introduction will then address the general problems arising from the contextualization of the ideal-type distinction between a civic and an ethnic conception of the state and the nation. Finally, it will examine how the question of sovereignty in a secessionist process, and the problem of the moral justification of wars of secession, may be contextualized.

SECESSION, SECESSIONIST MOVEMENTS, AND SECESSIONIST PROCESSES

Conceptual tools need to be specially chosen and refined for our purposes. The first level of differentiation concerns the concepts of secession, secessionist movement and secessionist process.[4] By secession we mean withdrawal from a state or society through the constitution of a new sovereign and independent state. Here secession has a clear-cut meaning. Thus, by 'the right to secession' we mean the right to constitute a new, independent state. We do not associate this expression with the right to live under other forms of self-government, such as in an autonomous region or in a federation.

A 'secessionist movement' is harder to define than the term 'secession', insofar as we are confronted with the difficulty of verifying the precise intentions of the leadership of such movements. Autonomy or a federal or confederal status is written into the programmes of many political movements, which may under certain conditions be described as secessionist. These objectives are often regarded by the movements themselves as an intermediate stage on the path to full independence. To take an example from the contributions to this volume, this was the case with the Abkhaz political leadership, which had advocated a confederal solution to the Georgian—Abkhaz conflict from the beginning of the 1990s, before proclaiming independence in 1999.

By contrast with the notions of 'secession' and 'secessionist movement', the term 'secessionist process' refers to a series of graduated actions or events directed towards (although not necessarily leading to) the withdrawal of an area from the aegis of a central government. Its forms may vary widely. Decentralization, the creation of an autonomous political unit through devolution, and federalization may all be seen as different stages in a secessionist process, which may or may not result in full independence. All these institutional forms may be seen as alternatives to secession which aim to take the edge off a secessionist drive. They may also be seen as stepping-stones leading to the radicalization of a secessionist conflict, and eventually to independence. It makes no sense, however, to describe the creation of autonomies or federalization as part of a secessionist process in cases where independence is not at stake in the political debate. This means that it is meaningful to speak about a secessionist process in the cases of Belgium, Spain, and the United Kingdom, but not in the case of the Federal Republic of Germany. Unlike the term 'secessionist movement', the term 'secessionist

---

[4] On the following see also Bruno Coppieters, Ivan Myhul, and Michel Huysseune, 'Introduction' to Bruno Coppieters and Michel Huysseune (eds.), *Secession, History and the Social Sciences* (Brussels, VUB University Press, 2002), 19–20, on the internet on http://poli.vub.ac.be.

process' thus does not refer to the intentions of the players involved, but rather to the consequences of their actions and to the institutional devices constructed over time.

Confronted with the impossibility of predicting the long-term consequences of federalization processes and other remedies for nationality conflicts, it is necessary to use not only a broad definition of a secessionist process—whose various stages may include both external and internal ways of exercising the right to national self-determination—but also a time-frame where choices are made in periods that may encompass several generations. For the political consequences of particular institutional choices may only become apparent over such long periods, and the principles morally relevant to the debate may then shift. Such long time-spans may even be part of the perspective of a particular political strategy. This has been expressed by the Tatar author Zufar Fatkutdinov: 'The patience of a nation is measured in centuries.'[5] The strategies of Flemish, Catalan, Basque, and Scottish nationalists, which count on the long-term erosion of the competences of the national state in a future 'Europe of the regions', are based on the knowledge that state-building is generally not the work of a single political generation.

Broadening the meaning of the term 'secessionist process' and the timeframe for its analysis makes it possible to extend the scope of the debate from a simple acceptance or rejection of secessionist claims to a differentiated discussion of feasible options. This may encompass a discussion of steps in constitutional reform that stop short of self-governance: for example, the present volume includes a contribution by Gunter Lauwers on the French debate on a limited form of autonomy for Corsica. However limited this reform may be, in comparison with regionalist developments in other European Union member states the long-term consequences of this discussion, and the modification of the traditional French republican (Jacobin) interpretation of the nation and national sovereignty as being one and indivisible, should not be underestimated.

THE NORMATIVE DEBATE ON SECESSION

While the need for a comprehensive normative framework for judging secessionist claims is often highlighted, the nature of the principles that should inform such a framework remain controversial. Secession studies deal with a number of questions, foremost among them being the extent to

[5] Zufar Fatkutdinov, 'Terpenie naroda izmeryaetsya stoletiyami', *Idel* 11–12 (1995), 20–3, quoted in Alexei Zverev ' "The Patience of a Nation is Measured in Centuries": National Revival in Tatarstan and Historiography', in Coppieters and Huysseune, *Secession, History and the Social Sciences*, 70.

which the ethics of secession should be based on the principle of self-
determination (Daniel Philpott),[6] and whether democratic institutions are
more likely to flourish when it is made difficult for a group on a particular
territory to withdraw from it (Allen Buchanan). In the present debate on
the legitimacy of unilateral declarations of secession there are two main
currents, which offer different answers to the above questions. The first is
the *choice* approach, which assumes the universal validity of the right to
self-determination and maintains that, under certain conditions, any group
aspiring to it has the right to claim a separate political identity up to and
including independence. According to this school of thought, which follows
the liberal 'rights' tradition, unilateral secession is a free (albeit strongly
conditioned) choice. Xiaokun Song, in her contribution to this volume, sees
scholars in this school as adopting an *a priori* approach in which the right
to self-determination is rooted in the free choice of the individuals constituting a national community. The principle of self-determination and its
application to concrete cases stem is from the nature of political freedom
itself and is not to be deduced *a posteriori* from concrete experiences in the
history of the nation. But there are formal conditions that must be met when
this right is being exercised. These conditions have to do with the extent to
which the seceding group adheres to democratic rights and values, its
respect for minority rights, whether it has a civic understanding of nation-
building, the lack of better alternatives such as the granting of increased federal rights, and possible compensation for the remainder of the state. These
formal conditions must be fulfilled before it is legitimate to accede to the
wish for independence clearly expressed by the majority of a population.

Scholars belonging to the second current are labelled *just cause*
theorists by Margaret Moore and are regarded by Song as defending an
a posteriori approach. These writers point out the contentious nature of the
principle of national self-determination, and in particular the problematic
meaning of 'self' in this concept. This current, whose most prominent representative is Allen Buchanan, stresses the disruptive nature of secessionist
crises and their generally negative consequences for the individuals and
minorities involved. Although the writers supporting this position frequently share the liberal outlook of the first current, they refuse to recognize
the absolute right to self-determination, and the philosophy of 'choice'
behind it, as an adequate point of departure for formulating a judgement on
secession. They defend the thesis that a verdict on the question can only be
reached after a careful analysis of the experience of living together in a particular state. A number of criteria have to be applied when judging whether,

---

[6] Daniel Philpott, 'Self-Determination in Practice', in Moore, *National Self-Determination
and Secession*, 79–102.

in a concrete historical case, secession may be considered a legitimate outcome of tensions between distinct communities or conflicts. In order to build up a case for secession, cases of flagrant injustice, ranging from deeply entrenched discriminatory policies in the economic and social fields to genocide, would have to be included in a list of grievances. The right of a government to oppose a secessionist movement and to defend the principle of territorial integrity has to be analysed according to the same criteria.

Notwithstanding their contrasting arguments, both currents adopt a remedial approach to secession: it is legitimate only as a last resort. Less radical alternatives have to be explored before a unilateral declaration of independence may be considered acceptable. For a 'choice' theorist such as Philpott, the universal validity of the principle of national self-determination does not necessarily include the right to external self-determination. Other means are available for redressing most well-founded grievances. Philpott concedes that his approach ends up by limiting the number of nations entitled to statehood to an extent similar to that allowed by the normative framework proposed by Buchanan—who belongs to the 'just cause' school. In his own words, he doubts 'that there are many cases to which my own theory would give a green light, but to which Buchanan's would grant a red or yellow light'.[7] In Philpott's view, a federal structure, in which a nation may exercise its right to internal self-determination, should as a rule be quite adequate for satisfying the legitimate claims of secessionists. More moderate forms of conflict management—such as power-sharing or electoral reform—are also considered in all these debates.

Despite the awareness of the writers involved in such discussions that the analysis and application of the principles should be contextualized,[8] concrete cases of secession are generally taken as mere illustrations of logical arguments. Many cases are hypothetical, and therefore have the same status and exemplary value as imaginary tales. The ethics of secession are analysed by describing its consequences for the fate of freedom-seeking people X living in oppressive state Y. This kind of approach, which avoids tackling the innumerable difficulties inherent in the precise description and analysis of a concrete case of secession, does have clear advantages. It makes it possible to clarify the moral debate on secession when discussing the hierarchical order of various legal and philosophical principles and arguments within a systematic framework. There is a need for such a framework, as no analysis of a concrete case can prescribe rules with normative validity across cultures.

---

[7] Philpott, 'Self-Determination in Practice', in Moore, *National Self-Determination and Secession*, 90.

[8] As Margaret Moore states in her Introduction, 'many of the writers in this volume argue that thinking about self-determination should be contextual'. Margaret Moore, 'Introduction' to ibid. 11.

Such an approach, however, may be subject to criticism. To begin with, it entails the risk that the discussion of the general principles and foundations for judging the validity of a right to secession will lack the insights that can be achieved by methods and research results from other disciplines, which also assess demands for and opposition to secession. An interdisciplinary approach would emphasize above all the need for a historical and legal analysis of specific cases. Second, it may be argued that philosophical reflection on the guiding principles applicable in a normative analysis of the legitimacy of secession cannot be made in a way that is entirely abstracted from practical experience. Third, from a consequentialist position, the lack of attention devoted to a comparative analysis of the effects of secession on social cohesion, individual well-being and the institutional coherence of the polity itself may be criticized. In these discussions it can be assumed that precedents do have a certain value for judgements on future cases. Fourth, discussions on secession and its alternatives are part of a problem-solving endeavour, in which a lack of attention to the particular circumstances surrounding each case cannot lead to a reasonable resolution.[9] Fifth, a comparative analysis of the moral considerations relevant to particular circumstances increases our capacity to perceive, discern and assess. This may help us avoid repetition and sterility, which constitute a permanent risk in moral debates on timeless rules for regulating secession.

In the continuing theoretical debate on secession, the moral relevance of the specific features of individual cases is not denied. Some authors even go so far as to argue that the discussion of general principles is now exhausted, and that further progress can only be expected from a contextualized debate.[10] It is precisely the aim of this collective volume to explore the potential of a contextualized normative discussion. A comparative study of moral cases of secession should be seen as complementary to the type of discussion characteristic of current studies of secession. Some of the myriad difficulties surrounding the application of general principles to secession and its alternatives will be analysed. Attention will be paid to the traditional list of questions dealing with the circumstances: 'who, what, where, when, why, how, and by what means?'[11] The contextualization of the normative discussion on secession through a comparative analysis should also lead to a more differentiated approach.

---

[9] For the following discussion we have borrowed arguments in favour of a casuistic approach to questions of practical reasoning, such as just war or medical ethics, from Albert Jonsen and Stephen Toulmin, *The Abuse of Casuistry: A History of Moral Reasoning* (Berkeley, University of California Press, 1988), and Richard B. Miller, *Casuistry and Modern Ethics: A Poetics of Practical Reasoning* (Chicago and London, The University of Chicago Press, 1996), 3–16.

[10] 'The debate over principles has been fruitful. Perhaps it is now time that the social scientists and lawyers take over', Philpott, 'Self-Determination in Practice', 100.

[11] Jonsen and Toulmin, *The Abuse of Casuistry*, 253.

ETHNIC AND CIVIC CONCEPTIONS OF NATIONHOOD

The broadening of the field of research allows traditional themes in ethical debates on secession to be examined from new perspectives. The distinction between an ethnic (or cultural) and a civic understanding of nation- and statehood has been analysed by philosophers in the ethics of nationhood. It has also been used for analytical purposes by historians and social scientists.[12] A civic understanding of the polity has been associated with defining characteristics such as rationalism, voluntarism, universalism, liberalism, an inclusive concept of citizenship and respect for the rights of individuals and minorities. An ethnic understanding of the polity has, by contrast, been associated with defining characteristics such as romanticism, nationalism, particularism, an exclusive concept of citizenship, and the historic rights of a national group over a particular territory. Literature on nationhood in general and on secession in particular is clearly dominated by authors who formulate judgements with the help of 'civic' notions of policy-making. But a normatively nuanced use of this opposition is also to be found in literature on particular national identities.

The opposition between an ethnic and a civic type of nationhood is, of course, not necessarily used to formulate moral judgements. In Rogers Brubaker's research on the French and German conceptions of the state, the nation, and citizenship, this opposition is considered to constitute a difference of degree and not one of inner principle. Brubaker argues against Manichean views whereby the ethnic representation of a political community is seen as 'faulty' and civic conceptions as 'ideal'.[13] Avoiding the caricature is not easy. In one of his later writings, Brubaker concedes that the traditional opposition between a civic and an ethnic understanding of nationhood does have some analytical and normative merits, but points out that using it in practice is extremely problematic.[14] This is due primarily to the unclear meaning of the terms 'ethnic' and 'cultural nationalism': they are defined either too narrowly (when identified with an understanding of nationhood that emphasizes common descent), or too broadly (when identified with political culture at large). In the latter case, a cultural understanding of

---

[12] On the following see Bruno Coppieters, 'Ethno-Federalism and Civic State-Building Policies. Perspectives on the Georgian—Abkhaz Conflict', in *Regional and Federal Studies* 11:2 (2001), 72–3.

[13] Rogers Brubaker, *Citizenship and Nationhood in France and Germany* (Cambridge, Mass., Harvard University Press, 1992), 2–3; Bernard Yack, 'The Myth of the Civic Nation', *Critical Review* 10:2 (1996), 193–211; Brubaker, 'The Manichean Myth', 55–71.

[14] On the following, see Rogers Brubaker, 'Myths and Misconceptions in the Study of Nationalism', in Moore, *National Self-Determination and Secession*, 257–60.

nationhood would even include France and the United States—which count
as paradigmatic models of civic nationalism. Because of this analytical
weakness, Brubaker favours the application of another type of distinction—
that between a conception of the nation that is congruent with the state and
one that is conceived in opposition to an existing state or states—which
would allow a more differentiated approach to concrete realities.

Two problems referred to in this discussion are relevant for normative
studies on secession. In this context a distinction has to be made between
the use of the civic/ethnic dichotomy as a conceptual tool for making moral
judgements and its use as a conceptual tool for gaining a better understanding of secessionist movements and processes. The first problem is that
of method in the use of ideal types in the social sciences, such as an ethnic
and a civic understanding of nationhood, and whether this method is also
relevant for a moral use of this distinction. The second problem deals with
the question whether normative studies should abandon the civic/ethnic
dichotomy in favour of other kinds of distinctions, as proposed by Rogers
Brubaker for studies not having a moral judgement as their purpose.

Max Weber's methodological writings on ideal types are relevant in this
context, even though they do not deal with the ethnic/civic distinction.[15] In
his view, ideal types do not make it possible to subsume social reality under
particular concepts, as is the case with conceptual schemes constructed
according to the principle of 'genus proximum, differentia specifica'.[16] This
Aristotelian principle allows the classification of objects according to a specific difference (*differentia specifica*), which distinguishes them from closely
related objects that are subsumed under a more general concept (*genus
proximum*). This hierarchical principle, according to which concepts of a
lower order are subsumed under concepts of a higher order, makes it possible to classify phenomena unequivocally under a particular concept. In
Weber's view, this type of classification is suitable only for the natural and not
for the social sciences. Ideal types are based on a different classificatory
approach. They are not to be seen as reflecting reality in themselves, but rather
as useful tools for achieving such an aim. An ideal type is a synthesis of diverse
individual phenomena in which some characteristics are emphasized one-
sidedly. Such an accentuation—or even exaggeration—of particular traits is

[15] On the following see Max Weber, 'Die "Objektivität" sozialwissenschaftlicher Erkenntnis',
in Max Weber, *Schriften zur Wissenschaftslehre*, ed. Michael Sukale (Stuttgart, Philipp Reclam
jr., 1991), 21–101 and 'Der Sinn der Wertfreiheit der soziologischen und ökonomischen
Wissenschaften', ibid. 176–236. See also Talcott Parsons, *The Structure of Social Action* (New
York, The Free Press, 1967), 601–10 and D. Lockwood, 'Ideal-type Analysis', in Julius Gould and
William L. Kolb (eds.), *A Dictionary of the Social Sciences* (New York, The Free Press of Glencoe,
1964), 311–13.
[16] See Michael Sukale, 'Einleitung' in Weber, *Schriften zur Wissenschaftslehre*, 16–17.

useful to the extent that in reality phenomena are found in a confused state. The idealization of particular phenomena, in which they are elevated to form a consistent mental construct or 'type', makes them useful for comparative analysis and systematic scientific purposes. As 'ideas' or utopias, ideal types may be compared with individual phenomena, and historical research may then enquire to what extent ideal types approximate to or diverge from this observation.

This excursus on the utopian character of ideal types is quite relevant to the present discussion on the use of the ethnic/civic distinction. The representation of particular conceptions of nationhood, or even nations, as unequivocal expressions of either civic or ethnic views is based on a mistaken use of ideal types. For Weber, regarding ideal types as being empirically true is generally a sign of the immaturity of a particular scientific discipline.[17] This means that the ethnic/civic dichotomy is a conceptual distinction that is as 'unreal' as any other, and that this is not a reason for abandoning it in favour of other distinctions. Its use does not preclude a high degree of nuance in a descriptive analysis. It may, to use Brubaker's expression, seek to express sensitivity 'not only to the gross features or differing contexts but to finer details as well; it presupposes relatively "thick" understanding of the local contexts in which it is to apply'.[18]

Max Weber considered it impossible to decide *a priori* whether or not particular ideal types should be regarded as fruitful for scientific analysis. Ideal types abstract from different concrete situations according to particular criteria, and the particular kind of abstraction they make may be criticized. Ideal types are intended to help clarify the meaning of particular characteristics of social reality, and their degree of success can only be judged on the basis of scientific results. They are themselves not goals of scientific research, but simple tools to be used in such research. They are not even to be taken as a scientific hypothesis—a proposition about social reality that is empirically verifiable—but merely as facilitating the construction of such a hypothesis. There can be no progress in the social sciences without criticism of existing conceptual tools. The fact that particular ideal types are constantly deconstructed in favour of new ones is even a sign of 'eternal youth'.[19] Seen from this perspective, Brubaker's criticism—that the ethnic/civic dichotomy emphasizes the meaning of cultural characteristics in conceptions of nationhood too vaguely, or even wrongly—and the use of alternative distinctions in order to build up hypotheses, are fully legitimate. It has to be asked, however, whether such a criticism is also valid for the use of the civic/ethnic dichotomy in moral judgements.

---

[17] Weber, 'Die "Objektivität" sozialwissenschaftlicher Erkenntnis', 91.
[18] Brubaker, 'Myths and Misconceptions in the Study of Nationalism', 240.
[19] Weber, 'Die "Objektivität" sozialwissenschaftlicher Erkenntnis', 91–2.

Max Weber has constantly warned against the danger of mixing up the two distinct meanings of an 'idea'. The idealization of phenomena can be aimed either at the construction of conceptual tools for understanding reality or at the construction of moral ideals, taken as meaning 'what something should be'. Only the first type of idealization can properly be regarded as the construction of ideal types.[20] The relationship between moral values and ideal types is a complex one. According to Weber, researchers can work scientifically with ideal types that correspond, oppose or are indifferent to their moral ideals. But in all these cases it remains possible to compare reality with the ideal type in order to gain a better understanding of it.[21]

The ethnic/civic dichotomy can be used as an ideal-type distinction or as a distinction between moral ideals (given that it is also possible to regard an ethnic understanding of nationhood as a 'counter-ideal'). Both approaches are to be found in this volume, and it is important to distinguish between the two forms of usage.[22] The ethnic/civic dichotomy, for instance, is of primary importance in identifying the holder of the right to self-determination. Secessionist movements throughout the world have a very diverse understanding of this problem. Divisions appear even among the leaders of these movements. Some defend a predominantly exclusive and ethnic view, while others have defined or redefined the self on the basis of an inclusive and territorial conception of nation building. The ethnic/civic distinction is also a prominent issue in the implementation of a plebiscitary right to secession. In cases where international organizations such as the United Nations feel that a referendum on secession should take place, they generally defend a territorial conception of the electorate, in which every inhabitant has the right to participate. Some secessionist movements, on the contrary, wish to limit the collective right to decide on the future of a territory to a more limited constituency of its citizens. This problem was central to the disintegration of Yugoslavia, as analysed in this book by Raymond Detrez, and is also a core issue in the public debates on the future of Abkhazia. The ethnic/civic distinction is further present in discussions on the extent to which ethnic conflicts may be mediated through the process of European integration. The idea of Europe is underpinned by an inclusive and multicultural understanding of a civic identity. As will be shown in this volume by Richard Kearney and Nathalie Tocci, the secessionist conflicts analysed by them—concerning the reunification of Ireland and Cyprus, respectively—may cease

---

[20] Weber, 'Die "Objektivität" sozialwissenschaftlicher Erkenntnis', 84.

[21] Weber, 'Der Sinn der Wertfreiheit der soziologischen und ökonomischen Wissenschaften', 230.

[22] The extent to which Max Weber would consider each of them either as scientific or as being beyond the reach of scientific analysis, and to what extent our use of the distinction between ideal types and ideals may properly be considered as 'Weberian', should not concern us in this context.

to be intractable once they are perceived by the political players themselves as being part of the construction of a European institutional framework. For this whole complex of problems to do with the values and norms defended by secessionist movements throughout the world or embedded in national or European institutions, it remains fruitful to use the ethnic/civic distinction as an ideal-type distinction.

Normative studies on secession may also deal in a different way with the ethnic/civic distinction. In this case, an opposition to the ethnic and an identification with the civic view of the nation, on moral grounds, is most common. Such an approach is also to be found in the present volume. The ethnic/civic dichotomy is used in normative frameworks to make a distinction between justified and non-justified claims to secession. A claim that is based on a civic understanding of nationhood is then considered to be more morally justified than one based on an ethnic understanding. A solution to a secessionist crisis that is based on civic ideals—such as the idea of a supranational European level of governance—will also be regarded as more legitimate than one based on the territorial separation of ethnic groups. Such moral approaches do not use the ethnic/civic distinction as an ideal-type distinction, but as a distinction between ideals. But their application will inevitably lead to a comparison between these ideals and reality, for whose understanding ideal types remain important. It may be concluded not only that it is necessary to distinguish between the use of civic and ethnic conceptions of nationhood as ideals (or as an ideal and as a 'counter-ideal' respectively) for formulating moral judgements and their use as ideal types without such a purpose, but also that it is important to stress that both types of use remain closely interrelated in any normative study on secession. It may further be concluded that it would be difficult to formulate a judgement on the legitimacy of secessionist claims with the help of the civic/ethnic distinction if this judgement is based on an analysis of reality that operates primarily with an ideal-type distinction other than the ethnic/civic one.

SOVEREIGNTY

In his introduction to *Leviathan*, Thomas Hobbes aptly characterized sovereignty as the 'artificial soul' of the state.[23] The question as to whether several souls may peacefully coexist in one body politic—and if so, how—is addressed in all the contributions to this volume. This question is at the heart of relations between Tatarstan and Russia, Chechnya and Russia, the Turkish and Greek communities in Cyprus, Taiwan and Mainland China,

---

[23] Thomas Hobbes, *Leviathan*, ed. C. B. Macpherson (Harmondsworth, Middlesex, Penguin Books, 1982), 81.

Abkhazia and Georgia, Corsica and France, and Ireland and Britain (concerning Northern Ireland), and between the various constituent nations and minorities of the former Yugoslavia. The question of how the principle of sovereignty may fit into a multi-tiered political system is further addressed in the contribution on the future of Cyprus in a unified and regionalized Europe.

Hobbes's definition of the principle of sovereignty points both to its theological origins and to the artificial character of the modern state. The capacity of humanity to create and construct social and political mechanisms of peaceful co-existence was at the heart of his writings. But he was sceptical about the possibility of dividing sovereignty artificially among domestic institutions. Nor, in his view, did the creative power of mankind extend to the international system, which was doomed to reproduce an eternal state of nature. Since the publication of *Leviathan*, the thesis that sovereignty is indivisible and that it is impossible to overcome the anarchic nature of interstate relations has been challenged by many other approaches, but it has retained its significance to this day, in particular for the debate on secession. The question of whether sovereignty should still be conceived as being one, indivisible and inalienable, is central to French parliamentary discussions on the devolution of legislative power to the Corsican Assembly, and to the attempt by the Chinese government to apply the formula of 'one country, two systems' in the process of reunification with Taiwan. From the perspective of secessionist movements, the claim to independence is made because it is assumed that sovereignty cannot or should not be shared. The view that sovereignty is ultimately indivisible is also at the heart of proposals for a confederal solution to a secessionist crisis, since a confederation is not one unified state but a union of states, based on treaty-type relations in which the constituent units do not lose their sovereignty. Moreover the sovereignty of the individual member states is then recognized by the international community.[24] The confederal option has been favoured by secessionist movements in Tatarstan, Abkhazia, the Turkish Republic of Northern Cyprus and Taiwan—to take some of the cases analysed in this volume.

The debates about the lasting significance of sovereignty as the core institution in the international order are no less important for secessionist studies than those on the meaning of sovereignty in the domestic order. The thesis of an erosion of—or even an end to—sovereignty in a globalizing world figures most prominently in these debates. An acceptance of this thesis would generally imply diminished significance for the act of secession. It is also used as a forceful argument in attempts to persuade secessionist

---

[24] On the popularity of the confederal model in the post-Soviet world see Bruno Coppieters, *Federalism and Conflict in the Caucasus* (London, The Royal Institute of International Affairs, 2001).

movements to abandon the demand for independence and to accept non-sovereign status within a federal framework. But this view is far from generally accepted. It has been rightly stated that the diminishing importance of sovereignty may only be asserted if this concept is defined as 'interdependence sovereignty'.[25] This particular type of sovereignty refers, in the words of Stephen D. Krasner, 'to the ability of public authorities to regulate the flow of information, ideas, goods, people, pollutants, or capital across the borders of their state'.[26] States have, for instance, to a great extent lost their ability to regulate international movements of capital, and consequently to control the consequences of their monetary policies.[27] But this form of sovereignty is concerned with state control, power and institutional capabilities, and not with state authority or right.[28] Where sovereignty in the latter sense is concerned, there is no indication that sovereignty is now becoming outdated or is even being outstripped by rival forms of international political arrangements. State authority and right are prominently at stake when we speak about international legal sovereignty, which concerns 'the practices associated with mutual recognition, usually between territorial entities that have formal juridical independence'.[29] This is the particular kind of sovereignty that is at stake in secessionist conflicts.

In speaking about '*de facto*' independence or '*de facto*' sovereign statehood, we have to bear in mind that an independent or sovereign state is not a fact in the way that a chair is a fact, but rather, as formulated by Crawford, 'a legal status attaching to a certain state of affairs by virtue of certain rules'.[30] The term 'sovereignty' may be taken as shorthand for a state's full competence, whose legal consequences stem from the quality of statehood itself. Sovereignty in this sense should be differentiated from sovereignty as a competence within a state, in the sense used when speaking about the sovereignty of parliament.[31]

The leaderships of the *de facto* independent states studied in this volume are convinced that they have good reason to strive for international recognition of their entity as a sovereign state. Full powers to perform acts in the domestic and international spheres through sovereign status do indeed bring obvious formal advantages in comparison with the various types of non-sovereign status, such as that of a federated state, for instance. Sovereignty, as the independence of a self-governing authority from all other authorities, translates into practice the principle of equality with all

---

[25] Stephen D. Krasner, *Sovereignty: Organized Hypocrisy* (Princeton, Princeton University Press, 1999), 12. [26] Ibid. 4. [27] Ibid. 12.
[28] On this distinction see Robert Jackson, 'Introduction' to his *Sovereignty at the Millennium*, 2. [29] Krasner, *Sovereignty: Organized Hypocrisy*, 3.
[30] Crawford, *The Creation of States in International Law*, 4. [31] Ibid. 27.

other states in the international community. The principle of non-intervention in the internal affairs of a sovereign state applies. No other state would—at least formally—be entitled to dictate its policies.[32]

These advantages derive not only from independence, but also from sovereign status in a confederation. Seen from this perspective, the question of sovereign statehood is indeed critical in all attempts to achieve a settlement in a secessionist crisis. The question of the precise type of federal arrangement has to be answered on the basis of this statehood. For James Crawford, the state is a legal concept, whereas concepts such as confederations or federations are to be regarded merely as classifications.[33] It is for this reason that the status of a confederated state is envisaged as being acceptable by secessionist movements in a number of non-recognized states, such as Taiwan, the Turkish Republic of Northern Cyprus, Montenegro, or Abkhazia. In some of these cases, it would be legitimate to speak of 'sovereignty movements' rather than 'independence movements'. Crawford's remark also helps explain why the Chinese, Greek-Cypriot, and Georgian leaderships refuse to envisage the option of a confederation.

The question of the recognition of international sovereignty is related to the question of the recognition of states. In debates on the nature of statehood and the effects of recognition, international legal theory is divided into a 'declaratory' school and a 'constitutive' school. The 'declaratory' school holds that statehood is a legal status based on a set of objective criteria, and is independent of recognition. The 'constitutive' school, on the other hand, holds that statehood is a legal status that can only be granted by international recognition.[34] The leaderships of non-recognized states generally claim that they fulfil the general criteria of statehood as prescribed by declaratory theory, which include a reasonably well-defined territory, a permanent population, a stable government, the capacity to enter into relations with other states and substantial independence from other states.[35] An examination of this claim requires in all cases an analysis of the extent to which the various criteria apply. In many cases, the degree of dependence on outside powers undermines a state's claim to being *de facto* sovereign and *de facto* constituting an independent state. Moreover, international recognition has to be seen as a political act, which is regulated by a number of normative criteria. In this respect, the factors which are relevant for recognition and which require a contextualized approach include the types of claims made by the authorities of these states themselves, their willingness to respect international law, the implications for regional security and the entire set of international circumstances in which the claim to independence is put forward.

---

[32] Crawford, *The Creation of States in International Law*, 32.   [33] Ibid. 422.
[34] See on this discussion ibid. 1–25.   [35] Ibid., p. viii.

Radical movements for secession claim sovereign status with the firm conviction that the right of nations to self-determination is an inalienable right and non-negotiable. Their claims are further made in the certainty that international recognition of the rights of nations to sovereign statehood is generally not based on substantial individual merits, but depends on accidents of history. In making such accidents happen, the use of force may sometimes be decisive. If such radical movements striving for national self-determination do not have sufficient force to impose a solution that is in their interest, they may still expect that a more or less distant future will bring about an international situation more favourable to their recognition.

Such movements are certain that the subjective will of the nation to constitute a sovereign state and the fulfilment of the objective criteria of *de facto* statehood mentioned above are sufficient to create a state. They reject the approach adopted in the constitutive theory of statehood. At the same time, they do not deny the significance of international recognition, which is not seen as a necessary condition for sovereign statehood but rather as one that would make it more complete. Recognition by other states would give strong evidential value to the question under dispute.[36] As sovereignty is a matter of authority and right, its international recognition has a deep symbolic meaning. It increases a government's domestic legitimacy.[37] International recognition gives states the right to engage in international activities on a par with other states. Relations with other states then become more stable and predictable. At the economic level, the transaction costs for agreements with the outside world are radically reduced. As self-determining units, these states become members of multilateral organizations, which gives them access to grants, loans, and foreign capital, and thus the interests of the domestic constituency may be upheld by securing external resources. States that are weak and failing can obtain substantial support from the international community, partly because sovereignty gives a certain bargaining power. Internationally recognized sovereign status makes it possible for states to make their voices heard and to negotiate in international organizations.[38]

It is true that some of these advantages are also given to political entities that do not have sovereign status. Federated states, for instance, may have cultural and trade relations with the rest of the world. They may also have a limited international personality and a certain amount of treaty-making power in the field of their constitutional competences. But their non-sovereign status reduces their role to 'para-diplomacy', excludes reciprocity on the basis of equality when dealing with sovereign entities, and denies them direct access to all those international organizations for which sovereignty

---

[36] Crawford, *The Creation of States in International Law*, 421.
[37] Krasner, *Sovereignty: Organized Hypocrisy*, 17.
[38] James, 'The Practice of Sovereign Statehood', 41

is a condition of membership. This is primarily the case with international security organizations. As security is a primary concern for many secession-ist movements, in particular when the breakaway has resulted from violent conflict, the status of a federated state may not be attractive. Sovereignty means membership of the superior class of states, as opposed to the inferior class of dependencies.[39]

In seeking recognition, sovereignty movements are of course strong defenders of sovereignty as the founding principle of international relations. They are reluctant to acknowledge, however, that they are being denied recognition by the international community precisely because this principle can only be safeguarded by restricting as far as possible other nations' access to independence. The viability of the club of sovereign nations depends entirely on its exclusivity. Sovereignty movements are conservative—they do not seek to revolutionize the international system by establishing new principles, nor even to reform it to make it more amenable to the many demands for national self-determination.[40] This exclusive club may stay as exclusive as it is: the only request sovereignty movements have is to be part of it.[41]

JUST WAR THEORY

Secessionist studies highlight the dramatic nature of the choice for or against independence. Most authors stress the disruptive consequences of this choice and the intensity of the political conflicts in which it is embedded. Even in those cases where such choices can be made in an environment sufficiently peaceful for no lives to be lost in the transition to independence, a judgement on the legitimacy of this type of secession remains highly emotional and dramatic. Despite the typically disruptive consequences of both types, a distinction has to be made between peaceful and violent secessionist crises.

The present volume includes case studies of both forms. Peaceful cases include those of Tatarstan and Quebec. The example of Tatarstan raises the ethical question of the legitimacy of the use of force in a secessionist conflict, and demonstrates the reasons why the political players involved have consciously adopted the principle of non-violent conflict resolution. Most of the cases chosen for this volume, however, deal with secessionist crises that have turned violent or have become outright secessionist wars. The contributions on Chechnya, British—Irish relations, Corsica, Cyprus, the former Yugoslavia, and Abkhazia deal with cases where the use of force has been chosen as a deliberate political strategy. Such cases confront both players and external observers with very different types of moral choices from the peaceful cases mentioned above. In this respect, the present volume differs

[39] Georg Sorensen, 'Sovereignty: Change and Continuity in a Fundamental Institution', in Jackson (ed.), *Sovereignty at the Millennium*, 174.
[40] See Jackson, 'Introduction' to his *Sovereignty at the Millennium*, 12.   [41] Ibid. 27.

from other literature on the ethics of secession, which refers to both kinds
of secessionist conflicts but fails to draw any normative consequences from
this distinction.[42] A more differentiated approach requires the application
of ethical discourses on the legitimacy of the use of force, such as pacifism,
realism, or just war theory. Few of the arguments from these traditions is
typically present in secession studies.

In the present volume, the contributions on Abkhazia, Chechnya, Cyprus,
and Taiwan apply the criteria to be found in just war theory in order to judge
the legitimacy of the use of force, or the threat to use force, in secessionist
crises. Unlike pacifism, which considers the use of force to be immoral, the
just war tradition regards it as a legitimate means in particular cases. This
moral tradition refers to justice in thinking about war, and is thereby distinguished from realism, which dissociates war and morality as two kinds of
activity that have little or nothing to do with each other. From the realist perspective, the use of force is a non-moral activity, whereas from the perspective
of just war thinking it is a moral activity. Arguments in the pacifist, realist, and
just war traditions are all present in public debates on secession. The focus on
just war theory in this volume does not reflect the primacy of this type of
moral discourse in secessionist crises, or its acceptance by political leaders, but
rather the conviction that this particular theory may facilitate a fair judgement of opposing claims.

The just war tradition analyses the ethical foundation of the criteria to be
used in any judgement on the legitimate use of violent means. Both the decision to start a war and the use of military means on the battlefield have to be
in accordance with these principles if the war is to be a just one. A war should
therefore be seen not as an extra-legal activity—an outburst of irrational
violence—but as a legal instrument. Just war thinking deals with the use of
force between political units, irrespective of whether or not they are recognized
as sovereign states. This aspect is crucial in those secessionist crises where only
one of the warring parties enjoys recognition by the international community.
The right of a party to the secessionist conflict to wage war derives only from
its commitment to the common good and to the rule of law. Force against a
central government or against a secessionist movement may only be used if it
can be construed as a defence of the international order and a way of securing
international peace and security.[43]

In the case of a war to achieve or oppose secession, the just war tradition
constrains the use of force as a legitimate means of action. Each of its principles must be respected for the use of force to be considered just. The six

[42] Only occasional references to just war theory are to be found in secession studies
(cf. Philpott, 'Self-Determination in Practice')

[43] An excellent discussion of the question of who has the legitimate authority to wage war
is to be found in A. J. Coates, *The Ethics of War* (Manchester, Manchester University Press,
1997), 126–8.

jus ad bellum principles that determine the conditions on which such a war may be started are as follows:[44]

1. A war should have a 'just cause'. This means that the injustice to be prevented or remedied should be serious enough to justify the use of force. Some examples here are self-defence and the defence of the territorial integrity of the country.
2. The decision should be guided by 'right intentions'. This means that a war should not primarily be fought for motives other than those considered to be a just cause.
3. Only a 'legitimate authority' may launch a war. Such an authority should not be understood formalistically as including only legally appointed officials and internationally recognized states: anti-colonial movements, for example, may in some circumstances be regarded as having the legitimate authority to use force as a last resort in order to defend their nation against oppression and to exercise their right to self-determination and secession.
4. A 'reasonable chance of success' is a prerequisite for starting military operations. The use of force against secessionist movements or by them is justified only if commensurate outcomes are to be expected from it. The probability of a military defeat rules out the legitimate use of force.
5. The principle of proportionality should be respected. The anticipated moral costs of fighting the war should not be disproportionate to the benefits.
6. The use of violence can only be a 'last resort' solution. Before resorting to war, it should be clear that any further diplomatic and other non-violent efforts would be useless and that the use of force is the last reasonable resort for remedying or preventing injustices. Alternatives include federative arrangements.

The two principles to be followed in the war itself (the *jus in bello*) include:

1. The principle of 'discrimination'. Combatants should spare the lives of non-combatants.
2. The use of particular military means should respect the principle of 'proportionality', with respect to their costs (costs in human lives, costs of destruction) and their military benefits.

Each party in a war of secession may be deeply convinced that it has a just cause (which may be the defence of either the principle of territorial integrity or that of national self-determination). It may further claim to fulfil all the other conditions for a just war: that it has good intentions, that it represents a legitimate authority, that all peaceful alternatives have failed, that it enjoys

[44] On the following see Bruno Coppieters and Nick Fotion (eds.), *Moral Constraints on War: Principles and Cases* (Lanham, Md., Lexington Books, 2002).

reasonable chances of success on the battlefield, and that the use of force is proportional to its political objectives. Thus, from a subjective point of view, both parties may claim to be fighting a just war on secession. A sceptic could conclude that just war thinking should therefore be regarded as having merely a legitimizing function, justifying the actions of any party.

Such a sceptical view may, however, be refuted. It is true that just war thinking is often used for purposes of ideological legitimization, a characteristic it shares with all moral theories. The case studies in this volume analyse some ideological justifications of the threat to use force in secessionist conflicts and of the use of force in secessionist wars. Just war theory may, however, also be used by outside observers for critical purposes. This is the intention of the contributors to this volume when they apply the theory. With the help of this theoretical tradition they aim to achieve a more differentiated analysis of the conflict and to reach new conclusions about the validity of rationalizations of war.[45]

Authors working in the just war tradition use the term 'theory' in a sense similar to that used by authors discussing the ethics of secession. In both cases, the theory endows the field of research with a certain structure, systematizes the research questions and provides a coherent set of concepts on which ethical judgements can be based. The theory delivers a bare framework for the ethical analysis, antecedent to the choices that have to be made.[46]

Just war thinking and secession studies share other characteristics. They both need to contextualize their abstract principles. They have common concerns when analysing intra-state conflicts in post-Cold War Europe. Above all, they share common perspectives in analysing such cases, as it is often hard to dissociate a judgement on the legitimacy of secession from a verdict on the legitimacy of the use of force in a war of secession. It is therefore remarkable that the ethics of just war and the ethics of just secession constitute separate traditions in ethical thinking. Despite the many affinities between the two traditions, they have rarely been systematically compared with one another. A contextualization of secession, of the kind to which we aspire in this volume, necessarily links both forms of ethical thinking, even if the format of the contributions does not permit a systematic clarification of the many connections between the two traditions. Such a comparison will be made in the conclusion to this volume.

---

[45] Moreover, just war theory may lead political forces envisaging the possible use of force to take a prudential attitude. Just war principles such as proportionality or reasonable chance of success favour this kind of behaviour.

[46] Jeremy Waldron, 'Minority Cultures and the Cosmopolitan Alternative', in Will Kymlicka (ed.), *The Rights of Minority Cultures* (Oxford, Oxford University Press, 1996), 98. See also Coppieters, Myhul, and Huysseune, *Introduction*, 12–13.

2

A Nation Confronting a Secessionist Claim: Italy and the Lega Nord

Michel Huysseune

INTRODUCTION

The Lega Nord, the movement campaigning for the secession of northern Italy, emerged as a central political player in the early 1990s. It came to the fore in the context of a crisis of Italy's political system, caused by the disclosure, beginning in 1992, of the widespread and deeply entrenched practices of corruption pervading the Italian state. It gained political prominence as an anti-system movement, whose secessionism offered the most radical alternative to the crisis-ridden Italian political system. Although the Lega (as it is usually referred to) has receded more into the background in recent years, it nevertheless continues to be a presence on the Italian political scene. As a junior partner of Silvio Berlusconi's *Casa delle Libertà* ('House of Liberties') alliance, it acceded to several regional governments in northern Italy in 2000, and to national government after the victory of this alliance in the national elections of May 2001.

In comparative studies of contemporary secessionist movements, the Lega's demand for the independence of northern Italy—'Padania'—on behalf of a 'Padanian' nation is generally interpreted as the anomalous case of a movement acting on behalf of a group not previously identified as a 'nation'. Its secessionism can thus be dismissed out of hand as an instrumentalist political manoeuvre, as when Ronald S. Beiner expressed the opinion that 'there is little reason to think that Umberto Bossi's dream of a republic of Padania is anything other than a cynical fabrication'.[1] This negative evaluation, frequently shared by students of the Lega and of Italian politics, nevertheless begs the question of how the Lega's construction of a national identity has made itself credible to a broader audience. The impact

[1] Ronald S. Beiner, 'National Self-Determination: Some Cautionary Remarks Concerning the Rhetorics of Rights', in Margaret Moore (ed.), *National Self-Determination and Secession* (Oxford, Oxford University Press, 1998), 158–80, at p. 160.

achieved by the arguments of the Lega is not confined to its sometimes considerable electoral impact (in the general elections of 1992, 1994, 1996, and 2001 the Lega polled 17.3, 17.0, 20.5, and 8.2 per cent respectively in the northern regions).[2] The Lega has undoubtedly been able to attract votes and mobilize a considerable amount of militancy around the issue of the independence of northern Italy. Whatever the intentions of its leadership may have been, its public defence of Padanian secessionism was taken seriously both by its rank-and-file and by its electorate.[3] The secessionist stance of the Lega Nord moreover coincided with a broad movement of critique of the Italian state. Comments on the Lega Nord have hence highlighted how '[t]he Lega's success is essentially based on its convincing reinterpretation of old grievances in Italian society'.[4] Students of the Lega frequently interpret it as a player voicing—albeit in a distorted and instrumentalist way—the justified complaints of the North.[5]

[2] The 'northern regions' are those included in the official statistical categories of North-West and North-East: Valle d'Aosta, Piedmont, Lombardy, Liguria, Trentino-Alto Adige, Veneto, Friuli-Venezia Giulia, and Emilia-Romagna. The Lega has generally obtained its best results in Lombardy, Veneto, and Friuli-Venezia Giulia: in the elections of 1996, it emerged as the strongest party in these three regions, polling respectively 25.5, 29.3, and 23.2 per cent (all these percentages refer to the elections for the chamber of deputies). The Lega has been less successful in the regional elections of April 2000. It polled 15.5 per cent in Lombardy, 7.6 per cent in Piedmont, 12.0 per cent in the Veneto, 4.3 per cent in Liguria, and 3.3 per cent in Emilia-Romagna (*Corriere della Sera*, 18 April 2000). In the national elections of 2001, it polled 12.1 per cent in Lombardy, 5.9 per cent in Piedmont, 10.1 per cent in the Veneto, 8.2 per cent in Friuli-Venezia Giulia, 3.9 per cent in Liguria, 2.6 per cent in Emilia-Romagna, and 3.6 per cent in Trentino-Alto Adige.

[3] The persistent attachment of the Lega's militants to Padanian independence was revealed at the recent (March 2002) congress of the Lega Nord. A proposition to abandon the reference to independence in the party's name (the Lega is still officially named 'Lega Nord per l'indipendenza della Padania', the 'Northern League for the independence of Padania') was withdrawn when it roused violent protests of its rank-and-file (Giovanna Pajetta, 'Più poltrone, meno voti: Lega a congresso', *Il Manifesto*, 2 March 2002).

[4] Oliver Schmidtke, 'The Populist Challenge to the Italian Nation-State: The Lega Lombarda/Nord', *Regional Politics and Policy* 3:3 (1993), 140–62, at p. 141.

[5] The most comprehensive studies of the Lega Nord are Ilvo Diamanti, *La Lega. Geografia, storia e sociologia di un soggetto politico* (Rome, Donzelli, 1995 (1993)); id., *Il male del Nord* (Rome, Donzelli, 1996); Roberto Biorcio, *La Padania promessa* (Milan, Il Saggiatore, 1997); and Vittorio Moioli, *Sinistra e Lega: processo a un flirt impossibile* (Milan, Ed. Comedit, 1997), in English Damian Tambini, *Nationalism in Italian Politics. The Stories of the Northern League, 1980–2000* (London, Routledge, 2001) and Anna Cento Bull and Mark Gilbert, *The Lega Nord and the Northern Question in Italian Politics* (Basingstoke, Palgrave, 2001). The relation between the Lega's discourse and the 'Northern Question' is emphasized by Ilvo Diamanti in *Il male del Nord*. This relation is also outlined in Piero Bassetti, *L'Italia si è rotta? Un federalismo per l'Europa* (Rome and Bari, Laterza, 1996); and Roberto Mainardi, *L'Italia delle regioni. Il Nord e la Padania* (Milan, Bruno Mondadori, 1998). In this paper, I focus on the relation between the Lega Nord's and mainstream discourses as it developed in the late 1980s and 1990s. After the centre-right's return to power in 2001, intellectuals have started to play an important role in mobilizations against the Berlusconi government (which includes the Lega Nord). This may lead to important paradigm shifts in mainstream discourses that remain to be ascertained.

This focus on what is now called the 'Northern Question' reveals that, notwithstanding the strong opposition of Italian mainstream public opinion to the northern nation-building programme of the Lega, the existence of a 'northern' identity is nevertheless accepted. The complaints made on its behalf are moreover frequently considered credible and important. This raises the question of the relevance of sub-national identities in Italy, and of the ways to address the grievances voiced on behalf of them. In the context of the institutional reforms Italy is undergoing at present, moreover, the Lega's claim and the mainstream focus on the 'Northern Question' coincide with more general critiques of the centralism of the Italian state. The dynamics of a political situation in which reforms of the state interact with demands for federalism thus create a context in which secessionist demands may have an effective impact.

In the first section of this chapter, I analyse the content of the northern Italian or 'Padanian' identity as constructed by the Lega. The second section discusses the grievances against the Italian state its discourse articulates. The third section considers how the Lega's secessionist claim can be evaluated within the two normative frameworks for judging secession, the 'just cause' remedial approach and the 'choice' approach. The final section examines the alternatives to secession proposed in Italy, which focus both on institutional reform and on critical re-evaluations of national and sub-national identities. I conclude by discussing normative frameworks for the analysis of secession in the light of the Italian case.

THE AFFIRMATION OF A NORTHERN ITALIAN IDENTITY

Throughout its existence, the Lega Nord has proposed several definitions of the northern Italian nation it claims to represent.[6] The Lega has its origins in movements in northern Italy presenting themselves as the defenders of regional identities; the *Liga Veneta* in the Veneto, the *Lega Lombarda* in Lombardy (the most prominent and successful of them), and various groups in Piedmont. These regional identities were defined as corresponding to the institutional regions into which Italy is divided.[7] The Lega Nord, founded in

---

[6] The Lega's programme is outlined in the books published by its leader, Umberto Bossi, generally written together with the journalist Daniele Vimercati. Those co-authored with Vimercati include: *Vento dal Nord* (Milan, Sperling & Kupfer, 1992); *La Rivoluzione* (Milan, Sperling & Kupfer, 1993); *Processo alla Lega* (Milan, Sperling & Kupfer, 1998). Authored by Bossi alone: *Tutta la verità. Perché ho partecipato al governo Berlusconi. Perché l'ho fatto cadere. Dove voglio arrivare* (Milan, Sperling & Kupfer, 1995); *Il mio progetto. Discorsi su federalismo e Padania* (Milan, Sperling & Kupfer, 1995).

[7] Italy is divided into twenty regions, five of which (Sicily, Sardinia, Valle d'Aosta, Trentino-Alto Adige, and Friuli-Venezia Giulia), have a special statute, while the others are referred to as 'ordinary-statute regions'. The five 'special-statute regions', inhabited by ethnic minorities or

1991 by merging these regionalist movements, has claimed to represent a generic northern Italian identity, which is at the same time understood as an aggregate of regional identities. The Lega has defined the 'North' in territorial terms, either as including all the regions north of Rome, or alternatively in the light of a tripartition of Italy between the North, the Centre, and the South, excluding the 'central' regions of Tuscany, Umbria, and the Marches from the North. This latter 'limited' version of northern Italy corresponds to the regions included in the official statistical categories of North-West and North-East.

Finally, the Lega has also defined an ethnic 'Padanian' identity.[8] This last articulation of a northern identity, which in territorial terms broadly corresponds to the 'limited' version described above, assumes that northern Italians, or 'Padanians', are an ethnically distinct group which has, in particular, its own dialects and cultural traditions. The Lega associates these traditions with the Celtic roots of northern Italy, highlighting how these territories were colonized by Celts before being occupied by the Romans. This myth of descent is, however, rarely interpreted in a strict genealogical sense, and the issue of northern purity in a racial sense is only marginally present in the Lega's official discourse. For the Lega, these Celtic ancestors are important because of their struggle against Rome, which means that they exemplify what is, for the Lega, characteristic of the people(s) of northern Italy: their struggle for autonomy against central government.[9] The original name of its most important branch, the *Lega Lombarda*, and its symbol, the *Carroccio* or battle-wagon, thus refer to the twelfth-century struggle of the northern Italian cities, united in the Lombard League, against the emperor Frederick Barbarossa. The Lega hence positions its struggle against the Italian state in the historical continuity of traditional struggles for self-government.

ones that have experienced secessionist tendencies, were granted autonomy after World War II (Friuli only later, in 1964), and have a larger measure of autonomy than the others (which obtained regional self-government in 1970).

[8] The Lega's viewpoint on this 'Padanian' identity is most extensively elaborated in Gilberto Oneto, *L'invenzione della Padania. La rinascita della comunità più antica d'Europa* (Bergamo, Foedus Editore, 1997). The position of ethnic minorities in northern Italy is not systematically addressed by the Lega Nord. In his book, Oneto accords the ethnic minorities within northern Italy (i.e. the northern regions, see above, n. 2)—the South Tyrolians, Ladini, Friulians, Slovenians, and the French-speaking inhabitants of Valle d'Aosta—the right to self-determination, including secession. Analogously, 'Padanians' living outside the borders of northern Italy should, according to Oneto, be given the right to choose inclusion in the new 'Padanian' state. This concerns inhabitants of the central Italian regions Tuscany and Marche, but also of neighbouring states, namely Switzerland, France, Slovenia, and Croatia. See Oneto, *L'invenzione della Padania*, 155–73.

[9] See Guido C. Bolla and Luigi F. Imperatore, *Da Ambrosio a Bossi. Lotte per la libertà nella Padania* (Milan, Edi B.I., 1992).

It is not difficult to demonstrate the artificiality of several of the identities proposed by the Lega. The regional identities it puts forward in opposition to the national identity have weak historical roots: the institutional regions they refer to date from Unification, and rarely correspond to previously rooted identities. In so far as they have acquired cultural or political relevance, they tend to be perceived as complementary to Italian identity, not in opposition to it. The entity of 'Padania'—in both its territorial and ethnic versions—undoubtedly forms a geographical unity around the Po river, separated from the rest of Italy by the Apennines. It has, however, no historical unity (it was united in the same years as the rest of Italy), and no common cultural identity (it has in fact been marked by political divisions between the 'red' region of Emilia-Romagna, and the generally 'white'—i.e. Christian-Democrat—other regions). Linguists are prepared to acknowledge the common linguistic roots of the dialects spoken in northern Italy, as distinct from dialects of the rest of Italy.[10] The political relevance of this fact, however, is limited, not only because the use of dialects in daily life is diminishing, but also because of the complete absence of a common 'Padanian' language around which a common identity could be constructed. Revealingly, the Lega itself—except for local propaganda, where it can make use of local dialects—has tended to favour Italian for its political communication, developing for its particular purpose a populist language that contrasts with the traditional jargon of political parties.

Denunciations of the artificiality of the Lega's historical recon-struction of a 'Padanian' national identity have, however, one crucial weakness: namely, that they can likewise be applied to Italian identity. While the latter can rely on a long-standing cultural and literary tradition with its roots in the Middle Ages, the *Risorgimento* movement that sought to create a united Italian nation-state cannot be traced back further than the late eighteenth century. As Benedetto Croce already argued at the beginning of the last century, Italy's history (understood as political history) is 'not ancient or centuries old but *recent*, not outstanding but *modest*, not radiant but *laboured*'.[11] At least some of the identities the Lega defines (particularly the 'Venetian' identity, associated with the Venetian Republic that dominated most of north-eastern Italy from the fifteenth century to 1797) have roots as solid as the Italian one.

The pertinence of identities can thus be evaluated only by focusing on their contemporary political content and relevance. From this viewpoint, the

---

[10] Tullio Di Mauro, 'Linguistic Variety and Linguistic Minorities', in David Forgacs and Robert Lumley, *Italian Cultural Studies. An Introduction* (Oxford, Oxford University Press, 1996), 88–101, esp. pp. 95–8.

[11] Benedetto Croce, quoted in Mauro Moretti, 'The Search for a "National" History: Italian Historiographical Trends Following Unification', in Stefan Berger, Mark Donovan, and Kevin Passmore (eds.), *Writing National Histories: Western Europe Since 1800* (London, Routledge, 1999), 111–22, at p. 118.

ethnic version of the 'Padanian' identity emerges as a partisan construction with as yet little or no relevance for outsiders. The more generic 'northern' identity based on the contrast between northern and southern Italy can, on the contrary, be considered both politically and culturally significant. Unlike the other identities the Lega defines, these northern and southern identities have a long tradition as interpretative categories of diversity within Italy. These categories have moreover carried a strong political meaning almost since Italy's unification in 1860–1. They derive their significance from the important and persistent differences between the two parts of the country.

Northern Italy has undergone a successful process of modernization. The recent industrialization of the peripheral regions of northern Italy, the so-called Third Italy, is frequently regarded as a model of endogenous regional development.[12] It has a well-entrenched tradition of civic culture and of (relatively) competent local and regional government.[13] Southern Italy, on the contrary, has consistently lagged behind, and has suffered from a poorly performing economy, high unemployment, a weak civic culture, bad government, and the strong presence of organized crime.

The economic divide between the two parts of Italy has frequently been interpreted as a political and cultural divide, with northern Italy considered to be close to Western models and southern Italy more backward, less European. The journalist Luigi Barzini, for example, in a book written in 1964 to explain the Italians to an Anglo-Saxon readership, distinguished the northern *homo economicus*, very similar to his fellow Europeans, from the southerners, who were attached to un-economic values such as honour and respect, and were hence less efficient and enterprising.[14] This juxtaposition has been translated into the popular images—which originated in the nineteenth century—of a 'European' North as opposed to an 'African' South, frequently deployed by the Lega Nord. It acquired particular saliency in the early 1990s, when Italy's huge public debt caused general anxiety about whether the country would be admitted into the European Monetary Union (which it joined in 1998). This anxiety gave added weight to the Lega's proposal to liberate the North from the burden of the South, held to be responsible for this debt.

The Lega's definition of a northern Italian identity hence follows a well-rooted tradition of identity-construction within Italy. This discursive tradition

---

[12] Sergio Conti and Fabio Sforzi, 'Il sistema produttivo italiano', in Pasquale Coppola (ed.), *Geografia politica delle regioni italiane* (Turin, Einaudi, 1997), 278–336; Mainardi, *L'Italia delle regioni*; Gioacchino Garofoli, 'Les systèmes de petites entreprises: un cas paradigmatique de développement endogène', in Georges Benko and Alain Lipietz, *Les régions qui gagnent. Districts et réseaux: les nouveaux paradigmes de la géographie économique* (Paris, PUF, 1992), 57–80.
[13] Robert D. Putnam, *Making Democracy Work: Civic Tradition in Modern Italy* (Princeton, Princeton University Press, 1993). The revelations of corruption scandals in the 1990s, however, revealed the involvement of many local and regional governments in the North in these practices. [14] Luigi Barzini, *Gli italiani* (Milan, Mondadori, 1985 (1964)), 266–7.

is, like the Lega, imprecise in defining the North. The South is in fact the better-defined unit of Italy: it is associated with the regions of the former Kingdom of the Two Sicilies,[15] although it also includes Sardinia, which resembles those regions in its socio-economic and cultural profile.[16] The status of the central regions has, however, historically been unclear, since their 'central' geographical location does not correspond to any form of identity. In the juxtaposition of the North and the South, Rome and its region (Lazio) have tended to be excluded from the North, without, however, being included in the South, while nowadays the other central regions are often assimilated to the North.

The 'northern' and 'southern' identities emerge as admittedly ill-defined but nevertheless relevant interpretative categories of Italian social reality. They have been incorporated into the 'imagined geography' of Italians, both by scholars and by the public at large. As Silvana Patriarca argues in a critical review of the emergence of the South as a statistical category after Unification, it would be absurd to deny regional differences within Italy, or the deep roots they often have in history: 'But these differences tend to be become naturalized and taken for granted instead of being properly historicized and subjected to questioning.'[17] Viewing Italy exclusively through the prism of its North–South divide, associated with the modern-backward dichotomy, is in fact to overlook the similarities and different forms of interdependence linking the two parts. These result from the common historical experience within the unified Italian state, and particularly from the strong economic development both parts of Italy have experienced, especially since World War II.[18]

The potentially divisive dynamics of interpreting the differences between northern and southern Italy as consequences of 'northern' and 'southern' Italian identities have been acknowledged for a long time. In 1935 Antonio

[15] Until its absorption in 1860–1 into the Italian kingdom, the Kingdom of the Two Sicilies, governed by the Bourbons, included the territories of the contemporary southern mainland regions: Abruzzo, Molise, Puglia, Campania, Basilicata, and Calabria, and the island of Sicily. Notwithstanding the frequent separation of Sicily from the mainland South (the last one dating from the French occupation of the mainland in the early nineteenth century, when Sicily remained unoccupied), the territories of the Kingdom of the Two Sicilies have a long history of political unity, dating from the Norman conquest in the eleventh century.

[16] Sardinia, which never belonged to the Kingdom of the Two Sicilies, was ceded by Spain to Piedmont in 1720, and thus formed a core territory of the Piedmontese Kingdom before the latter incorporated the rest of Italy. Notwithstanding its different history and its cultural—and especially linguistic—particularities ('Sardinian' is claimed to be a separate language), it is normally included in the 'South', which it resembles in many of its socio-economic characteristics.

[17] Silvana Patriarca, 'How Many Italies? Representing the South in Official Statistics', in Jane Schneider (ed.), *Italy's 'Southern Question': Orientalism in One Country* (Oxford and New York, Berg, 1998), 77–97, at p. 92.

[18] Carmine Donzelli has drawn attention to the fact that, in the post-war period, both parts of the country have had almost the same growth rates. See Carmine Donzelli, 'Mezzogiorno tra "questione" e purgatorio. Opinione comune, immagine scientifica, strategie di ricerca', *Meridiana* 9 (1990), 13–53, esp. pp. 29–32.

Gramsci commented thus upon northern prejudices against the South and
southerners: 'The poverty of the Mezzogiorno was historically "inexplic-
able" for the popular masses of the North...The ordinary man from
Northern Italy thought...that, if the Mezzogiorno made no progress after
having been liberated from the fetters which the Bourbon régime placed in
the way of modern development, this meant that the causes of the poverty
were not external, to be sought in objective economic and political conditions, but natural, innate in the population of the South...the organic incapacity of the inhabitants, their barbarity, their biological inferiority.'[19] In
1962 the historian Luciano Cafagna pointed out how a northern identity
could be constructed in opposition to the South, as a discourse highlighting
the moral superiority of the North over the South, a North that was dissoci-
ated from the dysfunctional Italian state.[20] Luigi Barzini argued in 1964 that
the mutual mistrust and lack of understanding between northerners and
southerners could ultimately jeopardize the—always fragile—national unity
of Italy.[21]

The centrifugal dynamics of an interpretation of Italy through its
North—South divide are, however, by no means a given. They are in fact
dependent on the political content of the discourses that interpret this divide.
At several points in Italian history, discourses promoting North–South solidarity have played an important role. In the first decades after Unification, the
South was perceived as a victim of misrule by the Bourbons, and hence
the nation's duty to redeem it prevailed.[22] The post-war policies designed to
modernize the South have likewise received frequent public support, as an
act of national solidarity. Interpretations of the North–South divide can, however, easily be inserted into discourses vaunting northern superiority. These
discourses rely on two important value judgements: the vindication of the
moral superiority of northern Italian society, and the opposition between a
sane northern society and both a 'deviant' or 'backward' South and an Italian
state contaminated by southern vices. The latter dissociation has facilitated
the Lega's construction of a 'northern' identity, symbolically incorporated into
Europe and separated from the South.

[19] Antonio Gramsci, 'Notes on Italian History', in *Selection from Prison Notebooks* (London, Lawrence and Wishart, 1978), 52–120, at pp. 70–1.
[20] Luciano Cafagna (ed.), *Il Nord nella storia d'Italia. Antologia politica dell'Italia industriale* (Bari, Laterza, 1962), 332–3.   [21] Barzini, *Gli italiani*, 266.
[22] It should be noted, however, that this official vision was frequently accompanied by strong, privately voiced prejudices against the South, considered to be 'backward' and 'barbar-ian'. The widespread banditry in the South after Unification particularly encouraged the cre-ation of this negative image. See John Dickie, 'A World at War: the Italian Army and Brigandage 1860–1870', *History Workshop* 33 (1992), 1–24; and id., 'Stereotypes of the Italian South, 1860–1900', in Robert Lumley and Jonathan Morris (eds.), *The New History of the Italian South* (Exeter, University of Exeter Press, 1997), 114–47.

NORTHERN GRIEVANCES

The Lega Nord has been able to activate the latent opposition between northern and southern Italy, especially in the late 1980s and the early 1990s, by linking it with a number of specific grievances. The first set concerns the dysfunctional features of the Italian state: on the one hand its lack of efficiency and the slowness of its bureaucracy, on the other, the corruption of Italy's political establishment. For the Lega, the vices of the Italian state are a consequence of its strongly centralized structure, where the government and the central bureaucracy control the decision-making process at lower levels. According to the Lega's second set of grievances, the Italian state favours the South, especially in its redistribution policies. In this interpretation, these policies reflect the fact that the Italian state is a southern institution that colonizes the North. The Lega hence directs itself against what is interpreted as the predatory Italian state (*Roma ladrona*, 'Rome the thief') and the South, accused of leading a parasitic existence financed by the North.

As far as the first set of grievances is concerned, there is general agreement with the Lega's critique of the inefficiency of the Italian state. The link it makes between inefficiency and over-centralization can also be considered justified. Throughout the history of post-Unification Italy, its strongly centralized administration and bureaucracy have discouraged initiatives by local authorities, but have at the same time been unable to provide for adequate and timely government intervention.[23] The regional governments established after 1970 have likewise remained subordinate to the state's centralism, although they have introduced dynamics leading towards autonomy, which matured in the 1990s.

Sidney Tarrow has highlighted how the inefficiency of the Italian state derives from its particular structure as both an adaptation and a modification of the French Napoleonic model. Italy's post-Unification political élite adapted a state structure that copied the autocratic French model of territorial administration, without having the French tradition of functional unity in administration at the level of the *département*, and instead used administration to exert political control.[24] While the Italian prefects were an extension of the Interior Ministry and its interest in public order, '[t]he other ministries could exercise their powers in the provinces practically free of his [i.e. the Interior Minister's] command, and there was no equivalent of

---

[23] Raffaele Romanelli, 'Centralismo e autonomie', in Raffaele Romanelli (ed.), *Storia dello stato italiano dall'Unità a oggi* (Rome, Donzelli, 1995), 125–86.

[24] Sidney Tarrow, *Between Center and Periphery: Grassroots Politicians in Italy and France* (New Haven/London, Yale University Press, 1977), 61. This 'combined' model was itself chosen because of the negative Italian experience of the Napoleonic model, which was felt to be too authoritarian.

the Napoleonic myth to weld the state together'.[25] The Italian model thus combines obscure power lines from Rome to the periphery with the absence of an institutional focus that would enable communities to regulate their relationship with the state.

The inefficiency of the Italian state is thus located in the very roots of its organizational structure. While until recently the state has maintained a strongly centralized structure inherited from its semi-absolutist origins, it is at the same time characterized by the weakness of its centre. It has in fact always been obliged to negotiate its dominance with peripheral élites, who have thus been able to manipulate the state to their own advantage. Within this system, 'clientelistic centre-periphery relations...are essential to the system's operation; short of a political alternative, no other viable mechanisms have existed in Italy to overcome the stalemate at the centre and the blockages of the bureaucracy between centre and periphery'.[26] As a consequence, extra-legal relations between centre and periphery developed, together with clientelism, the privatization of state power and in some regions organized crime. Local élites (and, after World War II, political parties) acted in this structure as mediators between centre and periphery, and their consolidated position in that structure may have played an important role in helping them resist secessionist temptations.

Although corruption has been an endemic problem in the Italian state, the critique of corruption became especially relevant in the political context of the late 1980s and the early 1990s.[27] The Lega has combined a critique of the Italian state and the domineering role of the traditional political parties (the *partitocrazia*, 'partitocracy') with a proposal for dissolving the Italian state. Particularly after the *Mani Pulite* ('clean hands') operation, which brought a large number of political leaders before the courts, revealed the widespread and deeply entrenched practices of corruption that pervaded the Italian political system in the 1980s and the early 1990s, the Lega's discourse proved to be politically effective.[28] The squandering of the subsidies allocated for the reconstruction of the regions in the South hit by an

---

[25] Ibid. 61–2.   [26] Ibid. 195.

[27] It is commonly assumed that the endemic corruption of the Italian political system was exacerbated in the 1980s, an aggravation generally associated with the central political role played by Bettino Craxi's Socialist Party (PSI, *Partito Socialista Italiana*). As a relatively small party, lacking the traditional financial backing enjoyed by both the Christian Democrats and Communists, it is claimed to have resorted to this means to finance its activities.

[28] The *Mani Pulite* operation started during the electoral campaign of 1992, with the arrest of a minor official in the Socialist Party. The inquiry soon expanded, uncovering proof of the large-scale involvement of Italy's political class in corrupt practices. Although almost all parties, including the Lega Nord, were involved in this corruption to a certain extent (the spoils of corruption tended to be divided according to party quotas), the dominant government parties, the *Democrazia Cristiana* and the *Partito Socialista Italiana*, were hit particularly hard. Many of their leading figures came to be accused, which accelerated the dissolution of these parties.

earthquake in 1980 became the most visible example of how public spending was characterized by waste and corruption. This emphasis on the post-earthquake waste in these regions may, however, have contributed to two undue generalizations: first, that government intervention policies in the South were all marked by inefficiency and corruption, and second, that the North was untouched by such corruption. The *Mani Pulite* investigations in fact revealed how corruption was also well entrenched in the North, especially in Milan, until then often referred to as 'the moral capital of Italy'.

The second justification for secession proposed by the Lega, discriminatory redistribution, takes a prominent place in its rhetoric. The Lega argues that northern Italy's contribution to national taxes is proportionally much higher than the percentage of state expenditure it receives. Discussions on discriminatory redistribution in Italy are bedevilled by uncertainty about the choice of data for evaluating it. They are moreover highly controversial politically, because they entail a value judgement on the criteria to be adopted for redistributive policies. The Lega's argument is based on the principle that regions should be awarded means according to the income they produce, and that interregional transfers should be abandoned or at the very least radically reduced. Determining regional per capita tax incomes is, however, as Giuseppe Cotturi points out, problematic: the incomes to which these data refer to are not necessarily generated within the region. Firms in fact pay taxes in the region in which their headquarters are located, which is disproportionately the North, especially Lombardy.[29] Taking into consideration this distortion and the difficulty of establishing accurate per capita tax incomes, there is nevertheless little doubt that the northern regions do generate higher incomes, and are thus on the donor side of interregional redistribution.

The Lega's argument concurs with a more widely shared critique of the redistributive policies of the Italian state. This revisionism questions the assumption upon which redistributive policies have been based up to now, namely, that the constitutional principle of the equality of Italian citizens should be reflected in equal per capita spending by the state in each region, a principle that implies interregional transfers.[30] Whether the principle of equal per capita spending has been respected is, however, itself a matter of controversy. Most overviews of per capita spending argue that, according to this criterion, the North and the South receive more or less equal

[29] Giuseppe Cotturi, 'Federalismo dal Mezzogiorno', *Democrazia e Diritto* 2 (1999), (Federalismo e Mezzogiorno), 9–19, esp. p. 14.

[30] Alessandro Pizzorusso, *La Costituzione ferita* (Bari and Rome, Laterza, 1999), 45–6 and 97–9. This principle can in fact also be invoked to demand a higher per capita investment in southern regions, because of their developmental backlog. Because of the specific dynamics of the present public debate, with its focus on a 'Northern Question' and its critique (frequently justified, at least in part), of 'southern waste', such claims are nowadays extremely rare.

amounts.[31] Giancarlo Pagliarini, one of the spokespersons of the Lega and ex-budget minister, has contested this conclusion. He argues with some justice that data on per capita spending include repayments of state debts (repayments that are higher in northern regions). A comparison should thus be made on the basis of per capita spending without those repayments. Pagliarini's data for the years 1992 and 1993 indeed reveal that four northern regions—Lombardy, Piedmont, Veneto, and Emilia-Romagna—received the least. A closer look at his data shows, however, that the greatest beneficiaries were not the southern but the special-statute regions (with Valle d'Aosto and Trentino-Alto Adige on top, and Sardinia, Friuli, and Sicily lower down the ladder), and Lazio (including Rome). The most densely populated southern mainland regions—Campania, Puglia, and Calabria—received more than the four northern regions mentioned above (with Lombardy, which received least, rated at 100, they received respectively 124.5, 115.4 and 119.3 in 1992; and 140.9, 137.2 and 148.4 in 1993). However, this amount is substantially the same as that received by several central regions, such as Tuscany and Umbria, which are included in the 'large' version of northern Italy, and less than northern Liguria (which scored 149.0 in 1992, and 165.9 in 1993).[32] Following Pagliarini's interpretation of data on per capita spending, the Lega can justly claim that several northern regions receive per capita less than average. Its representation of the redistributive policies of the Italian state as being marked by a North–South dichotomy in which all southern regions are favoured and all northern regions disadvantaged, however, can only be regarded as misleading.

Social scientists who have analysed the territorial dimension of the redistributive policies of the Italian state confirm this more nuanced picture. The large investments made from the 1950s to the early 1990s for the development of southern Italy, the Mezzogiorno (within the framework of the so-called *intervento straordinario*, the 'extraordinary intervention')—often used as an argument to demonstrate the disproportionate profits the South has derived from the state—implied a specific organization of these investments, not a higher per capita allocation of resources to southern regions. Social scientists have also highlighted the complexities of redistributive processes, which cannot be limited to tax levels and government expenditure.[33] They point out that

[31] Raffaele Brancati, *La questione regionale. Federalismo, Mezzogiorno e sviluppo economico* (Rome, Donzelli, 1995), 68. In 1995 Bossi himself gave (without references) a comparison of the per capita spending—including social transfers, public spending, and investments—for the South (5 million lire), and the North (5.2 million lire), that would confirm this viewpoint. See Bossi, *Tutta la verità*, 190.

[32] Giancarlo Pagliarini, 'Le ragioni della Lega', *Nuvole* 6:3 (1996), 35–48, esp. p. 41.

[33] Federico Rampini, 'Conviene alla Padania la secessione?', *Limes* 1 (1996), 31–6; Giulio Scaramellini, Elena dell'Agnese and Guido Lucarno, 'I processi redistributivi', in Pasquale Coppola (ed.), *Geografia politica delle regioni italiane* (Turin, Einaudi, 1997), 337–400.

other redistributive mechanisms (e.g. welfare expenditure) tend to favour the North, rather than the South.[34] All these elements justify the view that it is difficult to establish with certainty which part of the country (with the exception of the special-statute regions, which are clearly favoured) benefits most from redistributive policies, when benefits are measured in terms of per capita spending.[35] There is, however, little doubt that, in the light of the economic differences between the North and the South, sustaining this equality in per capita spending will mean continuing interregional transfers, mainly from the North to the South.

Notwithstanding the mixed results of research on the redistributive policies of the Italian state, confirmed even by the data produced by the Lega, the latter's view of the North as being fiscally exploited by the Italian state in order to subsidize the South has become a commonplace, used rather unthinkingly even by many social scientists and intellectuals.[36] The Lega's viewpoint derives its credibility from the well-known fact that because of the pervasive role of clientelism, money invested in the South has often been instrumental in creating and maintaining widespread state-supported corruption, of which organized crime is just the most visible aspect. The Lega's arguments against unequal redistribution can therefore be regarded as having a certain degree of legitimacy, even if they do not justify secession, since other possibilities for redressing these wrongs may be taken into consideration. The fact that inhabitants of the South have often been the first victims of this mismanagement gives an additional reason to consider alternatives to secession.

The Lega has, however, also argued that the state is beyond reform. This line of argument is in fact closely associated with the traditional construction of the northern identity, which perceives the Italian state as 'southern' and, in the Lega's version, unreformable. I would argue, however, that there are several serious problems with such a vision. In the first place, the 'southern-ness' of the Italian state results from an inappropriate interpretation of an acknowledged fact, the strong presence of southerners in the state appara-tus (itself a consequence of the economic underdevelopment of the South, which has traditionally attracted southerners to state employment). This overrepresentation facilitates two erroneous deductions: namely, that the

---

[34] This goes against a commonly held opinion on the issue (see e.g. Pagliarini, 'Le ragioni della Lega'). The South, notoriously, does indeed have more civilian invalids (often alleged to be fraudulent welfare recipients), but these extra expenses are more than compensated for by the (more invisible) ordinary welfare expenses, very favourable to the North (see Scaramellini et al., 'I processi redistributivi').   [35] Ibid.

[36] For examples outside Italy, see e.g. Allen Buchanan, *Secession: The Morality of Political Divorce from Fort Sumter to Lithuania and Quebec* (Boulder, San Francisco, and Oxford, Westview Press, 1991), 115; Milica Zarkovic Bookman, *The Economics of Secession* (New York, St Martin's Press, 1992), 106–7.

inefficiency of the state is a consequence of 'southern' overrepresentation in the state apparatus, and that the policies of the government are dominated by southern interests. The former statement is an example of cultural stereotyping, since there is no causal connection between 'southernness' and inefficiency. The successful integration of southerners in northern Italy outside the state apparatus (or abroad, as emigrants) is solid proof that the problem of state inefficiency lies within its organizational structure, rather than with its regional composition.

The second claim puts the burden of proof on the Lega Nord: since northern Italians are in fact a majority within Italy, they should be able to sustain their political interests, especially since economic power is also located in the North. The Lega generally refers to the fact that the South has always voted in favour of government parties and, it claims, must therefore have received more favours from the government. In the period preceding the emergence of the Lega Nord, from Liberation to the late 1980s, the government parties could indeed generally count on a majority in most southern regions. Differences in voting patterns acquired a particular relevance in the early 1990s, when the government coalition first came under heavy criticism in the North. In the national elections of 1992, the government parties suffered heavy losses in the North, while advancing in the South. This voting pattern has not been confirmed, however, since the traditional parties suffered a similar decline in the South very shortly afterwards. In later elections the South divided its vote more or less evenly between the two major political alliances, the centre-left and the centre-right, with a slight preference for the latter. This explanation, moreover, overlooks the fact that for most of the post-war period many northern regions also voted consistently for government parties. Ironically, the regions and provinces that have given the strongest support to the Lega Nord correspond with those that for the whole post-war period were most faithful to the Christian Democrat party (*Democrazia Cristiana*, DC)—more than any southern region—giving this quintessentially governmental party strong majorities in all elections.[37]

This ignorance of past allegiances best symbolizes the distorted vision of Italian history defended by the Lega. It exemplifies how the wrongs of governments are projected outside the North, with a suitable amnesia of their northern connection. Similar amnesia also characterizes interpretations of partitocracy and the corruption of the 1980s. However much the partitocracy may have connived with southern interests, including organized crime, the political predominance in those years of the socialist Bettino Craxi (whose main power base was located in Italy's business capital, Milan) symbolizes its connection with northern interests. The Lega, however, argues

---

[37] On the Lega's electorate, see Diamanti, *La Lega*; and Biorcio, *La Padania promessa*.

that the government was more interested in defending the interests of big
capital than small entrepreneurs, whom the Lega purports to represent.
This claim is at best only partially true, since Italian governments have a
long tradition of catering for the interests of small industry. At the local
level, governments 'provided not only basic services, but, from the beginning of the 1960s onwards, expanded their activities by setting up networks
of social services and developing policies and infrastructures of direct
concern to industry'.[38] Their development took place in a context of 'little
interference by governments in the life of companies',[39] a euphemism meaning that the government tolerated tax evasion by companies and their
disregard for labour legislation.

At the national level, the Christian Democrats (who governed Italy
without interruption between 1945 and 1993) systematically implemented
policies in favour of artisans and small industry, offering them generous
tax facilities and subsidies. Moreover, northern regions received, when compared with the South, a disproportionately large amount of subsidies in the
framework of these policies, particularly for artisans and small industries.[40]
The Lega's claim may nevertheless have some plausibility in the specific
context of the late 1980s and early 1990s. Research on voting patterns in the
early 1990s in towns where the Lega was strongest—marked by the strong
presence of small enterprises, and the important role of small entrepreneurs—does indeed reveal that their concerns played an important role in
the transfer of political allegiance from the DC to the Lega. They motivated
this defection by referring to the fact that the DC no longer defended their
interests as it used to do in the past.[41]

The theory that supports both the mainstream interpretation of the
North–South divide and the Lega Nord's secessionist claim—namely, the
dissociation of northern Italy from the dysfunctional Italian state—hence
emerges as a specious self-justification. The vision of a state interested only in
the South is indeed a myth, since the Italian state—including its dysfunctions—is historically as 'northern' as it is 'southern'. This does not mean, of
course, that the grievances voiced against the Italian state are not relevant or

---

[38] Bruno Dente, 'Sub-National Governments in the Long Italian Transition', *West European Politics* 20:1 (1997), 176–93 (quotation p. 178).   [39] Ibid. 177.

[40] Linda Weiss, *Creating Capitalism: The State and Small Business since 1945* (Oxford, Basil Blackwell, 1988), esp. ch. 4, 55–80. Appendix I, Table F 216 shows the relation between firms registered and firms financed in 1971, and Table H 218, the regional distribution of loans and finance granted between 1952 and 1960 under Law 949 of 1952. Within northern Italy, these subsidies particularly favoured the regions outside the industrial triangle of Milan-Turin-Genoa, the so-called Third Italy.

[41] Anna Cento Bull, 'The Lega Lombarda: A New Political Subculture for Italy's Localized Industries', *The Italianist* 12 (1992), 179–83; and id., 'The Politics of Industrial Districts in Lombardy: Replacing Christian Democracy with the Northern League', *The Italianist* 13 (1993), 204–29.

should not be addressed: it only means that their translation into identity politics that dissociate the North from the Italian state should be understood as a self-serving discourse.

This self-serving and instrumentalist approach also characterizes the Lega's attitude towards Europe. The Lega has admittedly frequently highlighted its identification with European values, and stressed how the economic successes of northern Italy revealed its adaptation to European standards of economic modernity (while the 'failures' of the South allegedly revealed its non-European status). In recent years, the Lega has emphasized the cultural specificity of Europe, contrasting it both with the Third World (and particularly the Islamic countries) and the United States (whose 'melting pot' culture of immigration is considered as a negative example compared to an allegedly culturally homogeneous Europe). Both discourses, however, intend to construct European identity as instruments of exclusion, of southern Italians and of immigrants of non-European origins respectively.

While endorsing a European framework, the Lega has nevertheless always been critical of the institutions of the European Union, considered as examples of bureaucratic centralism reproducing the deleterious features of nation-states. Bossi contrasts the Europe of small peoples, of small enterprises, of minorities, of cultural liberty, of cities and of regions with the Europe of strong nationalisms, of an uncontrollable centralism, subordinated to the interests of its bureaucracy, of big finance and multinational corporations.[42] More specifically, the Lega has located its 'northern' and later 'Padanian' nation-building programme within a European framework, the construction of a Europe of the peoples, based on regional states.[43]

These lofty ideals have not been reflected in the political practice of the Lega. Until the acceptance of Italy in the European Monetary Union, the Lega subordinated its critique of the European Union to that of the Italian state, deemed incapable of achieving the country's entrance into the EMU. This incapacity was a consequence of the unpreparedness of the South, and hence justified the secession of the North, ready for an immediate insertion in the EMU.[44] When Italy was nonetheless accepted into the EMU, the Lega drastically modified its discourse. It now argues that the Euro will weaken the competitive position of Padanian entrepreneurs. According to the Lega, the new currency has been imposed by the large European states, especially France and Germany to facilitate their economic penetration of Padania, with the connivance of the Italian state. The Lega vindicates the right of Padania to an autonomous economic policy, including the management of its own currency. It claims the right to protect the Padanian economy and

---

[42] Bossi and Vimercati, *La Rivoluzione*, 208–9.   [43] Ibid. 208.
[44] Pagliarini, 'Le ragioni della Lega', 48.

in particular to enhance its competitiveness by the devaluation of its currency.[45] In practice, its ideal of a Europe of peoples is thus contradicted by an approach in which the cooperation between regions and peoples is subordinated to economic self-interest and cut-throat economic competition, and by a view of globalization as a struggle for the survival of the fittest.

AN EVALUATION OF THE LEGA'S CLAIM

My discussion of the arguments deployed by the Lega has highlighted how most of them can be interpreted as partisan constructions. The speciousness of the arguments certainly diminishes their relevance as acceptable justifications for secession. From a 'just cause' perspective, which accepts a 'remedial right of secession…for groups that have suffered certain kinds of injustices and for which secession is the most appropriate remedy',[46] the Lega's claim cannot carry much weight. Its arguments about discrimination against the North do not withstand critical scrutiny. Its justified critiques of the Italian state, with its inefficiency and over-centralization, and in the late 1980s and the early 1990s also its rampant corruption, give good grounds for demands for reform, not for secession. Even if one accepts the Lega's claim that the Italian state is beyond reform, such an acceptance would be a justification for revolution rather than for secession, since, contrary to what the Lega argues, the dysfunctional features of the state are not the consequences of 'southern contamination'.

The 'choice' perspective, which accords regions the right to secede if a majority expresses this intention, at first sight appears to give more justification to the Lega's claim. Even from a 'choice' perspective, however, several objections to this claim can be raised. To begin with, the group the Lega claims to represent is ill-defined, and the territorial delimitation of the North is highly problematic. In the highly unlikely event that the Italian government were prepared to organize a referendum on secession, delimiting the territory concerned would immediately create almost insoluble problems.

From the perspective of choice, moreover, the Lega presents another problem: its attitude towards democratic values. In the early 1990s especially, it presented a public profile respectful of these values. It has professed its attachment to cultural pluralism, reflected for example in the organization of a 'Padanian' gay movement, and a movement of 'Padanian' immigrants, and it has expressed its attachment to anti-fascism.[47] The Lega has no record of

[45] Bossi and Vimercati, *Processo alla Lega*, 46–62.

[46] Wayne Norman, 'The Ethics of Secession as the Regulation of Secessionist Politics', in Margaret Moore (ed.), *National Self-Determination and Secession* (Oxford, Oxford University Press, 1998), 34–61, at p. 41.

[47] It should be noted, however, that this 'anti-fascism' may just have been 'anti-Southernism' in disguise, since the Italian fascist party, the MSI (*Movimento Sociale Italiano*, now transformed into the post-fascist *Alleanza Nazionale*, AN) traditionally attracted most of its votes in the South.

discriminatory attitudes towards most of the minorities that have long been established in the North, especially those that can be regarded as belonging to 'Western' culture, such as the Friulians, the South Tyrolians, or the inhabitants of the Valle d'Aosta. Public statements deprecating southern Italians, the Slovenian minority in Friuli-Venezia Giulia, immigrants from the Third World and cultural deviants have, however, frequently contradicted its professions of liberalism. In particular, it has systematically defended discriminatory policies towards immigrants, such as barring their access to social services.[48] The same negative attitude can be found towards groups that are regarded as cultural deviants, especially when these groups are critical of the culture the Lega represents. It has, for example, frequently voiced its violent hostility towards the *centri sociali*, cultural centres well represented in the North, which play an important role in organizing alternative cultural events and left-wing opposition activities. In recent years, the Lega has moreover accentuated its illiberal inclinations, expressing its support for foreign right-wing populist movements such as Jorg Haider's *Freiheitliche Partei Österreichs* (FPÖ), and campaigning against immigrants, especially those of Islamic faith. The Lega would certainly not qualify for the condition Kai Nielsen requires for recognizing a nation's right to secession, namely the acceptance of other national identities on an equal footing.[49] The exasperated discourse of cultural superiority (geographically identified with 'Europe') that lies behind the Lega's construction of national identity is in fact translated into an attitude that excludes such equality.

PROPOSING ALTERNATIVES TO SECESSION

Unless one accepts the principle of self-determination as an absolute right and grants it to every group claiming to represent a 'self', that is a nation, regardless of its attitude towards democratic values, from a normative viewpoint the Lega's claim for secession should be rejected. Since at least some of its grievances can be considered justified, especially its critiques of the inefficient and over-centralized Italian state, discussing alternatives to secession is nevertheless a relevant exercise. Such discussions have in fact been prominent in both public and scholarly debates in recent years.

Discussions in Italy on institutional alternatives to secession centre first upon 'federalism'. The exact meaning of this term in the Italian debate is imprecise. When the Lega refers to federalism—as in its proposal of the early 1990s to reorganize Italy as a federation of three macro-regions, the North, the Centre, and the South—it conceives of the state as a confederation, based

[48] Biorcio, *La Padania promessa*, 145–65.
[49] Kai Nielsen, 'Liberal Nationalism and Secession', in Moore, *National Self-Determination and Secession*, 103–33, at p. 108.

on a freely established association, whose parties retain the right to dissolve it at any time.[50] For its centralist opponents, 'federalism' functions as a verbal substitute for reform. Its meaning is thus stretched from relatively minor administrative reforms to the reorganization of the Italian state as a loose confederation. Scholarly and intellectual efforts to give the concept a more precise interpretation have foundered on the dynamics of the public debate, where the imprecision of the concept has actually been an asset. The concept of 'federalism' can nevertheless be understood as expressing a generic intention to reform the centralized Italian state. Expressing a similar intention, 'subsidiarity' is the second concept that has marked the public debate in Italy. According to this principle, sponsored by the European Union, the central state would be ascribed a 'subsidiary' function, exercising only those competences that lower levels of governance would be unable to fulfil effectively. It also implies visualizing the role of the state as 'subsidiary' to community and/or private initiative.[51]

Both concepts have had a considerable impact on the public debate, and have promoted a series of reforms of the state. Of these reforms, the most straightforward and relatively least controversial have been concerned with administrative decentralization. Since 1990, several laws have been passed for this purpose, for example on the simplification of administrative procedures, and the weakening of central control over local authorities. Their implementation is generally credited with having had positive effects on local and provincial authorities.[52] Institutional reforms are certainly more complex and controversial. In the first place, they entail a re-evaluation of the role of the Italian regions.[53] Most assessments of the process of regionalization have

[50] Gaspare Nevola, 'La politica della secessione', *Rivista italiana di scienza politica* 28:1 (1998), 119–56, esp. p. 145.

[51] This doctrine has its origins in social Catholicism, and played a role in the Italian Christian-Democrat party in the early post-war years. Cf. Raffaele Romanelli, 'Centralismo e autonomie', in id. (ed.), *Storia dello stato italiano dall'Unità a oggi* (Rome, Donzelli, 1995), 125–86 (p. 163). See also Marco Cammelli, 'La sussidiarità preso sul serio', *Il Mulino* 49:3 (2000), 447–55.

[52] Dente, 'Sub-national Governments', 182–6. See also James Newell, 'L'inizio di un viaggio: passi sulla strada della decentralizzazione', in Luciano Bardo and Martin Rhodes (eds.), *Politica Italiana. I fatti dell'anno e le interpretazioni*, *Edizione 1998* (Bologna, Il Mulino, 1998), 175–96; and Giuseppe Cotturi, 'Federalismo dal Mezzogiorno', *Democrazia e Diritto* 2 (1999) (Federalismo e Mezzogiorno), 9–19, esp. pp. 13–14. Marco Cammelli gives a still positive, but more critical appreciation of these reforms: Marco Cammelli, 'Autonomie locali e riforme amministrative: due letture', *Il Mulino* 49:2 (2000), 313–22.

[53] This debate focuses almost exclusively on the ordinary-statute regions. The special statute of each of the other regions is guaranteed by the constitution. For three regions (Valle d'Aosta, Trentino-Alto Adige, and Friuli-Venezia Giulia), their special status is moreover related to the post-war settlements. Contrary to the ordinary-statute regions, these regions have always possessed exclusive competences. Notwithstanding their larger measure of autonomy, they have faced many of the same problems as the other regions.

highlighted its limits. Since their establishment in 1970, the regions have undoubtedly acquired legitimacy, particularly where there has been a continuity of stable government, but their possibilities for policy-making have been seriously hampered by financial problems and by the intervention of the central government. The regions were only given competences shared with the central government, or executive competences, and financially they have (until recently) remained largely dependent on the central state. The national instability of the party system frequently has repercussions at the regional level, leading to changes of coalition and causing the endemic instability of many regional governments in both northern and southern Italy.[54] The regions have for some time been demanding reforms that would enable them to function in a more efficient way, and they have also played an important role in developing and proposing plans for such reforms.[55] At the same time, the regions themselves have frequently been criticized for their centralism, their limited willingness to share competences with a lower level of governance—the provinces or local authorities—and thus for not applying the principle of subsidiarity.[56]

Of the attempts to reform the Italian state, the most ambitious has been undertaken by the (unsuccessful) *Bicamerale* (Bicameral) commission, constituted after the national elections of 1996 for the purpose of drawing up a proposal for constitutional reform.[57] Its final proposal would have given the regions legislative powers and exclusive competence on issues not explicitly reserved for or shared with the central state.[58] Following the German model, it also aimed to reorganize the Senate as a Chamber of Regions.[59] The constitutional law 1999, N. 1 has given regions the right to outline their own electoral systems and statutes (within the framework of the Italian constitution), and it established the direct election of the *presidente* of the region. Changing regulations and practices have in the meantime given regions greater financial autonomy while they started to acquire the right to

---

[54] Luigi Mariucci, 'L'elezione diretta del Presidente della regione e la nuova forma di governo regionale', *Le istituzioni del federalismo* 20:6 (1999), 1149–64.

[55] The project of the Emilia-Romagna region has been published in Luigi Mariucci, Roberto Bin, Marco Cammelli, Adriano Di Pietro, and Giandomenico Falcon, *Il federalismo preso sul serio. Una proposta di riforma per l'Italia* (Bologna, Il Mulino, 1996). See also the reflections of the ex-president of Tuscany, Vannino Chiti. Vannino Chiti, 'L'Italia fra federalismo vecchio e nuovo', *Nuova Antologia* 132:2204 (1997), 39–63.

[56] See e.g. Cesare Damiano, 'Federalismo o devolution? Il caso del Veneto', *Quale stato* 4 (2000), 69–80; Domenico Pantaleo, 'Dal punto di vista del Sud', *Quale stato* 4 (2000), 95–100.

[57] For the text adopted by the commission, see Jader Jacobelli (ed.), *Il federalismo degli Italiani* (Rome and Bari, Laterza, 1997), 223–34. The proposal failed to get through parliament. For the *Bicamerale*, however, the issue of federalism was clearly of less importance than strengthening the power of the executive. Cf. Gianfranco Pasquino, 'Reforming the Italian Constitution', *Journal of Modern Italian Studies* 3:1 (1998), 42–54: see p. 46.

[58] Jacobelli, *Il federalismo degli Italiani*, 227. The list of competences attributed to the central government (pp. 226–7), remains, however, very extensive. See also Newell, 'L'inizio di un viaggio', 181–7.   [59] Jacobelli, *Il federalismo degli Italiani*, 233.

act as autonomous subjects vis-à-vis the European Union.[60] It created a hybrid situation, on the one hand reinforcing regional governments while on the other maintaining central control over them, producing a system that is still strongly centralized but in which regional presidents are nonetheless given a good deal of authority.[61] A law passed on 8 March 2001 amended the Constitution, largely following recommendations made by the *Bicamerale* commission. This has given the regions exclusive legislative competence on issues not reserved for or shared with the central state, the right (shared with central state) to develop international relations and it introduced the principle of subsidiarity into the constitution. It has not, however, entailed a reorganization of the Senate.[62] The law was voted for by the centre-left Ulivo then in power, no doubt to affirm its federalist credentials for the forthcoming electoral campaign.[63] This act was itself a response to a campaign by the regional governments of several northern regions controlled by the centre-right Casa delle Libertà alliance, which includes the Lega Nord), for more autonomy.

At the moment of writing (December 2002), the Italian parliament is discussing a project for devolution sponsored by the Lega Nord. This project proposes to modify the constitution by attributing regions exclusive legislative competencies for education, health, and local police.[64] It is unclear to what extent these constitutional changes will effectively put an end to a situation where the autonomy of regions (but also, partly, that of local and provincial authorities) remains conditional on the policies of central government, and the possibility of centralist reactions, particularly since the Berlusconi government is at the same time drastically reducing its financial contribution to regions.[65] This continued concern with institutional reforms reveals, however, the political importance the issues of 'federalism' and 'subsidiarity' have acquired in recent years.

[60] Mariucci, 'L'elezione diretta del Presidente della regione e la nuova forma di governo regionale'; Valentino Parlato, 'I poteri forti della nuova Regione', *Il Manifesto*, 16 April 2000; Massimo Bordignon, 'Federalismo fiscale? Riflessioni in merito alle recenti riforme in Italia', *Il Mulino* 49:2 (2000), 323–31.

[61] Paolo Nerozzi, 'Il federalismo necessario', *Quale stato*, No. 4, 2000 46–53. See p. 49.

[62] For the text of the amendments, see *Il Sole/24 Ore*, 8 March 2001. This law has since then been approved by a referendum, held on 7 Oct. 2001 (64.2 per cent of approvals, with a participation of 34 per cent of the electorate).

[63] Comments on this law have in fact highlighted that it introduced a precedent, by amending the constitution without a broad political consensus (in the Chamber of Deputies the amendments obtained an extremely narrow majority, 316 deputies out of a total of 630). The practice is itself legal, but it has clearly broken an implicit pact that such amendments should not be made under these conditions.

[64] Claudio De Fiores, 'Controriforme. Devolution, il principio di dissoluzione', Il Manifesto, 6 December 2002.

[65] Mariucci, 'L'elezione diretta del Presidente della regione e la nuova forma di governo regionale', 1163–4, Ilvo Diamanti, 'Quello Stato lontano dalle Regioni', *la Repubblica*, 10 November 2002.

A third issue in the debates in Italy concerns *federalismo fiscale*, 'fiscal federalism'. This concept may simply involve allocating more resources to the regional governments, and diminishing central tutelage over their expenditure. In its most drastic interpretation, it comes close to the abolition of interregional financial transfers. The implementation of such a reform would in all probability deepen the economic North–South divide. Most southern regions would be faced with serious financial problems, and would be obliged either to raise more taxes or to cut down drastically on their welfare expenditure. Such a reform would probably aggravate North–South differences in economic performance and standard of living, and would almost certainly reinforce centrifugal dynamics. In practice, proposals for fiscal federalism moderate this radical interpretation, leaving space for exceptions or for a balancing out to be decided on annually.[66] Such proposals nevertheless clearly question the principle that, to guarantee the equality of Italian citizens, all regions should have an equal per capita spending capacity.

The controversies over 'fiscal federalism' reveal most clearly the ideological issues that are involved in institutional reforms. One important category of proposals for federalist reforms belongs to a more generic critique of the welfare state.[67] Its defenders share with the Lega Nord the association of federalism with economic neo-liberalism (*liberismo*). They propose the abandonment of existing national standards of wage levels and social security, and frequently include their proposals in a vision of competitive federalism, interpreted in the context of a model of European integration based on competition between regions. Such proposals, voiced for example in the aforementioned campaign for autonomy launched by northern regional governments, tend to endorse the 'northern' viewpoint of the Lega Nord, since they are almost always designed to free the North from contributing to the South. The issues this campaign has highlighted and the rhetoric of devolution and autonomy it has deployed correspond in many ways with

---

[66] See e.g. Furio Boselli, 'Federalismo fiscale: da dove cominciare', *Federalismo & Società* 2:4 (1995), 53–5; and Giuseppe Valditara, 'La Bicamerale e il federalismo', *Federalismo & Libertà* 5:1 (1998), 35–44. See p. 39.

[67] Liberal federalism is proposed by adherents of both the centre-left and the centre-right. The former mayor of Venice, Massimo Cacciari, is the most prominent spokesperson on liberal federalism for the centre-left. See e.g. Massimo Cacciari and Mario Carraro, 'Dialogo sul Nord-Est', *MicroMega* 4 (1997), 17–25. The review *Federalismo & Società*, recently rebaptized *Federalismo & Libertà*, gives voice to the liberal federalism of the centre–right. See e.g. Gianfranco Morra, 'Il federalismo che vogliamo', *Federalismo & Società* 2:2–3 (1995), 11–14; Furio Boselli, 'Federalismo fiscale: da dove cominciare', *Federalismo & Società* 2:4 (1995), 53–5; Giuseppe Valditara, 'La Bicamerale e il federalismo', *Federalismo & Libertà* 5:1 (1998), 35–44. For a more critical evaluation, from a liberal point of view, of competitive models of federalism and fiscal federalism, see Giorgio Ragazzi, 'Federalismo fiscale e questione meridionale', *Federalismo & Società* 2:1 (1995), 29–57.

the Lega's nation-building discourse, and it in fact advocates a vision of 'federalism' based on more limited national solidarity. The new proposal for devolution, presently discussed in the Italian parliament, likewise follows this logic. The new competencies of the regions would be financially sustained according to the region's fiscal capacities, thereby introducing a mechanism privileging the richer and penalizing the poorer regions.[68]

By no means all proposals for federalism interpret it as a neo-liberal reform intended to dismantle the welfare state and interregional solidarity. Other proposals for federalism emphasize solidarity and, on the contrary, highlight the co-operative intention of their project. Like defenders of neo-liberal federalism, they take as their starting-point a critique of the inefficiency of the centralized state, but in addition they highlight its incapacity to sustain a more equal development of its territory.[69] Such visions of federalism are favourable to local autonomy, but are at the same time deeply concerned with maintaining national standards for wages, welfare and labour protection in order to prevent the aggravation of national income discrepancies and, hence, to maintain national solidarity.

In this light, the most interesting rethinking of Italian—and specifically southern—identity has recently come from intellectuals and students of southern Italy.[70] They have revealed how the Lega's nation-building discourse and the 'northern' vision of the South are often based on stereotypes and erroneous generalizations. The Lega's discourse and the northern vision highlight the deficiencies of the South, understood as the failures of a deeply-rooted southern culture, without analysing them in the context of the contemporary political history of the Italian state. Southern intellectuals and students of southern Italy draw attention to the consequences of intervention by the Italian state, its projects for developing the South, and particularly the *intervento straordinario*, the post-war 'extraordinary intervention' to modernize and industrialize the South. This intervention has indeed played an important role in modernizing the South, releasing it from the poverty trap and providing it with the infrastructure necessary for further development. Yet the political constellation in which this intervention occurred, and particularly its conception as a means to exercise political and

---

[68] De Fiores, 'Controriforme. Devolution, il principio di dissoluzione'.

[69] Pantaleo, 'Dal punto di vista del Sud'.

[70] The most significant discussions on the contemporary South are to be found in reviews such as *Meridiana* and *Nord e Sud*. The former especially has published important contributions, e.g. Carmine Donzelli, 'Mezzogiorno tra "questione" e purgatorio', 13–53; the special issues on 'Mezzogiorno Oggi' ('The Mezzogiorno Today', NS 26–7, 1996), and on development (31, 1998). See also the special issue of the review *Democrazia e Diritto* (2, 1999), on 'Federalismo e Mezzogiorno', ed. Franco Cassano and Giuseppe Cotturi. As the author of *Il pensiero meridiano* (Rome and Bari, Laterza, 1996). Franco Cassano is regarded as the intellectual founding-father of new 'southern' or 'Meridian' thought.

social control over southern Italy, has produced undesirable side-effects such as the proliferation of clientelism and corruption and the development of a culture of dependence.

The criticism of the 'northern' interpretation of southern backwardness voiced by these intellectuals continues what has always been an important quality of the *meridionalisti* (the generic name given to students of the 'Southern Question'), namely, interpreting the problems of the South not within a framework of victimization but as problems of Italy as a whole, deriving from the particular characteristics of the Italian political system. They acknowledge the deleterious features of southern society, but do not categorize them as the result of the negative inheritance of a supposedly unchangeable and homogeneous southern culture, as the 'Northern' viewpoint perceives it, but in the light of the South's political history.

More radically, one group of southern Italian intellectuals gives a positive content to a Southern or 'Meridian' identity. They have drawn attention to the specific cultural traditions of the South, in particular the resilience of the ties of community solidarity. These traditions may help in designing alternative models of development, unlike the *anomie* of modernity, which undermines such solidarity.[71] This vision in fact introduces a new element into the debate: a critique of the northern model of endogenous regional development. Especially in the regions where the Lega is strong, this development took place in the absence of coordination or regulation. It thus created an exclusively entrepreneurial culture, without regard for the social or environmental consequences of economic activities.[72] The harmful side-effects of this model are in fact rarely acknowledged in discussions of the 'Northern Question'. The polemical question raised by Sidney Tarrow—whether the separatism of the Lega Nord and the corruption scandals of the early 1990s should not be interpreted as indicating the 'collapse of the North's vaunted civic capacity'[73]—is rarely addressed. The impressive economic successes of the North render a discussion of its development model more difficult. Most commentators continue to highlight the virtues of northern Italy and assume that its—and implicitly the Lega's—grievances are justified, while they attempt to dissociate northern society from the Lega

[71] Mario Alcaro, *Sull'identità meridionale. Forme di una cultura mediterranea* (Turin, Bollati Bolinghieri, 1999), 46–9.

[72] This tendency can be related to the specific Christian-Democrat tradition of governance in these regions, sustaining development financially, but with little interest in creating institutions to regulate it. In the northern and central regions governed by the Communist Party, development has tended to be much more regulated. See Silvio Lanaro & Guido Crainz, 'Emilia, Veneto, Nord-Est: gli storici', *Rassegna di Storia Contemporánea* 7:1 (1997), 15–21.

[73] Sidney Tarrow, 'Making Social Science Work Across Space and Time: A Critical Reflection on Robert Putnam's Making Democracy Work', *American Political Science Review* 90:2 (1996), 389–97, at p. 392.

Nord. Only a minority points out how economic development in the North often took place—particularly in the regions where the Lega is strong—without concern for its social or environmental consequences. As the sociologist Aldo Bonomi has phrased it: the individualist entrepreneurial culture that characterizes some northern sub-regions is adept at 'making an economy', but lacks the capacity to 'make a society'.[74] The difficult relationship between such an entrepreneurial culture and a culture of responsible governance is in fact one of the elements behind the emergence of the 'Northern Question'.[75]

This new generation of *meridionalisti* and critical scholars from the North has the merit of proposing a viewpoint on national identity and reform that transcends a sterile North–South confrontation. With the question of identity as a starting-point, they propose redirecting the discussion towards the issue of models of society and of development. While critical of the predominantly economic focus of the northern model of development, the new generation of *meridionalisti* addresses the justified grievances of the North against southern inefficiency and waste. After an initial period of perplexity as regards federalism, they have started to look with more favour upon reforms of the centralized state.[76] They propose responsible self-government as an alternative to bureaucratic waste, inefficiency and corruption. They highlight how recent positive experiences in the South, like the emergence of a new civil society and entrepreneurship, and the renewal of local government in many cities may contribute to this goal.

These intellectuals suggest a refounding of Italy as a partnership between equals. They are particularly concerned to transform the South into a responsible political player within Italy, as an entity capable of making decisions by itself, instead of being a passive recipient of government subsidies. In the present context of economic inequality between the North and the South, they defend the legitimacy of continued redistributive policies on a national level, to guarantee the equal rights and opportunities of citizens, albeit in a context of accountability and responsibility.[77] Institutionally, they frequently express their scepticism of the present regions, not only because

[74] Aldo Bonomi, *Il capitalismo molecolare. La società al lavoro nel Nord Italia* (Turin, Einaudi, 1997).

[75] See e.g. Bruno Anastasia, Giancarlo Coro, and Enzo Rullani, 'La solitudine del produttore', *MicroMega* 4 (1997), 54–63; Gianfranco Bettin, 'La casa delle finestre che ridono', *MicroMega* 4 (1997), 26–32.

[76] See e.g. 'Federalismo. Discussione fra Raffaele Brancati, Carmine Donzelli, Salvatore Lupo e Carlo Trigilia, coordinato da Francesco Benigni', *Meridiana* 24 (1995), 143–71; Luigi Masella, 'Declino del meridionalismo unitario e centralista', in Franco Cassano and Giuseppe Cotturi (eds.), *Federalismo e Mezzogiorno* (*Democrazia e Diritto* 2, 1999), 28–36.

[77] Cotturi, 'Federalismo dal Mezzogiorno', 12 and 14–15. Daniele Petrosino, 'Il federalismo tra illusioni e necessità', in Cassano and Cotturi, *Federalismo e Mezzogiorno*, 37–49: see p. 45.

of the generally negative experience of regional governments in the South, but also because of the weak sense of identity with which they are imbued. Cities and local communities, as the locus of identity in the South and as examples of political renewal, play a more important role in their vision of autonomy and self-government.[78]

This 'southern' perspective offers a principled answer to the secessionist claim of the Lega Nord, one which not only deconstructs its rhetoric on the 'Padanian nation', but also effectively criticizes the mainstream interpretation of Italy's problems through the prism of the 'Northern Question'. The programme they propose is Utopian, in the sense that it relies on a vision of the South (and concurrently Italy) as it ought to be, rather than in its present state. This Utopian vision, however, is itself based on a critical assessment of the southern present, and the awareness that the achievement of federalism or of institutional reform implies a programme to transform southern society. Such a programme can already rely on its newly emerging civic culture and the appearance of a new political class. It remains, however, confronted with the challenge of achieving a wider consensus on its vision of the South's future.[79]

Like its counterpart, the secessionist discourse of the Lega Nord, this 'southern' viewpoint embeds institutional reforms in a more general vision of society. More than a debate on institutional engineering, the debate initiated by the secessionist claim of the Lega Nord is concerned with creating institutions that would enable a 'virtuous' development that would reinforce national cohesion, as against the centrifugal tendencies resulting from the inefficient centralism of the Italian state. While proponents of the 'southern' standpoint view institutional reform in the light of a critical assessment of southern society and a programme of social reform, this self-critical dimension is much weaker in the North. Because of the economic successes of the North, the virtues of northern society are frequently taken for granted, not assessed, and the dysfunctions of its institutions thus tend to be understood exclusively as resulting from external factors.

CONCLUSIONS

An analysis of the Italian debate certainly gives an additional admonition against a generic right to self-determination. It highlights how the definition of those 'selves', i.e. nations, is already problematic in itself. The identities the Lega proposes are constructs, and its different definitions of 'Padania' actually compete with each other. At the same time, however, the

---

[78] Cotturi, 'Federalismo dal Mezzogiorno', 10.
[79] Petrosino, 'Il federalismo tra illusioni e necessità', 48–9.

'invented' northern Italian identities cannot merely be reduced to a cynical fabrication. They rely on strongly entrenched interpretative categories, and address widely shared grievances, especially against the Italian state. The Lega's discourse in fact derives its strength from its correspondence with common-sense interpretations of the Italian state and of Italy's North–South divide.

The Italian case highlights both the necessity and the dangers of interpreting grievances through the prism of national identities. The whole perspective of the 'Northern Question' is based on a juxtaposition of the virtues of the northern people and the vices of the Italian state. The Lega's discourse has merely radicalized this framework, made explicit its inherent negative value-judgement on southern Italians, and given this juxtaposition an extreme political expression—secessionism. The regional differences referred to in the Lega's discourse are real enough and the discussion of their meaning and origins is legitimate. These differences, however, should be interpreted without resorting to their reified juxtaposition in the framework of the North–South dichotomy, which contrasts a modern and superior North with a backward and inferior South. The Lega's capacity to include justified grievances in a nationalist discourse is in fact greatly enhanced by the mainstream acceptance of this reified juxtaposition, which relies at least partially on a self-congratulatory historical narrative. Without leading to an endorsement of the existence of a 'Padanian nation' and its right to secession, this acceptance facilitates an interpretation of Italy's problems in the light of the 'Northern Question'.

In this context, it is also clear that discussing alternatives to secession cannot be limited to considering institutional reforms—whatever the merits of such reforms may be, and despite the undoubted relevance such discussions obviously have. The process of identity-building within Italy, when centred on a polarized North–South dichotomy, weakens mutual solidarity and thus strengthens centrifugal tendencies. Considering alternatives to secession can be effective only when the issues raised by the Lega are tackled and when the interpretative framework of Italy's North–South divide—in which the Lega's claim is embedded—is challenged. This implies re-evaluating the meanings attributed to northern and southern identities, as a way of imagining a common future for Italy.

3

Discussing Autonomy and Independence for Corsica

Gunter Lauwers

Corsica has been the scene of separatist violence for decades. Assassinations and bomb attacks seem to be an ingredient of everyday politics on this island. A comparison with Northern Ireland or the Basque Country is never far away. But in the long run the Matignon Agreement of 2000, negotiated between the French government and the local political élite, could well represent a first decisive step towards a lasting peace on the island. This compromise has met some of the main demands put forward by the Corsican nationalists in pursuit of their ultimate goal: self-determination for the Corsican people.

The aim of this chapter is to examine whether Corsicans have a moral right to self-determination and, if so, to determine whether they are entitled to autonomy or even independence as a consequence of this right. In the first section, I will give a short historical overview of Corsican secessionism. The second part deals with the legal interpretations of the right to self-determination, and its relationship with the right to autonomy and the right to secession. A third section gives an overview of the moral interpretations of the right to self-determination in contemporary political theory, making a distinction between two different schools of thought in this respect: the 'just cause' versus 'choice' theories. The subsequent and final sections consist of an application of these normative theories to Corsican nationalism, with an overview of the situation since the acceptance of the Matignon Agreement by the National Assembly of the French Republic.

THE CORSICAN QUESTION

The emergence of the Corsican demand for independence dates back to the mid-1970s. Until that time, nationalist Corsicans did not seek independent statehood but merely political autonomy within France. However, violent street clashes and the fact that this demand for autonomy was not given due consideration led to a radicalization of the movement. Several terrorist organizations made their appearance resulting in a gradual shift from a quest for autonomy towards a struggle for independence. In an attempt to weaken this secessionism, the French government implemented some institutional reforms in 1982, leading to an autonomous Corsican 'parliament'. Initially, Paris wanted this special status to approximate that of Sicily and Sardinia, by granting some limited legislative powers, but the final status diverged considerably from this original intention. The '*Assemblée de Corse*' (Corsican Assembly), directly elected through a proportional representation system of voting, had no legislative power whatsoever. It could merely solicit the Prime Minister, without any guarantee that he would give its proposals serious consideration.[1] The same was true at the fiscal level: the Assembly was granted the opportunity to present Paris with an annual list of its priorities on how to spend the state budget for Corsica, but the government was not in any way obliged to follow this advice. Since the island could hardly fall back on its own financial resources, it thus remained dependent on subsidies from the mainland. Certainly, 'in all areas relating to sovereignty over the island', the Assembly had only 'consultative, not decision-making, power'.[2] It was further granted some administrative competence in areas such as culture, transport, energy, planning, and education, but these powers were limited.[3] In addition, these minor responsibilities were ill defined, and there has been confusion and overlap in their allocation.[4]

The institutional reforms of the French government thus failed to satisfy the Corsican nationalists. In response, in 1991 the central authorities decided to upgrade the powers of the Assembly. This transformed Corsica into a '*Collectivité territoriale*' or Territorial Community, a *sui generis* authority with spheres of competence fairly similar to those of a French '*Territoire d'outre-mer*' (Overseas Territory, also known by the acronym 'TOM'). These TOMs had previously been part of the French colonial empire but in the period of decolonization their populations had decided not to separate and had opted to remain closely associated with France.[5] Corsica's new statute, which was modelled on that of the TOMs, introduced only a modest extension of the existing administrative and fiscal powers of the Corsican Assembly, and still conferred no legislative power on the latter.

---

[1] Helen Hintjens, Sean Loughlin, and Claude Olivesi, 'The Status of Maritime and Insular France: The DOM-TOM and Corsica', *Regional Politics & Policy* 4:3 (1994), 123–4.

[2] VANINA, *La revendication institutionnelle en Corse. Collectivité territoriale et mouvement nationaliste* (La Bussière, Acratie, 1995), 54.

[3] Hintjens, Loughlin, and Olivesi, 'The Status of Maritime and Insular France', 123–4.

[4] Peter Savigear, 'Corsica', in Michael Watson (ed.), *Contemporary Minority Nationalism* (London and New York, Routledge, 1992), 91.

[5] Today there are only three such TOMs: New Caledonia, French Polynesia and the Wallis and Futuna Islands, all three located in the Pacific region.

The successive steps taken by the French government to provide Corsica with its own institutions have therefore traditionally never gone far enough to meet autonomist and secessionist demands on the island. Quite the contrary, since these institutional reforms have been met by waves of criticism, and not only in political rhetoric. Paul Hainsworth and John Loughlin stated in 1984 that 'one fairly common verdict on the Assembly is that little of a significant nature has been achieved in Corsica due to the unwillingness of Paris to grant enough autonomy to it'.[6] Although their analysis was concerned with the institutional framework of 1982, this statement was still relevant after the reforms of 1991. In 1994, Loughlin—together with his co-authors Helen Hintjens and Claude Olivesi—concluded that 'the new institutions and the new special statute will do little to remedy the chronic political backwardness and instability of the island'.[7]

As a result, the demand for self-determination never faded, and separatist terrorism remained a feature of Corsican politics. Following an intensification of this violence in 1999, French Prime Minister Lionel Jospin entered into direct negotiations with the Corsican Assembly, including the elected deputies of A Cuncolta Indipendentista. This was regarded as an extraordinary event, for A Cuncolta—the most radical nationalist party in Corsica— is the political representative of the Front de Libération Nationale de la Corse (FLNC), the major terrorist organization on the island.[8] The aim of these negotiations was clear and ambitious: to achieve a final settlement of the Corsican problem through an open and direct debate between the central and local political élites, including members of a party with links to an armed, underground group.

These negotiations eventually led to the Matignon Agreement between prime minister Lionel Jospin and the Corsican Assembly in July 2000. The key provisions of this compromise, which was supported by A Cuncolta and will be discussed in more detail below, included the transfer of some limited legislative powers to the Corsican Assembly, as well as the more widespread teaching of the Corsican language. This Matignon Agreement was reworked into a bill, which was adopted by the National Assembly in December 2001.[9] Corsican nationalists and separatists thus took a significant step forward in the struggle they justify by invoking the right to self-determination. But the question remains: do Corsicans have such a right?

---

[6] Paul Hainsworth and John Loughlin, 'Le problème corse', *Contemporary French Civilization* 8:3 (1984), 362.
[7] Hintjens, Loughlin, and Olivesi, 'The Status of Maritime and Insular France', 128.
[8] In May 2001, A Cuncolta Indipendentista merged with three minor political organizations (U Cullettivu Naziunale, Corsica Viva and l'Associu per a Suvranità) and adopted the name Indipendenza.
[9] The Loi No. 2002-92 was published 22 Jan. 2002 in the *Journal officiel de la République française*.

THE RIGHT TO SELF-DETERMINATION: AN AMBIGUOUS CONCEPT

Self-determination has always been a controversial issue—not only in political science but also in legal studies—and, consequently, different schools of thought competed to set their seal on this concept when it was evolving from a political aspiration into a principle of international law. As a result, legal commentators cannot avoid confronting differing interpretations of the so-called 'right to self-determination' and are compelled to enter an arena of Babel-like confusion when addressing the subject. Although such legal opinions are of rather limited use for a normative analysis like the one presented here, particular elements of this wide-ranging debate on international law may be of special interest when assessing the Corsican case, since a large proportion of nationalist Corsicans translate the right to self-determination into a putative right to autonomy, and even a right to secession.[10]

The right to secession

One may question whether the internationally recognized right to self-determination encompasses a right to unilateral forms of secession. Secession is an issue on which international law has always remained silent, unless it concerned the liberation of overseas colonies. With the collapse of the Soviet Union and the subsequent dismemberment of the Yugoslav federation, however, secessionist self-determination in a non-colonial context has shaken international law. Indeed, most of those involved in the disintegration processes in these countries have endeavoured to legitimize their struggle by invoking the right to self-determination.[11] Secession and revolution, however, are political rather than legal concepts. Lawyers tend to conclude that—except in the colonial context—unilateral secession is not recognized as a right under international law. The issue of secession is a lacuna in international hard law. Nonetheless, some scholars argue that the UN 'Declaration on Friendly Relations'[12] of 1970 suggests a right to secession (albeit a strictly limited one). This declaration stipulates that the principle of territorial integrity can only be invoked by 'States conducting themselves in compliance with the principle of equal rights and self-determination ... and thus *possessed of a government representing the whole people belonging to the*

---

[10] On the distinction between the right to autonomy and the right to secession see also Gunter Lauwers and Stefaan Smis, 'New Dimensions of the Right to Self-Determination: A Study of the International Response to the Kosovo Crisis', *Nationalism and Ethnic Politics* 6:2 (2000), 43–70.

[11] See Dietrich Murswiek, 'The Issue of a Right of Secession—Reconsidered', in Christian Tomuschat (ed.), *Modern Law of Self-Determination* (Dordrecht, Boston, and London, Martinus Nijhoff Publishers, 1993), 28.

[12] In full: 'Declaration on Principles of International Law Concerning Friendly Relations and Co-operation Among States in Accordance with the Charter of the United Nations.'

territory without distinction as to race, creed or colour.[13] Hence, one could, *a contrario*, conclude that an ethnic entity has the right to secede from a sovereign and independent state if the latter does not possess a representative government or if members of the ethnic group concerned are systematically excluded from the political institutions of that state.[14] This radical view is not frequently expressed, however.

The right to autonomy

Whether the international right to self-determination comprises a right to autonomy is yet another controversial topic. Most scholars in the field maintain that autonomy is not as such a matter of general international law.[15] It belongs rather in the domain of constitutional law, regarded as an internal matter for a sovereign state. Hurst Hannum, however, states that there is an increasing tendency to interpret international minority rights as encompassing a right to territorial autonomy. But he admits that it is doubtful whether this 'right to autonomy' has yet achieved the status of international law.[16] Nevertheless, the concept of autonomy is an important issue for the international community, since the implementation of autonomy could well act as an efficacious cure for many ethno-political conflicts throughout the world, whether they are dormant or provoking violent acts.[17] Most international lawyers agree that granting autonomy has to be seen as one way—although not the only possible one—of recognizing a valid claim to the right to self-determination.

Legal instruments, however, grant a state extensive discretionary power in putting this internal form of self-determination into practice. Autonomy may therefore take different forms. James Crawford defines autonomous areas rather generally as 'regions of a State, usually possessing some ethnic or cultural distinctiveness, which have been granted separate powers of internal administration, *to whatever degree*, without being detached from the State of which they are part'.[18] Indeed, the degree of autonomy of

---

[13] GA Res. 2625 (XXV) of 24 Oct. 1970, section on self-determination, para. 7. Emphasis added.
[14] Frederic L. Kirgis, 'The Degrees of Self-Determination in the United Nations Era', *American Journal of International Law* 88:2 (1994), 306.
[15] Lauri Hannikainen, 'Self-Determination and Autonomy in International Law', in Markku Suksi (ed.), *Autonomy: Applications and Implications* (The Hague, London, and Boston, Kluwer Law International, 1998), 86.
[16] Hurst Hannum, *Territorial Autonomy: Permanent Solution or Step toward Secession?* 1–4. Paper presented at the international conference 'Facing Ethnic Conflicts', 14–16 Dec. 2000, Bonn University.
[17] See Ruth Lapidoth, *Autonomy. Flexible Solutions To Ethnic Conflicts* (Washington DC, United States Institute of Peace Press, 1997), 3 and Kjell-Åke Nordquist, 'Autonomy as a Conflict-Solving Mechanism—An Overview', in Suksi (ed.), *Autonomy*, 59–77.
[18] James Crawford, *The Creation of States in International Law* (Oxford, Clarendon Press, 197 , 211. Emphasis added.

so-called 'autonomous' regions can differ significantly. It is important to bear in mind that the concept of autonomy in the present chapter has to be understood as genuine *political* autonomy: granting some form of legislative power to the autonomous area. A merely *administrative* form of autonomy ('deconcentrated' or 'decentralized administration' are more appropriate labels) falls short of the contemporary political/philosophical definition of autonomy as it is currently used. With these arguments we have gradually left the path of the legalistic approach and entered the field of political theory. In a normative or moral debate on self-determination, other arguments have to be taken into account in addition to legal perspectives.[19]

THE CONCEPT OF SELF-DETERMINATION FROM A MORAL PERSPECTIVE

Wayne Norman rightly points out that, because of the legal vacuum with regard to secession, 'what we need in the meantime are clear moral theories based on sound principles in order to judge, in the absence of institutions, which groups have a right to secede'.[20] But the content of these theories— and theories of self-determination in general—can vary extensively, as the following short overview will attempt to show.

Jane Stromseth finds two situations in which reasons for unilateral secession seem particularly compelling. First, 'secession may be justified in order to undo past injustice when a distinct people has a legitimate claim to territory that was wrongfully annexed by another state'. Second, 'secession may be justified in order to undo present repression when a distinct people or minority is systematically repressed within an existing state and denied equal opportunity to participate in the political process or subjected to ongoing gross violations of human rights'.[21] The latter form of secession has been labelled by many scholars as an *ultimum remedium* or last resort when all other, less radical, options have failed. Under these circumstances, the 'right' to secede appears to be a right to self-defence—for the very survival of the people or minority is at stake—and even the use of force might be considered legitimate in such a situation.[22]

This 'just cause' approach is shared by many political theorists. They deny that self-determination (up to and including the right to secession) is a general right. The concerns of this school of thought are multiple when it

[19] Henceforth, the notion 'right to self-determination' will no longer be applied in the *legal* but in the *moral* sense, unless otherwise stated.
[20] Wayne Norman, 'The Ethics of Secession as the Regulation of Secessionist Politics', in Margaret Moore (ed.), *National Self-Determination and Secession* (Oxford, Oxford University Press, 1998), 45.
[21] Jane E. Stromseth, 'Secession and Humanitarian Intervention by the United Nations', *American Society of International Law Proceedings* (1993), 44.
[22] Murswiek, 'The Issue of a Right of Secession—Reconsidered', 26–7.

comes to granting such a general right to secession, for the following reasons: (1) the fear of Balkanization, or the domino theory; (2) the negative effect such a right could have on a democratic state system, as a minority would always have an opportunity for blackmail by threatening to secede if its wishes were not taken into account; (3) the possibility of the endless divisibility of a state, since very few states are ethnically homogeneous and secessionist territories are not usually ethnically homogeneous either; (4) the danger that it might lead to the creation of small, non-viable state entities; (5) the problem of 'trapped' minorities which could be prevented from seceding in their turn and (6) the issue of the stranded majorities who see the economically or strategically most important part of their territory seceding.[23] These authors regard the right to secession as a 'remedial right only'.[24]

At the other end of the spectrum lies the 'choice approach'. This trend considers self-determination (including secession) to be a 'primal right', rooted in liberal democratic theory and available to any group in which a majority of its members want it, regardless of whether the particular group is suffering injustice or not. Adherents of this school of thought also lay down some strict conditions in this matter.[25] The 'choice' theorist David Miller enumerates six conditions that need to be fulfilled before self-determination is granted: (1) the group concerned has to be a nation with an identity that is clearly separate from that of the larger nation from which it wishes to disassociate; (2) this entity must be able to exercise authority over the territory it seeks to occupy; (3) a (super-)majority of the group must approve the self-determination claim in a referendum; (4) respect for (new) minorities must be guaranteed in its enhanced institutional status; (5) the principles of distributive justice must be respected, and (6) the group claiming self-determination must have a territory and resources from which a viable political community can be created.[26]

Clearly, the conditions invoked by the 'just cause' and the 'choice' schools are very different.[27] Nevertheless, there is one aspect that most authors

[23] Lee C. Buchheit, *Secession: The Legitimacy of Self-Determination* (New Haven, Yale University Press, 1978), 20–30 and Alexis Heraclides, *The Self-Determination of Minorities in International Politics* (London, Frank Cass, 1991), 28.

[24] Apart from a right to secession acquired through a negotiated settlement (e.g. the former Czechoslovakia), or through constitutional provisions that explicitly grant such a right (e.g. the Ethiopian constitution of 1994).

[25] An unconditional form of the choice approach is absent from the academic discussions on self-determination and is articulated only in nationalist rhetoric. As a consequence, this unconditional variant is not taken into account hereafter.

[26] David Miller, 'Secession and the Principle of Nationality', in Moore, *National Self-Determination and Secession*, 69–75.

[27] Although it has to be stressed here that the descriptions of the just cause and the choice currents given above are mere illustrations, as different scholars may lay down (slightly) different conditions in this respect.

belonging to both tendencies have in common: they restrict their paradigm of self-determination to groups whose members 'share a common identity, ethnic, linguistic, or cultural, and have determined that this identity is important to their political fate...Sharing some sort of cultural trait, desiring to govern itself more directly, the group is almost always a "nation"'.[28] Apart from this, the gap between the two points of view remains wide and differences of opinion abound. This will also be demonstrated when applying the two different approaches to the discussion on autonomy and independence for Corsica.

THE CORSICAN NATION

The main thread running through this chapter is the question of whether Corsica has a moral right to self-determination and, if so, whether it is entitled to autonomy or even independence as a consequence of this right. One of the first requirements in answering this question is to ascertain whether the Corsicans form a 'nation', for Miller defends the idea that 'if the minority group in question regards itself as a separate nation, then the principle (of self-determination) seems to support its claims'.[29] This may prove hard to demonstrate in many cases throughout the world, but does not raise insurmountable problems when considering the Corsican example. Although many scholars in the field of nationalism use very different theoretical concepts and characterizations when it comes to defining a nation, Corsica clearly fits the 'cultural' definition of a nation as put forward by some theorists in both the just cause and the choice schools.[30] Allen Buchanan, for instance, characterizes nations as 'encompassing cultural groups that associate themselves with a homeland, and in which there is a substantial (though not necessarily unanimous) aspiration for self-government of some kind (though not necessarily for independent statehood)'.[31] Corsica undoubtedly meets the criteria for this definition. First, the Corsicans do indeed form an *encompassing cultural group* with a common culture that differentiates them from other peoples, insofar as philological and even anthropological research has established a distinctly Corsican ethnic identity.[32] The most important particularity in this respect is to be

[28] Daniel Philpott, 'Self-Determination in Practice', in Moore, *National Self-Determination and Secession*, 81–2.
[29] Miller, 'Secession and the Principle of Nationality', 62.
[30] Cf. Meinecke's distinction between *Kulturnation* and *Staatsnation*.
[31] Allen Buchanan, 'What's So Special About Nations?', in Jocelyne Couture, Kai Nielsen, and Michel Seymour (eds.), *Rethinking Nationalism* (Calgary, University of Calgary Press, 1998), 287–8.
[32] Klaus Engelhardt, 'The Autonomist Movement in Corsica', *Contemporary French Civilization* 4:2 (1980), 211.

found at the linguistic level. In recent times Corsican has been accepted by linguists as a language in its own right[33]—they have found sufficient similarities with other Romance languages, apart from Italian, and enough direct links with Latin, to conclude that Corsican is more than just a Tuscan dialect.[34] This linguistic distinction is, however, only one element in a whole set of cultural characteristics that create a distinctive Corsican identity.

Second, Corsicans do indeed *associate themselves with a distinct homeland*, geographically as well as administratively. Corsica is an island that has achieved the status of a 'Territorial Community', and has been endowed with its own institutions. As a consequence, Corsica is sometimes described as a 'territorial minority' whose territory is a primary reference-point in determining its identity.[35]

Finally, that the Corsicans share a *substantial aspiration for self-government* is also an established fact. A survey in 2000 showed that the demand for political autonomy in Corsica is backed by no less than 49 per cent of the island's population—with 31 per cent against and 20 per cent indifferent ('no opinion')[36]—as well as a majority of 59 per cent in France as a whole.[37] The results of the regional elections of 1999 can also give an indication in this respect: in the first round, all nationalist lists together took more than 23 per cent of the votes cast on the island. Far from a majority, of course, but nonetheless a very significant share. Owing to an electoral threshold of 5 per cent, all moderate autonomist lists were prevented from taking part in the second round of these '*régionales*', and only the radical Corsica Nazione coalition (composed of the separatist A Cuncolta Indipendentista and the Greens of I Verdi Corsi) ran the electoral gauntlet a second time. Ultimately, it gained about 17 per cent of the vote (after a result of 10 per cent in the first round). This was less than the overall nationalist score in the initial round, but still a remarkable result for a coalition with a political party that acts as the political representative of the FLNC.

It is thus clear that Corsica is to be considered a nation, at least in the cultural sense of the concept. The defenders of the French Jacobin perspective on nationhood are nevertheless vehemently opposed to such an argument.

---

[33]　Grace L. Hudson, 'Corsica', *World Bibliographical Series* 202 (1997), xxix.

[34]　Nicolas Giudici, *Le problème Corse* (Toulouse, Éditions Milan, 1998), 32.

[35]　Hintjens, Loughlin, and Olivesi, 'The Status of Maritime and Insular France', 121.

[36]　Survey conducted by *Louis Harris* on 1, 2, and 3 Dec. 1999 among 600 persons constituting a representative sample of the Corsican population of voting age. The results were published in the monthly *Corsica* of January 2000.

[37]　Survey conducted by *Louis Harris* on 25 and 26 Feb. 2000 among 1,002 persons constituting a representative sample of the entire French population of voting age. 33 per cent were against and the remaining 8 per cent had no opinion. The results were published on the internet (http://www.louis-harris.fr/version_f/autres_s/sondagecorse/sondage1.htm, consulted on 1 December 2002).

58   *Gunter Lauwers*

They still uphold the idea that the only nation in the French Republic is '*la nation française*' or the French nation, encompassing the entire territory and population of France as a whole. Consequently, the concept of nation is an important element in the contemporary debate on the decentralization of '*la France une et indivisible*' or the 'one and indivisible France'. It is important, however, to bear in mind that the political theorists of the just cause as well as the choice current use the term 'nation' in its cultural sense. This allows us to conclude that Corsica can be regarded as a nation, and thus the most elementary condition in order to be eligible for self-determination is met. But this condition is not the only one and, to be legitimate from a moral point of view, further requirements are placed upon a demand for self-determination through secession or autonomy.

CORSICA AND SECESSION: AN APPLICATION OF CONFLICTING THEORIES

A 'just cause' perspective

In a normative assessment such as the one presented here, it has to be admitted that the call for secession by Corsican separatists falls too far short of the requirements stipulated by the just cause current to be legitimate. This is particularly true with regard to the condition that to gain the right to self-determination a group must be suffering severe systematic repression and must have been denied an equal opportunity to participate in the political process. Certainly, several anti-racist and human-rights organizations in Corsica may frequently accuse the French authorities of violating the civil rights of Corsican citizens,[38] and elsewhere in France the negative stereotypes of Corsicans do indeed usually outweigh the positive ones,[39] but it is nonetheless clear that this does not correspond to the kind of injustices regarded by the just cause school as sufficient to justify secession. All the more so as the most fundamental complaints of these organizations are primarily related to the treatment of both putative and convicted terrorists, and only to a lesser extent concern the treatment of ordinary citizens or the Corsican population as a community.

Corsican nationalists also use the argument that Corsica was unlawfully annexed in the past, and was subsequently colonized by France. This is an important element, since the just cause theory grants the right to self-determination to a distinct people that has a legitimate claim to territory wrongfully annexed by another state. From the perspective of the just cause

[38] Principally '*Ava Basta!*', the '*Comité anti-répression*', and the '*Ligue des droits de l'homme*'.
[39] Alexandra Jaffe, *Ideologies in Action. Language Politics on Corsica* (Berlin and New York, Mouton de Gruyter, 1999), 45.

current, this allegation by the Corsican nationalists does not stand up either, when it comes to secession. France annexed the island in 1769, but this process cannot be considered a violation of the legal principles of that time. From the thirteenth century up until 1768 Corsica had been under the control of the city-state of Genoa. Repeated attempts by the islanders to overrule this authority finally succeeded in 1755, when Genoa withdrew its troops, leading to *de facto* independence for Corsica. From a purely legalistic point of view, however, the island remained *de jure* a part of Genoa, which decided to cede its sovereign rights over Corsica to Louis XV of France in the Versailles Treaty of 1768.[40] One year later, the island became an integral part of the French state.[41] But even if we were to consider this annexation as being 'historically unjust', most adherents of the just cause current still uphold the requirement that the group and its territory have to have been wrongfully incorporated into the state *within recent memory*.[42] It is clear that this condition is not met in the Corsican case.

Corsican nationalists also maintain that the island is now being colonized by the French state. This anti-colonization discourse emerged in the late 1960s, after the Occitan intellectual Robert Lafont devised the notion of 'internal colonialism', a concept later adopted by several Marxist scholars—such as Michael Hechter—when addressing the rise of ethno-nationalism throughout Europe during the 1960s and 1970s. Lafont's argument was that, in the same way as the colonies, the underdeveloped regions of France had been exploited by the centre for their natural and human resources. The analogy with colonialism emphasized both the cultural distinctiveness and the right to political sovereignty of the 'exploited' groups. The first comprehensive public manifesto by the Corsican nationalists, *Main basse sur une île* (1971), written by the Front Régionaliste Corse, explicitly declared Corsica a victim of such internal colonialism, an argument that was taken up by many other nationalist organizations.[43] The transfer to Corsica of nearly 18,000 '*pieds-noirs*'—French colonists who had to leave Algeria when the latter gained independence from France and who were heavily subsidized by the central authorities—was one of the key reasons for this view, all the more so as this operation was accompanied by the massive development of tourist infrastructure by French developers, without direct benefit for the Corsican population.

Gérard Marcou, however, contests the idea of a colonized Corsica. He stresses that a colonial regime is based on discrimination as well as

---

[40] Emmanuel Bernabéu-Casanova, *Le nationalisme corse. Genèse, succès et échec* (Paris, L'Harmattan, 1997), 29.   [41] Engelhardt, 'The Autonomist Movement in Corsica', 212.

[42] Allen Buchanan, Secession: *The Morality of Political Divorce from Fort Sumter to Lithuania and Quebec* (Boulder, San Francisco, and Oxford, Westview Press, 1991), 110–14.

[43] Jaffe, *Ideologies in Action*, 68.

economic exploitation, which was not and is not the case in Corsica.[44] The nationalist movement nevertheless points to exactly such exploitation and discrimination to support its claim, as seen above. But at least one aspect is clear in this discussion: Corsica has never been regarded as a colony in the legal and institutional framework of France—unlike, for example, Algeria or other overseas territories—at least from the rule of Napoleon III beginning in 1852.[45] Corsican citizens have traditionally enjoyed all political rights in the French Republic, unlike the vast majority of the population of Algeria or other overseas territories in the colonial period. As Michel Huysseune puts it, 'minorities within Europe rarely if ever experienced the same degree of subordination as colonies, since their élites were not systematically excluded from metropolitan power'.[46] The latter remark is undoubtedly true of Corsica, where numerous citizens seized the opportunity to make a career in the public administration of the Republic.

Thus, while discussing the alleged 'colonial status' of Corsica, one could ask whether the island is not an example of a case theoretically described by Miller as one 'where the X's, although perhaps always having certain features that distinguished them from the Y's, have been free and equal partners in the building of the community. Their new-found nationalism is a result not of historic exploitation but of cultural developments that make them now want to have greater control over what happens in their particular territory (for instance their language is in danger of being eroded)'.[47] It may be doubtful whether Corsica has always been regarded by France as an 'equal partner' in the development of the island, but equally it would be going too far to conclude that it has been treated as a 'colony' in this respect.

The foregoing paragraphs have led us to the conclusion that, if one takes a just cause approach, Corsica is not entitled to secede. But from the choice perspective, the picture can look very different. Most adherents of this current specify several other conditions which they require to be fulfilled before they consider a call for secession to be just.

A 'choice' perspective

When applying the conditions put forward by the choice perspective—outlined above—it becomes clear that two of them are unlikely to undermine

---

[44] Gérard Marcou, 'Déléguer un pouvoir législatif à l'assemblée de Corse?', *Pouvoirs Locaux* 47 (2000), 116.

[45] Isidre Molas, *Partis nationalistes, autonomie et clans en Corse*, Working paper no. 181 of the Institut de Ciències Polítiques i Socials (Barcelona, Universitat Autònoma de Barcelona, 2000), 14.

[46] Michel Huysseune, *An Analysis of the Relation between Research in the Social Sciences and Nation-Building Discourses: the Case of the Lega Nord in Italy*, Ph.D. Diss. (Brussels, 2001), 76.

[47] Miller, 'Secession and the Principle of Nationality', 69.

the legitimate character of the claim for independence in Corsica as seen from this point of view: (1) Corsica is *a nation with a distinct identity*, and (2) it is also *able to exercise authority over the territory* thanks to its own institutions. The remaining four conditions, however, merit a more thorough assessment, namely: (3) *respect for (new) minorities after secession*, (4) the *(super-)majority clause*, (5) the *distributive justice requirement*, and (6) the *viability condition*.

Concern for *the fate of (new) minorities* in an independent Corsica may stem from the violent character of some parts of the nationalist movement, in particular the FLNC.[48] Since its creation in 1976, this organization must be held responsible for hundreds of attacks annually, although—at least until the beginning of the 1990s—only occasionally have there been fatalities. The last decade, however, has revealed another picture. Owing to an increasing rivalry between the different factions of the underground nationalist scene, dozens of people have been killed in a *'guerre fratricide'* and the number of fatal attacks on French officials of the 'colonial state' such as mayors, police officers, etc., has also risen. This culminated in 1998 in the assassination of *préfet* Claude Érignac, the highest representative of the French Republic on the island.

Although loath to minimize the seriousness of these violent developments, one has to admit, however, that this kind of violence is not likely to threaten the position of (new) minorities in Corsica. The armed nationalist struggle is almost exclusively aimed at state representatives and public infrastructure. Unlike in Northern Ireland or the Basque Country, inter-communal violence or blind terror is not a common feature in Corsica. Ordinary citizens of non-Corsican origin are—contrary to what happened to some *pieds-noirs* in the 1960s and 1970s—not as such the target of direct coercive action or hostile political rhetoric, except in a few isolated incidents. Jean-Guy Talamoni, one of the leaders of A Cuncolta Indipendentista and a member of the Corsican Assembly, declared that 'not one political organization—public or underground—defines the Corsican people in ethnic terms. All nationalist groups defend the idea of a community that consists of *Corses d'origine et Corses d'adoption'*.[49] In 1988, the Corsican Assembly approved a motion to that effect, which was actually proposed by the nationalist representatives.[50] In this respect, Xavier Crettiez also stresses that Corsican nationalism is devoid of ethnic extremism. Never in the past has the FLNC advanced the superiority of the Corsican people or the desire

---

[48] There are several distinct terrorist groups active in Corsica, although the FLNC is by far the most important, oldest and also most radical one.

[49] Jean-Guy Talamoni, 'Le fantasme d'un régionalisme ethnique', *Pouvoirs Locaux* 47 (2000), 99.

[50] Marianne Lefèvre, *Géopolitique de la Corse. Le modèle républicain en question* (Paris, L'Harmattan, 2000), 120–1.

to 'deal with' French citizens. The famous slogan '*I Francesi fora!*' ('Out with the French!') and some other xenophobic expressions are thus more propagandist than prophetic.[51]

A possible explanation for the lack of inter-communal violence is the fact that the Corsican community consists to a high degree of a mixed population, and the island therefore possesses a large proportion of inhabitants who have a dual or 'nested' identity. Alexandra Jaffe points out 'that these two identities (being French and being Corsican) exist in tandem, albeit not always in harmony'.[52] A 1999 survey conducted among a representative sample of the entire Corsican population revealed that no fewer than 53 per cent regard themselves as being equally Corsican and French, while 15 per cent answered 'first Corsican, then French' and 8 per cent identified themselves as 'first French, then Corsican'. Only 8 per cent felt 'only Corsican', whereas 14 per cent felt they were 'only French'.[53] Violent polarization along ethnic lines within Corsican society is therefore not to be expected.

Such findings allow one to conclude that respect for (new) minorities is unlikely to be jeopardized by an independent Corsica and that the current acts of terrorism are not to be regarded as detrimental to the legitimate character of the Corsican call for secession, at least not from the choice perspective. Moreover, international recognition of an independent Corsica could be made conditional upon respect for the rights of (new) minorities, which would be monitored by the international community.

Another concern of the choice current is the *(super-)majority clause*, requiring that a claim for self-determination has to be approved in a referendum by a majority or even a super-majority of the seceding region's inhabitants. This is a very important aspect when discussing separatism in Corsica. According to a 1998 survey of a representative sample of the whole Corsican population, only 6 per cent of the respondents declared themselves in favour of independence, while a striking majority of 92 per cent was against.[54] Hence it is clear that the demand for independence voiced by radical Corsican nationalists is by no means backed by a majority of the island's population. With the support of only 6 per cent of the electorate, such a majority is not even within reach. Some may invoke the argument that 'genuine' Corsicans—born of a Corsican parent—represent only an

[51] Xavier Crettiez, 'Violence et politique de la reconnaissance', *Pouvoirs Locaux* 47 (2000), 63.

[52] Jaffe, *Ideologies in Action*, 58.

[53] Survey conducted by *Louis Harris* on 1, 2, and 3 Dec. 1999 among 600 persons constituting a representative sample of the Corsican population of voting age. The remaining 2 per cent of respondents did not express an opinion. The results were published in the monthly *Corsica* of January 2000.

[54] Survey conducted by *Ifop* on 9 Feb. 1998 among 501 persons constituting a representative sample of the population of Corsica. The remaining 2 per cent of the respondents did not express an opinion. The results were published in *L'Evénement du Jeudi* of 12 Feb. 1998.

estimated 60 per cent of the total community living on the island,[55] causing a certain 'bias' in opinion polls. Even if one were to take this aspect into account, it would not alter our conclusion that an overwhelming majority of Corsicans—whether '*Corses d'origine*' or '*Corses d'adoption*'—rejects the claim for independence put forward by Corsican separatists. Furthermore, the choice current in theories on secession requires that the constituency for such a referendum must be defined on a territorial and not an ethnic basis, to include *all* inhabitants of the secessionist region.

When judging a case of secession, one also has to bear in mind the *principle of distributive justice*. According to Miller, the concept of distributive justice entails two principles when applied to the particular context of secession. First, that the secession of territory X should not deprive remainder state Y of some valuable resource that has been created collectively. In such a case, the problem could be solved by a transfer payment from state X to remainder state Y, although it may prove difficult to agree exact terms. Second, the pursuit of national self-determination and justice for the inhabitants of seceding territory X should not lead to a state of affairs in which the inhabitants of remainder state Y are so deprived that they cannot achieve justice among themselves, and as a result are forced to contract an alliance with some colonial power or other neighbouring state, and thus have to give up a large measure of self-determination.[56] But neither of these concerns proves to be problematic with regard to Corsica. This is not an instance of a rich, prosperous region wishing to secede from an economically backward mainland. On the contrary: the regional per capita income of Corsica is roughly 23 per cent less than national per capita GDP, the island has hardly any primary resources or industry, and the unemployment rate fluctuates at around 13.5 per cent, slightly higher than the national average. Corsica is—from an economic point of view—one of the least successful regions in France.[57] Direct investment in Corsica by Paris, to increase the economic strength of the island, amounts to 1.3 billion euros annually, social benefits excluded.[58] It is therefore inconceivable that the secession of Corsica should lead to a situation where continental France is deprived of *vital* resources. As a consequence, the principle of distributive justice is no impediment to the possible legitimacy of the separatist aspirations voiced by some parts of the Corsican nationalist movement, at least not from a normative point of view.

---

[55] Peter Savigear, 'Corsica: Regional Autonomy or Violence?', *Conflict Studies* 149 (1983), 10.

[56] Miller, 'Secession and the Principle of Nationality', 74–5.

[57] Jean Glavany (ed.), *Corse: l'indispensable sursaut. Rapport fait au nom de la commission d'enquête sur l'utilisation des fonds publics et la gestion des services publics en Corse* (Paris, Assemblée nationale, 1998), 32–54.　　　　　　　　　　　　　　[58] Ibid. 81–3.

It is perhaps paradoxical that a backward region, benefiting to such a large extent from financial support by the central government, should have a significant separatist movement. But as Donald Horowitz rightly points out, 'there are several paths to secession, and rich regions are not the leading secessionists. They are far outnumbered by regions poor in resources and productivity'.[59] Quite simply, many groups throughout the world are determined to gain independent statehood, and are willing to pay the price.

The foregoing paragraphs inevitably raise the question of the *viability* of an independent Corsica. Apart from its precarious economic situation, the island is also weighed down by an unfavourable demographic structure. Corsica is the only French region—and the only major island in the Mediterranean—whose present population is smaller than it was at the beginning of the twentieth century. The population in 1901 came to no less than 296,000, but thereafter a decline set in, resulting in a figure of barely 200,000 by 1960. Massive emigration—in particular to continental France—was the main cause of this evolution, although the population has risen steadily since then.[60] This situation, which has stabilized at around 260,000 inhabitants over the past few years, is still far from propitious, however—all the more so because the present population of Corsica is also, increasingly, an aging one.[61]

But rather than reaching a final verdict on the viability of the island, I would prefer to question the practical utility of such a viability condition when assessing a claim to secession (in Corsica). The economic performance and social texture of a region within a larger state often depend on the specific position this particular region has had in the centrally managed economic and financial framework of this state. This is certainly the case in Corsica which—being an island—has always been regarded by Paris as a peripheral and insignificant entity when it comes to economic policy. It is, therefore, inappropriate to use mere social and economic indicators to 'determine' the viability of a region wishing to secede. It thus remains an open question whether an independent Corsica would fail in this respect if it were to have the powers and political institutions to adapt such a policy to its own particular needs. Eleonore Kofman rightly observes that for a long time only outsiders were in control of the development of the island, and were the beneficiaries of growth.[62] Peter Savigear illustrates this by

[59] Donald L. Horowitz, 'Patterns of Ethnic Separatism', *Comparative Studies in Society and History* 23:2 (1981), 170.

[60] As a consequence, the majority of Corsicans lives outside the borders of the island, principally in metropolitan France. It is estimated that their numerical strength is no less than 400,000 to 500,000 individuals, although this figure is very difficult to ascertain.

[61] Glavany, *Corse: l'indispensable sursaut*, 33–5.

[62] Eleonore Kofman, 'Differential Modernization, Social Conflicts and Ethno-Regionalism in Corsica', *Ethnic and Racial Studies* 5:3 (1982), 305.

stating that—at least until the 1980s—such a major economic activity as tourism was over 80 per cent controlled by French investors, and mainly non-Corsicans were employed in this sector.[63] Hence the allegation by Corsican nationalists that France has been practising a policy of 'internal colonialism', which siphons resources and people from the periphery to the centre. They therefore regard themselves as not responsible, either individually or collectively, for leaving Corsica or for the negative economic and social consequences on the island's demographic frailty.[64]

Following on from this analysis, we may state that, from a choice perspective, one particular requirement thwarts the legitimacy of the Corsican call for secession: the (super-) majority clause. Are we now forced to present the overall conclusion that a moral right to self-determination is a delusion with regard to Corsica, and this in both a just cause and a choice approach? All the more so since one might argue that unilateral secession by Corsica would be detrimental to France's self-determination. Miller stresses that the concept of national self-determination may also be appealed to in defence of the political status quo, although he admits that such a conservative interpretation of the principle can lead to a situation where the idea of self-determination loses much of its original moral appeal.[65]

In the final parts of my contribution, I will address some elements that might prevent us from drawing such a radical conclusion. After all, independent statehood is only one possible form in which to implement the right to self-determination, and before reaching a final verdict in this respect we still have to examine the concept of autonomy.

CORSICA AND AUTONOMY: THE REPUBLICAN NATION CONTESTED

The implementation of autonomy in Corsica began with the 1982 reforms setting up a regional Assembly whose competences were upgraded by a modification of its statute in 1991, as outlined above. The Matignon Agreement of July 2000 and the adoption of a bill on a new statute for Corsica by the National Assembly in December 2001 represented a new milestone in this development, as it introduced far more autonomous rights for Corsica. This bill stipulates—*inter alia*—that the Corsican Assembly would gain the right—in order to take account of the specific characteristics of the island—to adapt French national laws in those matters for

---

[63] Peter Savigear, 'Corsica and the French state', in Charles R. Reid (ed.), *Nations without a State: Ethnic Minorities in Western Europe* (New York, Praeger, 1980), 120–4.

[64] Jaffe, *Ideologies in Action*, 57.

[65] Miller, 'Secession and the Principle of Nationality', 62–3.

66   *Gunter Lauwers*

which it has been given competency by the legislator. Such adaptations would be possible on condition that they remain in conformity with the French Constitution. The Matignon Agreement may thus be seen as the first effort by the French Republic to give the island a—although modest—degree of political autonomy, and this constitutionally guaranteed from 2004 on.

It is clear that the autonomy granted to Corsica before the Matignon Agreement did not coincide with the paradigm of 'genuine political autonomy' as we use it in the current debate on self-determination. In his comparative study on different structures of autonomy in Europe, Ulrich Schneckener confirms that Corsica's specific institutional framework of 1991 puts it somewhere between being part of a centralized state and having 'real' territorial autonomy in the sense of 'self-rule'.[66] The Corsican Assembly had no legislative or fiscal powers.

These inhibitions had far-reaching consequences. Walter Kälin rightly states that attempts to solve conflicts by granting ethnic groups the right to self-governance at the regional or local level fail if such self-governance and autonomy exist only in form but not in substance. Under these conditions, the minority in question will be frustrated and the conflict will continue.[67] Such is indeed the case in Corsica, where the successive half-hearted attempts by the French government to grant autonomy never succeeded in putting an end to ethnic terrorism on the island. The granting of legislative powers therefore remained one of the most important demands of the nationalist movement in Corsica.

The Matignon Agreement was designed—*inter alia*—to meet this demand. The call for legislative powers has, however, been just one element in the programme of the Corsican nationalists. Another major demand—backed by a motion passed by the Corsican Assembly in 1988—concerns official recognition of the Corsican people.[68] Any attempt by the French government to meet this demand has been inhibited by the provisions of the French Constitution, Article 2 of which stresses the 'egalitarian principle', which ensures the equality of all citizens before the law without distinction of origin, race or religion. Because of this article, Paris has more than once declared officially that 'France cannot recognize the existence of ethnic groups, whether minorities or not'.[69] This is the reason why the expression '*peuple corse*', mentioned in the original drafts of both the 1982 and 1991 statutes, was in each case removed from the final text following a verdict of the French

---

[66] Ulrich Schneckener, *Auswege aus dem Bürgerkrieg. Modelle zur Regulierung ethnonationlistischer konflikte in Europa*, (Frankfurt. Suhrkamp, 2002), 357–67.
[67] Walter Kälin, *Decentralized Governance in Fragmented Societies: Solution or Cause of New Evils?*, 9. Paper presented at the international conference 'Facing Ethnic Conflicts', held from 14 to 16 December 2000 at Bonn University, Germany.   [68] Jaffe, *Ideologies in Action*, 128.
[69] See *inter alia* UN Doc. E/CN. 4/Sub. 2/384/Rev. 1 (1979), para. 67.

Constitutional Council. The constitution recognizes no people other than '*le peuple français*'.[70] Following these successive rectifications by the Constitutional Council, the Matignon Agreement and the subsequent bill with the provisions of the new statute contained no further reference to '*le peuple corse*'.

Yet another substantial demand by Corsican nationalists concerns an improved status for the Corsican language. The latter inevitably remains under pressure from French, the only official language in the public administration of the Republic. It was not until 1974 that Corsican was included in the provisions of the 'Deixonne law' of 1951, which provided for limited instruction in the language to be included in educational curricula and then only on an optional basis and supplementary to regular class hours.[71] Despite this improvement, Corsican language use is still being eroded. Throughout the 1970s, an estimated 70,000 people were capable of holding a wide-ranging conversation in Corsican, whereas by the end of the twentieth century this figure had decreased to a mere 20,000.[72] Many therefore share the belief that the survival of the language depends on co-officiality, or at least on the mandatory teaching of it—demands backed by a motion passed by the Corsican Assembly in 1992 but never put into practice.[73] The new statute only slightly complies with this demand: one of its provisions entailes the teaching of the Corsican language in kindergarten and primary schools during regular class hours, but still on an optional basis.

Although language is a topical and most important issue in Corsica, this grievance was in fact articulated decades ago, when it concerned all culturally distinct regions in France. At that time the issue was especially highlighted by Robert Lafont, who claimed in 1975 that reconquering the language was essential because it had to be regarded as the foundation of the nation and would legitimize political and economic autonomy.[74] The language has therefore remained a key element in the Corsican demand for self-determination, as shared linguistic/cultural unity has dominated European definitions of nationhood ever since the French Revolution. '*Morta a lingua, mortu u populu*', reads an early slogan on posters—'the death of the language is the death of the people'—whereby the Corsican

---

[70] Hintjens, Loughlin, and Olivesi, 'The Status of Maritime and Insular France', 123–6.

[71] This Deixonne law (Loi No. 51-46 of 11 January 1951), which had allowed public schools to teach one hour a week in Basque, Breton, Catalan or Occitan since 1951, initially excluded Corsican on the grounds that it was considered to be not a regional language of France but an Italian dialect for which the government was not responsible. A decree of 1974 altered this law by including Corsican (Décret No. 74-33 of 16 January 1974).

[72] Giudici, *Le problème corse*, 33. But these figures are difficult to ascertain and should be regarded as mere estimates.

[73] Hervé Guillorel, 'La langue corse: histoire et enjeux actuels', *Pouvoirs Locaux* 47 (2000), 73.

[74] Cited in Jaffe, *Ideologies in Action*, 68.

nationalists asserted the intrinsic link between language and people, as the Romantic philosophers Herder, Fichte, and Humboldt had done before them.[75] Or, in the words of Alexandra Jaffe, 'language can be the metaphor for the experience of nationality and the nation can be a metaphor for the language and self'.[76]

French monolingualism has, however, been the foundation of the French ideology of cultural and political identity and unity since the edict of Villers-Cotterêts (1539), which stipulated that the language of the *Île de France* was the official language of the kingdom, to be used in all administrative and legal texts. This very first piece of language legislation in France prefigured the Jacobin conviction that the unity of the Republic demanded unity of speech, and it refused to countenance any variety in this respect. The value of the edict was merely symbolic, however, as millions of French people still spoke languages or dialects other than Parisian French by the time of the Revolution in 1789. The Revolutionaries soon seized on language as a symbol of national unity, though, and 1794 rang in the period of 'linguistic terror', when defenders of dialect were labelled 'counter-revolutionaries'. All public documents were required to be in French, although Corsica and other regions 'where they speak idioms that have no illustrative merits and are only leftovers of the barbarisms of centuries past'[77] were exempted from implementing these decrees. But this was only a temporary measure, and the Frenchification of all the provinces continued—an operation that was thus regarded as a means of moral and cultural elevation. The guiding light was the link between language and rationality, civilization, culture, virtue, and citizenship.[78]

The latter age-old conviction—however moderated throughout history—is still of importance for contemporary adherents of the Jacobin Republican ideology in France, whether left- or right-wing. As a consequence, the language issue remains a strategic element in current French politics. Nevertheless, since the late 1990s the French government has pledged its support for the so-called 'regional languages'. On 7 May 1999, it signed the European Charter on Regional and Minority Languages.[79] But the *ratification*

---

[75] Cited in Jaffe, *Ideologies in Action*, 122.   [76] Ibid. 124.

[77] Quote from Abbé Grégoire, who had conducted a nationwide survey on language practices and who presented a report to the National Assembly in which he asked the government to annihilate the *patois* and universalize the use of the French language. See Jaffe, *Ideologies in Action*, 79.   [78] Ibid. 78–80.

[79] The European Charter on Regional and Minority Languages—in force since 1 March 1998—originated in the Council of Europe. The Charter's purpose is to prevent the decline of regional or minority languages in Europe and to help them develop by promoting their spoken and written use in public life and in social and economic contexts as well as through the teaching of them. States Parties are requested to introduce measures to recognize and promote such languages (including in areas of public life such as in education, the courts, the public administration, the media, economic and social life, etc.) and to provide facilities for teaching and studying them.

of this Charter—necessary to make it a legally binding commitment—was impeded by a ruling of the French Constitutional Council.[80] Article 2 of the French Constitution declares that French is the only language of the Republic, thereby ruling out the use of regional or minority languages in the courts and the public administration, and thus effectively obstructing the ratification of the Charter. For the very same reason the status of co-officiality for the Corsican language—a nationalist demand beyond the provisions of the Charter—is equally unconstitutional.[81] And the same goes for the compulsory teaching of it, since this has to be seen as contradicting the egalitarian principle enshrined in Article 2 of the Constitution as outlined above.[82] These demands were consequently not incorporated into the Matignon Agreement.

An overwhelming majority of the Corsican Assembly—including the members of A Cuncolta Indipendentista—approved the new draft statute on Corsica following the Matignon Agreement of 2000, and the subsequent bill that was adopted by the National Assembly in December 2001. But a considerable proportion of the political establishment in France fears that the new statute will jeopardize 'indivisibility' and 'national cohesion' in France and will also encourage other secessionist movements in the country, for instance in Brittany or the French Basque areas. Owing to his discontent in this matter, the left-wing Interior Minister Jean-Pierre Chevènement—an influential and highly regarded defender of the Republican ideological heritage—decided to resign from office in August 2000. For the defenders of Republicanism believe that allowing Corsicans to adapt national laws could damage the nation's sovereignty, will undermine the definition of France as a community of equal citizens and will lead to a return to the *Ancien Régime* where every province made its own laws. Some are therefore inclined to conclude that the new statute on Corsica following the Matignon Agreement implied the recognition of ethnic regionalism in French institutions and a break with the notion of citizenship on which the Constitution is based.[83] As a result of this opposition, Corsican nationalists are still doggedly determined to defend the institutional autonomy of the island. While the most radical militants still tirelessly pursue their quest for an independent Corsica, whether this is to be achieved through bullets or ballots.

TOWARDS A FINAL VERDICT?

In accordance with the results of our enquiry, it can be stated that Corsica does not have a moral right to self-determination through independence,

---

[80] Décision No. 99-412 DC of 15 June 1999. [81] Guillorel, 'La langue corse', 72–3.
[82] Roland Debbasch, 'L'avenir institutionnel de la Corse et la Constitution', *Pouvoirs Locaux* 47 (2000), 92. [83] Marcou, 'Déléguer un pouvoir législatif à l'assemblée de Corse?', 118.

either from a just cause or from a choice perspective. Our conclusion that Corsica is not entitled to independence, however, does not mean that it is not entitled to self-determination. Norman points out that—because of the radical character of the right to self-determination through independence—there have been several recent philosophical attempts to ground a more moderate theory of national self-determination. In the liberal tradition, these theories explain why so-called 'encompassing groups', particularly national minorities with a different language from the majority in their state, have a special claim to self-determination—through a degree of political autonomy in which they can protect their language and culture, and which falls short of secession. Political autonomy is then seen as conducive to improving equality of opportunity and the individual autonomy of members of the national minority.[84]

The implementation of self-determination through political autonomy may be regarded as the appropriate solution for Corsica—all the more so since a majority in favour of political autonomy is present in both Corsica and France as a whole, as shown through opinion polls. And the advantages of genuine political autonomy for Corsica—achieved in a modest form by the new statute—are very clear, since such a concept is responsive in this respect to both majority concerns (preserving the integrity of the state) and minority demands (exercising a meaningful degree of self-government), as expounded by Hurst Hannum.[85] Furthermore, the transfer of decision-making power to autonomous units 'facilitates the possibility for people belonging to minorities to identify with state institutions, to adequately express their will and to shape their way of life' and thus 'to influence those matters which concern them most directly'.[86] Such a point of view seems to gain importance in France as well, where the new statute of Corsica in recent political debates even appears as a 'model' to implement a general decentralisation in the entire Republic.

Considering all the particularities of the analysis, from a theoretical as well as a contextual point of view, I am thus inclined to conclude that the moral right to self-determination of the Corsicans may be best achieved through *genuine political autonomy*, even if the political reforms aimed at achieving it may in the future entail the necessity of amending the French Constitution. Such an alteration would then show that the 'peripheral' island of Corsica actually lies at the very heart of politics in the French Republic.

---

[84] Norman, 'The Ethics of Secession', 36.   [85] Hannum, *Territorial Autonomy*, 3.
[86] Asbjørn Eide, 'Ethno-Nationalism and Minority Protection', in La Laguna University, *The Reform of International Institutions for the Protection of Human Rights* (Brussels, Bruylant, 1993), 130.

4

Self-Determination in Cyprus: Future Options within a European Order

Nathalie Tocci

INTRODUCTION

This chapter provides an analysis of the 'Cyprus question' during the latter half of the twentieth century through the application of critical normative debates on secession. The particularly interesting aspect of the Cyprus conflict from an analyst's point of view is its longevity and the tense no-peace, no-war situation that has persisted on the island for almost three decades. The conflict presents several major phases across different time periods—such as the outbreak of ethnic conflict, war and the attainment of *de facto* secession, the stalemate in the negotiating process and the continuing search for a constitutional solution. It thus lends itself to a rich and multi-faceted normative discussion.

The chapter begins with a discussion of Allen Buchanan's remedial theory of secession. The theoretical insights are applied to the situation of Cyprus in the decade between 1963 and 1974, i.e. from the time of the outbreak of an explicitly inter-communal conflict up until the Turkish military intervention of 20 July 1974, which effectively partitioned the island. In particular, in a case such as Cyprus—where *de facto* secession was achieved through war, military occupation, and the substantial displacement of ethnic populations—do remedial rights arguments continue to hold? We then move on to the period during and immediately following the Turkish invasion and the *de facto* secession of the Turkish Cypriot community from the internationally recognized Republic of Cyprus. The events in Cyprus during the critical year of 1974 will be examined in order to raise several questions that need to be tackled by any normative theory of secession. Finally, the paper turns to the present. Given the situation on the island today, contrasting normative theories could be said to provide more arguments against a full reintegration of the two communities than in favour. Do 'radical pluralism' theories provide more appropriate justifications of Turkish Cypriot demands for separate sovereignties in Cyprus?

The lack of clear normative answers to all of the above questions leads to an exploration of alternative scenarios for conflict resolution, which move away from the black-and-white 'secession' question. An analysis of the Cyprus question contributes to the theoretical debate on the achievement of self-determination outside the straitjacket of the nation-state. Hence the chapter ends with a discussion of the possible status of Cyprus within the European Union's regional framework, which could provide greater flexibility than that allowed within the well-defined world of sovereign nation-states. To what extent could the European Union's multilevel system of governance represent an alternative means of self-determination and facilitate conflict resolution on the island in the near future?

NORMATIVE JUSTIFICATIONS OF THE RIGHT TO SECESSION: CHOICE AND REMEDIAL THEORIES OF SECESSION

The choice and remedial theories of secession are the two main schools of thought providing for normative justifications of the right to secession. The choice approach derives from an application or extension of the notion of liberal democracy, although it is also applied to concepts of nationalism and national self-determination.[1] It argues that self-determination through secession simply represents an extension of liberal democratic rights. It is thus inconsistent to advocate one principle without also defending the other. Daniel Philpott suggests that both democracy and the plebiscitary right to secede are justified by the value of individual autonomy, while David Copp holds that a fundamental and equal respect for persons justifies both notions. However, as Allen Buchanan aptly rejoins, both views can be mutually invalidated since, in a democracy, it is not the case that each individual is self-governed. Rather, individuals are governed by the majority of the community.[2] But who is to decide on the composition of the overall group that should vote on the question of secession? Equal respect for all individuals would indicate an all-encompassing group, rather than a select group which happens to correspond to the one demanding secession in the first place.

[1] See Wayne Norman, 'The Ethics of Secession as a Regulation of Secessionist Politics', in Margaret Moore (ed.), *National Self-Determination and Secession* (Oxford, Oxford University Press, 1998), 36–41.

[2] Allen Buchanan, 'Democracy and Secession', in Moore, *National Self-Determination and Secession*, 14–34.

The second approach in the literature that examines the normative grounds for secession is the 'remedial' or 'just cause' theory. In particular, I will focus on Buchanan's remedial theory of secession in the following section. Buchanan holds that a right to secession exists when a particular minority has been treated unjustly by the state to which it currently belongs. In other words, an existing state's legitimacy may be questioned, and a particular minority within that state may have a right to secede only if this represents a 'last resort to escape serious injustices'.[3] The author sets out the precise conditions under which this may be the case. These include a persistent violation of human rights, systematic discrimination and inhibited access to participation in democratic governance, and/or the unjust appropriation of territory. When such conditions are not fulfilled, a state is considered to be legitimate and secession is deemed impermissible, as self-determination may be adequately attained within the confines of the democratic state. In the following, I will apply the various criteria to be found in this approach to the case of Cyprus.

REMEDIAL THEORY AND THE JULY 1974 PARTITION OF CYPRUS

Turning to the early years (the 1960s and early 1970s) of the Cyprus question, can Buchanan's theory of legitimate statehood and remedial secession provide a normative basis for the effective partition of the island in 1974? In the light of the events that had taken place in this period, was the partition of the island justified?

Following the 1959 Zurich and London Agreements between Britain, Greece, Turkey, and the Greek and Turkish Cypriot communities, Cyprus was transformed from a Crown Colony of the British Empire into an independent, joint and bi-communal Republic. The 1959 Agreements formulated a Basic Structure for the Cypriot state, which was then further developed and incorporated into the 1960 constitution signed in Nicosia. The constitution aimed to construct a 'partnership' Republic that would ensure the self-determination of both ethnic communities via an intricate and finely balanced arrangement of community representation and power-sharing. A few examples may be useful to illustrate how the concepts of partnership, representation and power-sharing were translated into practice. First, the executive was set up as a presidential system, where the president would be a Greek Cypriot and the vice-president a Turkish Cypriot, and both would have the power to veto questions relating to foreign affairs, defence, and security. The executive also included a council of ten ministers, seven of

---

[3] Ibid. 25.

whom would be Greek Cypriots appointed by the Greek Cypriot president and the remaining three of Turkish Cypriot origin, appointed by the vice-president. Secondly, in the legislature, representatives of the two communities would be elected separately, and any laws concerning electoral, fiscal, or municipal issues would require separate majorities. Furthermore, communal councils were set up to deal with matters affecting education, religion, culture, recreation, and charitable and personal status. Any amendments to the constitution (other than to the basic articles, which were 'unalterable') would require a two-thirds majority of *both* Greek and Turkish Cypriot members of parliament. Thirdly, the civil service, the law-enforcement mechanisms, the military, and the judiciary would also have a distinctive bi-communal character, with specified community quotas.

In addition to the constitution, the London and Zurich agreements included two further treaties, the Treaty of Guarantee and the Treaty of Alliance. The Treaty of Guarantee granted Britain, Greece, and Turkey the right to intervene either jointly or unilaterally to re-establish 'the state of affairs established by the treaty' and prevent 'any activity aiming at promoting, directly or indirectly, either the union of Cyprus with any other state or the partition of the island'.[4] Both *enosis*, i.e. union with Greece, and *taksim*, i.e. the partition of the island into Greek and Turkish Cypriot states, were prohibited. Peace and stability in the eastern Mediterranean rested upon this condition.

From the early 1930s *enosis* had been the dominant Greek Cypriot objective, supported by motherland Greece from the mid-1940s through its bilateral relations with Britain and diplomacy in UN forums.[5] The Turkish and Turkish Cypriot aim of *taksim* was developed later in the mid-1950s. It was articulated primarily as a reaction against the Greek Cypriot goal.[6] Given the emergence of these irreconcilable positions, the 1959 Zurich and London Agreements expressed a delicate compromise. Britain renounced its claims to sovereignty on Cyprus. In order to retain peace on the island and in the volatile eastern Mediterranean region, Cypriot independence had to be achieved and any form of irredentism and secession had to be explicitly prohibited by the constitution. The Treaty of Alliance, instead, was a defence pact, which allowed Greece and Turkey to station troops in Cyprus and allowed Britain to set up two military bases there.

The equal political partnership and internationally sanctioned regime enshrined in the constitution and the treaties lasted only until 1963–4.

---

[4] Treaty of Guarantee, Article 2, 1960 available on http://kypros.org/Constitution/treaty.htm.

[5] See Ioannis Stefanidis, *Isle of Discord: Nationalism, Imperialism and the Making of the Cyprus Problem* (London, Hurst & Company, 1999).

[6] Andrew Borowiec, *Cyprus: A Troubled Island* (Westport, Praeger Publishers, 2000).

Almost immediately after their finalization in 1959–60, the Greek Cypriot community led by president Makarios began to signal its discontent with the existing arrangements. The president of the Republic contested the legitimacy of the 1960 constitution and agreements, which in his view violated the self-determination of the Cypriot people enshrined in the UN Charter, in so far as they had not been approved by the population. Moreover, Makarios also contested the substance of the arrangements. He argued that Turkish Cypriot rights and responsibilities were both inefficient, given that they implied a costly duplication of positions and functions, and unworkable, since they provoked tensions and gridlock in the decision-making process. He claimed that because of their inherent potential for tension, the governing arrangements had created a state but precluded the formation of a nation.

More fundamentally, however, the Greek Cypriot authorities argued that the constitution encouraged the effective partition of the island. They contested the concessions granted to the Turkish Cypriot community, which they believed to be over-generous in relation to the demographic structure of the island. According to the Greek Cypriots, the Turkish Cypriot community, which at the time represented 18.5 per cent[7] of the island's population, should have been granted merely adequate minority rights, rather than being allowed an almost equal share in governing arrangements. The Greek Cypriot élite saw the relationship between the two ethnic communities as one of a majority to a minority, in which both enjoyed equal individual rights but in which the former community would enjoy supremacy in government. The Greek Cypriots also contested the intervention rights granted to the three protector states, which they said allowed for the violation of the sovereignty, independence, and territorial integrity of Cyprus and was thus at odds with international law. More specifically, they feared the effects of Turkey's rights of intervention on the latter's foreign policy vis-à-vis Cyprus.[8]

Dissatisfaction with the arrangements enshrined in the 1960 constitution led to the non-implementation of many of its provisions by Greek Cypriot authorities. Finally, in 1963 Archbishop Makarios—as president of the republic—proposed thirteen 'reasonable and just' amendments to 'improve' the constitution, despite the disapproval of the Greek government led by Konstantin Karamanlis.[9] The amendments significantly reduced the

---

[7] As recorded by the official census on the island for 1960.

[8] The Greek Cypriots felt threatened by Turkey's continuous provision of weaponry and military training to the Turkish Cypriot armed forces. In October 1959 the Cypriot authorities detected the Turkish ship *Deniz* in the Karpass peninsula, allegedly carrying weaponry for the Turkish Cypriots.

[9] Glafcos Clerides, *Cyprus: My Deposition*, 2 vols. (Nicosia, Alithia publishers, 1989), vol. i.

guarantees of political equality to the Turkish Cypriot community by modifying several of the 'unalterable' articles of the constitution. The amendments proposed removing the veto powers of the president and the vice-president,[10] eliminating the requirement of separate parliamentary majorities,[11] reducing Turkish Cypriot quotas in the civil service, the police and the military,[12] altering income tax legislation,[13] and explicitly unifying the military forces[14] and municipal councils.[15] They thus paved the way for a unitary state in which the Turkish Cypriots would be granted minority community rights.

At this stage it must be stressed that Makarios's constitutional amendments effectively demonstrated that the Greek Cypriot acceptance of the 1960 constitution had been nothing more than what the Greek Cypriot President Glafcos Clerides (in office since February 1993) defines in his memoirs as a 'tactical retreat'.[16] In his autobiographical *My Deposition*, Clerides argues at length that Makarios never fully entered into his role as a statesman of a bi-communal state aiming to build inter-communal confidence: instead he remained the national leader of one community and as such never fully accepted the compromises of 1960. He therefore stressed the unworkability of the constitution without having given it sufficient time to demonstrate its efficacy; 'prematurely [using] his newly acquired powers as president of the republic to press for constitutional reforms'.[17]

An honest evaluation of the situation during the period 1960–3, divorced from propagandistic tendencies, would lead to the conclusion that, with the exception of the provisions for separate majorities when voting on tax legislation, there was no need to press for constitutional amendments, and that such a move was premature, that it was made before bridges of confidence were built between the two communities, and that it was prompted by the resentment the Greek Cypriots felt at the excessive rights granted to a minority and the need felt by Makarios to vindicate himself in the face of his opponents' constant accusations of capitulation both on the issue of *enosis* and on that of minority rights.[18]

Ankara, followed by the Turkish Cypriot vice-president Fazil Kuçuk, rejected the proposed amendments. Tensions within public institutions grew until Turkish Cypriot officials either left or were made to leave all public offices. Instead of preventing the outbreak of inter-communal violence, both sides inflamed it by arming paramilitary groups, and ultimately both lost control of the situation. Paramilitary organizations were initially defensive in nature, but as the tension mounted they adopted more aggressive

---

[10] Article 50 of the constitution of the Republic of Cyprus, 1960.
[11] Ibid., Article 78/8.   [12] Ibid., Article 123/3.   [13] Ibid., Article 78/2.
[14] Ibid., Article 129/5.   [15] Ibid., Article 173/2.
[16] Clerides, *Cyprus: My Deposition*, i. 328.   [17] Clerides, ibid. ii. 24.
[18] Ibid. 130.

positions. The outbreak of inter-communal violence between Greek Cypriot police forces and the Turkish Resistance Movement, and between Greek and Turkish Cypriot paramilitary groups, led to numerous deaths and the forced displacement of over 30,000 Turkish Cypriots from mixed villages to enclaves. The government imposed an economic embargo on the sending of strategic goods and services to the enclaves, it directed no public expenditure to the Turkish Cypriot community living in enclaves, restricted the latter's freedom of movement and denied it most forms of employment. The problem intensified with Greece's efforts to destabilize Makarios's government. Tensions between the two had grown following the events of 1963, when Greece had openly expressed its disapproval of Makarios's intention to revise the constitution unilaterally. The distance grew following the 1967 military coup in Greece and the growing interference by that country in the internal affairs of the island. Finally, on 15 July 1974 the Greek National Guard staged the 'Apollo coup', ousting the Archbishop's regime and extending the dictatorship to Cyprus. In response to the coup by the Greek military, 40,000 Turkish troops invaded the island on 20 July 1974. Following the first attack and the subsequent failure of negotiations in Geneva, the Turkish army led on 14 August 1974 a second attack that ended with the occupation of 37 per cent of the island's territory.

In the light of the above events, does the remedial theory of secession justify the partition of the island in 1974? As indicated above, this theory argues that secession is morally justified only when it represents the last resort in exercising the right to self-determination. Under conditions of systematic discrimination, violation of human rights, and denied access to democratic governance, the aggrieved segment of the population has a right to secede from the unjust state.

In the period 1963–74, were these conditions fulfilled in the case of the Turkish Cypriot community? The Greek Cypriot policy against the Turkish Cypriot enclaves could be viewed as the natural response of a 'legitimate government' towards an effectively self-proclaimed 'state within a state'.[19] In fact, in 1967 the Turkish Cypriot population living in enclaves began to be governed by a separate provisional administration. On the question as to whether access to democratic governance was being denied to the Turkish Cypriot community, one could argue that Turkish Cypriot officials voluntarily left the institutions of the Republic of Cyprus in response to Makarios's proposed amendments. In other words, the Turkish Cypriot leadership seized this opportunity to abandon the implementation of the 1960 constitution in order to further a secessionist cause.

[19] In fact limited employment opportunities mainly concerned the Turkish Cypriots living in enclaves: non-enclaved Turkish Cypriots were comparatively freer in their economic activities. A notable example in this respect is the Turkish Cypriot community in Limassol.

There may indeed be some truth in such an interpretation. Nonetheless, it cannot be denied that the proposed amendments did effectively remove most of the constitutional provisions implementing the concept of a 'partnership' republic and which, in the eyes of the Turkish Cypriots, allowed for the self-determination of both communities on the island. Moreover, the internal migration of Turkish Cypriots, in 1963, to economically blockaded enclaves was a natural response to the continuing inter-communal violence. The treatment of these citizens within the blockaded enclaves undoubtedly violated their human rights and indicated a policy of systematic ethnic discrimination against them. As for the argument that the Turkish Cypriot leadership exploited events to further their own separatist cause, it must be noted that it was not until 1967 that the Turkish Cypriot leadership, in the absence of an agreement with their Greek Cypriot counterpart, formed a provisional administration to govern the enclave communities. Finally, even if the departure of the Turkish Cypriot officials from the republic's institutions may not have been forced on them by the Greek Cypriot authorities, the coup by the Greek military regime against Makarios on 15 July 1974 certainly implied that access to democratic governance was denied to the Turkish as well as to the Greek Cypriot community in Cyprus.

One may thus be inclined to conclude that in 1974 the Turkish Cypriots did have a remedial right to rebel against the existing regime. Such a justification does not question either the effectiveness of the 1960 constitution or the exact apportionment of blame for the outbreak of inter-communal conflict in the decade between 1963 and 1974. Whether the Greek Cypriots were justified in their moral objections to the constitution (i.e. as a *sui generis* constitution with inappropriate or unjust aspects in relation to segregation, balance of political power, unalterability of basic articles and rights of external interference), becomes secondary. Also of lesser importance to the argument is the question of precisely where the blame for the inter-communal strife lies. Clerides in his memoirs rightly argues that 'lots of ink has been spilt to prove the guilt of one side or the other. The truth is very simple...Both leaderships were captives of their previous policies and very sensitive to the pressures from military organizations, which had been created to support those policies'.[20] Hence, rather than attempting to formulate an argument based on the historical blame of one community or the other, it may be more fruitful to observe what the outcome of their actions was by July 1974. The undeniable end result was discrimination against the enclaved Turkish Cypriot community and the existence of an undemocratic Republic of Cyprus which, in July 1974, seemed about to be formally incorporated into the Greek military regime.

[20] Clerides, *Cyprus: My Deposition*, ii. 208.

Was the partition of the island, nonetheless, really a last resort in attempting to achieve justice? The last resort condition is itself a questionable one. It is far more difficult to assess *ex ante*, at the time when the relevant decisions were being taken, whether or not secession is indeed the last resort in the effort to achieve justice than to make such informed judgements *ex post*. In the case of Cyprus, the Greek military coup on 15 July 1974 was viewed by Turkey as the final trigger for decisive action. If the coup and not the events that preceded it (i.e. the period of inter-communal strife and failed negotiations from 1963 to 1974) are viewed as having necessitated a last resort to secession, then following the collapse of the Greek military regime on 24 July 1974 the remedial right to secession ceased to exist. Of course the Turkish victory was itself a decisive factor in the ultimate demise of the Greek dictatorship, and one cannot predict what course events in Greece would have followed without it. If one assumes that the regime would have fallen in any case, at some later date, then after the collapse of the regime the Turkish Cypriot right to secede as a last resort no longer holds. If 15 July 1974 and not December 1963 is chosen as the date on which secession was deemed to be the last resort in achieving justice, given the establishment of the Greek military dictatorship, then the Turkish Cypriot right to secession since the collapse of that regime on 24 July 1974 would be highly questionable.

WAR, OCCUPATION OF TERRITORY, AND HUMAN RIGHTS VIOLATIONS: ARE THE CONSEQUENCES OF THE REMEDIAL RIGHT TO SECESSION JUSTIFIABLE?

So far it has been argued that a group has a right to secession when it is governed by an 'unjust' state. In the case of Cyprus one may initially be inclined to argue that, given the events of the 1960s and early 1970s, the minority ethnic community had a remedial right to rebel against the existing regime, and perhaps, following the Greek military coup of 15 July 1974, to secede from the state. In the light of the collapse of the Greek military regime of 24 July 1974, however, the territorial partition of Cyprus as a 'last resort' in the attempt to achieve justice is debatable. Yet the 1974 division of the island becomes even more questionable once we move on to an analysis of a second period—that during and immediately following the Turkish military intervention. The questions raised by these events need to be addressed. Does exercising the remedial right of secession morally justify war, territorial occupation, and the forced displacement of people?

First, can the remedial right to secession be exercised by force? Or—to go further—does it allow invasion and continuing occupation by the army of a third country in defence of the seceding minority? The argument below does not deal with the legal justification of the Turkish invasion, which was defended by Turkey on the grounds of its obligations under the Treaty of Guarantee. The normative questions raised below are not legal ones.

The 'just cause' theory of war establishes—as described in the Introduction to this volume—the conditions under which one may morally use force. The first and most critical condition is the existence of a 'just cause' for resorting to war. In the case of Cyprus, we have already discussed how the years of segregation in blockaded enclaves, the absence of a Turkish Cypriot representation in government, and finally the Greek military coup, gave the Turkish Cypriot community a remedial right to separate both communities, as part of an effort to oppose the Greek dictatorship and to restore constitutional order. In so far as the Greek/Greek Cypriot authorities contested this right by force, the Turkish Cypriot minority had the right to defend themselves. In this case, self-defence constituted a 'just cause' for the use of force.

Second, the question is whether force is a last resort to achieve justice. Quoting the last resort condition to legitimize the use of force implies that all peaceful means to achieve justice have been explored and have failed. The just cause and last resort conditions become identical if the only peaceful and just alternatives are also alternatives to secession. Hence, when alternatives to just secession have been exhausted, then justice will only be achieved through force. The analysis above called into question the right to secession as a last resort in achieving justice after the collapse of the Greek regime on 24 July 1974. Below we shall examine the implications of this conclusion for the continuing presence of Turkish military forces on the island. Nonetheless, it may be granted that, in the light of the gross violations of Turkish Cypriot rights between 1963 and 1974 and the Greek coup on 15 July 1974, separating both communities at least temporarily through a partition of the island was indeed the last resort if justice were to be achieved. Therefore, given that a just partition necessarily entailed the use of force against the Greek and Greek Cypriot authorities, who opposed partition, the first Turkish invasion of 20–22 July was justified.

A third condition for the legitimate use of force is the existence of a legitimate authority. One may argue that under the 1960 Treaty of Guarantee the Turkish army had legitimate authority to prevent the unification of Cyprus and Greece. The prospect of *enosis* following the Greek coup on the island thus gave Turkey a legitimate right to intervene in the internal affairs of Cyprus.

Fourth, there must be a reasonable probability of success for the military operation, to prevent soldiers and civilians from being sacrificed in the name of an unattainable cause. Again, in the light of the relative strength of the Turkish army, this condition may be regarded as having been satisfied.

A fifth condition is the respect for the principle of proportionality. This condition was satisfied in the first Turkish attack of the island, which was followed by a troop withdrawal, and could have provided sufficient incentive for settling the problem. Indeed it triggered the collapse of the military junta in Athens. Yet the initial failure of talks in Geneva immediately triggered a second and more forceful attack on 14 August 1974, which culminated in the permanent occupation of a large proportion of the island's territory. If one asserts that war was the last resort in attaining the just cause, but that the just cause was not permanently to partition the island but rather to displace the current dictatorial regime and re-establish the constitutional Republic of Cyprus, then one may justify the first attack, but not the second, which resulted in the *de facto* secession of the Turkish Cypriots through the occupation of a disproportionate share of territory.

The sixth and final condition is that of 'right intention', in other words, the warring party must fight with the primary intention of attaining the just cause. No other objective may be decisive in launching military operations. One could argue that the just cause—and thus the violated rights and living conditions of the Turkish Cypriot community—was only one of the triggers for the Turkish invasion. Another, perhaps more salient, motive was the strategic value of Cyprus to Turkey, which was ultimately threatened by the Greek coup. It may in fact be useful to note that prior to 1974, Turkey had already twice planned military intervention in Cyprus. Both in 1964 and in 1967 it was deterred by the United States. Hence, arguably, the primary motive behind the Turkish invasion was not the 'just cause', which emerged following the Greek coup of 15 July 1974, but rather the strategic value of the island in a Cold War context. Of course it is not easy to separate the 'just cause' from the strategic value of the island to Turkey. Turkey's strategic interests would have been safeguarded *if* the Turkish Cypriot community had been recognized as co-owner of Cyprus and retained sufficient say in governing arrangements. However, in this case the rights of the Turkish Cypriots would not be considered an objective *per se* but rather a means to achieve Turkey's 'strategic' aims. Such a conclusion, while not invalidating Turkey's 'right intention' behind the war, does however cast doubt on its unambiguous fulfilment of this condition.

Even more morally questionable is the presence of Turkish military forces in northern Cyprus to this day, which has ensured the continued territorial division of the territory. In an island with fewer than 700,000 inhabitants there are approximately 35,000 Turkish troops and 4,500 Turkish Cypriot troops in northern Cyprus. Militarization in the Turkish Republic of Northern Cyprus (TRNC) considerably outweighs that in the Republic of Cyprus. The knowledge of such extensive militarization in the north exacerbates the fears of Greek Cypriots and confirms their view that the Cyprus problem is provoked by Turkey's strategic rather than humanitarian concerns. Even if one is prepared to justify an initial Turkish military response

to the Greek coup in 1974, can one morally sanction the strong presence of
the Turkish forces in northern Cyprus to this day, decades after the initial
invasion and the almost immediate collapse of Greek military junta thereafter? It was argued above that recourse to force could have been regarded
as a 'last resort' in an attempt to achieve a temporary separation of the population following the Greek coup. With the collapse of the regime a few days
later, however, the *de facto* secession of the Turkish Cypriot community can
no longer be viewed unambiguously as a 'last resort' in the struggle for justice. Consequently the persistent threat of force of the Turkish military presence in Cyprus becomes even less defensible. This is both because secession
is no longer an unambiguously 'just cause' and because military action
could no longer be viewed as a last resort.

The second question concerns territorial occupation. The Turkish invasion led to the occupation, as we have seen, of 37 per cent of Cypriot territory, inhabited ultimately by a mere 18.5 per cent of the total population of
the island. Normative theories argue that secession can be justifiable for territorially concentrated ethnic groups. In the case of Cyprus, the Turkish
Cypriot community was not only a minority in northern Cyprus but was
also scattered virtually throughout the entire island, without being even relatively concentrated in the north. Thus it did not have an obvious right to the
northern territories. Throughout the centuries, Greek Cypriots had also
inhabited that land, shaping it together with their Turkish Cypriot neighbours. One may be inclined to argue that the self-determination of the
Turkish Cypriots required some kind of territorial delimitation. But can one
justify the occupation of 37 per cent of the overall territory by 18.5 per cent
of the island's population? When a specified minority has a remedial right to
separate self-determination, and yet it is not unambiguously identified with
a particular territory, on what territory, and on how much of it, is it morally
justified to exercise its right?

This includes the question of the forced emigration and resettlement of
refugees. Above, it was suggested that if one recognizes the Turkish
Cypriots' remedial right to separate self-determination, then some form of
territorial delimitation of Cyprus may have been necessary. However, normative theories state that a recourse to secession as a last resort in order to
attain self-determination can only be justified provided it does not in turn
create further problems of minority repression or, worse still, an exponen-
tial multiplication of minority rights violations.[21] Drawing new territorial
boundaries through secession is unlikely to lead to new homogeneous

[21] Margaret Moore 'The Territorial Dimension of Self-Determination' and John McGarry
'"Orphans of Secession": National Pluralism in Secessionist Regions and Post-Secession States',
in Moore, *National Self-Determination and Secession*, 215–32 and 134–57.

nation-states, and new ethnic minorities will undoubtedly emerge. Specifically, what is to be the fate of newly created minorities belonging to the very ethnic group that had been in the majority in the former, unified, state? In the light of historical precedent, the latter may well be ill-treated by the new majority group, thus rendering the new post-secession state as unjust as its predecessor. Margaret Moore therefore concludes that 'in cases where two national groups are interspersed in the same territory, self-determination cannot take a secessionist form, but must be achieved by more complex arrangements'.[22]

In the case of Cyprus, there are almost no Greek or Turkish ethnic minorities in the 'TRNC' or the 'Republic of Cyprus', respectively. This is entirely due to the significant migration flows that took place in the immediate aftermath of the 1974 invasion and the Vienna agreements on the exchange of populations. Because of the non-territorial nature of the two ethnic communities, 160,000 Greek Cypriots and 60,000 Turkish Cypriots fled as internally displaced persons and refugees.[23] All the property formerly belonging to Greek Cypriots in the north was nationalized by the *de facto* Turkish Cypriot government and subsequently distributed to Turkish Cypriot inhabitants through certificates of usufruct. The problem worsened over time as a result of the deliberate policy of the Turkish Cypriot administration, which altered the demographic balance by encouraging well over 50,000 Anatolian settlers to immigrate to northern Cyprus and take over what had formerly been Greek Cypriot homes.

Does the existence of substantial refugee flows following partition invalidate the moral right to full secession? In Cyprus, moreover, the refugee flows and resettlement were forced, which once again opens up the normative debate on the 'just' use of force. We have already discussed how the criteria for a just war were only partially fulfilled by the Turkish military actions of 1974. The use of force to achieve migration and resettlement becomes even harder to justify. The Turkish Cypriot community may have had a remedial right to separate self-determination, which may have implied some form of territorial delimitation, but this does not mean that the separate territories should be ethnically cleansed. Assurances that the Greek Cypriot community would not dominate affairs in the Turkish Cypriot zone would by no means require reciprocal ethnic cleansing on the island.

So far we have argued that although the events between December 1963 and July 1974 may have justified the Turkish Cypriot community's remedial right to separate self-determination, one cannot conclude that by the end of

---

[22] Margaret Moore, 'Introduction: The Self-Determination Principle and the Ethics of Secession', in Moore, *National Self-Determination and Secession*, 154.

[23] Clement Dodd (ed.), *The Political, Social and Economic Development of Northern Cyprus* (London, Eothen Press, 1993).

July 1974, following the collapse of the Greek junta, effective secession was the appropriate means of exercising this right. First, Buchanan's criteria for a remedial right to secession are not wholly satisfied. The collapse of the Greek military regime by late July 1974 casts doubt on whether secession could have still been considered a last resort in the struggle for justice a few weeks after the effective partition of the island. Second, the events during and following the Turkish invasion raise further questions about the normative bases of the *de facto* partition of the island. Analysing just war theory, one cannot conclude that all conditions guaranteeing a justified recourse to force were satisfied by the Turkish armed forces in Cyprus during the summer of 1974. The fact that foreign armed forces continue to be present even now casts further doubt on the legitimacy of the military intervention. Its results are also highly questionable from a normative perspective. The disproportionate territorial occupation by the Turkish Cypriots and, most importantly, the forced migration and resettlement of ethnic populations, all give moral grounds for challenging the partition of the island in 1974.

RADICAL PLURALISM: THE GREEK- AND TURKISH CYPRIOT COMMUNITIES IN CYPRUS TODAY

The previous sections dealt with the application of Buchanan's remedial theory of secession and of just war theory. In this discussion, a specific time period for the Cyprus question was selected. The remedial right to secession of the Turkish Cypriot community was analysed for the period between 1963 and 1974, while the problems associated with the exercise of this right were highlighted for the period during and immediately after the Turkish invasion. We now turn to the present, and in doing so we focus on a different set of normative principles. This analysis attempts to draw some conclusions regarding the possible resolution of the problem in the near future.

A well-functioning democratic society is by no means necessarily a homogeneous one. On the contrary, cohesive democratic states may well be multi-lingual, multi-ethnic or multi-religious compounds, in which different sectors of society hold contrasting political views. Many political theorists argue that it is actually the process of channelling and reconciling diverse values and ideas that produces the best political results.[24] The existence of societal divisions does not in itself mean that state boundaries should be redrawn. That said, it must be stressed that if a democratic society is to function effectively it should comprise individuals and communities 'who

---

[24] Buchanan, 'Democracy and Secession', in Moore, *National Self-Determination and Secession*, 23.

have *enough* in common to be able to engage in meaningful participation in rational, principled political decision-making'.[25] When this condition fails to be met, the rationale for secession becomes qualitatively different. In these situations, which Buchanan describes as situations of 'radical pluralism', different communities may be unable to join in common, democratic decision-making to achieve even the minimal good common to both. Consequently it may be expedient to redraw the political map to reflect the existence of different political—and not simply ethnic or cultural—communities.

Turning to the present political situation on the island, do these ideas and conditions for building a functioning democratic society offer some insight into the problem of secession four decades after the Cyprus question first became an issue? Three decades after the territorial separation of the two communities on the island, and with a continuing no-peace no-war situation, several salient factors suggest that an all-encompassing reunification of the two communities would be unworkable. Real causes of division compounded by irrational fears and misperceptions of the 'other' explain the persistent inter-communal conflict and the existence of two clearly separate political identities and communities in Cyprus. We will now single out the conditions *sustaining* the inter-communal conflict today.[26]

Two separate systems of governance

The first divisive condition creating two antagonistic nations and two separate political communities is the existence of a *de facto* division in governance. Since 1967, Cyprus has effectively been subjected to two systems of governance: the formally recognized Republic of Cyprus, and the *de facto* but unrecognized Turkish Cypriot government, governing the Turkish Cypriot community. As the conflict was showing no signs of being resolved the latter was transformed from being an administration that had served the enclaved Turkish Cypriots in 1967–74 to declaring itself the government of a federated Turkish Cypriot state and, finally, in 1983, an independent state (the TRNC). The present situation—in which there are two distinct states with separate and non-communicating governments, administrations, judiciaries, police and military forces—has greatly exacerbated the division between the two peoples by precluding any experience of joint governance and the development of a joint political culture by their political élites.

---

[25] Ibid.
[26] For a more detailed exposition of these arguments see Nathalie Tocci, *The Cyprus Question: Reshaping Community Identities and Elite Interests within a Wider European Framework*, CEPS Working Paper available on www.ceps.be, 2000.

The absence of social, cultural, or economic contacts

The second condition conducive to division has been the almost complete lack of any social, cultural, or economic links between the two communities. Because of separate governance, and above all the impenetrable 'green line' cutting across the island, contact between the two sides is virtually non-existent. In the social and cultural spheres, linkages between the two peoples are inhibited by territorial separation, while in the economic sphere, the embargo imposed on the north by the Republic of Cyprus almost destroyed any economic links through trade or joint ventures. Hence, new generations of Cypriots are growing up without any form of contact with the other community. Most young Cypriots today have never met anyone from the opposing ethnic group living on the other side of the border. This in turn has encouraged radical political opinions built on biased evidence and prejudice, and has therefore hampered prospects for a peace built on the reintegration—or even peaceful coexistence—of the two communities in Cyprus.

Inter-communal socio-economic disparities

The third condition fostering contrasting identities and purposes is the great disparity in the economic standards of the two communities. Even during the period of Ottoman rule and the overt emergence of the inter-communal conflict, the economic levels of the two communities differed substantially, with the Greek Cypriot community effectively controlling the economy while the Turks controlled government. Existing disparities increased exponentially in the decades following the emergence of the conflict. The 1974 invasion and subsequent partition of the island left both ethnic communities in a state of total economic disarray. However, while the Greek Cypriot economy in the south underwent a vigorous recovery, leading to economic prosperity, the Turkish Cypriot economy in the northern region has stagnated.

The Greek Cypriot economic success has been facilitated by the status of the Republic of Cyprus as the only internationally recognized state on the island. As a small economy it has benefited hugely from trade and investment, specializing in light manufacturing goods, tourism, and offshore financial services. Northern Cyprus, on the other hand, presents a starkly contrasting scenario. The productivity of the TRNC is less than 40 per cent that of the Republic of Cyprus.[27] Agriculture remains largely subsistence-based, and tourism is underdeveloped[28] owing both to potential visitors'

---

[27] Dodd, *Development of Northern Cyprus*, 1993.
[28] Over 80 per cent of all tourists in northern Cyprus are in fact Turkish.

fear of travelling to a non-recognized state, and to the lack of international air links from places other than Turkey. The economy is dominated by a corrupt public sector, leading to serious fiscal imbalances. The stagnation in the economy has been caused to a large extent by the lack of international recognition for the TRNC and its resulting economic isolation.[29] The close ties between northern Cyprus and Turkey have not only been insufficient to offset the cost of international isolation.[30] They have also meant that northern Cyprus has inherited Turkey's macroeconomic imbalances, which has further hindered trade and investment, and thus overall growth.

These wide and all-encompassing economic disparities add to the conditions provoking inter-communal division, which in turn breed conflict. Economic disparities imply radically different ways of life and standards of living, which impose tight constraints on inter-communal contact and relations and contribute to the creation of separate political communities.

Moreover, conditions of economic disparity exacerbate concerns about reunification amongst the Turkish Cypriot people, who fear the economic domination of northern Cyprus by the more prosperous Greek Cypriot population. The Cyprus conflict is above all a security conflict for both communities. While the Greek Cypriot community fears direct or indirect domination by Turkey, the Turkish Cypriot community fears domination by the larger Greek Cypriot community. In this context, economic disparities become an important aspect of the conflict. The economic superiority of the larger community further exacerbates the security concerns of the smaller one, which fears political and economic control by the former. This explains why one of the principal items on the conflict resolution agenda is the liberalization of the three freedoms of movement, settlement, and property. While for the Greek Cypriot community the wish to return to the north requires the three-fold liberalization, the Turkish Cypriot community categorically rejects this. They argue that if these freedoms are achieved, northern Cyprus would be effectively 'bought over' by the richer Greek Cypriot community, and as such the communal survival of the Turkish Cypriots would be threatened.

Greek–Turkish rivalry

The final cause of division between the two ethnic communities on the island is the underlying conflict between their respective motherlands,

---

[29] For example in 1994 the European Court of Justice passed a ruling prohibiting the acceptance of goods originating in Cyprus without accompanying certificates from the authorities of the Republic of Cyprus.

[30] In 1998, Turkey formed an Association Council with the TRNC providing for close links in trade, political solidarity and budgetary support.

Greece and Turkey. Since the Ottoman conquest of Constantinople in 1453 and the ensuing four centuries of Ottoman rule over Greece, which terminated with the Greek war of independence in 1821–29, tensions between the two nations have been high. Rivalries were reinforced in the late nineteenth and early twentieth centuries by the wars of 1897, 1912–13, and 1919–23, and again since 1974 by conflicts over sovereign rights in the Aegean. In so far as the two communities in Cyprus will always to some extent identify with their respective motherland countries, the Greek–Turkish rivalry will prevent the creation of shared or even coexisting identities in Cyprus. Greek–Turkish relations underwent significant improvement following the earthquake diplomacy of August–September 1999 and the subsequent meetings between the two countries' foreign ministers in early 2000. However, the rapprochement remains extremely fragile, with any minor crisis in Cyprus or the Aegean endangering the entire process.

It may be concluded that separate systems of governance, the lack of social, cultural, or economic relations, the differing levels of economic well-being, and the underlying Greek–Turkish rivalry have reinforced perceptions of separate identities and have fostered deep-rooted distrust and fear of the 'other' amongst both communities. This has cemented a situation of 'radical pluralism' on the island.

In this context it may be interesting to note some of the results of a poll carried out in March 2000 in the Republic of Cyprus.[31] Seventy-five per cent of the Greek Cypriots interviewed said that they would not agree to a marriage between a member of their family and a Turkish Cypriot. Over 80 per cent said that in the event of a federal solution they would not live in the Turkish Cypriot unit. Finally, between 30 and 40 per cent of interviewees were against working in the same place as a Turkish Cypriot, living in a mixed village, or allowing their children to attend the same schools as Turkish Cypriot children. These figures highlight how conditions have transformed the mindset of the two peoples, in a way that would prevent the proper functioning of an immediate solution based either on a shared Cypriot identity or on the peaceful and complementary coexistence of two communities within the same political entity.

Media and books have selected primordial elements of division such as ethnicity, language, and religion in order to define and legitimize the respective communities, conveniently neglecting other elements that are common to both peoples, such as shared colonial history, customs, and traditions on the island. The communities on Cyprus have chosen to forget those aspects of everyday life, which they continue to share despite separation and disparity, thus compounding real causes of division with imaginary differences

[31] Jean Christou, *Cyprus Mail*, 10 April 2000.

fuelled by irrational fear and prejudice. Hence, while the initial causes of the conflict are rooted in the decades preceding 1974, the conditions of division which have emerged since then have sustained the inter-communal conflict. Real and imaginary divisions have generated support for rigid negotiating positions by the two community leaderships, which have prevented the materialisation of an agreement. The longer an agreement is delayed, the more entrenched do divisions become, locking Cyprus in a vicious no-peace no-war circle.

MOVING BEYOND THE NATION-STATE: SELF-DETERMINATION IN CYPRUS WITHIN THE STRUCTURE OF THE EU

The polarized pluralism that exists in Cyprus today is the consequence of decades of separation and lack of contact. Greek and Turkish Cypriots may in the long term gradually eliminate the current conditions of division and feasibly form one political community under a democratic system of governance. As discussed above, the existence of a multi-ethnic, multi-religious and multicultural society could well improve the functioning of a democratic state. Provided there is sufficient commonality between the communities, the existence of a heterogeneous society can represent an asset to democratic decision-making.

Where does this leave us? Our argument so far has run as follows: the historical trends in the decade 1963–74 may, on initial analysis, be interpreted as suggesting that the Turkish Cypriot community had a remedial right to secession. However, the highly debatable fulfilment of the 'last resort' condition for achieving justice through secession in 1974, and the events during and after the Turkish military intervention—in particular the creation of two separate, ethnically cleansed entities on the island—argue against international recognition of the TRNC as it exists today. On the other hand, it could be maintained that the current existence of two distinct political communities on the island warns against the creation of one unitary democratic state. While that may be a possibility in the more distant future, as the grounds for conflict erode, such a state would probably be unsustainable today.

We thus return to Moore's call for 'imaginative' and 'complex' solutions. McGarry argues that the way to address the existence of national diversity is to move away from the rigid model of the nation-state based on the legal principle of indivisible external sovereignty.[32] Such a shift of paradigms

---

[32] See Kypros Chrysostomides, *The Republic of Cyprus: A Study in International Law* (The Hague and London, M. Nijhoff Publishers, 2000), 350–69.

would dismiss ideas both of reintegration into the unitary state and of secession to form two separate states. In other words, secession does not in itself resolve the problem of national diversity, but simply transplants it to another, equally state-centred context.

Conventional federal and confederal models, however, are just as rigid. Again, international public law prescribes that, in the case of the former, external sovereignty resides wholly in the federal state, while in the latter it rests with the separate confederated states. A federation remains one externally sovereign state (albeit with an internal division of sovereign competences), while a confederation entails two externally sovereign states (albeit with some sovereign powers delegated to a centre). In circumstances of ethnic conflict, these legal distinctions acquire critical significance. Mutual insecurities tend to place conflicting parties in opposite camps. While the community representing the original state insists upon the model of a federation, whose single sovereignty would prevent future secession, the seceding community, fearing domination and seeking for equality, demands separate sovereignties and at most accepts a confederal arrangement. The appropriate way to address the problem may be to seek a different framework within which to articulate federal ideas, one within which concepts of indivisible sovereignty and territorial integrity gradually change meaning. How can such a step be taken?

In July 1990 the Republic of Cyprus applied for full membership of the European Union on behalf of the whole island, and in March 1998 accession negotiations began. The conclusions of the Helsinki European Council of December 1999 formally removed the resolution of the Cyprus conflict as a precondition to full accession to the Union. The Turkish Cypriot authorities opposed this initiative. Although the Turkish Cypriot community favours EU accession in the long run, the majority held that accession should only take place once the conflict has been resolved. In parallel with the evolution of Greek Cypriot–EU relations during the 1990s and up until January 2002, the conflict on the island deteriorated considerably. The negotiating positions of both parties hardened, negotiations were stalled between 1997 and 2002 and the TRNC and Turkey proceeded towards greater integration. This does not mean, however, that the EU could not ultimately act as one of the principal factors facilitating peace on the island.

The transformation of Cyprus from a conflict-ridden state, in which 'state' and 'nation' do not coincide, into a federal state with single sovereignty and territorial integrity as advocated by UN resolutions, is an unlikely outcome.[33]

---

[33] For a review of UN mediation efforts in Cyprus in the search for a federal settlement see Hugo Gobbi, *Rethinking Cyprus* (Tel Aviv, Editorial Aurora, 1993); A. J. R. Groom 'The Process of Negotiation 1974–1993', in Dodd, *Development of Northern Cyprus*, 15–45; Polyvios G. Polyviou, *Cyprus in Search for a Constitution* (Nicosia, Chr. Nicolaou & Sons, 1976), and Oliver

On the few occasions in which the UN almost secured an agreement,[34] the contradictions between the interpretations of sovereignty and self-determination of the two sides were masked by vague wording. This could have led to impasse during the implementation stage. The continuation of conflict for over three decades has in turn promoted the increasing entrenchment of inter-communal division. New and more imaginative constitutional constructs are called for. In view of the accession of Cyprus to the EU, these could be envisaged within the existing structure of European multilevel governance.[35] Such constructs could prove better suited to the actual situation on the ground than the conventional federal or confederal models so far suggested by the conflicting parties.

As several cases in Western Europe suggest (such as Belgium and Northern Ireland), the EU could play a role in easing the perennial tensions between different 'nations' within one 'state'. While there is no consensus concerning a definite EU impact upon the settlement of intra-EU conflicts, some research shows that the EU factor has at least been one of the elements contributing towards conflict resolution in cases such as Northern Ireland.[36]

Turning to Cyprus, if past positions of the two community leaderships are assessed (for example during the 1992 Set of Ideas talks), it becomes clear that EU membership, while not providing a magic formula for conflict settlement, could facilitate the ultimate achievement of a win-win agreement on the island. This occurs through inclusion in a wider regional

Richmond, *Mediating in Cyprus* (London, Frank Cass, 1998). For literature on federal solutions in Cyprus see Clement Dodd 'Confederation, Federation and Sovereignty', in *Perceptions: Journal of International Affairs*, 4:3 (1999) (http://www.mfa.gov.tr/grupa/percept/IV-3/dodd.htm); Nanette Neuwahl 'Cyprus, Which Way? In Pursuit of a Confederal Solution in Europe', *Harvard Jean Monnet Working Paper 4/00* (2000); Zenon Stavrinides, 'Is a Compromise Settlement in Cyprus still Possible? Revisiting the Ghali Set of Ideas', and Ergun Olgun, 'Response to Zenon Stavrinides', *Journal of Cyprus Studies*, 14/15 (1999), 51–72 and 73–80; Andreas Theophanous, *The Political Economy of a Federal Cyprus* (Nicosia, Research and Development Centre, Intercollege Press, 1996).

[34] Such as Perez de Cuellar's Draft Framework proposals in Jan. 1985, April 1985, and April 1986, or most importantly Boutros Ghali's 'Set of Ideas' in 1992.

[35] On EU multilevel governance see Liesbet Hooghe, 'Sub-national Mobilization in the European Union', *West European Politics*, 18:3 (1995), 175–98; Liesbet Hooghe (ed.) *Cohesion Policy and European Integration: Building Multi-Level Governance* (Oxford, Clarendon Press, 1996); Gary Marks, François Nielsen, Leonard Ray, and Jane Salk 'Competences Cracks and Conflicts: Regional Mobilisation in the European Union', in Gary Marks et al. (eds.), *Governance in the European Union* (London, Sage, 1998), 40–63; Inger-Johanne Sand, 'The Changing Preconditions of the Law and Politics: Multi-Level Governance and Mutually Interdependent, Reflexive and Competing Institutions in the EU and the EEA', *Arena Working Paper*, no. 29 (1997); Fritz W. Sharpe, 'Community and Autonomy: Multi-level Policy Making in the European Union' in *Journal of European Public Policy*, 1:1 (1994), 213–42.

[36] See Elizabeth Meehan '"Britain's Irish Question: Britain's European Question?" British–Irish relations in the context of European Union and the Belfast Agreement', *Review of International Studies*, 26 (2000), 83–97.

framework, characterized by multiple levels of government, including a powerful supra-national tier. Within such a framework, concepts of indivisible sovereignty and territorial integrity gradually change meaning, and as such could create the scope for new and more complex constitutional alternatives to be formulated in Cyprus. However, this would first require a more balanced approach of the EU towards the conflict in general and the engagement of the Turkish Cypriot community in Cyprus–EU relations in particular. If these preconditions were satisfied, the EU could contribute to the resolution of the Cyprus problem in the following ways.

First, EU membership could facilitate an agreement on constitutional arrangements, where the Turkish Cypriot insistence on political equality and the Greek Cypriot insistence on single statehood have prevented an agreement for decades. Within the EU, while remaining full-fledged 'states', member states delegate several important competences to Brussels, where many decisions are collectively taken on the basis of majority rule. Predominantly in the economic sphere, but increasingly in the justice and home affairs as well as the security and foreign policy spheres, the EU level of government lies at the fore of policy-making. Many competences would be transferred from the member state to the European level, thereby reducing the problem of hierarchy between levels of government and competition for the allocation of competences. During past negotiations in Cyprus, issues of contention between the two communities concerned decision-making in monetary and trade policy affairs. Within the EU, these points of disagreement would be removed automatically, as these policy competences would be transferred to the supra-state level. To a lesser extent the same would be true for an entire range of policy competences, ranging from budgetary questions, to the environment, agriculture and immigration.

Not only are many decisions now taken at the EU level. In the Council of Ministers, where EU decisions are ultimately taken, participation is no longer restricted to official representatives of the central governments. Since the 1991 Maastricht Treaty, member states can choose to send sub-state representatives to Council meetings so long as these are empowered to speak and vote for the entire country.[37] Belgium in particular has made extensive use of this provision since 1993, elaborating a complex system of internal coordination which allows regional or community representatives to participate in those Councils, when these deal with policy issues falling either wholly or predominantly in their sphere of powers. Without necessarily advocating such an

---

[37] Article 146 of the Maastricht Treaty does not specify that Ministers participating in Council meetings should be State Ministers (and thus Federal Ministers in the case of Federal States). Hence, ministers of federated entities can participate in Council meetings provided that in doing so they represent the entire country.

arrangement in Cyprus, the Belgian example illustrates how the EU, by effectively allowing some sharing of external sovereignty (in addition to shared internal sovereignty within a state), could facilitate an agreement in Cyprus based upon two politically equal communities within a single EU member state. It is interesting to note that in the latest draft UN Plan for the settlement of the conflict, proposed to the parties on 11 November 2002, the UN explicitly endorsed the 'Belgian model' for Cyprus' future representation in EU institutions.[38]

In less substantive ways, but nonetheless worth mentioning, the EU framework also enhances the status of sub-state actors, through regional policies/structural funds and institutions such as the Committee of the Regions. This is so particularly for those regions that already have pronounced roles within their member state (i.e., federal states or those with autonomous regions). If and when regional levels of government play important roles within their member state (as a result of institutional set-up, fields of competence, economic capacity, or regional distinctiveness), their role is further enhanced within the EU. In other words, the emerging system of multi-level governance rather than developing into a homogeneous system throughout the Union, is being shaped according to the internal features of each member state. A 'Europe with some regions' rather than 'of the regions' is in the making.[39]

Within the EU context, and particularly in the case of highly decentralized member states, the difference between single and divided sovereignty becomes fundamentally blurred. Decision-making and implementation in a given policy domain is determined by a particular allocation and sharing of competences between different levels of government. These include the state, the supra-state, and (particularly in the case of federal states) the sub-state levels of government. While different levels of government remain legally distinct, through different channels of communication and policy procedures they become practically interrelated and mutually interdependent. As such the notion of statehood and sovereignty fundamentally alters. Within the EU framework, a hybrid constitutional model containing federal and confederal principles could be envisaged. The political equality of the two Cypriot communities could be endorsed, thus satisfying the essence of Turkish Cypriot demands, but Cyprus would remain one formally recognized EU member state.

[38] The first draft of the UN Plan was reproduced on Cyprus Mail on 14 November 2002 (http://www.cyprus-mail.com/November/14/news2.htm). Article 2 of the draft states that: "In particular, the [component states] shall participate in the formulation and implementation of policy in external and European Union relations on matters within their sphere of competence, in accordance with Cooperation Agreements modeled on the Belgian example. The [component states] may have commercial and cultural relations with the outside world in conformity with the Constitution". [39] Hooghe (ed.), *Cohesion Policy and European Integration*.

Second, EU membership could facilitate an agreement on Cyprus by affecting the debate about territory, given the Union's pledge to assist the development of northern Cyprus through structural funds of the EU budget and loans from the European Investment Bank. The rules and criteria of the existing structural funds of the EU would see the whole of northern Cyprus recognized as 'Objective 1 Priority Region'. The European Commission published on 30 January 2002 first indications of the likely scale of financial assistance to Cyprus.[40] The total amount foreseen in commitments for the northern part of Cyprus through structural funds and pre-accession aid over the course of three years was 206 million euros. A large part of these funds would be spent on investment in renewal of economic infrastructures specifically linked to territorial readjustments. Special attention would be paid to renewing transport and communications infrastructures between north and south across the 'green line', and rehabilitating Varosha for example. Loan finance for investment in the private sector, a well as public infrastructure, would also be available from the European Investment Bank (EIB), for example for rehabilitation and modernization of the tourist economy.

A third major item on the conflict settlement agenda is security and in particular the role and rights of Turkey in Cyprus. While discussions concerning the Treaty of Guarantee would remain an issue to be decided by the two communities and the three guarantor powers, the EU and its legal mechanisms could contribute to Cyprus's security system. The EU already has instruments at its disposal to respond to breaches of rights and constitutional provisions within its member states. In the event of a breach of the principles of 'liberty, democracy, respect for human rights and fundamental freedoms, and the rule of law' (article 6.1 of the Treaty of the EU), 'the Council, acting by a qualified majority, may decide to suspend certain rights deriving from the application of the Treaty' to a member state (Article 7.3 of the Treaty of Nice, ex article 7). In other words, upon Cyprus's accession to the EU, irrespective of the military guarantee agreement between the parties, Articles 6 and 7 of the Treaty on European Union (TEU) would effectively act as a first non-military EU guarantee of the constitutional order and of the respect for EU principles in Cyprus.

Such a non-military guarantee would facilitate a settlement of security questions for two main reasons. First, it would provide an extra element of security to the Turkish Cypriot community against a hypothetical recurrence of the events of 1963–74. Provided the EU non-military guarantee existed in

---

[40] EU Commission, *Commission offers a fair and solid approach for financing EU enlargement*, Press release, January 30, 2002. http://europa.eu.int/comm/enlargement/ docs/news.htm.

addition to any other guarantee freely agreed upon by the parties, EU membership would be an additional provider of security to the Turkish Cypriot community, given the strong deterrent force of possible EU sanctions. Second, the inclusion of a 'first-stop' EU non-military guarantee would reassure the Greek Cypriot community and thus increase their flexibility in accepting Turkey's role in Cyprus' security. In the hypothetical situation of a constitutional breakdown or an infringement of rights provoked by the Greek Cypriot community, the Greek Cypriot authorities would be sanctioned first by the EU and only as a last resort would military intervention be envisaged. The disincentives on all parties to infringe rights and agreements would be such that it would be virtually impossible to envisage a repetition of the 1963–74 scenario.

A final major issue of contention in the Cyprus conflict is the freedom to settle and acquire property in Cyprus. So far the EU *acquis communautaire*, providing for a liberalization of these freedoms, has generated a deep suspicion of the EU in the Turkish Cypriot community. However, the EU with its principles as well as its realities could actually facilitate an agreement in Cyprus on the 'freedoms'. While the EU *acquis* provides for the freedom of movement of goods, services, persons, and capital across the Union, viewed favourably by the Greek Cypriot community, in the implementation of these principles there have been several types of exceptions. In the current (fifth) enlargement negotiations, the European Commission has proposed a seven-year transitional period in candidate states on the freedom to acquire agricultural land, five years for the acquisition of second homes, and none for other investment, given the need of foreign direct investment in most of the candidates.[41] While viewed with much more scepticism, the EU has in the past also accepted some permanent exceptions to the full application of the *acquis*. In Finland, the Swedish inhabited Åland Islands only allow individuals with Åland 'official domicile' to participate in elections, stand for local office, own property or exercise trade or a profession. In the current round of enlargement Malta also succeeded in negotiating permanent restrictions on the purchase of property by foreigners and Maltese not residing in Malta. Following EU membership only foreigners and Maltese residing in Malta for more than five years will be able to acquire property freely on the island.[42]

Hence, in Cyprus, the menu of conceivable possibilities within the framework of the *acquis communautaire* could range from Polish-style transition periods to Finnish/Danish/Maltese permanent derogations. According to

---

[41] Poland in particular was demanding longer transition periods.
[42] The restriction on the right to acquire property on Malta had to be made non-discriminatory between Maltese citizens and other EU-citizens. Maltese citizens who are not residing in Malta have therefore no right either to acquire property.

the UN Plan of 2002, proposed restrictions on Greek and Turkish Cypriots to settle and acquire property in each others' 'component states' would be scaled down over the course of fifteen years. The Plan also foresees restrictions on the freedoms of Greek and Turkish nationals to settle and acquire property in Cyprus if their numbers exceeded 10 per cent of the populations of the two 'component states'. These restrictions were proposed to account for Turkish Cypriot concerns. Provided the two Cypriot communities agreed to a set of restrictions, the EU could feasibly accommodate these demands. On the other hand, the general framework of liberalization within the Union could increase Greek Cypriot acceptance of these restrictions in so far as their gradual phasing out would be more plausible within an EU context.

Within the international system of states, a minority group such as the Turkish Cypriot community in Cyprus argues that its security can only be guaranteed through separate statehood. The majority Greek Cypriot community responds to this demand with equally compelling arguments. As this chapter has attempted to demonstrate, a normative analysis of the Cyprus case does not reveal a black and white solution to the problem. The European Union, with its institutions and policies, could present a possible way forward, offering an alternative framework that could facilitate an integrative agreement on all the major headings of the conflict settlement agenda. While not automatically eliminating all sources of friction and disagreement in Cyprus, the EU could considerably aid the search for a win-win-settlement on Cyprus leading the way to conflict transformation and resolution. By opening up new prospects and possibilities within a multi-level structure of governance, the EU could act both as a facilitating factor in formulating and implementing an initial agreement, and as a catalyst for the achievement of an optimal settlement. In this way Cyprus's EU membership and the resolution of the deep-rooted Cyprus conflict could evolve together, each reinforcing the other in a virtuous circle of reconciliation and development.

5

Britain and Ireland: Towards a Post-nationalist Archipelago

Richard Kearney

Nation-states are rather like teenagers: fine when full of questions but impossible when they get too sure of themselves. What we were witnessing on the Irish–British archipelago at the cusp of this millennium is little short of a revolution in our political understanding. With the ratification of a peace agreement on Northern Ireland in April 1998—the so-called Good Friday Agreement—both sovereign governments signed away their exclusivist sovereignty claims over Northern Ireland—and came of age. This signalled the possible end of the constitutional battle over the territory of Ulster: that contentious piece of land conjoining and separating the islands of Britain and Ireland for so long. The Siamese twins could now, one hoped, learn to live in real peace, accepting that their adversarial offspring in Northern Ireland may at last be 'British or Irish or both'.[1]

Since April 1998, the power-sharing agreement between the two Northern Irish communities has repeatedly been confronted with the threat of breaking down. The members of the four-party Ulster executive have accused each other of actions in breach of the peace agreement. It may happen that the British government and the political parties in Northern Ireland will be unable to maintain the momentum of the peace process and fail to keep the new institutions alive. Even in such a worst case event, the Good Friday Agreement has challenged traditional political wisdom and introduced new principles in the discussions on the future of Northern Ireland, whose relevance for a future peace order cannot be exaggerated.

---

[1] *The Good Friday Agreement*, Belfast, April 1998, paragraph 6. On the agreement see Clem McCartney (ed.), 'Striking a Balance: The Northern Ireland Peace Process' in *Accord: An International Review of Peace Initiatives*, 8 (1999), also on http://www.c-r.org/accord8/; Duncan Shipley-Dalton, 'The Belfast Agreement', *Fordham International Law Journal*, 22 (1999), 1320–44; Brendan O'Leary, 'The Nature of the Agreement', ibid. 1628–67; Michael Cox, Adrian Guelke, and Fiona Stephen (eds.), *A Farewell to Arms? From War to Peace in Northern Ireland* (Manchester, Manchester University Press, 2000); John McGarry, *Northern Ireland and the Divided World: The Northern Ireland Conflict and the Good Friday Agreement in Comparative Perspective* (Oxford, Oxford University Press, 2001).

According to classical political wisdom, unitary sovereignty could not be exercised by two separate nation-states over the same place at the same time. Especially if we were talking 'absolutist' sovereignty—which we were—and understood this to mean something like 'one and indivisible' (as defined by Hobbes, Bodin, and Rousseau)—which we did. The Agreement marked the termination of the age-old conflict between the rival ideologies of a United Kingdom and a United Ireland: a conflict made inevitable by the fact that two into one simply won't go.

The British and Irish nation-states have been compelled to redefine themselves. The 'hyphen' has been reinserted into their relations, epitomised in the new British–Irish Council (BIC). This council, which was established in the framework of the Good Friday Agreement and had its first meeting on 18 December 1999, allows direct cooperation between Scotland, Northern Ireland, Wales, the Channel Isles, the Isle of Man, and the governments of Ireland and Britain.[2] Its aim, as the April 1998 Agreement tells us, is 'to promote the harmonious and mutually beneficial development of the totality of relationships among the peoples of the British and Irish islands'. The Irish government has endorsed the removal of articles 2 and 3 from the Constitution of the Republic (articles which made a claim on the territory of Northern Ireland); while the British government has rewritten the 1922 Government of Ireland Act which approved the partition of Ireland and held referenda to establish regional assemblies in Scotland, Wales, and Northern Ireland.[3] The zero-sum game of exclusive 'national identities' is over.

The emerging post-nationalist scenario allows, for the first time in history, that citizens of Northern Ireland can owe differing degrees of allegiance to an expanding range of identifications: from regional townland, parish, or province to national constitution (British or Irish or both) and, larger still, to the transnational union of Europe. As John Hewitt wrote foresightedly to his fellow Ulster poet, John Montague: 'I always maintained that our loyalties had an order: to Ulster, to Ireland, to the British archipelago, to Europe, and that anyone who skipped a step or missed a link falsified the total.'[4] How right he was.

---

[2] On the British–Irish Council see Vernon Bogdanor, *Devolution in the United Kingdom* (Oxford, Oxford University Press, 1999), 107–8. A report of the first meeting was published in the *Irish Times*, 18 Dec. 1999. See also Graham Walker, 'The Council of the Isles and the Scotland-Northern Ireland Relationship', *Scottish Affairs*, 27 (Spring 1999), 108–23.

[3] On Scotland, see Alice Brown et al., *Politics and Society in Scotland*, 2nd edn. (Basingstoke, Macmillan, 1998); Christopher Harvie, *Scotland and Nationalism* (London, Routledge, 1998); Jonathan Hearn, *Claiming Scotland* (Edinburgh, Polygon, 2000); Michael Keating, 'Britain—The United Kingdom?', in Don MacIver (ed.), *The Politics of Multinational States* (Basingstoke, Macmillan, 1999); Andrew Marr, *The Battle for Scotland* (London, Penguin, 1992); and Lindsay Paterson, *The Autonomy of Modern Scotland* (Edinburgh, Edinburgh University Press, 1994).

[4] See R. Kearney, *Postnationalist Ireland* (London and New York, Routledge, 1997), 105–6.

THE ORIGINS OF THE BRITISH–IRISH CONFLICT

How did the game of exclusive nationalities first originate? Like most stories of national genesis, the Irish and British one began with a mirror-stage. The peoples of our two islands first identified themselves as separate and unique by differentiating themselves from one another. One of the earliest chapters in this process, noted by the Welsh historian, R. R. Davies,[5] was the attempt to forge the notion of an English (proto-British) nation—*nacio* or *gens* in Latin—over and against that of a colonized Irish nation in the fourteenth century. The English–British settlers of the time felt so fearful of mingling with the natives, thereby becoming 'more Irish than the Irish themselves', that they invented the infamous Statutes of Kilkenny. These Statutes, passed into law in 1366, instigated segregation between colonizer and colonized, fomenting political divisions between two supposedly incompatible 'peoples'. Non-observance of the Statutes was called 'degeneracy'— that is, the falling outside the Pale of the *gens*. To marry outside the *nacio* or *gens* was to cease to be a proper English 'gentlemen', thereby forfeiting the attendant virtues of gentility and gentrification. Commingling with the so-called natives was, as the old phrase went, 'going beyond the Pale' (literally, exiting from the frontier-walls of the city of settlers, Dublin). To transgress this limit was to betray the tribe. The colonizing *gens* thus came to define itself over and against its *de-gens*, its alter-ego: namely the indigenous Irish. Thus, even though it was the venerable Bede who initially invoked the idea of an English *gens*, and while it was Alfred's expansion of Wessex (871–899) which opened the way, it was actually in the laboratory of Ireland that the English nation first saw itself in the glass and believed its image. In Ireland England originally earned its credentials and cried victory. If the Irish didn't exist, the English would have had to invent them.

By virtue of this mimetic logic, the Irish in turn began redefining themselves as an equally pure and distinct *nacio*. In response to the colonial campaign of segregation, King Donald O'Neill of Ulster wrote to the Pope in 1317 declaring himself heir of the 'whole of Ireland' and affirming an unbroken historical continuity of the Irish people (*gens*) through their laws, speech, and long memory of tribulations suffered at the hands of the colonial invaders. (This move conveniently masked the fact that the 'natives', no less than the colonial settlers, were a mongrelized ethnic mix of successive invasions, Viking, Anglo-Norman, Scots, Celts, Milesians, etc.) Ever since this act of reciprocal invention and definition in the fourteenth century, the Irish and English–British nations have evolved like twins, inseparable in

---

[5] R. R. Davies, *The Peoples of Britain and Ireland 1100–1400*, vol. i, in *Transactions of the Royal Historical Society* (London, Royal Historical Society, 1994).

their loves and hates, joined at the hip of Ulster and forever bound to a dialectic of conflict and reconciliation.

It is of course true that the Irish nation had some primitive sense of itself before this reaction to the fourteenth-century plantation. It has been argued, by Proinsias McCana for example,[6] that some form of unitary government began to emerge as early as the ninth century in response to the Viking invasions, and again in the twelfth century in response to the Anglo-Norman invasion. But these intermittent efforts at all-island structures of self-rule were largely a matter of self-defence rather than any self-conscious assertion of enduring national identity. After all, the term 'scotus' could as easily refer to an inhabitant of Ireland as of Britain up the eleventh century (e.g. John Scotus Eriugena from the former, Duns Scotus from the latter). In short, the first *successful* attempt to identify the Irish and British as two radically separate peoples really only took hold after the fourteenth century invasionary settlement made it in the interests of the colonizers, and the colonized, to differentiate themselves as two distinct *gens*.

The criteria of discrimination were conventional rather than natural. They were, in other words, largely of a cultural and legal character—e.g. apparel, name-forms, language, decorum, property rights—than of ethnic foundation. (Indeed it is well accepted that the inhabitants of our respective islands share a virtually homogeneous gene pool due to their common experience of successive invasions and migrations, pre-Celtic, Celtic, Viking, Anglo-Norman etc. The first book of Irish letters is, after all, called the *Book of Invasions*!) The *gens* actually 'looked' almost identical to the *de-gens*. But this absence of racial distinguishing marks made it all the *more* necessary to compensate at the level of contrived legislation and statute. Where nature could not segregate, law would.

But law in itself was not enough. The border of the Pale separating *gens* from *de-gens* remained constantly shifting, porous and indeterminable, requiring repeated recourse to propaganda. The stereotyping usually took the form of prejudice and snobbery ('the natives are not *gentlemen*'), drawing great ammunition from Giraldus Cambrensis' twelfth-century *History and Topography of Ireland*. Cambrensis himself was, tellingly, a secretary to Prince John on one of his invasionary expeditions to Ireland and his depiction of the natives as 'a wild and inhospitable people who live like beasts' well served its colonial purposes. As the Irish historian, Art Cosgrove, would later observe: 'The picture drawn by Gerald was unflattering; the Irish were economically backward, politically fragmented, wild, untrustworthy and semi-pagan, and guilty of sexual immorality. Doubtless the picture was

---

[6] Proinsias MacCana, 'Notes on The Early Irish Concept of Unity', in *The Crane Bag Book of Irish Studies (1977–1981)* (Dublin, Blackwater Press, 1982), 205–9.

much influenced by the need to justify conquest and dispossession.[7] But the prize for colonial stereotypes must surely go to the British historian, Charles Kingsley, who could still remark on a visit to Ireland in the nineteenth century: 'to see white chimpanzees is dreadful; if they were black, one would not feel it so much, but their skins are as white as ours!'[8]

The Irish, of course, responded with their own version of self-conscious national pride, their spalpeen poets and bards spinning tales of the virginal motherland being raped and plundered by the invading *Sasannach*. And this widening gender opposition between Ireland as female virgin (Roisin Dubh, Cathleen ni Houliahn, *Speirbhean*, etc.) and England as male master (fatherland, King and Country, etc.) served to aggravate the divide between the two peoples.

But while literary propaganda worked, it was as nothing compared to the divisive power of *religion*. Arguably, it was not really until the seventeenth-century plantation of Ulster, after the Reformation, that the colonization of Ireland ultimately succeeded—and with a vengeance. The disenfranchising of Irish Catholics *en masse* in favour of Planter Protestants, subsequently backed up with the infamous Penal Laws, was evidence of how fatally religion could be deployed as a galvanizing force of apartheid. Where neither nature, nor ultimately even law or propaganda, could succeed in separating the peoples of these islands—*faith* in the one true church would! After Cromwellian zeal and Elizabethan ruthlessness had taken their toll, there were many Protestants and Catholics in the island of Ireland who preferred to die rather than to commingle. And not even Wolfe Tone and the United Irishmen, with their valiant appeal to a single nation of 'Catholic, Protestant and Dissenter' in the 1790s, could put the hibernian Humpty Dumpty back together again. Sectarianism was here to stay.

It would take another two hundred years after the failed Rebellion of 1798 for Britain and Ireland mutually to renounce their separatist claims to Northern Ireland thereby permitting Irish Catholics, Protestants and Dissenters peaceably to cohabit for the first time since the Reformation. It was only when the two communities inhabiting Ulster acknowledged that they could be 'British or Irish or both' that they could be united once again. Not, to be sure, as a unitary national identity as Wolfe Tone hoped, but as a multiple post-national one.

UNITIES OF PEOPLE AND POLITY

The story of the genesis and evolution of the Irish and British nations might thus be said to run broadly in parallel. As R. R. Davies again points out in

---

[7] Art Cosgrove, 'Seeing Ireland First', in *Books Ireland*, Kilkenny, 71 (1983), 35–6, at 35.
[8] Cited in 'Introduction', Richard Kearney (ed.), *The Irish Mind* (Dublin, Wolfhound Press, 1984), 7.

his landmark study *The Peoples of Britain and Ireland 1100–1400*,[9] what the English, and later the 'British', had great difficulty accepting was that after the Viking and Norman invasions, the various parts of these islands were already countries of 'multiple' peoples, which included, in part at least, the culture of the colonizer who was so desperately struggling to retain (even if it meant reinventing) his own sense of pure, uncontaminated identity. The settlers in Ireland were so insecure and unsure of their own ambiguous status as a 'middle nation'—neither fully English nor fully Irish—that they demonized the native Irish as their 'other' in order to more emphatically insist on their belonging to the former. The planters bolstered up this separatist propaganda with legal statutes and racist rhetoric, determined to prove to themselves and others that they were right. This scapegoating campaign led to the exacerbation of existing conflicts.

The match between people and polity that was achieved in England (and to a lesser extent Scotland) was not replicated in Ireland. But while the peoples of England (including the Normans) were by the fifteenth century welded into an integrative unit by virtue of such strategies of alien-nation— namely, establishing oneself as a single nation over against an alternative one—the island of Ireland remained a victim of such divisions. What would continue, however, to haunt the contrived national unity of Englishness— and of Britishness after the unions with Wales and Scotland—was the ghost of their alien and alienated double: Ireland. The very *difference* from Irishness became part and parcel of English–British identity. Their Hibernian Other was uncannily mirrored in themselves, the familiar spectre hidden in strangeness, the original double they had forgotten to remember, the threatened *revenant* of their own repressed political unconscious.

Linda Colley provides further evidence for this mirror-imaging of Irish and British nationalism in the last two centuries. In *Britons: Forging the Nation, 1797–1837*,[10] she also argues that the peoples that made up the British nation were brought together as a national unit by confrontation with the 'other'. In keeping with the theses of the new British history advocated by Benedict Anderson, Hugh Kearney, Tom Nairn, and J. G. A. Pocock,[11] Colley suggests that British national identity is contingent and relational (like most others) and is best understood as an *interaction* between several different histories and peoples. Without necessarily endorsing the Four Nations

[9] Davies, *The Peoples of Britain and Ireland 1100–1400*.

[10] Linda Colley, *Britons: Forging the Nation, 1797–1837* (New Haven, Yale University Press, 1992).

[11] Benedict Anderson, *Imagined Communities: Reflections on the Origin and Spread of Nationalism*, rev. edn. (New York, Verso, 1991); Hugh Kearney, *The British Isles: A History of Four Nations* (Cambridge, Cambridge University Press, 1990); Tom Nairn, *The Break-up of Britain: Crisis and Neonationalism*, 2nd edn. (London, New Left Books and Verso, 1981); J. G. A. Pocock, *Limits and Divisions of British History* (Strathclyde, University of Strathclyde, 1979).

model of Britain, Colley contends that most inhabitants of the 'British Isles' laid claim to a double, triple or multiple identity—even after the consolidation of British national identity after 1700. So that it would not be unusual, for example, to find someone identifying him/herself as a citizen of Edinburgh, a Lowlander, a Scot, and a Briton. It was over and against this pluralist practice of identification, on the ground, that the artificial nation of Great Britain managed to forge itself, not only by its Tudor conquests and successive unifications with Wales in 1536, Scotland in 1707 and Ireland in 1800, but also by its homogenizing Industrial Revolution and a series of massive external wars between 1689 and 1815. Due to these latter especially, Britain managed to expand its empire overseas and to unify its citizens back home, replicating on a world stage what England had first tried out in Ireland in the fourteenth century. It galvanized itself into national unity by pitting itself against external enemies.

The strategic benefits of British imperialism were not just commercial and political, therefore, but psychic as well. And the biggest advantage of the 'overseas' African and Asian colonies was that, unlike Britain's traditional enemies closer to home (the Irish and the French), these 'others' actually *looked* entirely different. But as the empire began to fracture and fragment in the first part of the twentieth century, the British resorted to *religion* once again to cement the sense of real national identity. For some, what united the British above all else in their times of trouble and decline, was their 'common Protestantism'. Hence the emblematic importance of the famous representation of St Paul's during the Blitz—the parish church of the besieged empire *par excellence*—'emerging defiantly and unscathed from the fire and devastation surrounding it...a Protestant citadel, encircled by enemies, but safe under the watchful eye of a strictly English-speaking deity'.[12] The British nation thus emerged, like many another nation, as an 'imagined community' that invented itself in dialectical opposition to its 'others'—and none more fundamentally than Ireland, its first, last and most intimate 'other'. For Ireland was unique in combining the three most salient characteristics of alien-nation: (1) Ireland was majority *Catholic* (non-Protestant); (2) it was a *colony* (overseas if only a little over—but sufficiently so to be treated like a subordinate rather than an equal neighbour, *pace* Wales or Scotland); and (3) Ireland was a traditional ally of *France*, the main military rival to British imperial designs, and inspirational insurrectionary model, along with Ireland, for rebellious movements in India, Palestine, and

---

[12] Linda Colley, 'Britishness and Otherness', *Journal of British Studies*, 31:4 (Oct. 1992), 309–29, at 72. Of course, the Protestant motif in the World War II should not be taken too far, since Germany was predominantly a Protestant country and allies such as Poland and France were Catholic.

elsewhere. Thus Ireland came to serve as the untrustworthy 'poor relation' of the United Kingdom:

(Ireland's) population was more Catholic than Protestant. It was the ideal jumping-off point for a French invasion, and both its Protestant and its Catholic dissidents traditionally looked to France for aid. And although Irishmen were always an important component of the British armed forces, and individual Scots-Irishmen like Macartney and Anglo-Irishmen like the Wellesley clan played leading imperial roles as diplomats, generals and pro-consuls, Ireland's relationship with the empire was always a deeply ambiguous one. How could it not be, when London so persistently treated the country in a way that it never treated Scotland and Wales, as a colony rather than as an integral part of a truly united Kingdom? Ireland was in many respects the laboratory of the British empire. Much of the legal and land reform which the British sought to implement in India, for example, was based on experiments first implemented in Ireland.[13]

It is of course the very *ambiguity* of Ireland's insider–outsider relation with Britain that made it at once so fascinating for the British (witnessed in their passion for Irish literature from Swift and Sheridan to Wilde, Yeats, and Shaw) *and* so repellent (evidenced in the popular portrayals of the Irish as brainless simians in the British Fleet Street media). This paradox of attraction and recoil is typical of what Edward Said calls 'orientalism': Ireland serving as Britain's Orient in its own backyard. It also approximates to what Freud describes as the 'uncanny' (*unheimlich*)—the return of the familiar as unfamiliar, of friend as stranger. Ireland served, one might say, as Britain's unconscious reminding it that it was ultimately and irrevocably a stranger to itself: that its self-identity was in fact constructed upon the screening of its forgotten other—in both senses of 'screen': to conceal and to project.

The nature of this unsettling rapport was evident not only in the mirror-plays of Irish dramatists like Shaw and Wilde, but also in the works of English dramatists who reflected on the neighbouring island. Already in Shakespeare we witness traces of this. In *Henry V*, for example, we find Captain MacMorris, the first true-blue Irishman to appear in English letters, posing the conundrum: 'What ish my nation?'—thereby recalling not only that Ireland is a nation still in question, but that England is too. And we find an even more explicit example in *Richard II*, when the King visits Ireland only to regain the British mainland disoriented and dismayed. Having set out secure in his sovereignty, he returns wondering what exactly *is* his identity, and by implication, his legitimacy as monarch: 'I had forgot myself, am I not king?' he puzzles. 'Is not the king's name twenty thousand names? (III, ii). In short, Ireland takes its revenge on the king by deconstructing and multiplying the one and indivisible character of his sovereignty. Richard is shaken

[13] Linda Colley, 'Britishness and Otherness', *Journal of British Studies*, 31:4 (Oct. 1992), 309–29, at 72. Of course, the Protestant motif in the World War II should not be taken too far, since Germany was predominantly a Protestant country and allies such as Poland and France were Catholic, 76.

from his slumber by his sojourn in the Irish colony, discovering that the very notion of a united national kingdom is nominal rather than real, imaginary rather than actual.

Where Ireland had the advantage over England/Britain, then as now, is that it never achieved indivisible sovereignty as a unitary nation—and so never could mistake the illusion for a reality. For the Irish, from ancient legend to the present day, the idea of sovereignty was linked to the notion of a 'fifth province': a place of mind rather than of territory, a symbol rather than a *fait accompli* (the Irish for province is *coicead*, meaning a fifth, but there are only four provinces in Ireland). Or to put it another way: when it came to sovereignty, Ireland had less to lose than Britain because it never had it (all-Ireland political sovereignty) to lose in the first place. Ireland was never legally established as a single, united nation-state. The Irish knew in their hearts and souls that 'the nation' as some absolute and indivisible entity did not exist. (Which did not, of course, prevent it being often elevated to the status of theological mystique.)

The crisis of British sovereignty reached its peak in recent times. This was brought on by a variety of factors: (1) the final fracturing of the empire (with the Falklands, Gibraltar, and Hong Kong controversies); (2) the end of the Protestant hegemony (with the mass immigration of non-Protestants from the ex-colonies—Asian, African, Caribbean, and Irish); (3) the entry of the United Kingdom, however hesitantly, into the European Union, which ended Britain's isolationist stance vis-à-vis its traditional alien-nations, Ireland and France; (4) the ineluctable impact of global technology and communications (proving Nicholas Negroponte's point about the tremendous changes brought about by the digital age and globalization, leading to the creation of smaller entities on the European continent while much of this continent was uniting economically[14]); and finally (5) the devolution of power from over-centralized government in Westminster to regional assemblies in Edinburgh, Cardiff, and Belfast—and most probably, in time, to different English regions as well.[15] Britain is now a multi-ethnic, multicultural, multi-confessional community which can no longer sustain the illusion of an eternally perduring sovereignty.

To be sure, Thatcherism represented one last desperate exercise in 'denial' fantasy, finding its perfect foil in the IRA. Terrorist bombings of London and Birmingham momentarily served to rally the British people against the alien Irish in their midst: people who looked and spoke like them but were secretly dedicated to their destruction. But even the IRA at their most menacing—and however associated with similar anti-British 'monsters' like

[14] Nicholas Negroponte, *Being Digital* (New York, Knopf, 1995).
[15] See the March 1999 MORI poll, conducted by the *Economist*, showing 50 per cent versus 27 per cent of the English in favour of more devolved power to English regions.

Galtieri, Gadafy, and Sadam Hussein—could not save Britain from itself. Thatcher's last stand to revive Tory nationalism was just that, a *last* stand. It could not prevent the dissolution of absolute unitary power, ultimately leading to the formation of regional parliaments in Edinburgh, Cardiff, and Belfast. The break-up of Britain was as inevitable as it was overdue. So much so that the enormous outpouring of grief at Princess Diana's demise was not just mourning for a particular person but for the passing of an imperial nation.

If Ireland was present at the origin of the British *nacio*, as I have suggested, then it is equally present today—in the guise of the Ulster crisis and resolution—precipitating its end. Ireland is the deconstructive seed at the heart of the British body politic: the cracked mirror reflecting Royal Britannia's primal image of its split-self; John Bull's other island sending shock waves back to the mainland; the island behind the island returning to haunt its inventor.

NOTIONS OF SOVEREIGNTY

The British–Irish 'Council of the Isles' is becoming a reality. This third spoke of the Agreement's wheel—alongside the internal Northern Ireland Assembly and the North–South cross-border bodies—harbours enormous promise. What the transnational model effectively recognizes is that citizens of Britain and Ireland are inextricably bound up with each other—mongrel islanders from East to West sharing an increasingly common civic and economic space. In addition to the obvious contemporary overlapping of the sports and popular cultures of the two islands, the citizens of Ireland and Britain are becoming ever more mindful that much of their respective histories were shared during centuries when the Irish sea served as a waterway connecting the two countries rather than a *cordon sanitaire* keeping them apart. And this is becoming true again in our own time, with over 25,000 trips being made daily across the Irish sea, in both directions. It is not entirely surprising then that over eight million citizens in Britain today claim Irish origin, with over four million of these having an Irish parent. Indeed a recent survey shows that only 6 per cent of British people consider Irish people living in Britain to be foreigners. And we do not need reminding that almost a quarter of the inhabitants of the island of Ireland claim to be at least part British. Finally, at a symbolic level, few can fail to have been moved by the recent unprecedented image of the president of the Irish Republic, Mary MacAleese, standing beside the Queen of England on the battlefield of Flanders commemorating their respective dead—poppies and shamrocks no longer considered symbols of irreconcilable identity.

In light of this reawakening to our crossed memories and experiences, it was not surprising to find Tony Blair receiving a standing ovation from Dail Eireann, the Parliament of the Irish Republic, on 26 November 1998, in the wake of the Good Friday Agreement. Blair acknowledged openly on this occasion that Britain was at last leaving its 'post-colonial malaise' behind it and promised that a newly confident Republic and a more decentralized United Kingdom would have more common tasks in the scenario of European convergence than any other two member states. East–West reciprocity was back on track for the first time since the divisive Statutes of Kilkenny.

Though no one is shouting about it, a *practical* form of joint-sovereignty has now been endorsed by the Irish and British peoples. The pluralization of national identity epitomized by the BIC entails, I believe, a radical rethinking of our hallowed notions of sovereignty. In essence, it means the *deterritorialization* of national sovereignty—namely, the attribution of sovereignty to peoples rather than land. (A fact which finds symbolic correlation in the Agreement's extension of national 'belonging' to embrace the Irish diaspora, which now numbers over 70 million world-wide.)

The term sovereignty (from the Latin *superanus*) originally referred to the supreme power of a divine ruler, before being delegated to divinely elected 'representatives' in this world—kings, pontiffs, emperors, tsars, monarchs—and, finally, to the 'people' in most modern states. A problem arose, however, in that many modern democracies recognize the existence of several *different* peoples within a single state. And many peoples means many centres of sovereignty. Yet the traditional concept of sovereignty, as already noted, was always *unitary*, that is, 'one and indivisible'. Whence the dilemma: how divide the indivisible? This is why, today, sovereignty has become one of the most controversial concepts in political theory and international law, intimately related to issues of state government, national independence, and minority rights.

Inherited notions of absolutist sovereignty are being challenged from both within nation-states *and* by developments in international legislation. With the Hague Conferences of 1899 and 1907, followed by the Covenant of the League of Nations and the Charter of the UN, significant restrictions on the actions of nation-states were already laid down. A system of international checks and balances was introduced limiting the right of sovereign states to act as they pleased in all matters. Moreover, the increasing *interdependence* of states—in the interests of greater entente, social justice, economic exchange, and information technology—qualified the very principle of absolute sovereignty. 'The peoples of the world have recognised that there can be no peace without law—and that there can be no law without some limitations on sovereignty. They have started, therefore, to pool their sovereignties to the extent needed to maintain peace, and sovereignty is being

108   *Richard Kearney*

increasingly exercised on behalf of the peoples of the world not only by national governments but also by organisations of the world community.'[16]

If this pertains to the 'peoples of the world' generally, how much more does it pertain to the peoples of the islands of Britain and Ireland? This is why I argued in *Postnationalist Ireland* (1997)[17] for a transcending of the existing nation-states in the direction of both an Irish–British Council and a federal Europe of regions. The nation-state has become too large and too small as a model of government. Too large for the growing needs of regional participatory democracy; too small for the increasing drift towards transnational exchange and power-sharing. Hence the relevance of the Nordic Council as a model for resolving our sovereignty disputes—in particular the way in which these five nation-states and three autonomous regions[18] succeeded in sorting out territorial conflicts, declaring the Åland and Spitsbergen islands as Europe's two first demilitarized zones.[19] Could we not do likewise under the aegis of a new transnational British–Irish Council, declaring Northern Ireland a third demilitarized zone?

To date, such sovereignty sharing had been largely opposed by British nationalism, which went by the name of Unionism. It was, ironically, the Irish republican tradition (comprising all democratic parties in the Irish Republic as well as the Social Democratic and Labour Party (SDLP) and Sinn Fein in the North) which was usually labelled 'nationalist', even though the most uncompromising nationalists in the vexed history of Northern Ireland have often been the Unionists. It was the latter, after all, who clung to an anachronistic notion of undiluted British sovereignty, refusing any compromise with their Irish neighbours; until Tony Blair blew the whistle and moderate unionism realized the tribal march was over. John Hume's 'new republicanism'—a vision of shared sovereignty between the different peoples of this island—had little difficulty with the new 'post-nationalist' scenario. Indeed Hume, former leader of the moderate Northern Irish nationalist party, the SDLP and Nobel prize winner, had declared himself a 'post-nationalist' for many years without many taking heed. And, curiously, one might even argue that Michael Collins, one of the leaders of the original Sinn Féin

---

[16] 'Sovereignty' in *The New Encyclopaedia Britannica*, 15th edn. (Chicago, Auckland, and London, Encyclopaedia Britannica, 1998), xi. 57   [17] Kearney, *Postnationalist Ireland*.

[18] The Nordic countries are Iceland, Norway, Sweden, Denmark, with the self-governing Faroe Islands and Greenland, and Finland with the self-governing Åland Islands. Informal cooperation had been established at government level in the 1920s and 1930s and on the parliamentary level, through the Nordic Council, in 1953. See http://www.lysator.liu.se/nordic/mirror2/NIAS_1.html

[19] On the Nordic Council as a model for the British–Irish relations see Simon Partridge, 'Nordic-style institutions recommended for Irish–British islands', in *Eagle Street: Newsletter of the Finnish Institute in London*, January 1998 and various other papers published in the same newsletter. This publication is available on the internet site http://finnish-institute.org.uk/

movement for Irish independence, was himself something of a post-nationalist when he wrote in 1921 that as a 'free and equal country' Ireland would be willing to 'cooperate in a free association on all matters which would be naturally the common concern of two nations, living so closely together' as part of a 'real league of nations of the World'.[20]

That the Blair government seemed prepared to grasp the sovereignty nettle and acknowledge the inevitable long-term dissemination of Britain, qua absolute centralized state, is to its credit. But it was not a decision taken in a vacuum. There were precedents for sovereignty-sharing in Britain's recent experience, including Westminster's consent to a limitation and dilution of sovereign power in its subscription to the European Convention on Human Rights, the Single European Act, the European Common Defence and Security Policy, and the European Court of Justice. If Britain has been able to pool sovereignty in these ways with the other nation-states of the EU, surely it is only logical to do so with its closest neighbour, the Irish Republic! Moreover, the EU principles of subsidiarity and local democracy, promoted in the European Charter of Local Self-Government,[21] offer a real alternative to the clash of British–Irish nationalisms that paralysed Ulster for decades.[22]

In this respect, one should not forget either that the forging of Britain into a multinational state constitution was predicated, at its best, on a *civic* rather than *ethnic* notion of citizenship. We need only recall how radically the borders of the British nation have shifted and altered in history (e.g. in 1536, 1707, 1800, and 1921) to envisage how they may shift and alter yet again—perhaps this time so radically as to remove all borders from these islands. The fact that British nationalism was often little more than English nationalism in drag does not take from its salutary constitutional principle of civic (rather than ethnic) belonging.

POST-NATIONALISM: THE GOOD FRIDAY AGREEMENT

The implications of the Good Friday Agreement are especially relevant here: the conflict of sovereignty claims exercised over the same territory by two independent governments—issuing in decades of violence—has been superseded by a post-nationalist paradigm of intergovernmental power. The dual identities of Northern Ireland, which long belied the feasibility of

---

[20] *The Manchester Guardian*, Dec. 1921.
[21] http://conventions.coe.int/treaty/en/Treaties/html/122.htm
[22] On the contradictory effects of the Europeanization of Irish and British policies on the Northern Ireland peace process see Elizabeth Meehan, ' "Britain's Irish Question: Britain's European Question?" British–Irish Relations in the Context of European Union and The Belfast Agreement', *Review of International Studies*, 26:1 (2000), 83–97.

'unitary' government, show the necessity of separating the notion of *nation* (identity) from that of *state* (sovereignty) and even, to some extent, from that of *land* (territory). Such a separation is, I submit, a precondition for allowing the coexistence of different communities in the same society; and, by extension, amplifying the models of identity to include more pluralist forms of association—a British–Irish Council, a European network of Regions, and the Irish and British diasporas. In sum, it is becoming abundantly clear that Bossuet's famous seventeenth-century definition of the nation as a perfect match of people and place—where citizens 'lived and died in the land of their birth'—is no longer wholly tenable.

There are no pristine nations around which definitive state boundaries— demarcating exclusivist sovereignty status—can be fixed. (Germany's attempts to do this from Bismarck to Hitler led to successive and disastrous wars.) The new Agreement recognizes the historic futility of both British and Irish constitutional claims on Northern Ireland as natural 'national territories'. Instead, the Council of the Isles promises a network of interconnecting assemblies guaranteeing parity of esteem for cultural and political diversity and an effective co-management of practical common concerns such as transport, environment, social equity, and e-commerce. We are, in effect, being challenged to abandon our mutually reinforcing myths of mastery (largely British) and martyrdom (largely Irish), going back to the fourteenth century, and to face our more mundane post-imperial, post-nationalist reality. Might the BIC not, as Simon Partridge suggests,[23] even serve as an inspiration to other parts of Europe and the globe still enmired in the devastations of ethnic nationalism? Discussions on the search for federal alternatives to secessionism in the Balkans and in the Caucasus show that it may.[24]

What the 1998 Agreement indicated, in short, is that our ineradicable need for identity and allegiance may gradually be channelled away from an exclusive focus on the nation-state, where history has demonstrated its tenure to be insecure and belligerent, to supplementary levels of regional and federal expression. In the Irish–British context, this means that citizens of these islands may come to express their identity less in terms of rival nation-states and more in terms of *both* locally empowered provinces (Ulster, Scotland, Wales, North and South England, the Republic, etc.) *and* larger international associations (the BIC and EU). The new dispensation, I repeat, fosters variable layers of compatible identification—regional,

---

[23] Simon Partridge, 'Reimagining these Islands: The Need for a Britannic Framework' (London, European Regionalist Discussion Paper, 1995), 5.
[24] On the relevance of the BIC for regional integration in the Caucasus see Bruno Coppieters, 'A Regional Security System for the Caucasus', *Caucasian Regional Studies*, 5:1 & 2 (2000), http://poli.vub.ac.be/

national, and transnational—allowing anyone in Northern Ireland to declare allegiance to the Ulster region, the Irish and/or British nation, the European community, and in the widest sense, the cosmopolitan order of world citizenry.

Citizens of these islands might, I suggest, do better to think of themselves as mobile mongrel islanders than as eternal dwellers of two pure, god-given nation-states. There is no such thing as primordial nationality. If the nation is indeed a hybrid construct, an 'imagined community', then it can be reimagined again in alternative versions. The task is to embrace this process of hybridization from which we derive and to which we are committed willy-nilly. In the face of resurgent nationali-sms in these islands and else-where, fired by the rhetoric of purity and purification, we would do well to remember that we are all mongrelized, interdependent, and marvellously mixed up.

6

The Right to Self-Determination and Secession in Yugoslavia: A Hornets' Nest of Inconsistencies

Raymond Detrez

The Macedonian political theorist Vladimir Gligorov phrased the problem, which has been at the root of the tensions and conflicts in Yugoslavia since the end of the 1980s, as follows: 'Why should I be a minority in your state when you can be a minority in mine?'[1] Rephrased in terms of the theme of this book, this question would read: 'Why should I give up my right to self-determination on your account, if you can do so on mine?' The national communities in Yugoslavia did not manage to resolve this dilemma, and fighting broke out as a result. Ultimately, the international community decided to cut the many knots. However, its justification for granting a full right to self-determination and secession to some national communities, and not to others, was far from convincing, especially to those who were left out in the cold. In some cases, mediation by the international community led to increased violence, as the frustrated national communities refused to give in. This was the case for instance in April 1992 when recognition of the independence of Bosnia-Herzegovina, with the implied rejection of the Bosnian Serbs' claim to secession, provoked a dramatic escalation of the hostilities into full-scale civil war.

The international community had no consistent approach in addressing the question of national self-determination. It failed to find a satisfactory answer to the crucial question of whether the national communities in Yugoslavia that were to enjoy the right to self-determination and secession should be ethno-cultural communities or territorial entities. This inconsistency reflects the contradictory conceptions of national rights that were to be found in the

I am very grateful to Lidija R. Basta Fleiner for her comments on this paper.

[1] Vladimir Gligorov, 'Is What's Left Right? (The Yugoslav Heritage)', in János Matyás Kovacs (ed.), *Transition to Capitalism? The Communist Legacy in Eastern Europe* (New Brunswick, NJ, Transaction Publishers, 1994), 147–72, quoted in Susan Woodward, *Balkan Tragedy: Chaos and Dissolution after the Cold War* (Washington, DC, The Brookings Institution, 1995), 108.

former Yugoslavia. Rogers Brubaker, in an assessment of the choices open to the international community concerning the right to self-determination in Yugoslavia, addresses this question, on which the lives of hundreds of thousands of people depended:

How, then, were…self-determining units to be construed? Was the right of self-determination to be exercised by Serbia or by Serbs? By Croatia or by Croats? By Bosnia-Herzegovina or by Yugoslav Muslims? By territorial entities, that is, or by boundary-transcending ethno-cultural nations? Were all the inhabitants of the Croatian republic to enjoy a single right of self-determination? And similarly for all the inhabitants of the Serb republic, and of Bosnia-Herzegovina, by majority vote? Or rather, was self-determination to be exercised by the Croatian, Serb, and Muslim ethno-nations, whose populations spilled over the republican borders? In practice, the international community opted for the former—but perhaps without realising the tremendous difference between the two modes of construing self-determination for the same national units. And the consequences were catastrophic.[2]

In this chapter, I will deal with the many dilemmas that arose in the implementation of the rights to self-determination and to secession in Yugoslavia, and in particular the problem of whether these rights should be exercised by ethno-cultural nations or territorial entities, as they were defined in the Yugoslav federation. This problem was, as Margaret Moore has pointed out,[3] the issue 'at the heart' of the conflicts. I will examine to what extent the international community succeeded or failed in finding a consistent approach to these problems, and how its attitude should be explained. This will be done through an historical analysis, paying special attention to how the peoples involved perceived their own national rights within the Yugoslav framework and how they reacted to the way the international community dealt with these rights.

THE RIGHT TO SELF-DETERMINATION AND SECESSION IN THE FORMER YUGOSLAVIA

The issues of self-determination and secession, as dealt with in the 1974 Yugoslav constitution, were the complex result of the long and laborious process of federalizing the Yugoslav state. In the former Yugoslavia, the word 'nation' (*nacija*) or 'people' (*narod*) had at least three different meanings. First, there was a 'Yugoslav nation', which was based on a civic understanding of the nation, and on the acceptance of the normative principles of

---

[2] Rogers Brubaker, 'Myths and Misconceptions in the Study of Nationalism', in Margaret Moore (ed.), *National Self-Determination and Secession* (Oxford, Oxford University Press, 1998), 239.

[3] Margaret Moore, 'Introduction: The Self-Determination Principle and the Ethics of Secession', in Moore, *National Self-Determination and Secession*, 138.

Yugoslav socialism. Second, the nation was seen as being constituted by the 'proletariat'—the agents of the Yugoslav system of workers' self-government. Third, 'nation' had the meaning of an ethno-cultural or national community. So the 'Yugoslav nation' consisted of a number of 'ethnic nations'. While ideological allegiance to the former was more or less compulsory and taken for granted, allegiance to the latter was in no way regarded as secondary or questionable. One could (for example on census forms) declare oneself an 'ethnic Yugoslav', as was done mainly by children of ethnically mixed families and by some state and party officials. But the latter group could also find advantages in declaring themselves to be Croats, Serbs, Slovenians, or members of other constituent nations of the Yugoslav federation, since there was a quota system on the basis of ethnicity for almost all posts in state and party structures.

Within the ethno-cultural or national communities, a distinction was made between 'nation/people' (*nacija/narod*) and 'nationality' (*narodnost, nacionalnost*). In practice, a nation was a national community which had its own nation-state or 'fatherland' within Yugoslavia, while a nationality was a national community with its nation-state or 'fatherland' outside Yugoslavia. For instance, the Croats were a nation, because the state of the Croats was located within the borders of Yugoslavia and there was no Croat state outside Yugoslavia. The Albanians, on the other hand, were a nationality, because they had a state of their own, namely Albania, outside Yugoslavia. Other nationalities were the Bulgarians in Eastern Serbia, the Italians on the Adriatic Coast, the Hungarians in Vojvodina, and many others. It should be pointed out that no ethnic group in Yugoslavia constituted a majority in the federation. Yugoslavia was a country of minorities, which made it difficult to use the term 'minority' in the same sense as it is used in other countries.[4]

The Yugoslav approach to the national question had the undeniable advantage of flattering the national pride of the most important peoples that made up the federation by granting them the right to secession. Having a state of their own within Yugoslavia, they were expected to be less inclined to leave the federation. The right to secession was withheld from those nationalities which had their own state outside Yugoslavia. They were

---

[4] For example, the most frequently cited definition by Capotorti: 'A group numerically inferior to the rest of the population of a State, in a non-dominant position, whose members—being nationals of the State—possess ethnic, religious or linguistic characteristics differing from those of the rest of the population and show, if only implicitly, a sense of solidarity, directed towards preserving their culture, traditions, religion or language.' Francesco Capotorti, *Study on the Rights of Persons Belonging to Ethnic, Religious and Linguistic Minorities* (New York, United Nations, 1991), 96, quoted in Peter Malanczuk, 'Minorities and Self-Determination', in Neri Sybesma-Knol and Jef Van Bellingen (eds.), *Naar een nieuwe interpretatie van het Recht op Zelfbeschikking* (Brussels, VUB Press, 1992), 172.

presumed to cherish the idea of joining up with their fatherland and to be more prone to separatism. This unequal treatment led to a problem of legitimacy for those who received the—lesser—status of a nationality.

The distinction between nations and nationalities may appear artificial, superfluous and even discriminatory, as it in fact created two categories of citizens. Nations appeared to be higher up in the hierarchy than nationalities. This hierarchy was visible in two ways. First, the federal units of nations were called 'republics'; those of the nationalities, 'autonomous provinces' (or 'autonomous regions'[5]). Republics were on a higher level than the autonomous provinces. Among the various nationalities living in the Republic of Serbia, only the two major nationalities had the privilege of living in an autonomous province: the Albanians in Kosovo and the Hungarians in Vojvodina. Both of the autonomous provinces were territorially and constitutionally parts of the Republic of Serbia.

Secondly, although in terms of degree of autonomy and number of competences the differences between republics and autonomous provinces were in fact symbolic, and republics and autonomous provinces were 'for all practical purposes, equivalent',[6] one such symbolic difference was of the utmost importance. Nations were entitled to exercise the right to self-determination and secession, while nationalities were not. The 'Basic Principles' of the 1974 Yugoslav constitution stated that 'the *nations* of Yugoslavia, based on the right of every nation to self-determination, including the right to secession, on the basis of their freely expressed intention... have united in a federal republic of free and equal nations and nationalities'.[7] This principle was explicitly referred to in the constitutions of the republics of Croatia and Macedonia as well.

To be sure, this right was of a hypothetical nature as long as Yugoslavia was a stable state. By the end of the 1980s, when national communities were referring to constitutional principles in order to claim the right to secession, the statements in the part of the constitution dedicated to its basic principles were hotly contested. Some critics distinguished the Basic Principles from the constitution itself, and considered them to be devoid of any real legal validity. Others pointed out that the Yugoslav nations had forfeited

---

[5] Voivodina was an '*autonomna pokrajina*' and Kosovo until 1963 an '*autonomna oblast*' and after 1963 an '*autonomna pokrajina*'. Both '*pokrajina*' and '*oblast*' can be translated as 'province' and as 'region'.

[6] Sabrina Ramet, *Nationalism and Federalism in Yugoslavia 1996–1991* (Bloomington and Indianapolis, Indiana University Press, 1992), 77.

[7] See 'Introductory Part. Basic Principles' (*Uvodi deo. Osnovna nacela*) in the Yugoslav Constitution: 'Narodi Jugoslavije, polažeći od prava svakog naroda na samoopredeljenje uključujući i pravo na otcepljenje, na osnovu svoje slobodno izražene volje... ujedinili su se u saveznu republiku slobodnih i ravnopravnih naroda i narodnosti... *Ustav socialističke federativne republike Jugoslavija* (Belgrade, Službeni list, 1991), 9.

their right to self-determination and secession by becoming constituent peoples of the Yugoslav Federation. However, when the political situation deteriorated in the late 1980s, the 1974 constitution lost much of its importance as it was replaced by new constitutions in many of the Yugoslav republics.

The wording in the Basic Principles of the constitution contained some deceptive and dangerous subtleties. First of all, *nations*, and not *republics*, were entitled to exercise the right to self-determination and secession. Consequently, the right of the Croats to secede did not necessarily imply that the territory of the Republic of Croatia could be detached from the Yugoslav state. This distinction between nations and republics was invoked by the leaders of the Serb community in Croatia as soon as it became obvious that the leaders of the republic were heading for independence. As the right to self-determination and secession was assigned to nations, not only the Croats, but also the Serbs in Croatia could claim the same right. These Serbs desired to be united with their co-nationals in Bosnia-Herzegovina and Serbia proper, within the Yugoslav state.

In 1991, in order to support international mediation efforts, the European Community created an Arbitration Committee, consisting of five members from the French, German, Italian, Spanish, and Belgian Constitutional Courts and headed by the President of the French *Conseil Constitutionnel* Robert Badinter.[8] This committee was to advise upon the legal aspects of the dissolution of Yugoslavia. It recommended that Croatia should be recognized as an independent state within the former Yugoslav internal borders if it provided sufficient guarantees for the protection of minority rights, but it explicitly denied the right to self-determination of the Serb community in Croatia. The Basic Principles of the 1974 Yugoslav constitution were not even taken into account. The European Community, soon followed by the United States, took its advice and recognized the Republic of Croatia in January 1992. The Badinter Arbitration Committee further advised against recognizing Kosovo as an independent state, because it did not have the status of a republic. This meant that the Committee was basing its opinion on the Yugoslav distinction between 'nations' and 'nationalities', since Kosovo was not a republic precisely because the Albanian Kosovars were a nationality and not a nation.[9]

In point of fact, the term 'nationality' was used in Yugoslavia more or less as a synonym for 'minority'. That nationalities in Yugoslavia were not entitled to exercise a right to self-determination, which included the right to

---

[8] International Crisis Group, *Current Legal Status of the Federal Republic of Yugoslavia (FRY), and of Serbia and Montenegro*, ICG Balkans Report no. 101, Washington and Brussels, 19 Sept. 2000, 6.

[9] Although Western publications speak about Albanian and Serb Kosovars, for the local population of Kosovo a 'Kosovar' is always an Albanian from Kosovo (from Albanian *kosovar*, plural *kosovare*. In Serb, there is a specific term for Serbs from Kosovo: *kosovac* (plural *kosovci*).

secession was in accordance with European practice concerning minority rights. The Conference on Security and Cooperation in Europe (CSCE) Copenhagen Document says that persons belonging to minorities do not have 'any right to engage in any activity or perform any contravention of ... the principle of the territorial integrity of States'.[10] This means in effect that minorities have no right to secession.

CROATIA

According to the logic of the Yugoslav federal system, constituent peoples of Yugoslavia living outside their own federal unit (in compact communities) were not regarded by the various republican constitutions as minorities, but as constituent nations of the republics they lived in. So the Serbs were a constituent people in Croatia, and the Bosniaks, Croats, and Serbs were constituent peoples in Bosnia. No crucial decision about such important issues as secession could be made without the approval of all constituent peoples in a federal unit. This is why the Serbs, from the end of the 1980s, so fiercely insisted that they were not a minority in Croatia, but a constituent people. According to them, Croatia could not secede from Yugoslavia without their consent. The Serb nationalist leaders further demanded a separate autonomous region in Croatia, which was to remain part of Croatia as long as Croatia remained in Yugoslavia. In their view, the region was entitled to secede from Croatia as soon as Croatia seceded from Yugoslavia. During the dissolution of the Yugoslav federation, the Serbs created four autonomous regions in Croatia which, after the secession of Croatia in 1992, became united in the Serb Republic of Krajina. This unrecognized Serb mini-state sought secession from Croatia and unification with Yugoslavia. It was finally abolished in 1995 following the invasion of the Croat army, which drove out most of its population. In Eastern Slavonia, the Dayton Agreement mandated the United Nations Transitional Administration for Eastern Slavonia (UNTAES) to monitor the withdrawal of the Serb forces and to support the peaceful integration of the region into Croatia before January 1998. Here, too, most of the Serb population fled.

It may appear contradictory, or even cynical, that the Serb community of Croatia demanded extensive territorial autonomy for themselves whereas the Serb authorities abolished the autonomy of Kosovo in 1989. But in fact these choices were not at all inconsistent. According to the logic of the Yugoslav federal system, the Serbs, as a constituent people, were entitled to exercise the right to secession (in other words, to leave Croatia and join Yugoslavia), but

---

[10] See Article 37 of the CSCE Copenhagen Document, Minorities, Part IV. Cfr. Eric Suy, 'De VN-praktijk op het stuk van het zelfbeschikkingsrecht der volkeren', in Sybesma-Knol and Van Bellingen (eds.), *Naar een nieuwe interpretatie van het Recht op Zelfbeschikking*, 273.

the Albanian Kosovars, as a nationality, were not. On the other hand, as soon as Croatia's independence was internationally recognized, the Serb community in Croatia actually became a nationality in the Yugoslav sense of the word, which means a minority. The Croat government preferred the word 'minority' (*manjina*) and announced that it was prepared to give the Serbs all the national rights minorities enjoy in developed European countries. These rights did not include the right to secession. To the Serbs in Croatia, this was not only a humiliating demotion but also, obviously, a drastic limitation of their traditional political rights.

BOSNIA-HERZEGOVINA

Bosnia represented an even more complex problem. In Bosnia, there were three constituent peoples: Bosniaks (officially called Muslimani),[11] Croats, and Serbs—all three entitled by the constitution to exercise the right of self-determination and secession within Yugoslavia as a whole. The Bosniaks were officially recognized by the Yugoslav government as a constituent people in 1969. However, this recognition did not go unchallenged. Many Croats and Serbs continued to regard the Bosniaks as a religious and not an ethnic community. At the beginning of the 1990s, Croat and Serb nationalist ideologists explicitly denied the existence of a Bosniak nation. Thus the Bosniaks' right to self-determination and secession was challenged at its very basis: did a distinct national community, which could claim the right to self-determination and secession, actually exist at all?

In the nineteenth century, national identities started developing among the speakers of Serbo-Croat on the basis of religion. Catholic speakers of Serbo-Croat, living in the Habsburg Empire, identified themselves as Croats, whereas the Orthodox speakers of Serbo-Croat, living scattered throughout the Habsburg and Ottoman Empires and in their own Principality of Serbia, considered themselves Serbs. The development of a Bosniak national consciousness among the Muslim speakers of Serbo-Croat was delayed, due to the fact that, traditionally, being a Muslim was far more important to the Bosniaks than belonging to one or other of the national communities. The Serbs' and Croats' attempts to incorporate the Bosniaks into their own respective national communities as Serb or Croat Muslims also hampered the development of their national consciousness.[12]

---

[11] Yugoslav terminology distinguished between *Muslimani* (Muslims) in the ethnic sense (*u etničkom smislu*), written with a capital, and *muslimani* (Muslims) in the religious sense, written in lower-case. The Washington Agreement in March 1994 first mentioned the traditional name, Bosniaks (*Bocšnjaci*) again.

[12] On this see e.g. Francine Friedman, *The Bosnian Muslims: Denial of a Nation* (Boulder, Colo., Westview Press, 1995); Noel Malcolm, *Bosnia: A Short History* (London, Macmillan,

The formation of a Bosniak national consciousness was accomplished only in post-war Yugoslavia. The official recognition of Bosniak nationhood in 1969 had resulted largely from the political need of the Yugoslav authorities to counterbalance Croat separatism and Serb hegemonism. The Bosniak representatives were expected to play a stabilizing role for the Yugoslav Federation both at the level of the federal government and in the government of the Republic of Bosnia-Herzegovina. This does not mean, however, that the Bosniak nation should be regarded primarily as a product of the communist regime. Even at that time, the Bosniaks constituted a very distinct national community, defining itself through its religious identity. Islam's self-identifying role for the Bosniaks was similar to that played by Catholicism for the Croats and Orthodoxy for the Serbs.[13] There were thus three nations in Bosnia, competing to exercise their respective rights to self-determination and secession. Each of these nations had a very different view of their right to national self-determination and how it should be implemented.

The Bosniak view of Bosnia-Herzegovina

When the Yugoslav Federation began to find itself in crisis at the end of the 1980s, the Bosniaks were in favour of preserving it. Yugoslavia had recognized them as a nation and had offered them protection. The Bosniak position depended, moreover, on the balance of power between Croats and Serbs within Bosnia and Yugoslavia. As soon as Croatia left the federation, the Bosniaks (and Croats) in Bosnia felt threatened by Serb domination in the rump state, which they derisively but significantly called 'Serboslavia'. Under these circumstances, the Bosniak leaders opted for secession. They hoped for a peaceful coexistence of Bosniaks, Croats, and Serbs in an independent Bosnia. This choice of a multinational state was inspired not by the ideal of multiculturalism, but by pragmatic considerations. The Bosniaks had neither the military power nor the diplomatic support to create an ethnically and religiously homogeneous state. But the impossibility of creating an ethnically homogeneous Bosniak state did not mean that the Bosniaks could not have a dominant position in the new state. Bosnia, they felt,

---

1994); Mark Pinson, *The Muslims of Bosnia-Herzegovina* (Cambridge, Mass., Harvard University Press, 1994).

[13] In fact, the previous insistence by Croats and Serbs upon their respective religious affiliations as a basic component of their national identity was a major factor in preventing the Bosniaks from regarding themselves as Muslim Serbs or Croats, and facilitated the emergence of a proper Bosniak national identity. Moreover, just as Croats think of their nation as being part of Western European civilization and Serbs feel they belong to Slavic Orthodox Eastern Europe, the Bosniaks consider their nation a full member of the large family of Islamic peoples with their own age-old cultural traditions.

should be first and foremost a Bosniak state, just as Croats and Serbs had also acquired states of their own.[14]

The Serb view of Bosnia-Herzegovina

The point of view of the Bosnian Serbs was very much the same as that of the Serbs in Croatia. As a constituent nation, they claimed the right to self-determination and secession in order to establish autonomous regions. If Bosnia-Herzegovina left the federation, these regions were to be joined up to constitute an independent state, which would eventually be attached to the Republic of Serbia. Thanks to their military superiority (reinforced by support from Serbia proper) and to large-scale ethnic cleansing, the Serbs succeeded in bringing almost 70 per cent of Bosnia under the control of the *Republika Srpska* (Serb Republic). However, the Bosnian Serb Republic was never united with Yugoslavia. The 1995 Dayton Peace Agreement turned it into an 'entity'—a kind of federal unit with vast autonomy—within Bosnia.

The Croat view of Bosnia-Herzegovina

With the dissolution of the Yugoslav federation, the Croat nationalist ideologists in Bosnia and Croatia found themselves in a very difficult position. They had defended the viewpoint that the borders of the nascent independent states should coincide with the existing Yugoslav internal borders, established by the Jajce Conference in 1943. This would allow the Croats to keep the territories in the Krajina, populated by Serbs, within Croatia. In Bosnia, however, the situation of the Croats was very similar to that of the Serbs in Croat Krajina. Having subordinated the right to self-determination and secession of the Serb constituent people to the Croats' right to protect the territorial integrity of the Croat state, they now had to respect the territorial integrity of the Bosnian state and renounce the right to self-determination and secession of the Croat constituent people in Bosnia. Consistency in this case would be at the expense of Croat national interests.

The situation was further complicated by the fact that the Croats in Bosnia lived mainly in two distinct areas and in quite different circumstances. In Western Herzegovina, the Croats constituted a compact mass and, in most districts, an absolute majority of the population. In Central Bosnia, on the contrary, they were closely intermixed with Bosniaks (and

[14] It must however be added that, traditionally, Muslims generally have fewer problems than Christians in living together in one state with other religious communities. In the Ottoman Empire, the dominant Muslim administrators allowed Christians and Jews to have their own autonomous religious communities (*millets*) and to preserve their own religious identity and traditions.

Serbs). They constituted only a relative majority (as the largest of the three communities) in a few isolated districts.

These circumstances made the policy of the Croat leaders towards Bosnia somewhat ambiguous. On the one hand, moderate Croat politicians believed that the international community would support the cause of Croatia's independence more vigorously if Croatia clearly displayed its own readiness to respect the territorial integrity of the Bosnian state. Others, like President Franjo Tudjman and his supporters from the so-called 'Herzegovian lobby', were in favour of annexing at least the overwhelmingly Croat-populated Western Herzegovina. This was done notwithstanding the fact that this position contradicted the principles used to justify the Croats' determination to keep the Serb-populated Krajina within the borders of Croatia. In 1993, the proponents of annexing Western Herzegovina, claiming the right to self-determination and secession of the Croat constituent people in Bosnia, and following the example of the Serbs in the Krajina and Bosnia, established a Croat autonomous region, Herceg-Bosna. The intention was to unite this region eventually to Croatia. Some more extreme Croat nationalist leaders, like Dobrosav Paraga, who considered the Bosniaks to be merely islamicized Croats, pleaded for the annexation of the whole of Bosnia-Herzegovina. The Tudjman approach was widely supported by the Croats in Western Herzegovina, while Croats in Central Bosnia either agreed to live in an independent and territorially undivided Bosnian state, or preferred the annexation of the whole of Bosnia by Croatia.

This ambiguity explains many of the contradictions of the war in Bosnia. In some regions, Bosniaks and Croats fought together as allies against the Serbs and drove out the Serb population; in others, Bosniaks and Croats were enemies and drove each other out. Moreover, their relations underwent many changes as the war progressed, depending on the political and military situation, which pushed them into temporary alliances or, under international pressure, forced them to demonstrate a desire for reconciliation.

The international community's view of Bosnia-Herzegovina

Although Croat and Serb nationalist leaders were adversaries wherever the borders of the territories they coveted overlapped, they largely agreed in their perception of the Bosniak identity and upon a general 'solution' to the Bosnian problem. They regarded the Bosniaks as islamicized Croats or Serbs, respectively. As a religious rather than an ethnic or national community, the Bosniaks were not, in their view, entitled to have their own state. They consequently saw a division of Bosnia between Croatia and Serbia as being the best solution. Those of the Croat and Serb communities in Bosnia who advocated this division were supported by their co-nationals in Croatia and Serbia. Tudjman and Milošević met several times to discuss how this division could be achieved in practice. Their solution, however, was completely unacceptable to the Bosniaks and to the international community, which had already recognized the independence of Bosnia-Herzegovina in April 1992.

The implementation of the right to exercise national self-determination up to and including the right to secession faced insuperable problems in Bosnia. The exercise of the right of each of the three national communities excluded the exercise of the same right by the two others. The independence of Bosnia-Herzegovina (within its internal Yugoslav borders) was satisfactory to the Bosniaks, but not readily accepted by the Croats and Serbs. The secession of territories dominated by a largely Serb population would be applauded by the Serbs, but such a move would be unacceptable to the Bosniaks and Croats living in these regions as it would effectively turn them into minorities. In conditions of civil conflict this entailed the risk of being driven out or even exterminated. The secession of the region of Herceg-Bosna, overwhelmingly populated by Croats, would have the same dramatic consequences for the local Bosniak and Serb populations.

A 'mathematical' solution to the problem was thwarted by the fact that none of the national communities there had an absolute majority: 44 per cent of the total population of Bosnia was Bosniak, 32 per cent Serb and 18 per cent Croat, the remainder consisting of different small ethnic groups. Croats and Serbs lived in quite compact masses, while the Bosniak population was scattered all over the country. Two of the three parties involved agreed that the solution was to divide Bosnia between Croats and Serbs. The Bosniaks were alone in defending the integrity of Bosnian territory. Moreover, the two 'agreeing' parties constituted a majority—albeit a very small one—of the total population of Bosnia.

There might have been good reasons for adopting a solution which would enable two of the three parties involved, constituting the majority of the population, to exercise the right to national self-determination and secession. However, the international community was unwilling to change existing borders, and those of the former Yugoslav Republic of Bosnia-Herzegovina had to be preserved. The international community supported the Bosniak community, which was in favour of preserving a multicultural society. As opponents of the Serbs, who were held responsible for the bloodshed in Yugoslavia, and as victims of policies of ethnic cleansing and other atrocities, the Bosniaks had attracted a good deal of international sympathy. International diplomacy was concerned not to divide the Bosniaks among two states (Croatia and Serbia), although as a result of the recognition of the Croat and the Bosnian states the Serbs were to be divided between three states and the Croats into two.

The international community did not in fact accord the right to self-determination exclusively to the Bosniaks, since it does not apply an ethnic definition of nationhood. But that is how the decision to preserve the territorial integrity of Bosnia was interpreted by Croats and Serbs. This choice seemed to them both arbitrary and partial. One could even argue that the lack of a convincing legal and moral legitimization of the international community's decision in fact helped to provoke the conflict in Bosnia. As the international community had failed to uphold their perceived rights, Serbs and Croats took the law into their own hands and employed extensive measures to expel the 'other' community, which was the holder of a competing right to self-determination.

KOSOVO

As we have seen, the Albanians in Kosovo could not claim the right to self-determination and secession because they were a 'nationality' and not a 'nation'. The international community initially adopted the Yugoslav point of view, treating the Albanian Kosovars as a minority. The borders of the autonomous province of Kosovo were not regarded as 'state borders' in the same way as the borders between the Yugoslav Republics. However, the autonomous province of Kosovo had been all but an equal member of the Yugoslav federation, on the same footing as the republics. The Albanian Kosovars, alleging on the one hand that they had always been treated as second-class citizens in Yugoslavia, referred on the other hand to their *de facto* equality in the Yugoslav federation. This was done in order to convince the international community that they had the same right to secede as the Slovenes, the Croats, and the other Yugoslav nations.

The 1974 Yugoslav constitution offered the autonomous provinces great autonomy, largely meeting the Albanian Kosovars' demands for internal self-determination. But radical Kosovar activists continued to work hard for the autonomous province to become a republic. According to the constitution, the status of republic would have implied that the Albanian Kosovars were a nation and consequently entitled to exercise the right to secession. In 1981, riots at the university of Prishtina resulted in mass demonstrations for 'Kosovo-Republika'. The conflict between the two main national communities of Kosovo escalated during the 1980s, leading to severely repressive policies by the Serb government. In 1989 the autonomy of Kosovo was all but abolished, even though the 1989 constitutional amendments and the new Serbian constitution of 1991 granted minorities the cultural rights they were entitled to by virtue of international conventions and treaties. In September 1990 the Albanian Kosovar members of the Kosovan parliament, who constituted a large majority, unilaterally decided to adopt a new

Kosovan constitution, which created a Kosovan Republic, still within Yugoslavia. In October 1991, the Kosovan government proclaimed full independence. It was not recognized by any other state except Albania.

Thus the issue of self-determination and secession was at the very heart of the Kosovan question. The Albanian Kosovars, supported by the Albanians in Albania, claimed to be a nation and to be fully entitled to exercise the right to self-determination.[15] To the Serbs as well as the international community, the Albanian Kosovars were a minority. Consistently, the international community favoured a solution that would restore the Kosovars' former autonomy within the borders of Yugoslavia. In an attempt to preserve the territorial integrity of the Federal Republic of Yugoslavia, the international community actually backed Serbia's claims to Kosovo and encouraged the Albanian Kosovars to be satisfied with a 'limited' right to self-determination, namely internal self-determination without the right to secession.

Only from 1998 on, when the Kosovo Liberation Army (KLA) tried to enforce a violent solution to the Kosovan question and the international community had begun to consider military intervention, were the Albanian Kosovars treated in the Western media and by international security organizations as deserving self-government. This meant that the political status to be granted them went beyond the traditional approach to minority rights. The new approach could be interpreted as an implicit recognition of their reality as a nation. This conceptual shift led to a new paradox: if indeed the Albanian Kosovars were a nation and not a minority, why were they not entitled to exercise a right to secession? The international community favours a solution that keeps Kosovo within the borders of what from February 2003 became Serbia and Montenegro. The rejection of new border changes seems to be inspired by a number of considerations, such as the creation of a precedent on the international scene and the fear that independence for Kosovo and the creation of a 'Greater Albania' through the unification of Kosovo with Albania would provoke the Albanian community in (the Former Yugoslav Republic of) Macedonia. In the event, ethnic conflict there from 2001 destabilized Macedonia and threatened to throw the entire Balkan region into disarray. The creation of a Greater Albania is also strongly opposed by Greece, which is influential in the European Union.

A further aspect that deserves special attention is the connection between the Kosovan problem and the situation in Bosnia after Dayton. The secession of Kosovo would create a precedent the Bosnian Serbs could seize on to demand the secession of the *Republika Srpska* from Bosnia-Herzegovina—to

---

[15] Asked his opinion on the parallelism between the situation of the Albanian community in Yugoslavia and the Greek community in Southern Albania, an Albanian politician told me that the Albanian Kosovars are without any doubt 'a nation' and the Greeks in Albania without any doubt 'a minority'. He was not able to explain why exactly.

the embarrassment of the international community. This is why the Kosovar leaders have always opposed any linkage of the Kosovan question with the problems arising from the Dayton Peace Agreement.

Obviously, the reasons why the right to self-determination and secession is not fully granted to the Albanian Kosovars have little to do with theoretical considerations concerning this right. The principle of the protection of the territorial integrity of the state, though invoked by the international community, is not a very convincing argument in the case of Yugoslavia, as it has already been violated many times during the Yugoslav crisis. Again, to the Albanian Kosovars, the reason why they and only they were not allowed to secede from Yugoslavia appears quite arbitrary. And this perception was reinforced by the fact that, as long as Milošević was in power, the international community encouraged the Albanian Kosovars' opposition to him. This gave the impression that they also supported secessionist policies. Opposition to Serbian rule and its repressive policies was regarded as a kind of 'just cause'. After the fall of Milošević, this 'just cause' expired and more reservations were expressed when it came to dealing with the claims of the Albanian Kosovars. To the Albanians, their cause is just, with or without Milošević.

MACEDONIA

In the Republic of Macedonia the problems are twofold. In the first place there is the contested national identity of the Slavic Macedonians. According to traditional Bulgarian and Serb historiography, respectively, the Slavs in Macedonia are Bulgarians or Serbs. In the past, both groups produced ample historical, linguistic, and ethnographic arguments to advance their own territorial claims. Bulgaria did not accept the partition of Macedonia between Bulgaria, Greece, and Serbia (later Yugoslavia) in 1913, and in both World Wars it occupied both the Serbian part of Macedonia and adjacent territories in Greek Macedonia. Only in 1999 did Bulgaria reluctantly recognize the existence of a Macedonian language, but the 'Bulgarianness' of the Macedonians seems to have remained one of the cornerstones of the Bulgarian perception of the history of the region. After 1992, the Serbs learned to live with the idea of a separate Macedonian nation, but hard-line Serb nationalists still think of the Macedonians as Serbs. Greece, meanwhile, fearing the existence of a Macedonian nation, and in particular an irredentist Macedonian state on its northern borders, supports the thesis that there is no Macedonian nation, regardless of whether the Macedonian Slavs are Bulgarians or Serbs. Although the Badinter Arbitration Committee considered that Macedonia met all the requirements for recognition as an independent state, for many years the international community refused to grant this recognition because of the objections of Greece. Again, principles held to be sacrosanct in one case were relinquished in another case because of considerations of *Realpolitik*. The Republic of Macedonia has been recognized by its three neighbours and by the international community, but the continuing academic disputes about whether the Macedonians are a nation or not continue to challenge the legitimacy of their right to national self-determination: a nation that does not exist cannot invoke this right.

The second problem is the Albanian minority in the Republic of Macedonia—an estimated 30 per cent of the total population—whose leaders demand autonomy, preferably territorial autonomy. The Albanians in Yugoslav Macedonia never had the same territorial autonomy as the Albanian Kosovars, but enjoyed only cultural rights. The Macedonians in the new independent Republic of Macedonia were not inclined to give them much more than cultural autonomy. After Albanians in northern and western Macedonia took up arms in 2001, the international community, which had praised the Macedonian government earlier for their respect of the Albanians' minorities rights, forced the Macedonian state to introduce far-reaching amendments to the constitution (Agreement of Ohrid, 13 August 2001). Macedonia is now defined as 'the state of the citizens of Macedonia'. Albanian demands to be designated a 'constituent nation' in the constitution were rejected by the Slav-Macedonian majority as this would assign to them—in the spirit of the old Yugoslav perception of constituent nations and nationalities—the right to secession.

MONTENEGRO

The international community has proved unable to apply a principled approach to the political tensions between Montenegro and Serbia, which together constituted the Federal Republic of Yugoslavia.[16] Montenegro is a poor country, with a territory the size of Northern Ireland and a population of fewer than 700,000 people. In 1991–2, when the former Socialist Federal Republic of Yugoslavia disintegrated, Montenegro decided to remain within the renewed Yugoslav federation. It did not adopt a Declaration of Sovereignty. In the second half of the 1990s, however, tensions between the Serb and Montenegrin leaderships increased. These had to do with party-political disagreements, which gained momentum in 1998, after

---

[16] The following analysis of relations between Serbia and Montenegro is largely based on Bruno Coppieters, 'The Proliferation of Security Actors and the Fragmentation of the International System: The Cases of Massachusetts, Flanders, Montenegro and Abkhazia' (working title), manuscript. See also International Crisis Group, 'Current Legal Status of the Federal Republic of Yugoslavia (FRY) and of Serbia and Montenegro', ICG Balkans Report No. 101, 19 September 2000, Washington and Brussels.

Milo Djukanović, a defector from the Montenegrin branch of Milošević's Serbian Socialist Party who had become a fierce opponent of Milošević's policy, was elected President of Montenegro in October 1997.[17] Two significant steps in loosening the ties with Serbia were the decision by the Montenegrin government in March 1999 not to support Serbia's war against NATO on Kosovo, and in November 1999 to make the Deutschmark and later the Euro, its official currency.[18] In 1999 relations between the institutions of the two federated entities in the Yugoslav federation were already very loose. In August the Montenegrin government formulated a proposal to replace the existing federation by a confederal association of sovereign states.[19] According to the government, a referendum on independence would be the eventual legal confirmation of an objective process of dissolution. The Yugoslav armed forces, under the control of Milošević, remained the only significant responsibility of the federation.[20]

In Western capitals serious consideration was given to support attempts to achieve the peaceful separation of Montenegro. The argument that the Montenegrin government had distanced itself from Serb policies in Kosovo and followed a pro-Western line was used by some in favour of Montenegro's right to unilateral secession. But Western governments did not underestimate the risk of an armed confrontation. Though supporting Djukanović's government, and despite NATO's war against Yugoslavia, they regarded the demand for independence and the final dissolution of the Yugoslav federation an unnecessary provocation. Nor were the high levels of corruption in Montenegro, which impeded attempts at reform, or the difficulty of constituting an economically and politically viable state, overlooked in Western discussions. Furthermore, those in Western capitals who favoured a cautious line towards this new conflict pointed out that a significant part of the population was opposed to complete separation from Serbia. The fact that roughly half of the population of Montenegro considered themselves Serbs made any hope of a large majority in a referendum futile. Lack of cohesiveness in a future Montenegrin state, owing to this heterogeneity, and the worst-case scenario of a civil war in Montenegro itself, which could be triggered by a unilateral declaration of independence, were also taken into account.[21]

The tensions between Montenegro and Serbia reached a peak in July 2000 when Milošević had the Yugoslav constitution changed in order to be able to succeed himself as president. The Djukanović line was then encouraged by the international community, which thereby hoped to weaken the

---

[17] He was officially inaugurated as President in January 1998.
[18] *Financial Times*, 3 Nov. 1999. [19] *The Economist*, 14 Aug. 1999.
[20] *Financial Times*, 23 Nov. 1999. [21] *The Economist*, 29 Jan. 2000.

position of Milošević. The declarations by the Montenegrin government that the democratization of Serbia was the *conditio sine qua non* for the survival of the federation received open support in Western capitals. This meant implicitly that Milošević's authoritarian rule was considered a 'just cause' for Montenegro's gradual steps towards separation. But the Montenegrin government criticized the West's policies as being inconsistent: it supported Montenegro's policies towards Serbia but did not acknowledge Montenegro's right to withdraw from the Yugoslav federation. The West had even failed to take concrete measures to exempt Montenegro from the economic sanctions imposed on Yugoslavia.[22]

After the fall of Milošević in October 2000, however, the international community seemed more inclined to seek a solution to the Kosovan problem within the borders of the Yugoslav federation. The secession of Montenegro, which would entail the disappearance of the Yugoslav federation, would render that option obsolete. A renewal of the constitutional relationship between the various entities of Yugoslavia reached on the basis of common agreement was the preferred Western option. In April 2000, the Contact Group on the former Yugoslavia warned Montenegro that a unilateral declaration of independence would lead to the loss of political and financial support from the international community.[23] The European Union declared that it wanted Montenegro and Serbia to seek an accommodation by reforming the Yugoslav constitution within a federal framework.[24] Two positions were defended in the debates. The Yugoslav President Vojislav Kostunica proposed a Serbian-Montenegrin 'functional federation' with single statehood (a 'joint state'), a minimal number of functions to be performed at the federal level and a large number of co-operative structures between the two entities in the federation.[25] The Montenegrin president, on the contrary, proposed a confederal framework with two sovereign entities, which presupposed international recognition of Montenegro's statehood.

The international community expressed criticism of the procedures conceived by the Montenegrin authorities for a referendum on independence. The participation of half of the registered voters and approval by a simple majority of the participants was considered sufficient by the Montenegrin government. The United States declared that they found this threshold for participation and approval in a referendum on independence as required by the Montenegrin authorities to be too low.[26] But it was difficult for the international community to dismiss out of hand the democratic value of a

[22] *The Economist*, 14 Aug. 1999.   [23] *Financial Times*, 26 April 2001.
[24] Radio Free Europe/Radio Liberty (RFE/RL), *Newsline*, 5:40, Part II, 27 Feb. 2001.
[25] 'Yugoslav President's Proposal for Reconstruction of Yugoslavia', Tanjug, 10 Jan. 2001.
[26] RFE/RL, *Newsline*, 5:43, Part II, 2 March 2001.

Montenegrin referendum on independence. The European Union declared that it did not want to deny the democratic character of a referendum and declared that it would not oppose its results.[27] The April 2001 elections, which were presented by Djukanović as a test case for independence, proved that the supporters of independence only slightly outnumbered the opponents and that the majority obtained by the pro-independence parties in parliament would not be sufficient to guarantee a majority in a referendum. This allowed the international community to increase its pressure for reform along the lines of a joint federation.[28] Javier Solana, the EU's High Representative for Foreign and Security Policy, mediated in the conflict between Serbia and Montenegro. In March 2002, an agreement on the basic principles of the 'Restructuring of Relations between Serbia and Montenegro' was reached between the federal authorities and the authorities of Serbia and Montenegro. The Yugoslav state received a new name—'Serbia and Montenegro'—and preserved its own federal institutions (a parliament, a president, a Council of Ministers, and a Court). This agreement was only made acceptable for the Montenegrin government under the provision that Serbia and Montenegro would each be entitled after three years to institute proceedings for secession, which would then have to be legitimised by a referendum. For the European Union, which clearly expressed its preference for a common federal state, it was of the utmost importance that the re-integration of the Balkan region, together with its integration with the EU, would take place without a disruption of the existing state structures. From the European Union's perspective, the 'just cause' for Montenegrin secession seemed to have expired.[29]

ALTERNATIVE POLICIES

In addressing the problem of how the right to self-determination should be exercised in the Yugoslav context, the international community opposed a non-ethnic vision of the 'self' to the ethnic meaning of this right found in the interpretation of the concept of 'nation' shared by all the peoples of Yugoslavia. Such an ethnic meaning of the 'self' was to be found for instance in the 'Basic Principles' of the Yugoslav constitution. The normative discourses on the right to self-determination used by the international community and the warring parties in Yugoslavia were completely at odds with one another. Such

[27] RFE/RL, *Newsline*, 5:16, Part II, 24 Jan. 2001.

[28] The pro-independence parties won no more than a relatively slim majority of 44 of the parliament's 77 seats, *Financial Times*, 26 April 2001.

[29] See the document 'Proceeding Points for the Restructuring of Relations Between Serbia and Montenegro', available on http://www.mfa.gov.yu/Bilteni/Engleski/b150302_e.html; for a criticism of the EU position see 'An Open Letter to Dr Javier Solana re Montenegro, signed by thirteen prominent European politicians and activists (February)' on http://www.ceps.be/index.ph

discrepancies had drastic political consequences. The international community, for instance, strove for the recognition of the right to self-determination for the whole population of Bosnia-Herzegovina, as a multi-national entity. This policy was perceived by the Croats and Serbs in the republic as indicating unconditional support for the Bosniaks alone. This provoked the delegitimisation of the mediatory role of the international community and to an escalation of the conflict.

A second problem was raised by the question of a right to unilateral secession. In Yugoslavia, and especially in Bosnia-Herzegovina, such a unilateral right to secession was not accorded in a consistent manner to all the national communities demanding such a right. In 1992, it was granted to Slovenia and to Croatia, but not to Kosovo. In 1995, it was granted to Bosnia, but not to the Bosnian Croats or Serbs. In 1999, the Albanian Kosovars and the Montenegrin government cherished hopes of an independent Kosovo and Montenegro respectively, but these options were opposed by the international community. During the 1990s, choices concerning the right to secession were dictated by *Realpolitik*, rather than being based on a consistent, normative approach. But decisions inspired by *Realpolitik* vary over time, depending on concrete circumstances. The logic of *Realpolitik* may include a revision of a judgement on the conditions on which a people's right to secession may be exercised.

Inconsistency in respect to principles was the price to pay for Western *Realpolitik* towards the Yugoslav crisis. It should be emphasized, however, that none of the two main normative theories of secession—choice theories and the just cause theories[30]—offers a ready-made recipe for a consistent solution to the problems posed by secessionist movements in Yugoslavia. It would theoretically be possible to apply the choice theory of secession in such a way that the right to secession would be applied to all nations and national groups desiring it. This would have the merit of acknowledging the legitimacy of the principle of national self-determination—which has had such a strong mobilizing power in the Yugoslav context—and to link it to the search for commonly accepted rules and procedures for its implementation. But it would have been impossible to have the majority principle accepted by all parties in drawing new state borders. None of the parties would accept a minority status in a territory where ethnic and state borders are not congruent. It would also be impossible for the parties—and for the international community—to agree to 'voluntary' population exchanges.

The application of choice theory by the international community would thus not have avoided civil war in Yugoslavia. The international community

---

[30] See Wayne Norman, 'The Ethics of Secession as the Regulation of Secessionist Politics', in Moore, *National Self-Determination and Secession*, 34–61.

would moreover have had great difficulties in applying it consistently. A radical version of choice theory would assign the right to unilateral secession to ethnic groups, independently of their size and the viability of the new state structures. This would have resulted in a chaotic and unworkable dismemberment of the territory of the former Yugoslavia. Some restrictions to the application of the choice theories in terms of numbers, compactness, etc. would appear to be unavoidable. However, when subjected to restrictions, choice theory cannot be applied consistently.

Just cause theory, that requires the grounds for secession to be sought in the form of systematic discrimination, exploitation, or a gross and systematic violation of constitutional rights,[31] may seem to be more readily applicable in a consistent way. However, if applied logically the outcomes are quite at odds with the actual policies of the international community. The application of just cause theories would have challenged the international recognition of the independence of Slovenia and Croatia. As Norman states, most just cause theorists consider that 'the existence of a sufficient degree of sub-state autonomy precludes a right to secede'.[32] At the end of the 1980s Yugoslavia was turning into a confederal state (if it had not become one already). It can thus be argued that there was a sufficient degree of sub-state autonomy to preclude a unilateral right to secession, although it always remains disputable what is 'sufficient'. Moreover, in none of the federal units did 'systematic discrimination', 'exploitation', or 'gross and systematic violation of constitutional rights' take place. On the contrary, Yugoslavia was going through a radical process of democratization and liberalization, which significantly increased constitutional rights. The abolition of the one-party system, the creation of a free market economy, the first free elections, the establishment of free media, etc. all occurred by the end of the 1980s, at the very moment that claims for independence were raised in Slovenia and Croatia. This means that the rise of secessionist movements cannot be seen as a result of state repression, but their emergence had been made possible by democratization and liberalization. Even in Serbia, Milošević's conservative and authoritarian regime could not prevent these developments. This means that there was, strictly speaking, no 'just cause' for secession.

This conclusion may be opposed by the argument that, in practice, the violent intervention of the Yugoslav National Army (YNA) in Slovenia and especially in Croatia in June 1990 was considered at the time as 'just cause' to legitimate their secession. But is this really the case? Slovenian and Croat secessionist policy was not provoked by the YNA's intervention, but *vice versa*, the YNA's intervention was provoked by Slovenian and Croat secessionist policy. Even if we accept the argument that military intervention

---

[31] Ibid. 41.   [32] Ibid. 36.

by the YNA demonstrated the essentially undemocratic character of the Yugoslav state, it remains problematic whether we can consider the YNA's behaviour as an adequate 'just cause' to acknowledge Slovenia's and Croatia's right to independence.

Kosovo, however, offers a very different picture. We have here to differentiate between the various stages in the Kosovar crisis. The 1981 demand of the Albanian Kosovars to enhance the status of their autonomous province to become a republic—and, by doing so, to achieve the status of a nation and gain the right to secession—cannot necessarily be considered as legitimate from the point of view of just cause theory: the 1974 constitution gave Kosovo a considerable degree of sub-state autonomy and was then still fully operative. Even the curtailment of Kosovo's autonomy in 1989 by the Belgrade authorities, intended to restore Serb dominance in the region and to suppress Kosovar secessionism, cannot be considered 'just cause' for the right to secede. The territorial autonomy assigned by the new 1990 Serbian constitution to the autonomous provinces of Vojvodina and Kosovo still provided a 'sufficient degree of sub-state autonomy' to minorities, as compared to other countries in the world. But the harsh Serb repression and the many civil and human rights violations in Kosovo in the 1990s—extensively reported by *Amnesty International* and other human rights organizations— may indeed be considered as 'just cause' for secession. So if there was a just cause for secession in any of the federal units, it was only in Kosovo—the only former Yugoslav federal unit whose international recognition as an independent state is still pending![33]

The outcome of the consistent application of 'just cause' theory to the situation in Kosovo would thus fully contradict the actual policies of the international community. This approach would also have had other significant consequences. The logical and consistent application of just cause theory, in the form of a readiness to acknowledge the right of secession when human and civil rights were grossly and systematically violated, but *only* if they were grossly and systematically violated, combined with a serious monitoring mission that would report violations of human and civil rights as well as deliberate provocations by the state's military forces, could have had a remedial and moderating effect on the parties involved. However, the international community was apparently not prepared to apply such a just cause approach, while the communities claiming the right to secession may have felt rather more constrained than supported by it to achieve their final goal.

---

[33] It can also be argued that the KLA actually 'created' a just cause by provoking violent retaliations by the Serb security forces during the 1998 guerrilla war. The international community tried to overcome this problem by introducing the notion of 'excessive violence' as a just cause for the 1999 military intervention, apparently accepting the use of 'violence' against a guerrilla army as legitimate.

7

Special Status for Tatarstan: Validity of Claims and Limits on Sovereignty

Alexei Zverev

INTRODUCTION

The speed with which the unravelling of the Soviet Union came about exceeded its citizens' capacity to understand it. To people in Russia, who in Soviet times had heard innumerable professions of 'centuries-old' Russo-Ukrainian, Russo-Georgian, or Russo-Tatar friendship from Communist leaders and official poets in the respective Soviet republics (but who often had real friends among the people of the various Soviet nationalities), the outpourings of mobilized nationalism from these quarters came as a rude awakening.

The potential for secession in Russia was not exhausted with the demise of the USSR. In 1990–1, most of Russia's autonomous republics—the second tier of Soviet administrative arrangement after Union republics—proclaimed their republics' sovereignty. In Soviet (and post-Soviet Russian) parlance, the word 'sovereignty' meant self-rule short of full independence and was often understood as ownership of mineral resources, autonomy in internal matters, budgetary concessions, and a measure of competence in foreign policy. Attempts by Russia's republics to implement their qualified sovereignty—and efforts by the federal centre to curb them—create an arena in which the secessionist process is played out.

Tatarstan, which had developed an active nationalist movement by the end of the 1980s, spearheaded the so-called 'parade of sovereignties' among Russia's republics. Inside the republic itself, president Shaimiev managed to rein in independence-seeking nationalists by using some of their rhetoric to entrench himself in power. Avoiding the perils of violent secession as seen in Chechnya, he used his patriotic Tatar credentials to maintain interethnic peace, modernize the economy (some experts say, South Korean-style) while trying to cushion the severity of market reforms, and cut a deal with Moscow to secure 'special status' for his republic.

Tatarstan is a classic case of the 'secessionist process' referred to in the introduction to this volume—a 'series of graduated actions or events directed towards (although not necessarily leading to) the withdrawal of an area from the aegis of a central government'. It is probable that not all the distinctive traits of the Shaimiev regime will outlast the Yeltsin period. In his first years in office, Russia's president Putin curtailed Tatarstan's prerogatives in relation to tax exemptions and began to reinstate Russia's control over its legal system. Attempts by the Tatar leadership to withdraw from central government authority will, no doubt, continue, and are a legitimate field of academic enquiry.

The object of this chapter is to give a normative assessment both of the arguments used by independence-seeking Tatar nationalists and of those that stem from the logic of a gradual secessionist process. In so doing, we base ourselves on the various criteria elaborated by the permissive and remedial schools of thought on secession. We ask ourselves if secession for Tatarstan is a morally justified option, whether a claim to sovereignty, as opposed to independence, can be established with greater justification, and what are the countervailing factors that limit the validity of such a claim. We assume that the secessionist potential stems from the social, cultural, and psychological factors that keep nationalist sentiments alive, and from the political and institutional realities of post-Soviet Russia. As for the former, the noted Russian ethnologist Sergei Arutyunov points out the persistence of ethnic grievances, feelings of being second-rate, sociocultural disadvantage, cultural incompatibility and religious discrimination in most ethnically-defined 'sovereign republics' as distinct from ethnically Russian *oblasts*.[1] These feelings generate a predisposition to eventual secession by ethnic groups in non-Russian regions. Despite the fact that these feelings were widespread in their republic, the Tatar government had—as we will demonstrate—good reason for seeking a compromise with Moscow. The federal arrangement gave the Tatar leadership the possibility to address ethnic grievances in an institutional framework, which provides for domestic sovereignty and limited powers in foreign affairs.

The chapter is divided into four sections. In the first, we take up the theoretical debate on secession, to enable us later to place Tatarstan squarely within that debate. The second and third sections trace the historical evolution of Tatar national and cultural identity and the Tatar struggle for sovereignty in the period 1987–94, when the republic came close to actual secession. This was the time when, in the words of President Shaimiev, the leadership of

---

[1] Sergei Arutyunov's remarks are taken from the transcript of a conference on ethnic relations in the Russian Federation held in Suzdal, Russia, on 27–30 June 1997 and organized by the Kennan Institute. Posted on the website http://www.kennan.yar.ru/materials/profi2/welcome1.html.

Tatarstan came closer than the width of a razor-blade to a major conflict with Russia, but just managed to prevent one. The fourth section weighs the remedial/just-cause and permissive/choice theories against the arguments for Tatarstan's secession and/or qualified sovereignty.

THEORETICAL DEBATE ON SECESSION

During the last decade, informed debate on secession has given rise to an interesting literature on the subject. The most comprehensive theoretical attempt to deal with secession to date has come from the pen of Allen Buchanan,[2] whose remedial secession theory holds that secession can be morally justified chiefly on the grounds of rectifying long-standing and continued oppression, non-representation in the governing bodies of the parent country, or lack of distributive justice. Another important condition to consider, which may invalidate secession, is that of the viability of a new secessionist state. In a recent revised Russian edition of Buchanan's work referred to above, he adds two more criteria that may justify secession: (1) the case where the central government unilaterally annuls the autonomy earlier accorded a federated state (which means that the centre breaks an agreement that had earlier been concluded with that federated state, thereby pushing it towards justified secession); (2) the case where the central state breaks up from within or is destroyed by outside forces (a situation that generates a *sauve qui peut* separatism among the minorities of the state that no longer functions).[3]

Buchanan (like most other theorists) does not see the need for a generalized right to secession, and puts the onus on the secessionists to prove that the communities on whose behalf they purport to speak actually are suffering long-standing injustice or discriminatory redistribution. The idea is to erect a series of hurdles in the path of secession in order to prevent massive human-rights violations, the break-up of existing international alliances or economic dislocation. Remedial theories also place on the secessionists the burden of proof that democratic rights, including those of minorities in a seceding territory, will not be trampled on. Remedial theorists hold that self-determination (at least in liberal societies) should not be couched in the rhetoric of rights. 'Rights talk', writes Ronald Beiner, 'is a form of political discourse that is intended as the verbal equivalent of shaking one's fist in the direction of those with whom one is in a state of political disagreement.' Beiner concedes,

---

[2] Allen Buchanan, *Secession: the Morality of Political Divorce from Fort Sumter to Lithuania and Quebec* (Boulder, Colo., Westview Press, 1991).

[3] Allen Buchanan, *Setsessiya. Pravo na otdeleniye, prava cheloveka i territorial'naya tselostnost' gosudarstva* (Moscow, Rudomino, 2001), 4–5.

however, that in countries whose regimes oppress their citizens the rights discourse is more justified.[4]

In contrast, some permissive/choice theorists like David Philpott hold that self-determination is a basic right rooted in liberal democratic theory. In Philpott's view, this right is 'also qualified, limited by the same liberal commitments which ground it'.[5] Like Buchanan, Philpott qualifies the validity of secessionist claims by saying that a seceding nation must be no less democratic and no less tolerant towards ethnic minorities than the parent country it secedes from. 'What justifies self-determination is not the mere fact of the members' choice, but their realisation of democratic autonomy, their increased ability to steer their fate.'[6] Contrary to Buchanan, Philpott deems that a group need not suffer an injustice in order to warrant self-determination. Injustices perpetrated by that group itself, however, may invalidate its *prima facie* right.

David Miller, in one of the choice theory interpretations, holds that in cases where citizens form a national community—that is, where part of the country's population feels ethnically or culturally alien to the majority and does not share its ethnocultural identity—it may establish a valid claim (like Buchanan and unlike Philpott, a claim, not the right) to secession. However, this claim may be defeated by countervailing factors: for instance, a nation may not lay a valid claim to land it once ruled if it is currently inhabited, is being developed and is politically administered by another nation which now feels an attachment to that land.[7]

The Russian ethnographer and politician Galina Starovoitova believed that in assessing the validity of claims to secession the international community should take the following criteria into account: (1) intolerability of existence for a population of any territory (permanent oppression or discrimination); (2) historical rights (arguably the most contentious criterion: it serves to identify (outside the classic colonial context) the earlier inhabitants of a region conquered or unjustly ruled by a foreign nation); (3) ethnic composition of a population (an absolute percentage of the seceding nation on a seceding territory); (4) a clear popular mandate for secession (a vote for independence by an absolute majority in parliament or a referendum); (5) consequences of secession (a transitional period for self-determination movements may under certain conditions be desirable in order to prepare the seceding population for self-government).[8] In Starovoitova's

[4] Ronald Beiner, 'Self-Determination and Rights', in Margaret Moore (ed.), *National Self-Determination and Secession* (Oxford, Oxford University Press, 1998), 164.

[5] Daniel Philpott, 'Self-Determination in Practice', in Moore, *National Self-Determination and Secession*, 80.   [6] Ibid. 82.

[7] David Miller, 'Secession and the Principle of Nationality', in Moore, *National Self-Determination and Secession*, 65.

[8] Galina Starovoitova, *Sovereignty after Empire: Self-Determination Movements in the Former Soviet Union*. Posted on the website http://www.usip.org/pubs/pworks/pwks19/pwks19.html.

opinion, secession may be allowed only if all the above criteria, not just two or three, are taken into account. This latter demand effectively limits justified secession to a relatively few seemingly 'clear-cut' cases.

Thus, as we can see, various theoreticians, even those who consider that secession is a right, recognize its limited character and place various restrictions on it to prevent new grievances. Both permissive/choice and remedial/just-cause theories have much to offer for the analysis of self-determination claims advanced both by the moderate Tatarstan leadership and proponents of outright independence for that republic. Below we shall explore the relevant criteria that warrant or restrict secessionist claims for Tatarstan, but first we have to explore the evolution of Tatar identity and the Tatar nationalist movement. From the standpoint of a methodological analysis of secession, a factual outline of this evolution is important. For example, it would be necessary to establish whether Tatars have valid grievances stemming from continued injustice (Buchanan), whether they have a clear-cut, separate national identity and what countervailing factors might weigh against Tatarstan's secession (Miller), whether the democratic rights of minorities would suffer as a result of secession there (Philpott, Buchanan) and whether the secession of Tatarstan meets all the criteria established by Starovoitova that justify secession.

THE SHAPING OF TATAR IDENTITY

The main ancestors of the present-day Kazan Tatars—the Bulgars, a tribe of Turkic origin—came to the region of the Volga and Kama rivers from the shores of the Sea of Azov in the seventh and eight centuries AD.[9] There they founded the Bulgar Khanate, which was to exist from the eighth century to the first third of the fifteenth century (its capital was called Bulgar). Part of the khanate's population was also Finno-Ugrian. The Bulgars adopted Islam in 922. They were a settled people who engaged in trade (furs, wheat, handicrafts, slaves) with Kievan Rus, the countries of Central Europe, Byzantium, Egypt, and Central Asia.

The Bulgar Khanate was sacked by the Mongol hordes of Genghis Khan's son Batu in 1236–7. Part of the population was destroyed and part taken prisoner, while the rest escaped to Russian lands, where they were given refuge. The Mongol troops then laid waste the Russian principalities,

As a political figure, the late Starovoitova acted as a tough negotiator at talks between Russia and Tatarstan. As an expert, she is also remembered by the Tatars for having advised them to hold a referendum on sovereignty, which they eventually held in March 1992.

[9] Another section of the original Bulgars went to the Danube where, having mixed with local Slavs and adopted Christianity, they founded the Bulgarian Kingdom.

subjecting them to a 240-year domination. The invading Mongols called both themselves and the Turkic tribes they forcibly enlisted into their armies 'Tatars', as did the Arab, Persian, Armenian, and Russian chronicles of the day. In contemporary Western European sources the Mongols were called 'Tartars' by analogy with the 'Tartaros' (underworld) of the ancient Greeks—a fact still resented by modern Tatars, who feel humiliated at being unjustly associated with what Europeans see as the coarse, cruel, and bloody invader. As time went on, the Golden Horde—a state founded by the Tartars, extending from the Danube to Western China—became Turkicized and Islamized. Thus the alien name 'Tatar/Tartar' was in fact imposed on various Turkic tribes by the Mongols, and was later endorsed by Christians as a collective designation for the entire Turkic population of the Golden Horde.[10]

At the end of the fourteenth century, Tamerlane delivered a massive blow to the Golden Horde, destroying its capital Sarai on the lower Volga. As a result of Tamerlane's campaign and internecine struggles, in the fifteenth century the Golden Horde became fragmented into a number of separate hordes and khanates—the Greater Horde on the lower Volga (from which Russia finally freed itself in 1480), the Crimean Khanate, the Nogai Horde which spread from the Caspian to the Southern Urals (encompassing almost all of present-day Bashkortostan), the Kasimov Khanate in Russia's Ryazan region, the Siberian Khanate in Western Siberia, and the Kazan Khanate—each with a different ethnic stock. The Kazan Khanate, founded in 1439, comprised the lands of the Bulgars (including the Turkic but Orthodox-Christian Chuvash ethnic group) and the Finno-Ugrians (the present-day Mari, Udmurts, Komi, and Mordvins), and included a fair admixture of Kypchaks and Turkicized Mongols who came with the Golden Horde. The core of the Kazan Tatars—who called themselves *Kazanly* or *Kazan keshese* ('the Kazan people')—were directly descended from the Bulgars and used that name until the late nineteenth century.

The Kazan Khanate was larger than the present-day Republic of Tatarstan, reaching as far as Volgograd in the Middle Volga. Nowadays, Tatar historians like to remind us that the stones of the ancient cities of the Golden Horde and the Kazan Khanate lie beneath the foundations of Russian cities on the Volga such as Simbirsk (in Tatar Sinbir, now Ulyanovsk), Saratov (Sary Tau) and Tsaritsyn (Sary Tin, now Volgograd).

The Kazan Khanate was wiped out by Russia's Tsar Ivan the Terrible in 1552–6, after nearly a century of Muscovite attempts to destroy its independence. In 1552, Russian troops took Kazan by storm and then partly colonized

[10] Subsequently (up until 1917) the Russians used the term 'Tatar' to designate collectively not only the Turkic peoples of the Volga, the Urals and Siberia, but also those of Central Asia, the Dagestanis ('Mountain Tatars') and the Azeris ('Caucasian Tatars').

the newly conquered province. The late Russian scholar Vilyam Pokhlyobkin counted nineteen wars between Muscovy and the Kazan Khanate in the barely 120 years of the latter's existence.[11] In his opinion, only the first two of these wars were provoked by the Tatars' desire to strengthen their domination over Russia. The rest were aggressive wars on Russia's part, motivated by the desire to impose puppet governments in Kazan and ultimately to annihilate that kingdom—aggressive policies that are not vitiated by the fact that the Kazan warriors often mounted offensive operations in the course of these wars.

Nowadays, arguments based on historical justice in the Tatarstan case are important for enhancing the Tatars' dignity and self-respect. Each year on 15 October, Memory Day, members of Tatar national organizations, writers, singers, and actors hold a meeting to mark the anniversary of the fall of Kazan to the troops of Ivan the Terrible. Demanding a revival of Tatarstan's independence, they hold ceremonies to mourn the victims and join in Muslim prayer at a mosque. For those who called for sovereign status without secession from Russia, such symbols are likewise highly significant. For the authorities of Tatarstan, for example, harking back to the Russian conquest of 1552 serves to remind the public (and Moscow) that Tatarstan is not a region of Russia like any other but a state with a historical tradition of its own that should enjoy prerogatives to match its special status. History provides national symbols which serve as reference-points to highlight cultural, political and state identity. For a significant—though not a predominant—proportion of the Tatars in Tatarstan, this tradition of statehood has a positive value. A recent poll taken in Tatarstan revealed that 33 per cent of the Tatars polled regret the loss of statehood by their ancestors, 43 per cent have no such feeling and 15 per cent have no definite opinion about it.[12]

Thus there are two strands in the national identity of Kazan Tatars to this day—Bulgarism and Tatarism, each of which has its own conception of statehood and its historical reference points. In the late nineteenth and early twentieth century, Bulgarism—espousing Tolstoyan-type beliefs—represented a sect opposed to the official Muslim clergy. People who define themselves as 'Volga Bulgars' today still abhor the name 'Tatar' and hark back to the era of the Bulgar civilization. Apart from the fact that the Bulgars had long felt ethnically apart from the Tartar officials who ruled them, this opposition is motivated by a desire to dissociate themselves from the opprobrium associated with the 'Tartar yoke' in Russia and beyond. In addition, the Bulgar conception of Tatar identity was wilfully used in Soviet

[11] Viktor Pokhlyobkin, *Tatary i Rus'* (Moscow, Mezhdunarodniye otnosheniya, 2000), 180.
[12] Rafik Abdrakhmanov and Elvira Mavrina, *Respublika Tatarstan: Model' etnologicheskogo monitoringa*. Posted on the website http://federalism.soros.ksu.ru/publications/kateg_6.html.

times in the struggle against 'Tatar bourgeois nationalism'. This was meant
to 'localize' Tatar historical consciousness in the Bulgar Khanate, breaking
its pan-Turkic ties, and to prevent the Tatars of various tribes (including
those of non-Bulgar descent) from coalescing on an anti-Russian basis. In
fact, the Bulgar period was the only epoch in pre-Soviet Tatar history which
Soviet historians were allowed to see in a 'positive' light. According to the
present-day Bulgarist view, Tatarism is a 'chauvinistic current in the socio-
political thinking of the Volga Bulgars', a 'negative reaction to the pernicious
influence of Great-Russian chauvinism', and a 'distortion of the ethnonymic
consciousness of the Volga Bulgars with the ideas of Turkic solidarity and
confessional unity, a reaction to the destructive, assimilating influence of
the Russian yoke'.[13] Time has shown that the Bulgarist version can also be
nationalistic, defending its own conception of statehood. The Gorbachev
years saw the appearance of political organizations of Bulgarists: the Bulgar
al-Jadid[14] Club and the Bulgar National Congress. Both organizations are
opposed to Russian domination over Tatarstan (which they still call 'Volga
Bulgaria'). The Bulgar/Tatar cleavage, and the existence of local groups
of Tatars—the Mishars, the Kasimov and Astrakhan Tatars outside
Tatarstan and the Kriashens (baptized Tatars) inside it—shows that Tatar
ethnic consolidation is still far from complete.

  In contrast to Bulgarism, the Tatarist stance makes it possible to encompass
in the fold of Tatar ethnic identity not just the Bulgars but all other tribes historically designated as 'Tatars'. With the passage of time, most of the Tatars,
whatever their extraction (with the exception of Crimean and Siberian Tatars),
rallied around Kazan. Viewing all Tatars as a single nation makes it possible to
incorporate the Bulgar and Golden Horde periods into a single historical
narrative. Moreover, from the Tatarist (and particularly Turco-Tatarist) perspective, the Golden Horde—a brilliant civilization submerged by the sands of
history—may be presented as a state incorporating all the Turkic tribes on
earth. Thus romantic Tatar nationalists of the early twentieth century, such as
the political writer Galimjan Sharaf, saw the Golden Horde as a source of
national pride born of Turkic unity, with implications for national liberation:

In the historical writings left to us from the past we can take pride in the fact that
our ancestors were Turks by descent...that Genghis [Khan], in sending his troops to
the West, told them: 'If you see somewhere the son of a Turk held in bondage by others, do not go away until you have set him free...'[15]

---

[13] From the theses for the report 'Ethnonymic Consciousness of the Volga Bulgars in the
20th Century' (10.12.00) by G. Khalil, President of the Bulgar National Congress. Posted on the
website http://www.mi.ru/~bolgar/tezisy.html.

[14] Bulgar al-Jadid—'The New Bulgar'—was a medieval name for Kazan.

[15] *Ang*, 2 (1914), quoted from: G. Kasymov, *Pantyurkistskaya kontrrevolutsiya i yevo agentura
sultangalievshchina* (Kazan, Tatizdat, 1931), 14.

Nevertheless, the traditions of statehood handed down from the Bulgar Khanate, through the Golden Horde to the Kazan Khanate, important as they are in Tatar popular memory, were ruptured by the Tatars' incorporation into the Russian state, to be partially restored only later, when the Tatar Autonomous Soviet Socialist Republic (ASSR) was founded in Soviet times. Even then there was, of course, no continuity between the Soviet Tatar state and the Tatar/Tartar states of times long past.

After the fall of Kazan to the Russians, Tatar self-perception developed in opposition to national, social, and especially religious oppression. Loss of independence strengthened the Islamic component of Tatar identity. The centuries that followed the Tsarist Russian conquest saw repeated attempts to Christianize the Muslim population and, on the Tatars' side, to defend their mosques. Often, as the Russian missionaries left, Tatars who had been forcibly baptized would revert to their Islamic faith, frequently exposing themselves to subsequent retaliation by punitive Tsarist expeditions. Ruined mosques were tenaciously restored—and new ones built—by believers. Just as the Bulgars had 'tamed' the initially hostile Mongols by Islamicizing the Golden Horde, the Tatars of the Russian period, by hook and by crook, finally 'tamed' the Russian administration and won the right to practise their religion. This was achieved in the reign of Empress Catherine II (the Great). However, the Tatars' preoccupation with traditional Islam as the main feature of their identity, and with fighting encroachments upon it, hampered their development as a civic nation by embedding their sense of belonging in the *umma*. Until late in the nineteenth century and even beyond, most of the conservative Tatar mullahs opposed the teaching of Russian and the non-Islamic education of their flock, as well as any modernizing changes in Islamic teaching. In this, they were backed by the Russian administration, which prohibited secular teaching in the *medresses* (Islamic seminaries) on the assumption that it was easier to deal with Muslim fanatics than European-educated Muslims. The alternative—for Tatar students to enter Russian schools—was unacceptable to the Tatar élites, as such students, they claimed, would be integrated into Russian life in general and would abandon their Muslim community.

Towards the second half of the nineteenth century, Tatar identity began to be shaped by attempts to reform the Muslim community internally. The problems of modernization were at the heart of a movement of Tatar educational reformers, Jadidism (from the Arabic *jadid*, meaning 'new'). Socially, the Jadids based themselves on a far-flung network of rich Tatar merchants and entrepreneurs who operated in the Volga region, Central Asia, Siberia and the Far East as far as Mongolia and China. The early period of the Jadids' activity (*c.*1880–1905) may be seen as a cultural phase in the evolution of the Tatar national movement. The Jadids set up reforming *medresses*, which taught secular subjects and the Russian language in addition to the subjects pertaining to Islamic doctrine.[16] By the early twentieth century, Tatars had developed a network of print-shops, a Tatar press, secular literature in the vernacular, and national theatre. To allay the wariness of the Russian authorities, early Jadids such as Kayum Nasyri, Khusain Faizkhanov, Shigabutdin Marjani, and the Crimean Tatar Ismail Gasprinsky professed loyalty to Russia. They believed in enlightened monarchy, hoping that Russia would help them in their cultural and educational effort on behalf of the Muslim communities. This was a logical attitude, given the Jadids' initially narrow support-base among their Muslim compatriots, the majority of whom still followed the Kadimist (from the Arabic *qadim*, meaning 'old') conservatives. In their quest for European culture, the Jadids derived scientific knowledge not only from Russia but also from linguistically kindred Islamic Turkey and, directly, from Western countries where some of them received education (like Sadri Maksudi, who graduated from the Sorbonne). Thus in terms of Tatar national identity, Jadidism represented a European cultural (and ultimately political) influence.

Politically, the Jadids received an opportunity to express themselves freely after the first Russian revolution of 1905. They sided mostly with the Russian liberals and founded a Muslim faction in the four Russian Dumas. Their demands were distinctly more moderate than those of the other non-Russian nations—they called for cultural national autonomy on the Bauer–Renner model.[17] Other Tatar politicians (such as Gayaz Iskhaki) founded nationalist groups allied with Russian revolutionary parties. While continuing their struggle for political reform, the Tatar élites, representing the most educated Muslim nation in Russia, attempted to lead the country's other Muslim nations. Both strategies ultimately failed during the Russian revolutions of 1917—the former with the political demise of the Russian allies of the Jadids, the non-Bolshevik parties, and the latter with the manifest refusal of the Azeris, Kazakhs, Bashkirs, and other non-Tatar Muslims to be guided by the Tatar political leaders. Pan-Turkist and pan-Muslim ideals led some Tatar Jadids both in emigration (Yusuf Akchura) and in Russia (Gayaz Iskhaki) to side with Turkey in World War I. Lack of mass support from the Tatar populace (among whom the conservative Muslim clergy had held more sway, and for longer, than the Jadids) and a rift with the nationalists of neighbouring Bashkortostan also explain the failure of an attempt to

---

[16] But, while not knowing Russian, many Tatars knew Arabic and were well versed in Arab, Turkish, and Persian literature.

[17] Bruno Bauer and Karl Renner were Austrian Social Democrats whose concept of cultural national autonomy, developed in the late 19th cent., involved the transfer of schools and other cultural institutions to extra-territorial national committees in a multinational state, with education to be carried on in the native languages.

form an autonomous Volga-Ural State (Idel-Ural) in early 1918, which had been expected to comprise Tatar and Bashkir lands. Thus the Tatars, unlike the borderland nations of Russia (the Georgians, Ukrainians, or Balts) could not boast of a period of national independence even for the brief period of the Russian civil war (1918–21). The formation of the Tatar ASSR in 1920 by the Bolsheviks ultimately gave a territorial (not pan-Muslim) focus to Tatar nationalism and marked the closure of the Bulgarist–Tatarist debate on Tatar national identity (since the name 'Tatar' was now officially recognized as the designation of the territorially defined 'titular nationality' in the Tatar ASSR).

THE TATAR STRUGGLE FOR SOVEREIGNTY, 1987–94

The advent of Stalinism, after a brief spell of Soviet 'indigenization' policy in the 1920s, arrested the national development of non-Russian nations, moulding them, with greater or lesser success, into a 'Soviet people'. The gradual awakening of the Tatar intelligentsia under Gorbachev found them exactly where they had left off in 1918 with the failure of Idel-Ural—in an unfinished process of national renaissance. Unlike in the heyday of the Jadid movement, Tatarstan now had a mostly Tatar nomenklatura wielding power in a Soviet autonomous republic. Gone were the days when the Tatars could claim the leadership of Russia's Muslims—each Soviet Muslim ethnos had been territorially and politically compartmentalized and had developed a political identity and interests of its own. Both the Iron Curtain and Kemal Ataturk[18] had put an end to the pan-Turkist ideal to which the Tatars could aspire. Tatar society had become heavily industrialized with the resulting influx of many Russians into Tatarstan and thorough Tatar assimilation. The status of a Soviet Autonomous Republic for Tatarstan meant that it had fewer opportunities for cultural development than the Union republics—fewer hours on the local radio for Tatar-language broadcasts, no film studio, fewer cultural exchanges worldwide, fewer books published, no Soviet-wide Tatar newspaper, and so forth.

With the advent of Gorbachev's *perestroika*, sections of the Tatar intelligentsia felt free to express a pent-up sentiment of acute alienation from the Russian-dominated state. This can be graphically illustrated by an excerpt from an article in a Tatar youth magazine:

What fruits do we have from our closeness to the Russians? We have no state. Our language is in decline. There is neither a national army nor a national bank. One

[18] After coming to power in Turkey as a result of the revolution in 1923, Kemal Ataturk repudiated the pan-Turkic discourse that appealed to the common ethnic heritage of the Turkic peoples from China to the Adriatic, replacing it by civic Turkish nationalism within the borders of the Turkish Republic.

could say that our religion has just recovered from a long clinical death. As for education, only seven per cent of Tatar children are being educated in their native language. The hitherto glorious city of Kazan is lying in shambles. Instead of wealth from the oil we have nothing but costs: chemical poisoning, soil pollution, earthquakes provoked by the merciless and incompetent exploitation of our natural deposits and, finally, the feeling of desolation we have in our own hearts.[19]

Nationalist parties—the Tatar Public Centre (TOTs), Ittifak (Alliance), the Sovereignty Committee, the Iman ('Faith') Youth Islamic Culture Centre, Azatlyk (Freedom), and others—were quickly organized to press for full independence or, as Azatlyk's programme had it, the creation of two or three Tatar states in the Soviet Union, to ensure self-determination for Tatars living in different regions. The Tatar nationalists' greatest political success was the adoption by the Tatarstan parliament on 30 August 1990 of Tatarstan's Declaration of Sovereignty, which made no mention of the republic's affiliation to either the USSR or the Russian Federation, proclaimed all mineral wealth in the republic to be in its ownership and declared the pre-eminence of Tatarstan's laws on its own territory over those of the USSR and the RSFSR. The high points of the Tatar movement were the events in Kazan in May 1991: a 50,000-strong nationalist demonstration with the burning of Russian flags, a successful hunger strike to protest against the holding of the Russian presidential election in Tatarstan, and an attempt to storm the parliament building in October 1991, aimed at forcing the parliament to declare full independence for Tatarstan. Radical nationalists were beginning to organize an armed Tatar National Guard, and there were reports that the Russian population was starting to emigrate from the republic.

However, the Tatar independence drive, if it were triumphant, would mean a radicalization of society with an attendant reshuffling of the positions of the Tatar *nomenklatura*, which, by various estimates, constituted between 60 and 78 per cent of Tatarstan's political élite at the time of the fall of the Soviet Union (a much higher proportion than that of the Tatars in the republic's total population—48.3 per cent in 1989).[20] The Tatarstan élite, conscious of the dangerous example of Chechnya where the Soviet-era hierarchy had been overthrown, rallied around Chairman of the Tatarstan Supreme Soviet Mintimer Shaimiev (elected president of Tatarstan in 1991, re-elected in 1996 and 2000) who used the Tatar nationalist upsurge to strengthen Tatarstan's influence within Russia by entrenching the republic's sovereign constitutional rights. In March 1992 Shaimiev held a successful

[19] B. Rakhimova, 'Sosedi', *Idel*, 11 (1990).
[20] See Alexei Zverev, 'Qualified Sovereignty: the Tatarstan Model for Resolving Conflicting Loyalties', in Michael Waller, Bruno Coppieters, and Alexei Malashenko (eds.), *Conflicting Loyalties and the State in Post-Soviet Eurasia* (London, Frank Cass, 1998), 121 and 143 (nn. 5 and 6).

referendum on the status of Tatarstan to confirm the Declaration of Sovereignty. This was done against strong opposition from Russia's president and parliament and in defiance of a contrary injunction issued by Russia's Constitutional Court. Rumours of an impending Russian Military invasion of Tatarstan circulated. Shaimiev craftily declared that the referendum did not entail either the secession or the non-secession of Tatarstan from Russia. Finally, a little over half the electorate of the entire republic, local Russians included, voted in favour. In November 1992, Tatarstan's parliament promulgated the constitution of Tatarstan, Article 61 of which reproduced the wording of the March 1992 referendum on the status of Tatarstan: 'a sovereign state, a subject of international law, associated with Russia on the basis of a treaty on mutually delegated powers'.[21]

Based on this newly entrenched legitimacy (and fearful of unilateral steps towards outright independence), in February 1994, after protracted negotiations, the Tatarstan leadership concluded a power-sharing treaty with the Russian Federation that combined the contradictory wording of the Russian and Tatarstan constitutions ('The Republic of Tatarstan has been united with Russia on the basis of the constitutions of the two states'). Ever since it has remained the case that the Russian constitution considers the republic as its federated state, while the Tatarstan constitution (until the constitutional amendments of April 2002) deems it a state associated with Russia and having an international legal personality. A dozen agreements, mostly economic, were attached to the treaty. Tatarstan received substantial powers of taxation, the right to conduct its economic policy and foreign trade relations, a bigger quota of its own oil exports by comparison with other regions, and ownership of its mineral resources. Despite the lack of parliamentary approval of the treaty by either side, and its contradictory nature, the treaty did much to calm the conflict. The Tatar nationalist organizations (like their local Russian opponents, who believed that the situation was catastrophic, but the catastrophe did not happen) lost much of their influence. Between then and the end of Yeltsin's rule, the legal basis of relations between Russia and Tatarstan did not change. When Vladimir Putin assumed the presidency in Russia, what Russia believed to be excessive economic privileges for Tatarstan were rescinded (in 2000, Kazan paid Moscow twice as much in tax revenue as the previous year, with a commensurate disbursement from the federal exchequer to the Tatarstan treasury; to control the cash flow, a branch of the Federal Audit Chamber was established in Kazan),[22] and local branches of the Office

---

[21] On 19 April 2002, under pressure from the Putin government, the Tatarstan parliament adopted a more pliant version of constitutional provision on the status of Tatarstan: 'a democratic law-governed state, united with the Russian Federation…and a subject of the Russian Federation.' See *Nezavisimaya gazeta*, 23 April 2002.

[22] *Financial Times*, 25 April 2001.

of the Public Prosecutor, the Supreme Court and the Federal Security Service
were placed under greater federal control. The constitutional arrangements
governing Russo-Tatarstan relations (the reference in the Russian constitution to republics as 'states', not just provinces) and the power-sharing treaty,
however, have so far not been touched despite Putin's clear disapproval of
these treaties as a mechanism regulating federal relations. A small but symbolic detail is that the annual celebration of the Declaration of Sovereignty
in Kazan was held as usual in 2000 and 2001, under Putin, and was attended
by delegations of Russian federal officials.

ASSESSING THE VALIDITY OF TATARSTAN'S CLAIMS TO SECESSION AND SOVEREIGNTY

To be able to present a plausible case for secession from the choice-theory
perspective, it would be necessary to demonstrate that the Tatars are a distinct nation whose self-image is opposed to that of the Russian majority. To
put it simply, we would have to show that a sizeable proportion of the Tatars
want secession. From the perspective of remedial theory, we shall take up
such criteria as long-standing and continued injustice, cultural discrimination, discriminatory redistribution and economic viability. Both the choice
and remedial theories would also require us to prove that a breakaway Tatar
state would be viable.

We shall not, however, deal with the question of whether an independent
Tatarstan would be less or more democratic than a federated state. In our view,
it is difficult indeed to make such an assessment, even though both normative
approaches to secession regard this criterion as crucial. In 1989–93, at the
height of the secessionist upsurge in Tatarstan, the Tatar radical nationalists
(as distinct from the Shaimiev leadership) were not free from xenophobia.
Some of their leaders were opposed to mixed marriages, and even expressed
anti-Semitism. Such signs of political extremism and intolerance, however,
do not necessarily mean that an independent Tatarstan would be less
tolerant or democratic than the present republic.

A contextualized approach to the question of Tatar independence has to
take into account the difference between the political situation that led to the
secession of the Union republics from the USSR and the situation of the
secessionist process in present-day Tatarstan. If we turn to the former case, we
will see that the Soviet Union unravelled not primarily because of the historical grievances of its constituent nations, and not even because some of them
had been the object of Russian conquest in the past, but because the Soviet
economic system had exhausted its resources and could not provide incentives for development as it had done in the earlier decades of Soviet rule;
because the supranational idea that used to provide legitimacy for keeping the

republics together in a single state had crumbled with the demise of communism; because the local élites found they were free to 'go it alone', partly confident of their own strength and partly in the hope of Western aid; because the Russian economic liberals thought it easier to introduce a market economy into Russia without waiting for the other republics to do so; and, last but not least, because the Soviet 'power' agencies—the army, the police and the KGB, discredited in the wake of the August putsch of 1991—lacked both the power and the motivation to bring the republics back into the Soviet/Russian fold.

None of these factors that facilitated the disintegration of the Soviet Union is present in today's Russia or in Tatarstan. The introduction of the market economy has provided new incentives for development. The idea of Tatarstan sovereignty and civic nationalism (of the 'multinational people of Tatarstan') has replaced communism as an ideological cement. The Tatarstan élites cannot 'go it alone': on the contrary, they derive advantages from the central position of Tatarstan on Russia's map, with the republic straddling transport and commercial routes, and they enjoy the role of an influential power broker, a leader of Russia's regions and Russia's Muslims. Tatarstan does not suffer from Russia's identity crisis as the latter grapples with the legacy of the former empire, an anti-Western mentality, and Soviet-era ideological barriers which impede business activity (for instance, the sale of land). The Russian army and police, unlike their late-Soviet counterparts, would react strongly to any secession attempt, while the poverty in, and lack of crucial Western aid to, the former Soviet republics that did secede (as well as the tragedy of Chechnya) do not encourage the Russian republics to relive that experience. It is clear that these demographic and geographical factors and circumstances would not favour the secession of Tatarstan.

Do Tatars represent a distinct nation alien to the Russians?

It will be recalled that, according to David Miller, a national community ethnically or culturally alien to the majority, which does not share its ethnocultural identity, may establish a valid claim to secession and internal sovereignty. Let us now see whether the Tatars in Tatarstan constitute a regional nation in their own right and to what extent they have a dual or 'nested' identity which may be accommodated within the framework of the Russian Federation.

A contextualized approach to this question has to take a number of demographic and geographical factors into account. One is the existence of the Russian population in the republic, whose proportion never fell below 40 per cent throughout the twentieth century, who have been living in this area for 400 years and for whom these lands and rivers are a source of deep attachment. Another is the dispersal of most of the Tatars across Russia and Siberia (three-quarters of Tatars live outside Tatarstan). The Tatars know that if they secede from Russia they will become isolated from their kins-men. The land of Russia is not alien to them—on the contrary, Russian land outside Tatarstan is also Tatar land, the historic land of the Golden Horde, where three-quarters of the Tatar population now live.

A US–Russian poll conducted in 1994 in Tatarstan[23] asked respondents the question: What do you feel yourself to be: more a citizen of Tatarstan or more a citizen of Russia? Of the Tatars polled, 31.9 per cent said they felt more that they were citizens of both Russia and Tatarstan, 59 per cent felt more citizens of Tatarstan, and 2.7 per cent, more citizens of Russia. In our view, it would be premature to argue from these data that 59 per cent of Tatars are secession-prone. Given the official Tatarstan policy of 'parity nationalism' aimed at fostering a civic 'Tatarstani' nation in a polyethnic society, it is more likely that a large proportion of the people encompassed by that figure see themselves as a (nascent) dual nation desirous of internal sovereignty (Tatars and Russians combined make up 95 per cent of the republic's population). As we have seen, a further 31.9 per cent of the Tatars polled have a 'nested' identity. The argument in favour of an emerging dual, regional nation in Tatarstan seems to be corroborated by the figures in the same poll for ethnic Russians: 35.3 per cent of them identified themselves as citizens of both Russia and Tatarstan, 19.0 per cent felt that they were more citizens of Tatarstan and 36.1 per cent more citizens of Russia. In a more pes-simistic light, the above data could be interpreted differently: the relatively greater attachment of Tatars solely to Tatarstan and of local Russians solely to Russia (with a relatively low pro-Tatarstan identity) may conceal a latent potential for conflict.

Consider the data of another poll taken in Tatarstan by the Russian and Finnish Academies of Science in 1999.[24] The idea of full independence for Tatarstan eventually, along with secession from Russia, was supported by 21 per cent of the Tatars polled (34 per cent of those younger than 30 years of age, 15 per cent of those older than 60) and 8 per cent of the Russians polled. The poll showed that although the attitude of Tatar youth towards Russians is more open than that of the elderly Tatar respondents with respect to multi-ethnic coexistence and religious affairs (more tolerance of mixed marriages and of conversion from Islam to Orthodox Christianity), young people rather more frequently favour Tatar independence, because the idea of independence, as the pollsters remark, is being adopted by Tatar youth along with democratic ideas and is viewed as one of the 'freedoms',

[23] Rashit Akhmetov, 'Amerikantsy sobirayut dosye na Tatarstan', *KRIS*, No. 48 (1995). Quoted from: Lyudmila Tronova, 'Model kompromissov, mira i soglasiya', in *Tatarstanskaya model': mify i real'nost'* (Kazan, Ekopolis, 1997), 43.

[24] Kimmo Kaariainen and Dmitri Furman, 'Tatary i russkiye—veruyushchiye i neveruyushchiye, stariye i molodiye', *Voprosy filosofii*, 11 (1999), 70 and 78.

'rights' and 'equalities' inherent in humankind—the right to self-determination.

From the above data it may be easier to understand that the Shaimiev leadership, in its cautious sovereignizing policies and 'polyethnic' discourse, more or less reflects majority opinion in Tatarstani society on the question of how much sovereignty the republic needs and may actually claim. Given the sizeable proportion of the Tatar population with a nested identity and the low potential for interethnic conflict, the Tatarstan authorities may, as they did under Yeltsin, threaten Moscow with secession without actually seceding, in order to obtain economic concessions, or else, as they are doing under Putin, tone down their claims on Moscow without losing their popularity among the Tatar population. Meanwhile, local Russians are content with interethnic peace in the republic and Tatars feel pride at being citizens of a sovereign republic.

Long-standing and continued injustice

We have referred to Buchanan's view that illegal seizure, occupation by a foreign power and systematic political, cultural and economic discrimination *within recent-enough memory* constitute the only valid claim to secession. This recent memory, in the Tatar case, is undoubtedly the Stalinist period. Indeed, the roots of the secessionist movement in Tatarstan in the late 1980s and the early 1990s lay in a feeling of national humiliation engendered by Soviet and Tsarist policies on nationalities. It was also fostered by the negative social consequences of the Soviet industrialization model (which bred a perception of being second-class citizens among the Tatar rural dwellers who came to the urban Russian-dominated factories in search of work), by the imperilled state of Tatar culture, and by what were perceived as disproportionate economic burdens on Tatarstan citizens in the Soviet Union, who were endowed with oil deposits but lived a life of scarcity.

From a remedial theory standpoint, these complaints would perhaps constitute a valid claim for secession, if it could be proved that the Soviet state had wilfully engineered these injustices in order to create a privileged status for the Russians at the expense of the Tatars, to enable the Russians to rule them. But it is precisely this that cannot be proved.

First of all, Soviet rule had not only negative but also positive aspects for the Tatars. If the Russians had pursued a colonial policy towards the Tatars during the Soviet period, the Bolsheviks would not have created a Tatar Republic in the first place. A colonial Russian majority would have been better off if they had left a Tsarist-era Kazan province in place. For such a majority, a Tatar Republic would have been rather a nuisance, as it would only have created political problems in the event of a Tatar national revival.

The Tatar Bolsheviks had played a major role in making the revolution triumph, and some of them were among the first to be disappointed by its results.

Second, it cannot be proved that the Stalinist terror was a question of Russians against Tatars. Just as there were early Tatar Bolsheviks, so too were there Tatar Stalinists and members of Stalin's secret service. (As a Tatar woman wrote to a local newspaper in 1991: 'As for my father, a Tatar had squealed on him, Tatars tried him, and a Tatar shot him to death.')[25] At least in the case of Tatarstan, the answer to Stalinism is de-Stalinization, not secession.

While secession on the grounds of long-standing discrimination in Tatarstan is currently unwarranted, this cannot be said about the need to safeguard the republic's specific constitutional status within a federal framework as long as its population expresses the will to preserve it. Memories of past injustices, both in Tatarstan and in Russia as a whole, serve as a reminder that democratic consent should be the norm of governance.

Cultural discrimination

Russification policies towards the end of Stalin's era placed serious restrictions on Tatar cultural development. Arguments based on cultural discrimination make reference to the losses suffered by the Tatar intellectual élite and the constricted field of application of Tatar culture. By 1986 the number of books published in Tatar had become fewer than seventy years before. Whereas in 1913 more books were published in the Tatar language than in any other Muslim nation then in Russia's fold, in 1986 the number of book titles was far higher in the Kazakh, Turkmen, or Uzbek languages.[26] The Tatar language was inexorably losing ground, with Russian taking its place. Like some other Turkic peoples in the autonomous republics of the Soviet Union, a large percentage of Tatars (85.6 per cent) spoke their native language but few of them (3.6 per cent) knew it to perfection.[27] Tatar schools were being closed, often at the request of Tatar parents, because Tatar education carried less prestige. The number and circulation of Tatar newspapers and magazines were dwindling. Tatar writers were losing their readership among Tatar youth. These examples could be multiplied.

In the Gorbachev era, Tatar intellectuals linked this sorry state of affairs to the lack of Tatar independence, while Tatar officials ascribed it to the

[25] A. Valeeva, 'Mutanty-nelyudi', *Vechernyaya Kazan*', 13 March 1991.
[26] Quoted from A. Prazauskas, 'Natsional'noe vozrozhdenie v SSSR i postsovetskikh stranakh' in B. Yerasov (ed.), *Tsivilizatsii i kul'tury. Nauchnyi al'manakh*, Issue 2 (Moscow, Institut vostokovedeniya RAN), 1995, 128. It should be mentioned that the decreasing number of books published is a phenomenon of the late Stalinist to Brezhnev periods: in 1940 the number of books in Tatar (as in other national languages) exceeded pre-revolutionary levels.
[27] Data for 1989 cited in S. Klyashtornyi, 'Rossiya i tyurkskiye narody Yevrazii' in Yerasov (ed.), *Tsivilizatsii i kul'tury*, 186.

reduced status of Tatarstan as an autonomous republic rather than a Union republic like Latvia or Azerbaijan. Only the Tatars' own state—so argued the proponents of a sovereign or independent Tatarstan—could provide for the needs of Tatar culture. From perceived cultural discrimination one could argue for both internal sovereignty and independence.

There are good reasons to challenge this kind of discourse. It might be argued that the problems of Tatar culture in Soviet times lay in centralization on the one hand and industrialization on the other. Centralization meant that all decisions, including those on cultural development, were made in Moscow. The result was a disregard for local needs by the centre, the largely voluntary self-Russification of many Tatar parents and upwardly mobile students and professionals (a phenomenon common to most Union republics as well), and the marginalization of the national culture within the provincial framework. Industrialization led to the breakdown of the traditional way of life and a change in the Tatar readership from rural to urban—and to the decreased popularity of Tatar writers who still clung to rural subjects in their works. It may be expected that a less than fully sovereign Tatarstan in a decentralized Russia, along with a greater openness to international culture, will create a friendlier environment for the development of Tatar culture. In our opinion, Russification in the past is no more morally conducive to an independent Tatarstan than a compulsory French education is to the independence of Provence or Brittany. The level of internal autonomy in Tatarstan must naturally be substantial, for historical, cultural, and political reasons.

Discriminatory redistribution

Let us now come to the criterion of discriminatory redistribution. By the time of *perestroika*, Tatarstan could boast of an impressive industrial and agricultural capacity, built not just with its own resources but with funds and labour attracted from many Soviet regions. Its petroleum, chemical, automotive, and aircraft industries made it one of the most developed regions of the USSR. However, accelerated industrial development led to regional imbalances and environmental pollution. More importantly, the region felt that it was not getting adequate recompense for its contribution to the Soviet economy. One of the most commonly expressed claims was that, had Tatarstan been sovereign, the 2.5 billion tons of Tatarstan oil extracted between 1946 and 1990 would have been enough to make Tatarstan a 'second Kuwait'.[28] Instead, it was pumped along the Druzhba ('Friendship') Pipeline to bolster pro-Soviet regimes in Eastern Europe. (The oil of Tatarstan and Bashkortostan was the main source of fuel for the

---

[28] Venera Yakupova, *100 istorii o suverenitete* (Kazan, Idel Press, 2000), 28.

Soviet economy from the 1950s to the 1970s, until Western Siberian oil was discovered.) Another common claim was that Tatarstan was producing more wealth than the three Baltic Soviet republics combined, while its standard of living was markedly lower.

How well founded in the ethical sense are the arguments for secession based on discriminatory redistribution? In fact, every region in the Soviet Union or Russia that had extractive industries could say that it was unjustly treated and that its citizens were receiving less than they ought. Siberia and the Far East could claim that they had been *de facto* reduced to colonial status where the exploitation of mineral resources was concerned. Industrial regions lacking oil and gas deposits, like the Urals, could claim they were at a disadvantage precisely because they had no oil or gas. Tatar journalists and economic managers pointed to the fact that Tatarstan had a greater industrial output than Lithuania, Latvia and Estonia combined. When they did so, they were referring both to the former's lower political status as an autonomous republic, compared with Union republics like Estonia or Latvia, and to the latter's much higher living standards. The argument was heard in the Baltic republics, too, that the Soviet regime had deprived them of the European living standards they could have achieved had they been independent. So the mutual recriminations on economic grounds between Russian regions could be likened to a poor man trying to snatch a crust of bread from another poor man. In our view, the remedial action that these arguments suggest is not secession but economic reform.

Economic viability in the event of secession

Talk of secession for Tatarstan as a means of achieving remedial economic justice is vitiated by the extent to which its economy is integrated into that of Russia and the CIS. Soviet planners had included the republic's industry into the Volga economic region, which is popularly known as 'Russia's automobile workshop', representing a swath of land crossed from east to west by a network of rail and motorways, as well as oil and gas pipelines linking Russia's European portion with the Urals and Siberia. Tatarstan is home to Russia's largest plant producing supersize lorries (KAMAZ). It contains oil deposits (9 per cent of Russia's total) and, as elsewhere in the same region, machine-building, chemical, and petrochemical enterprises. In addition, Russia's arms industries located in Tatarstan are producing items like warplanes, helicopter gunships, and military optical equipment.

It should be noted that the economic base of Tatarstan had been created not *per se*, as one belonging to the Republic of Tatarstan, but as an integral part of the regional and nationwide economy. Raw materials and accessories for Tatarstan's industries come from allied industries of the Volga region and the country as a whole, while its own factories supply others elsewhere in Russia. The economist Padraic Sweeny, writing on Tatarstan in an electronic bulletin for US exporters, points out that its economy profits by close integration with the CIS countries and the regions of the Russian Federation. Conversely, Tatarstan's economy produces machines and products of organic chemistry, but lacks metal; it is endowed with considerable volumes of crude oil, but lacks petrol, kerosene, and other oil products, and much else besides.[29] These wide-ranging ties can hardly be broken, or perhaps they can in the improbable eventuality of an entire vast locality like the Volga region—mostly Russian-populated—seceding from Russia. However, there are academics in Russia who, like the sociologist Igor Yakovenko, believe that if economic decline in Russia continues, the country's break-up is inevitable.[30] In this case, what is improbable today may become probable tomorrow.

Without going into detailed economic analysis, let us note that the unity of the state requires a single labour and commodity market, monetary system, customs, transport infrastructure, and pipeline system. All these are now safely integrated within the nationwide network. For a small republic to break loose from that network, even if peacefully, in the knowledge that its people will surely have to endure economic dislocation ('Better be poor but independent'), would require a supreme effort of will, which—to the nationalists' dismay—is so far not in evidence. In the worst case, an attempt by Tatarstan to secede would mean bloodshed, while staying 'inside' would mean peace with incomplete sovereignty. Tatarstan's enclave position within Russia makes it an economic loser if it secedes from Russia, but a winner if it stays. The Tatarstan leadership knows full well which is the best alternative.

The impossibility and irrelevance of secession in the Tatarstan case does not mean that its internal sovereignty should not be defended. President Putin reversed the relatively lenient policy of his predecessor towards Russia's republics. The emphasis was now on 'gathering the lands' to prevent the perceived danger of the country's disintegration. This entailed harmonization of legislation between the centre and the federation subjects, the re-establishment of a 'power vertical' from top to bottom, and budgetary redistribution in favour of the government exchequer. The presidential authorities disapproved of the mention of sovereignty in local constitutions and sought to eliminate them. As for the power-sharing treaties, on 18 April 2002 in his state-of the-nation address Putin declared that, 'although the Russian Constitution provides for the possibility of concluding such

[29] Padraic J. Sweeney, *Regional Corner: Tatarstan*, posted on the website http://www.iep.doc.gov/bisnis/bulletin/9603tatr.html.
[30] *Argumenty i fakty*, 18–19 (2002), 7.

power-sharing treaties, they give rise to inequality among subjects of the federation, and consequently, among citizens of the country'.[31] Not surprisingly, many regions that had concluded such treaties had them 'voluntarily rescinded'.

As for Tatarstan, the Russian Constitutional Court repeatedly issued injunctions rendering the clauses on 'sovereignty' in the Tatarstan Constitution null and void. The Russian Federation (RF) and Tatarstan Procuracies insisted that the Tatarstan laws, the Power-Sharing Treaty and the Constitution be brought into line with the centre's wishes. The process of harmonization led to the introduction by the Tatarstan State Council of numerous amendments, mostly concerning matters of secondary importance. On issues of principle, however, the Tatarstan legislators did not yield. They retained the modified clause on sovereignty ('beyond the limits of the Russian Federation's competencies'), the controversial clause on Tatarstan citizenship, and rejected the motion of Tatarstan being a 'fully-fledged subject of the Russian Federation'. Thus the republic was not willing to renounce its hard-won sovereignty.

CONCLUSION

We have attempted to explore the relevant criteria that warrant or restrict secessionist claims for Tatarstan, analysing the secessionist process in Tatarstan from the standpoint of both the choice/permissive theory and the remedial/just cause theory. The yardsticks for this analysis were the degree to which Tatar national identity tends towards secession and is opposed to that of the Russian majority, as well as the presence or absence of long-standing and continued injustice, cultural discrimination and discriminatory redistribution. Also touched upon were the criteria of geopolitical, demographic, and economic viability. Within the contextual frame of reference, it was necessary to analyse the evolution of the Tatar national and cultural identity and to give a brief outline of the struggles for sovereignty carried on in Tatarstan in 1987–94. The context in which those struggles were waged was the break-up of the USSR and the first steps of the new, post-communist Russia. The difference between the two situations also explains the different outcome of secessionist battles by the former Union republics against the USSR and those by the Tatar nationalists against the Russian Federation in the early years of Yeltsin's rule.

It appears that both these theoretical approaches have much to offer for an assessment of the scope and limits of Tatarstan's struggle for sovereignty. The above analysis shows that, to take up the choice theory argument that a

---

[31] Quoted from RFE/RL Tatar-Bashkir Service. Daily Review From Tatarstan, 19 April 2002. www.azatliq.org

claim to secession may be generated by a separate region-nation that seeks autonomy or independence from the majority, the Tatars constitute a nation whose majority now wants internal sovereignty in a multi-ethnic society, not secession. Arguing from remedial theory, one can prove that various forms of past discrimination are, here, not of a nature to ground secession. They may be addressed by federal and economic reform.

What does Tatarstan need, after all? The fundamental demand is for the guaranteed opportunity to develop its culture to ensure its reproduction. Internal sovereignty coupled with limited external sovereign powers, the goal hitherto espoused by Tatarstan, means to have one's own constitution, parliament and government dealing with matters of the republic's exclusive competence as agreed in the 1994 treaty between Russia and Tatarstan; symbolic, dual Russian–Tatarstani citizenship; limited powers in foreign affairs; state symbols (flag, coat-of-arms, anthem and passport with pages written in the national language and bearing the republic's state emblems); and the right to legislate on and implement its own economic, cultural, and religious policies. Such limited sovereignty in internal matters is, for all the reasons mentioned above, preferable to striving to attain the goal of full independence.

In the Tatar view, the fact that the rights of the Tatar Autonomous Soviet Republic (the Tatar ASSR) were curtailed in the Soviet period requires special status for Tatarstan as a state associated with the Russian Federation. Satisfying these claims in some form or other appears to be justified. The best variant from the standpoint of safeguarding the rights of the federation subject would be to have Tatarstan's special status incorporated in the Russian constitution. The cherished goal of the advocates of Tatarstan sovereignty is to ensure that the rights formalized in the 1994 treaty be given a constitutionally guaranteed form in keeping with the concept of 'federalism from below'. But the federal centre is wary of contemplating the adoption such a constitutional provision. Fearing a split-off of Russia's ethnic groups, it is reluctant to accord one or several federation subjects the rights denied others. On the other hand, the Tatarstan leaders are unable to wrest such a constitutional reform from the centre. And this means that secessionist struggles, put on hold during Putinization, may erupt at some point in the future.

8

Chechnya: A Just War Fought Unjustly?

Richard Sakwa

INTRODUCTION

The Chechen bid for independence challenges existing theories of secession and ideas about national self-determination.[1] It has also come to threaten the basis of post-Cold War universalism, focused as it is on the ideology of human rights and the duty of international intervention in the internal affairs of states if they are perceived to be abusing their own population. The case, above all, focuses attention on the normative and political preparedness of a people for independence, while at the same time highlighting the limits of partition as the solution to the problems of divided communities. An associated question is the mutability and irreversibility of history from the perspective of the international community at large, and the perception of history in the eyes of the people who are the subject of secession. What is the basis for state sovereignty, and under what conditions should it be recognized by the international community? Under what conditions can 'world society' assert its proclaimed duty of defending the rights of individuals across state borders?

For the Chechen leadership independence appeared the natural conclusion of their centuries-long struggle against Russian domination; but the struggle also pitted one strand of international law (the right of nations to self-determination) against another (the territorial integrity of states and the inviolability of borders). The struggle threw into sharp relief the tension between the prerogatives of states to maintain their territorial integrity and the proclaimed rights of the international community to defend individuals within that state. From the perspective of international and domestic

---

[1] For a recent survey see Benyamin Neuberger, 'National Self-Determination: A Theoretical Discussion', *Nationalities Papers*, 29:3 (2001), 391–418.

law, the two Russian military campaigns in Chechnya are part of its internal affairs. The Russian authorities insisted that states have the right to defend their territorial unity and to combat terrorism. Throughout the campaigns there was a tension between arguments based on sovereignty and security, a tension that was exacerbated after the 11 September 2001 events and the creation of an international 'coalition against terrorism', of which Russia under president Vladimir Putin formed a willing part.

In so far as the right to wage war is concerned (*jus ad bellum*), the international community has not objected to the Russian policies. However, Western governments have insisted that the war should be conducted (*jus in bello*) within the framework of the considerable body of normative humanitarian values enshrined in numerous international documents and subscribed to by Russia itself, for example, when it joined the Council of Europe in February 1996. Russia's decision to wage war in 1994, while understandable because of the attempted unilateral secession of an area that was legally a part of the Russian Federation, tends to be regarded as ultimately politically and morally wrong, especially since the military campaign itself was waged in such an indiscriminate manner. The second war from September 1999, however, has garnered rather more support as a just war because of the more pronounced aspects of justified self-defence. The Chechen insurgents, from their side, considered that their overriding historically based claim to national self-determination transformed their own struggle into a just war. Within the framework of Allen Buchanan's remedial theory of secession,[2] the Chechens could argue that they had long been the victims of repression and inadequate representation in Russia's governing bodies. The Russian government could argue that this had nothing to do with them because the Russian Federation since 1991 had become a democracy based on universal citizenship, the federal separation of powers and the repudiation of communist and pre-Soviet excesses—and the defence of the integrity of this new post-imperial smaller Russia. The impeccable logic of various just war conceptions thus collided, exposing the contradictions in international law, political conventions, and mediatory practices.

The Chechen crisis erupted at the end of the Cold War. It was accompanied by one of the most intensive periods of nation-state formation of the twentieth century, comparable only to the period following World War I. The two largest communist federations disintegrated, according to Lukic and Lynch, because their federal systems had been constructed on the basis

---

[2] Allen Buchanan, *Secession: The Morality of Political Divorce From Fort Sumter to Lithuania and Quebec* (Boulder, CO, Westview Press, 1991). For a summary of his argument, see his 'Democracy and Secession', in Margaret Moore (ed.), *National Self-Determination and Secession* (Oxford, Oxford University Press, 1998), 14–33.

of ethnic rather than civic identities, imbuing the USSR and Yugoslavia with
the political characteristics of empires rather than the multilevel bargaining
typical of federations.[3] The Cold War had been accompanied by the freezing
of states, with only one successful case of secession between 1947 and 1991
(Bangladesh in December 1971).[4] Just as in the earlier period, new states
meant new minorities.[5] The establishment in 1991 of fifteen new states on
the basis of the old Union republics of the Soviet Union was relatively
unproblematic, but the question then shifted to the extent to which these
newly independent states would themselves fragment. Several Union
republics included autonomous entities or breakaway regions, which
claimed an enhanced political status. Georgian unity was challenged by
Abkhazia and South Ossetia, Moldova by the bid for independence by
Transdniestria, and Ukraine by the struggle for Crimean autonomy. The separation of one state was accompanied by attempts to achieve secession
within the secession: in the case of Russia by Chechnya and to a lesser degree
by Tatarstan. Unlike the Soviet constitution, which guaranteed Union
republics the right of secession (Art. 17 of the 1977 'Brezhnev' constitution),
the Russian constitution adopted in December 1993 grants no such right:
Article 27.2 guarantees individuals the right to leave the country but there is
no collective right of secession. The 1993 constitution, moreover, unlike the
1992 Federation Treaty (signed in March of that year between the units of
Russia), no longer views the ethnic republics as sovereign.

THE CHECHEN REVOLUTION

The distinctive legacy of Soviet ethno-federalism took the form of the
emergence of twenty-one republics within Russia, each dominated by a titular or group of titular nationalities (fourteen in the case of Dagestan).
However, in contrast to the USSR, where by 1991 ethnic Russians made up
barely 50 per cent of the population, in the Russian Federation at independence they comprised 81 per cent of Russia's 148 million population. In
only seven of the republics did the titular nationality comprise more than
half of the population.[6] One of these was Chechnya.[7]

---

[3] Reneo Lukic and Allen Lynch, *Europe From the Balkans to the Urals: The Disintegration of
Yugoslavia and the Soviet Union* (Oxford, SIPRI and Oxford University Press, 1996).

[4] The case of Singapore is rather different since it was expelled from the Malaysian
Federation in August 1965.

[5] In the post-World War I period, minorities made up 35 per cent of the newly-established
Czechoslovakia's population, 30.4 of Poland's and 25 per cent of Romania's.

[6] Chechnya, Ingushetia (these two were united at the time), Kabardino-Balkaria, Dagestan
(with many titular nationalities), North Ossetia, Chuvashia, and Tuva.

[7] According to the 1989 census the population of the Chechen–Ingush republic was 1.27
million, of whom 735,000 were Chechens, 164,000 Ingush and 294,000 Russians (including

Chechnya was the only republic in Russia where the transition to a post-Soviet order was accompanied by a national revolution that overthrew the old *nomenklatura* élites and the residual institutions of Soviet power. One of the reasons for the relative ease with which radicals seized the republic is that, unlike most other ethnic groups in the USSR, Chechens had not been allowed to have significant representation in the leading bodies of their own republic. There was no significant local ethnic élite trained in political management;[8] instead, the Chechen ruling group that came to power in the Chechen revolution was schooled in war rather than in the Soviet administrative skills of bureaucratic advantage and balance, let alone the pluralistic arts of compromise and negotiation.

It was only in the late 1980s that a Chechen for the first time was entrusted with power in a republic that was created in their name. Doku Zavgaev was elected first secretary of the Communist Party of the republic in June 1989, defeating Moscow's Russian candidate in an act typical of *perestroika's* cultivation of national-patriotic forces. The Supreme Soviet of Chechnya-Ingushetiya, with Zavgaev's support, adopted a declaration of sovereignty in November 1990. Russia itself had adopted its declaration of sovereignty on 12 June 1990, and although these declarations fell short of demanding independence they precipitated various 'wars of the laws' between the different levels of the Soviet federal structure. In the March 1991 referendum on the renewal of the Soviet Union, turnout in Chechnya-Ingushetiya (at 58.8 per cent) was lower than in any other of Russia's national republics, but three-quarters of those who voted supported the plans of the Soviet president, Mikhail Gorbachev, for a reformed Soviet federation. In the Russian presidential election of June 1991, 80 per cent of the vote in the republic went to Boris Yeltsin, who had campaigned in favour of the greater autonomy of Russia's national units.

The Chechen revolution, however, quickly outran any attempts at reform within the system. While structural and historical factors no doubt played their part, in the first instance it was intra-élite struggle that precipitated a revolutionary outcome, and not only in Chechnya.[9] In November 1990 the

Cossacks) (RSFSR v tsifrakh v 1989g. (Moscow, Finansy i statistika, 1990); 530,000 had been urban and 705,000 rural (*SSSR: administrativno-territorial'noe delenie soyuznikh respublik* (Moscow, Prezidium Verkhovnogo Soveta SSSR, 1987), 60). The population of Ingushetia alone was some 300,000, while in the capital, Grozny, about half the population of 400,000 was Russian.

8 Nabi Abdullaev, 'Chechnya is Facing Personnel Vacuum', The Jamestown Foundation, *Prism*, April 2001.
9 As Hahn comments, 'Dudaev's regime was encouraged by party apparatchiki to challenge RSFSR control as a way of making Yeltsin pay for his calls to Russia's autonomous republics to "take as much sovereignty as you can swallow"', Gordon M. Hahn, *Russia's Revolution from Above, 1985–2000: Reform, Transition, and Revolution in the Fall of the Soviet Communist Regime* (New Brunswick, NJ, Transaction Publishers, 2002), 473.

first draft of Gorbachev's Union treaty was published that conferred on 'republics that are part of other republics' the right to participate in the renewal of the Soviet Union on an equal footing with Union republics themselves.[10] In other words, Russia's declaration of sovereignty was to be countered by stimulating sovereignty aspirations of the Autonomous republics within Russia. In Chechnya, Zavgaev sought to deflect the challenge by co-opting the movements that in the summer of 1990 came together to form an Acting Committee of the All-National Congress of the Chechen People (the Chechen National Congress), an informal body made up of clan elders and excluding much of the urban population. This organization, with Yeltsin's support, had been intended to put pressure on the Soviet leadership and on Gorbachev personally. The Chechen National Congress, however, soon entered into opposition to its initiator, Zavgaev. In March 1991 Major-General Djohar Dudaev (1944–96) was elected leader of the Congress, and the Chechen revolution moved beyond attempts to liberalize and 'nationalize' the regime. Dudaev had been the first Chechen to attain the rank of general in the Soviet air force, having served in Afghanistan. He commanded a flight of strategic bombers stationed in Tartu in the late 1980s and early 1990s where, in January 1991, he had prevented Soviet special forces from attacking Estonian separatists and had thus become something of a local hero.

Zavgaev's equivocations during the August 1991 coup of Soviet conservatives against Gorbachev revealed the bankruptcy of his attempt to manoeuvre between Gorbachev's Soviet power and Yeltsin's nascent Russian state. The power vacuum was brilliantly exploited by Dudaev, who in effect staged a coup that was as farcical as it was effective.[11] Following the failure of the August coup the Chechen National Congress met in the Chechen capital, Grozny, to consider the implications for the republic. Under the leadership of Dudaev, who had resigned from the air force in May 1991, a group of armed men stormed the government buildings and overthrew the rule of Zavgaev. New presidential elections took place in Chechnya on 27 October. They were won by Dudaev, a victory that remains contested to this day, taking place as they did at gun point and with the electoral authorities appointed by Dudaev himself.[12] The subsequent unilateral declaration of

[10] *Pravda*, 24 Nov. 1990.

[11] By far the best analysis of the events of this period is by Dzhabrail Gakaev, 'Put' k chechenskoi revolyutsii', in D. E. Furman (ed.), *Chechnya i Rossiya: obshchestva i gosudarstva*, vol. iii of *Mir, progress, prava cheloveka* (Moscow, Publications of the Andrei Sakharov Museum and Public Centre, 1999), 150–76, at p. 168, who notes the farcical elements.

[12] Dudaev won 90 per cent of the votes cast, 63 per cent of the total electorate, *Moskovskie novosti*, 6 (19–26 Feb. 1995), 6. Gakaev, 'Put' k chechenskoi revolyutsii', 169 describes the irregularities. Dunlop, however, takes a rather more benign view, arguing that public opinion polls at the time in Chechnya suggested that some 60 per cent of the population supported Dudaev, John Dunlop, *Russia Confronts Chechnya: Roots of a Separatist Conflict* (Cambridge, Cambridge University Press, 1998), 114–15. While the flawed election may have reflected the popular will,

independence ('Act of Sovereignty of the Republic') of 1 November enjoyed far from universal support, although ratified the next day by the newly elected Chechen parliament (legislative elections had also taken place on 27 October). While the insurgency adopted the idiom of a national liberation struggle against an alien oppressor, a large proportion of the population (Russians and ethnic Chechens alike) were alienated by the violent manner in which power had been seized. Dudaev's rule lacked domestic legitimacy, shifting power from the urbanized, educated, and Sovietized élites of the lowland areas to the less urbanized and traditionally more anti-Russian and anti-Soviet groups of the Southern highlands.

The political struggles in Moscow itself were to have baleful consequences on Chechen-Russian relations, in particular the conflicts between Yeltsin and Gorbachev (Russia and the Soviet Union), and between Yeltsin and Ruslan Khasbulatov (the Russian executive and legislative), that paralysed attempts at forging a coherent and consistent response. Khasbulatov, an ethnic Chechen who had been deported to Central Asia in 1944[13] and who in 1990 had been elected to the Russian parliament as a deputy from Chechnya, was one of the most intemperate opponents of Chechen independence. At the same time, he sought to gain a privileged position in mediating between Moscow and Chechnya. According to the Chechen liberal Yusup Soslambekov, Khasbulatov in the late summer of 1991 had wanted to place his own team in charge of the Chechen government, but Yeltsin, fearing any augmentation of Khasbulatov's power, had preferred Dudaev.[14] The choice was fateful for both Russia and Chechnya, and reflected the factional infighting, corruption, and incompetence prevalent at the time. Russia's relations with Chechnya throughout were highly contradictory: ranging from a liberal response that was prepared to accept Chechnya gaining its independence, through to a neo-imperial approach that insisted on Chechnya remaining part of the country come what may. In between was the view that Chechnya could become independent as long as it negotiated a deal that ensured Russian economic interests (above all, protection of the pipelines and rail connections that crossed the territory), the rights of the non-Chechen population within Chechnya, and the security of the Southern borders of the country.

in the absence of any effective political checks and balances the voting was more a plebiscite than a democratic election where the rights of the minorities are protected and represented.

[13] 387,000 Chechens and 91,000 Ingush were deported to Central Asia (primarily to Kazakhstan), of whom at least a quarter died on the way. In 1991 a third of Chechens living at that time were returnees with memories of those bitter days. For his own description of the exile, see Ruslan Khasbulatov, *The Struggle for Russia: Power and Change in the Democratic Revolution*, ed. and introd. by Richard Sakwa (London and New York, Routledge, 1993), 3–4, 11–12.

[14] Liz Fuller, 'Death of a Chechen Pragmatist', *RFE/RL Newsline*, 4 Aug. 2000.

On 2 November the Fifth Russian Congress of People's Deputies, chaired by Khasbulatov, resolved that neither the presidential nor the parliamentary elections in the Chechen Republic were legal, and that their orders were not to be fulfilled. On 7 November 1991 Yeltsin declared a state of emergency in Chechnya (and then disappeared from view), but Gorbachev (after the failure of the August coup still president of the vestigial USSR) refused to allow the federal security and interior forces to support the Russian action.[15] This was allegedly in revenge for Russia's refusal to support his apparent attempts to subdue the Baltic republics by force in January 1991.[16] Russia's attempts to end dual sovereignty on its own territory was reiterated in Gorbachev's attempt to end dual sovereignty on Soviet territory, an irony that was lost on few. The lightly armed Russian troops flown into Grozny on the night of 8 to 9 November were captured and then sent back to Russia by Dudaev's forces. Lacking the military strength to subdue the insurgent regime, the Russian Supreme Soviet on 10 November reversed the decision to impose a state of emergency.[17] In three days Dudaev had been transformed from a comic operetta adventurer, with his gangster hat and strange moustache, into a genuine national hero. As Gakaev argues, it was Moscow's policies (or lack thereof) that ensured the victory of the Chechen revolution.[18] The Chechen crisis was transformed from an intra-Chechen élite struggle for power onto the plane of a Russo-Chechen national contest.

One of the reasons why Russia failed to find an adequate response to the Chechen crisis was that the post-communist trajectory of both Russia and Chechnya developed in parallel. In Furman's words,

These were problems associated with managing a society that had lost its totalitarian governing system but failed to establish a new democratic one; not knowing how to live in democratic conditions and hence shifting towards criminal anarchy. And both sought to resolve the problems by similar methods—through strengthening presidential power, which took on an authoritarian character (though not

---

[15] Gorbachev ordered an end to all troop movements in the region, Andrei Grachev, *Kremlëvskaya khronika* (Moscow, EKCMO, 1994), 277–8.

[16] According to Khasbulatov, Gorbachev directly stated: 'At that time [Jan. 1991] you did not allow me to introduce a state of emergency; do you remember how you [the Russian authorities headed by Yeltsin] got so excited?', reported by Gakaev, 'Put' k chechenskoi revolyutsii', in Furman (ed.), *Chechnya i Rossiya*, 170, from *Solidarnost'*, No. 13 (110), 1995. Russia's anger at Gorbachev's act of revenge contributed to the Belovezhskaya Pushcha (Minsk) secession of Russia, Belarus and Ukraine from the USSR on 8 Dec. 1991. It would be going too far to suggest that the Chechen secession bid was responsible for the disintegration of the USSR, but it was certainly one of the (often overlooked) nails in the coffin.

[17] It was precisely Russia's retreat at this moment that is seen by many Russian politicians, like Yabloko deputy Alexei Arbatov, as marking the fateful point when the legitimate use of force gave way to a cycle of Russian retreats that ultimately provoked catastrophic wars. Conversation with the present author, Tel Aviv, 7 April 2000.

[18] Gakaev, 'Put' k chechenskoi revolyutsii', in Furman (ed.), *Chechnya i Rossiya*, 171.

thereby becoming any more effective), the dissolution of parliaments, and strengthening their power through privatisation...to enrich and buy off whoever was required.[19]

Russia's state-building endeavours came into contradiction with Chechnya's nation-building aspirations, but both were mediated by the prevalence of group interests and élite struggles. Paradoxically, it was not the strength of the Russian government or of the Chechen insurgents that ultimately led to war, but their weakness.

NO WAR, NO PEACE

Dudaev gained time to consolidate his hold on the republic and to arm himself, especially since the withdrawing Russian forces later that year and into 1992, for reasons that have never yet been adequately explained, left behind the bulk of their weaponry.[20] Yeltsin now had three years to get used to Chechnya's *de facto* separation, although the republic's independence was not recognized by any state. The imposition of an economic blockade accelerated the descent of the republic into anarchy. The precise status sought by Dudaev for Chechnya remains a matter of controversy, veering between the demand for outright independence from Russia, membership of a reconstituted Soviet Union, to achieving for Chechnya no more than what Russia had granted Tatarstan.[21] A powerful lobby in Moscow, however, resisted all talk of making concessions to Chechnya. The group was led by Sergei Shakhrai, nationalities minister and later deputy prime minister; Nikolai Yegorov, who followed Shakhrai as nationalities minister; and Sergei Filatov, Yeltsin's chief of staff. Shakhrai in particular, according to Dunlop, was opposed to Yeltsin making concessions to Chechnya of the sort that had been on offer to Tatarstan. He allegedly whispered poison in Yeltsin's ear that Dudaev had insulted him as an individual. Given Yeltsin's personalized leadership style and highly developed *amour propre*, had devastating political consequences, leading to the adoption of an uncompromising negotiating stance that required the removal of Dudaev from power.[22]

---

[19] Dmitrii Furman, 'Samyi trudnyi narod dlya Rossii', in Furman, *Chechnya i Rossiya*, 6–7.

[20] For a discussion of the issue, see O. Orlov and A. V. Cherkasov (eds.), *Rossiya–Chechnya: tsep' oshibok i prestuplenii*, (Moscow, Memorial/Zven'ya, 1998), 103–8. One of the best accounts is the chapter by Robert Seely 'Dudayev's Regime: The Handover of Soviet Military Hardware', in his *Russo-Chechen Conflict, 1800–2000: A Deadly Embrace* (London, Frank Cass, 2001), 114–41.

[21] Rafael Khakimov, adviser to the Tatarstan president Mintimir Shamaev and witness to meetings of the Council of Heads of Republics in the early post-Soviet years, insisted that Dudaev would have been satisfied with the latter. Personal discussion with the author, London, 28 June 2001.

[22] Shakhrai may well have had a national animus against Dudaev. Shakhrai is a Terek Cossack, a group that had long been in conflict with Chechens.

Dudaev himself faced enormous problems in imposing his authority on the republic.[23] Large parts of Chechnya refused to accept Dudaev's authority, including Zavgaev's home region, Nadterechnyi district. One oppositional group after another was crushed. Chechnya (having formally separated from the Ingush Republic in 1992) soon became the centre of arms, narcotics, and money laundering operations as it spiralled into lawlessness. Trains passing through the region were regularly robbed. In April 1993 Dudaev violently dissolved the Chechen parliament and dispersed demonstrations and any institutional opposition to his rule.

Few in the Russian political establishment advocated war, and it was only when the threat to Russia itself from Chechen criminality became so great that direct action was undertaken. As Lieven insists, 'there was no question of a refusal to grant autonomy to Chechnya'.[24] The problem, however, was far deeper than that. Carl Schmitt talked in terms of the collapse of the political into the social in the Weimar Republic, where social forces overwhelm legal and political structuration.[25] In the context of relative state and political crisis, the idea of 'Weimar Russia' has been advanced.[26] However, it is in Chechnya that Schmitt's insight has the greatest validity. Banditry has deep roots in Chechen tradition, and for many was less a crime than a social tradition, which not only encapsulated resistance to a specific occupier but also represented resistance to the very idea of authority itself. While Khasbulatov may have characterized events in Chechnya under Dudaev as a 'peasants' revolt' (which he dismissed as 'the ugliest, the most stupid and most dangerous political phenomenon[27]), the reality is perhaps even worse: a bandits' revolt the like of which has rarely been seen before.

This prevented Chechnya signing a bilateral treaty with Russia in the period of transformation of the Russian Federation into an independent state, something that would have avoided war. In August 1990 Yeltsin had urged the federation subjects to 'take as much sovereignty as you can swallow'.[28] Consistent in this if in little else, the sovereignty of the centre was eroded in a process called by Katznelson in a different context the *parcelization of*

[23] For a perceptive and sympathetic analysis of Dudaev's dilemmas, see Taimaz Abubakarov, 'Mezhdu avtoritarnostyu i anarkhiei (Politicheskie dilemmy prezidenta Dudaeva)', in Furman (ed.), *Chechnya i Rossiya*, 177–96.
[24] Anatol Lieven, *Chechnya: Tombstone of Russian Power* (New Haven and London, Yale University Press, 1998), 84.
[25] See George Schwab, *The Challenge of the Exception: An Introduction to the Political Ideas of Carl Schmitt between 1921 and 1936*, 2nd edn. (New York, Greenwood Press, 1989).
[26] Notably by Alexander Yanov, *Weimar Russia: And What We Can Do About It* (New York, Slovo, 1995).   [27] Lieven, *Chechnya*, 79.
[28] Boris Yeltsin repeated this injunction to Russia's federation subjects on the eve of his impeachment vote in the Duma in May 1999.

sovereignty.[29] The continuing crisis of the state and the economy allowed some of the republics to expand their *de facto* sovereignty by adopting laws that created a legal space that became increasingly distinct from that established by Moscow. In the vanguard of this process, dubbed 'disassociation by default', were Tatarstan, Bashkortostan, Khakassia, and Yakutia. The unifying role of the military was lost, and indeed, the army became increasingly dependent on the regional authorities. The federal authorities were unable to guarantee basic civil rights in the regions, and even lost control over regional affiliates of state agencies. The local branches of the procuracy, the MVD (internal ministry) and other ministries fell into the hands of governors and local presidents.

The Chechen constitution, adopted in March 1992, proclaimed in its Preamble that the Chechen Republic was an 'independent and sovereign state'.[30] Such a unilateral formulation was clearly unacceptable to the Russian side, and various attempts to regularize Chechnya's status within some loose federal framework came to nothing. Hopes that an enhanced Tatarstan-type of bilateral treaty could be formulated foundered on the unilateral dynamics that informed the negotiating positions of both sides. Chechnya's status entered a limbo. As a *de facto* state it joined a rather large family (some 200) of putative actors on the world stage.[31] The Russian constitution of 12 December 1993 accepted the existence of a Chechen Republic (which was separated from Ingushetiya), but as one study argued from the perspective of Russian constitutional law: 'According to the constitution there is a Chechen Republic, but in practice, there isn't. There is no constitution, no president, no parliament, and no laws. Even its territory is not precisely defined.'[32]

Despite the competing sovereignty claims, war was not inevitable and some sort of federal solution may have been possible.[33] The Russian government and Chechnya on several occasions came close to agreement, but personality clashes prevented a negotiated political regularization of the conflict.[34] In 1992 the Russian Supreme Soviet and representatives of the

[29] I. Katznelson, *City Trenches* (Chicago, Chicago University Press, 1981).
[30] http://www.uni-wuerzburg.de/law/cc00000.html
[31] See Scott Pegg, *International Society and the De Facto State* (Cheltenham, Ashgate, 1998).
[32] Igor Zadvornov and Aleksandr Khalmukhamedov, 'Posle pobedy: o perekhodnom periode v politicheskoi istorii Chechenskoi Respubliki', *Osobaya papka NG*, 2:5 (29 Feb. 2000), 9.
[33] James Hughes, for example, argues against 'historicist' and 'ethnic' war accounts of the etiology of the Chechen conflicts of the 1990s: 'Chechnya: the Causes of a Protracted Post-Soviet Conflict', *Civil Wars*, 4:4 (Winter 2001), 1–48. However, Dudaev's insistence on a political settlement according to the principles of a confederation—which includes a unilateral right to secession—and his conception of sovereignty as being indivisible made a compromise solution very difficult. This is argued by Bruno Coppieters, *Federalism and Conflict in the Caucasus* (London, Royal Institute of International Affairs, 2001), 14–20.
[34] These are described, for example, by Dunlop, *Russia Confronts Chechnya*, ch. 4.

Chechen government conducted negotiations on at least ten occasions, and on one reached a political compromise that would have granted most Chechen demands.[35] The signing of the multiple Federation Treaty in March 1992 removed one of the main concerns of the Russian negotiators, the fear of the uncontrolled disintegration of the Russian Federation. Only Chechnya and Tatarstan remained out of the process. Relations between Tatarstan and the Moscow authorities were regularized by the signing of the bilateral treaty between the two parties in February 1994, granting Tatarstan extensive rights and affiliating Tatarstan to Russia on the basis of the treaty and the constitutions of the two states. Only Chechnya was left to formalize its status.

No region except Chechnya now sought outright independence. Instead, many turned towards 'legal separatism', the adoption of laws by regional and local governments that contradict federal legislation. By 1997, the constitutions of nineteen out of twenty-one ethno-federal republics violated the federal constitution, while about one-third of regional laws and regulations violated federal legislation or the constitution. By July 1998 the federal government had signed forty-six power-sharing treaties with forty-two regions and republics. Relations between the federal authorities and the other (non-Chechen) eighty-eight regions of Russia, however, remained political, in that a bargaining process was in operation, typically focused on Yeltsin's personal relationship with the regional leader in question. Politics is here defined as the structured and peaceful contestation of accepted legitimate alternatives. Elie Kedourie distinguished between constitutional and ideological politics,[36] with the former based on law and the acceptance of contestation, whereas the latter was directed towards the achievement of some perfect end state and considered society no more than a *tabula rasa* to achieve this goal. We build on this distinction to suggest that in Chechnya national-secessionism emerged as a particularly virulent form of ideological politics, fuelled not so much by utopian aspirations but by an uncritical historicism, closing down the scope for discussion of the past and the contestation of different policies for the future. According to Soslambekov, a member of the dissolved Chechen parliament and the chair of its Foreign Affairs Commission who split with the Chechen leader, Dudaev's methods ran counter to common sense: 'Rather than taking as his guidelines the norms of international law, from day one of his term as president he chose the path of confrontation...in regulating relations with the Russian Federation.'[37]

---

[35] The protocol drawn up by the Sochi meeting, 12–14 March 1992, Dunlop, *Russia Confronts Chechnya*, 169.

[36] Elie Kedourie, *Nationalism*, 4th edn. (Oxford, Blackwell, 1993), xiii–xiv.

[37] Soslambekov, the author of *Chechnya: The View From Within*, was gunned down in a Moscow street on 18 July 2000 and died nine days later at the age of 44. Cited in Fuller, 'Death of a Chechen Pragmatist'.

By contrast, in Tatarstan under Shaimiev similar goals—to achieve national autonomy and greater self-management—were achieved by constitutional and peaceful means.

If Zavgaev had remained in power, then Chechnya may have developed like Tatarstan; although it should be noted that leaders like Zavgaev *did* come to power in most of the republics of the North Caucasus, but none of them have been of the calibre of a Shaimiev able to conclude a Tatarstan-type economic, let alone political, treaty. The relative ease with which Zavgaev was overthrown, however, revealed precisely the weakness of *nomenklatura* rule in Chechnya, and thus the socio-political basis for the development of the Tatarstan variant in Chechnya was largely absent. Attempts in the 1980s to achieve the indigenization (*korenizatsiya*) of Soviet rule were belated, while the ethnically segmented pattern of economic development deprived the *nomenklatura* of broad support, allowing the insurgent part of the Sovietized élite (represented by Dudaev) to come to power by appealing to marginalized groups in society.

THE FIRST CHECHEN WAR, 1994–6

In the end, the Russian side decided that the only solution was a replacement of the Chechen leadership by exploiting the divisions within Chechen society. Throughout the spring and summer of 1994 a covert war was launched against the regime, managed by the Federal Counter-Intelligence Service (FSK) led by Sergei Stepashin. The use of proxies and clumsy direct intervention proved singularly ineffective (notably in a failed uprising on 26–27 November 1994), and indeed only strengthened the insurgent regime in Grozny. The extent of popular support for anti-Dudaev groups is difficult to gauge, but it is clear that opposition to the regime did not automatically translate into support for its opponents; while it is axiomatic that collaboration with Moscow tended to consolidate rather than erode support for Dudaev. By 1994 only Khasbulatov of the pro-Russian Chechens enjoyed any authority in the republic, but following his leadership of the 'parliamentary uprising' of October 1993 and subsequent incarceration in the Lefortovo isolator (until amnestied by the new Duma in February 1994), he remained beyond the pale for Yeltsin. Finally, on 11 December 1994 Russia launched a full-scale invasion of Chechnya, but rather than providing a 'short, victorious war' (as promised Tsar Nicholas II in 1904 in declaring war against Japan), the country became embroiled in a nearly two-year long savage struggle.[38]

---

[38] For background and above all a vivid account of the war, see Carlotta Gall and Thomas De Waal, *Chechnya: Calamity in the Caucasus* (New York, New York University Press, 1998).

Dunlop's view that a negotiated settlement to the Chechen crisis was possible is questioned by the account of the visit of a State Duma delegation
headed by Vladimir Lysenko to the republic in September 1994. The report
insisted that negotiations were impossible as long as Dudaev remained in
power, but urged that 'The Russian army must not take part in the resolution of the intra-Chechen conflict'. It recommended that since the political
crisis within Chechnya could not be resolved, a law imposing a 'special status'
on the Chechen Republic should be adopted.[39] Thomas de Waal defends the
contrary position that a settlement would have been possible, under the
condition that Russian negotiators would have had to have taken into
account Chechen views on history and past injustices:

> The tragedy of Chechnya is that the 1994 war was completely avoidable. Dudayev
> was a poor negotiator. But far more importantly, the administration in Moscow
> lacked any maturity and historical insight in their bargaining process with the
> Chechens. To achieve a peaceful settlement with Dudayev required a gesture of his-
> toric respect for what would have been the Chechens' first ever voluntary submis-
> sion to a Russian state. The failure to meet this challenge was the biggest failure of
> Yeltsin's new Russia.[40]

So why could no agreement be reached? A number of factors are usually
cited: domestic struggles in both countries between the executive and legislature; intrigues within the Kremlin that inhibited coherent policy formulation; and Moscow's threat of the use of force, including covert support for
Dudaev's opponents. Geopolitical factors certainly played their part, including broader questions of Caucasian security and Caspian pipeline politics.[41]
Above all, there were powerful personalities in Moscow (above all Shakhrai)
who opposed granting what they perceived to be excessive concessions to
Chechnya. All these factors suggest that the use of military force was not the
'last resort' solution.

In assessing the question of whether Russia respected the just war principle of 'just cause' when it launched its military operations, the question of
Russian war aims is crucial. While the Chechen insurgents asserted that
Yeltsin was continuing the centuries-long genocidal campaign against
Chechnya, there is no evidence that this was ever one of the Kremlin's purposes. Indeed, serious research on the origins of the Chechen conflict has
gradually moved away from 'abstract formulations of the national question

[39] 'Otchet o poezdke na severnyi Kavkaz gruppy deputatov Gosudarstvennoi Dumy RF dlya
izucheniya situatsii v Chechenskoi respublike i vokrug nee', in Vladimir Lysenko, *Ot Tatarstana
do Chechni (stanovlenie novogo Rossiiskogo federalizma* (Moscow, Institut sovremmenoi politiki,
1995)), 277.
[40] Thomas de Waal, 'Introduction', in Anna Politkovskaya, *A Dirty War: A Russian Reporter
in Chechnya*, trans. John Crowfoot (London, The Harvill Press, 2001), p. xxi.
[41] For a full analysis of these issues see the highly informative study by K. S. Gadzhiev,
Geopolitika kavkaza (Moscow, Mezhdunarodnye otnosheniya, 2001), esp. chs. 6 and 9.

to more concrete and at the same time broader ethno-political problemati-
sation of the question'.[42] The fear of annihilation nevertheless remained
strong in Chechen national consciousness. The deportation of the whole
Chechen population by Stalin in 1944 had framed the life experiences of the
Chechen post-communist élite (Dudaev and Khasbulatov were born in
exile in Kazakhstan). But Yeltsin was not Stalin, and 1994 was not a repeat
of the deportations of 1944. Russia's purpose (insofar as it had coherent war
aims) was not to destroy the Chechen people but to change the leadership
and provide Chechnya with a government amenable to agreement with
Moscow. As there is no evidence that the Chechen fear of annihilation was
still legitimate in 1991, Chechnya did not have a just cause when it proclaimed its independence unilaterally. Russia, to the contrary, had a just
cause when it claimed to protect its territorial integrity.

Notably absent, however, in Russia's normative justifications for armed
intervention was anything about the need to defend the rights of Russians
and other minorities in the republic, although nationalists in Moscow made
much of this factor. A further problem in assessing the just cause principle
is that under Yeltsin there appeared to be a symbiotic relationship between
corruption in Chechnya and in Russia at large: by turning a blind eye to the
latter, the former was allowed to prosper. According to Seely, 'The stumbling
into the 1994 war was a bloody attempt to stop the cancer of corruption in
Russian political and economic life from undermining the fragile foundations of the post-Soviet Russian state'—an incompetent attempt to put an
end to the 'corrupt failings of the previous three years'.[43] Even more, Yeltsin's
claim to be restoring constitutional order in Chechnya looked rather thin
when considered in the context of his ambiguous relationship with the constitution in Russia proper; and the legal basis for the use of regular forces in
a domestic conflict, although condoned by the Constitutional Court,
remained contentious.

Just war theory asserts the need to observe, besides the principles of 'last
resort' and 'just cause', the respect by the Russian executive of the constitutional procedures for launching military operations according to the principle of 'legitimate authority'. From this perspective, the normative basis of
the first war does not look fully secure. The Russian government had the
legitimate authority to protect its territorial integrity, but no attempt was

---

[42] This is the argument of A. N. Smirnov, *Etnopoliticheskie protsessy na Severnom Kavkaze:
osobennosti i osnovnye tendentsii* (Moscow, IMEMO RAN, 2001), 3. It is a view shared by Valerii
Tishkov (the director of the Institute of Ethnography and Anthropology of the Russian
Academy of Sciences), who condemns local, national, and international scholars studying the
region for their partisanship, scholasticism, and overemphasis on historico-cultural and historical debates, in V. A. Tishkov (ed.), *Puti mira na Severnom Kavkaze: Nezavisimyi ekspertnyi
doklad* (Moscow, Institute of Ethnography and Anthropology, 1999), 7.
[43] Seely, *Russo-Chechen Conflict, 1800–2000*, 213.

made to prosecute it in conformity with the 1991 Law on the State of Emergency; Yeltsin had already tried to impose a state of emergency on 7 November 1991, a decree which, as we have seen, had been rescinded by the Russian Supreme Soviet three days later.[44] Concerning the possibility of winning and the balance between costs and benefits of the war according to the normative principles of 'reasonable chance of success' and 'proportionality', liberals in Moscow had long argued that attempts to remove the secessionist Chechen leader by force would lead to high casualties and an Afghan-like guerrilla war against an implacable *mujahadeen* foe.[45] The enemy, moreover, was heavily armed, as we have seen, with weapons left behind when Soviet/Russian forces withdrew following Chechnya's declaration of independence. The costs of a war to the secessionist region are clear, but there are also important implications for the state from which the region is attempting to secede. Protracted warfare in Chechnya clearly degraded the quality of Russian political and social life, especially since there has been a tendency to dehumanize the Chechen insurgents, the Chechens as a people and Russian servicemen. The war poisoned Russian politics and threatened to inhibit Russia's further development as a democracy.

While only few cogent justifications for the operation can be found in terms of *jus ad bellum*, it cannot be justified at all in terms of *jus in bello*. The conduct of the campaign contravened the crucial principles of discrimination and proportionality. The decay of Russia's armed forces meant that discipline and training were appalling and that the army was in no condition to wage a coherent campaign. Instead, raw conscripts were sent into battle, armour was made to advance without infantry cover, and basic elements of reconnaissance and military intelligence were ignored. Brute force and indiscriminate violence were used to compensate for lack of military technique, leading to excessive military losses, large numbers of civilian deaths (many of whom were Russians, the group—predominantly pensioners—that the army had ostensibly come to protect, who had nowhere else to go), and the destruction of civil infrastructure and housing. Military operations used disproportional and indiscriminate force and failed to distinguish between armed fighters and the civilian population. War appeared to have been declared against the whole population of the Chechen Republic, Russians

[44] According to the Russian constitution, it is the prerogative of the Federation Council to confirm a presidential decree on introducing martial law (Art. 102.1.b) or a state of emergency (Art. 102.1.c); this procedure was not followed in this case. The normative basis of the war was finally only regularised with the adoption of a new Law on the State of Emergency in 2001.
[45] e.g. Egor Gaidar, *Dni porazhenii i pobed* (Moscow, Vagrius, 1996), 331. Gaidar himself adopted a strong anti-war position, resigning from the advisory Presidential Council after a year of fruitless protests. For Yeltsin's own position on the war, according to Aron, he 'lied to his former supporters about Chechnya, lied offensively, crudely and brazenly in a Soviet-like manner', see Leon Aron, *Yeltsin: A Revolutionary Life* (London, HarperCollins, 2000), 569.

and Chechens alike, irrespective of whether they had supported or opposed Dudaev's regime. The whole civilian population, above all men of fighting age, were considered legitimate targets. All civilians were effectively treated as 'bandits' and beyond the pale of the law.[46]

Despite brutal Russian tactics, including the use of filtration camps designed to separate combatants from civilians but where both categories suffered horrifically, the Chechen insurgents went on to force Russian concessions of the sort that had been mooted in 1992. It turned out that Russia had the wrong sort of army, one designed to fight great power wars with tanks and nuclear weapons and not guerrillas. The Chechen military leaders, including Dudaev and Aslan Maskhadov, had learnt the art of warfare in Afghanistan, while Shamil Basaev had been trained by Russian special forces in the early 1990s to support their operations in Abkhazia.[47] Russia at several points came close to military victory, notably following the capture of Vedeno in June 1995 that divided Chechen forces into four, a situation that was remedied by Basaev's raid on Budennovsk (Stavropol *krai*) on 14 June, when he took over a thousand hospital patients hostage. The act did much to salvage the fortunes of war for the Chechen insurgents. The Russian prime minister, Viktor Chernomyrdin, personally oversaw the negotiations with the hostage takers, the first time in Russian history (a history replete with terrorism) that the authorities entered into direct negotiation with terrorists. The raid bought the Chechen insurgents time to reassemble their forces to renew the struggle. It was Maskhadov's assault on Grozny in August 1996 that provoked the negotiations with Alexander Lebed, then Secretary of the Security Council, that led to what proved to be a temporary peace.

'DE FACTO' INDEPENDENCE: THE INTER-BELLUM 1996–9

The Khasavyurt agreement of 31 August 1996 effectively granted Chechnya *de facto* independence, stipulating that agreement on the republic's status was to be reached 'according to generally recognized principles and norms of international law' by 31 December 2001.[48] Within the framework of the

---

[46] The military aspects of the war are discussed by Stasys Knezys and Romanas Sedlickas, *The War in Chechnya* (College Station, Tex., Texas A&M University Press, 1999).

[47] Dunlop, *Russia Confronts Chechnya*, 144.

[48] The text of the main Khasavyurt agreement (*Principles*) is in *Nezavisimaya gazeta*, 3 Sept. 1996, 3. This document talked about the terms on which Russian troops would be withdrawn, the framework within which socio-economic relations with Russia would be developed, and insisted that 'The legislation of the Chechen Federation will be based on the observance of human and civic rights, the right of nations to self-determination, the principle of the equality of nations, the maintenance of civic peace, inter-ethnic consensus and the security of all citizens living in the Chechen Republic irrespective of their nationality, religion or other differences'

agreement, on 22 November 1996 the Russian army began to withdraw from the territory, with the last forces leaving on 4 January 1997. It was at this time that Pavel Baev noted that 'Russia's gradual strategic retreat from the Caucasus appears irreversible'.[49] Following presidential elections on 27 January 1997 Maskhadov assumed office for a five-year term with a popular mandate and Russia's tacit approval.[50] The parliamentary elections held at that time allowed the criminal and political worlds formally to merge, with a number of Chechnya's leading mafia figures entering the new legislature.[51] Maskhadov sought to incorporate the former commanders into the new order by offering them government posts (for example, Basaev became the deputy prime minister until his resignation on 9 July 1998); but instead of civilianizing the warlords, it was the government that was militarized. Maskhadov was unable to impose his authority on the field commanders. At the same time, warlords like Basaev increasingly fell under the influence of radical foreign Moslem militants (known as Wahhabis), in particular the Jordanian-born fighter Habib Abd al-Rahman, known as Khattab, who had previously fought in Afghanistan, a link that was retained in later years.[52] Basaev ultimately led a revolt against Maskhadov, and thus destroyed whatever fragile chance Chechnya had of establishing the foundations of statehood.[53]

By 1998 the population of Chechnya had officially fallen to 797,000,[54] but by then at least 300,000 had left, half of them even before the first war in 1994, including a large proportion of the Russians who had worked in the oil industry.[55] The proportion of Russians in the republic's second town, Gudermes, where before the war they comprised half the population, had

(Point 3). In addition, a *Joint Declaration* was issued, signed by Alexander Lebed, Aslan Maskhadov and some other Chechen leaders, outlining 'the principles on which negotiations would take place and on which relations between the Russian Federation and the Chechen Republic would be built', loc cit.

[49] Pavel Baev, *Russia's Policies in the Caucasus* (London, Royal Institute of International Affairs, 1997), 57.

[50] Maskhadov won 63.6% of the vote and Basaev 21.1 per cent on a turnout of 72.2 per cent, Robert Orttung (ed.), *The Republics and Regions of the Russian Federation* (Armonk, NY, M. E. Sharpe, 2000), 71.

[51] Anna Matveeva, *The North Caucasus: Russia's Fragile Borderland* (London, Royal Institute of International Affairs, 1999), 19.

[52] Khattab was born into a Circassian family in Jordan and graduated from the military academy in Amman, and served for several years in King Hussein's Circassian Guard (in the Middle East the term Circassian is used to describe all those originating from the North Caucasus). He fought with the Afghan *mujahadeen* in the 1980s against the Soviet forces, and at that time met Osama bin Laden. For a discussion of links with the Taliban and possibly with al-Qaeda, see The Jamestown Foundation, *Monitor*, 25 Jan. 2002.

[53] For analysis of Chechnya's period of de facto independence, see Timur Muzaev, *Chechenskii krizis-99* (Moscow, Panorama, 1999), and Isabelle Astigarraga, *Tchetchenie: un Peuple Sacrifié* (Paris, L'harmattan, 2000).

[54] Orttung (ed.), *The Republics and Regions of the Russian Federation*, 70.

[55] *Izvestiya*, 21 July 1998.

fallen to 2 per cent.[56] Few refugees chose to return home as the country sank into banditry and social catastrophe. Hostages were taken in order to obtain ransom or were used as slave labour. Their precise number is unknown, but estimates range from 500 to 2,000. Unemployment stood at least at 75 per cent, with all the main infrastructural elements of a modern state at a standstill, above all health, education, and law enforcement. The limited funds made available by Moscow for rebuilding disappeared without trace. No state recognized the independence of the republic, hence no major international funds were available for reconstruction. After three years of lawlessness even the chief mufti of Chechnya, Akmed-hadji Kadyrov, a hero of the first war, called for the permanent stationing of Russian troops in the republic to protect the population from the endemic lawlessness. The warlords had destroyed the opportunity for Chechnya to develop into a viable and independent society. The victory was a Pyrrhic one indeed. The war that had made the Chechen state possible rendered its existence untenable.

On taking control of Chechnya for the second time in August 1996 the 'secular' judicial system was in effect replaced by *sharia* (Islamic) courts. This ran counter to the human rights policy proclaimed in the Russian constitution and later normative acts and obligations, above all those undertaken as part of membership of the Council of Europe.[57] Secession in the Chechen case led to a retrogression in the normative framework of human rights and was accompanied by wholesale 'demodernization'. The war had already provoked a return to the archaic elements within Chechen society, focused above all on its pre-modern clan structure. The traditional division of Chechen society into highlanders and lowlanders (*gorskikh* versus *mirnykh*) was intensified. This was accompanied by the strengthening of *adat* or customary law, to fill the vacuum left by the collapse of civil institutions.

Above all, the *teip* as a social institution took on new life, although in modified forms. A *teip* is an extended kinship community (there were about 130 in Chechnya) consisting of a number of family groups who can trace their origins to a single individual. Every Chechen is obliged to know the history of his own clan (up to seven generations back) and the *teip* to which they belong. In the late Soviet period *teip* identification had become eroded and played little political role, whereas once Dudaev came to power *teip*-like social institutions (what could be called mimetic *teip*ism) became central both to political life and in personal relations.[58] In other words, there was a

---

[56] Vladimir Pozharskii, 'Zhiteli Chechni ustali ot boev', *Nezavisimaya gazeta*, 18 May 2001, 1.

[57] As part of its adjustment to membership, Russia imposed a moratorium on the death penalty in May 1996.

[58] Khasbulatov insisted that the role of the *teip* in Chechen society was greatly exaggerated: 'for a long time neither the *teip*s nor respected elders have played any role at all in social life', 'Gosudarstvo, politika i separatizm', *Nezavisimaya gazeta*, 14 Dec. 2000, 8. Plenty of evidence

wholesale retreat to earlier Chechen traditions: 'the ethnic swallowed up the social.'[59] The leaders of the *teip*s are often referred to as 'elders' (*starosty*), and many of them had far greater authority than any elected leader, and certainly over-shadowed president Maskhadov, who in social terms was regarded as no more than one leader among equals. During the first war each of the field commanders sought the support of his own village and region and considered himself the rightful leader of the country; in practice, they usurped the authority of the elders. The *starosty* were largely marginalized by the leaders of the insurgency. The martial residue of the *teip* system—the war had replaced traditional *teip* values with militarized ones—only reinforced the fragmentation of political authority. Chechen social structure, in short, inhibited the development of an authoritative state which could act as an interlocutor with Moscow and as the focus of Chechen national aspirations.[60]

The fundamental question at this time was procedural. For the first time in its modern history Chechen independence was on the verge of becoming a legal reality. But who or what would come to power? How could secession be managed? A large body of opinion in Russia at that time would have welcomed Chechen independence as long as the country posed no threat to its neighbours and if the civil rights of the entire population living in Chechnya could be guaranteed. The emphasis shifted from the normative to the empirical plane. How could civil peace, government, and the rule of law be restored within Chechnya and the activities of marauders and kidnapping gangs from the republic in neighbouring regions be stopped? The question at this point was not *if* Chechnya would become independent, but *how*: the mechanism of secession was crucial.

The status of the Khasavyurt agreement on 31 August 1996 was controversial. For some (above all the military), seen from the perspective both of Russian state interests and the majority of the Chechen people, it was considered an act of betrayal.[61] For others it was perceived as an act of enlightened statesmanship by the main Russian negotiator, Lebed. Maskhadov's own role proved tragic, in the real sense of the term. Having proved himself to be the architect of Chechnya's victory in the first war, Maskhadov proved himself unequal to the demands of peace. He was Russia's favoured candidate in the

---

suggests that traditional sources of authority were undermined by the first Chechen war; thereafter authoritative relations became militarized and, to a degree, criminalized.

[59] Zadvornov and Khalmukhamedov, 'Posle pobedy', 14.

[60] This argument is made by many, including Robert Bruce Ware, who goes further in arguing that Dudaev's radical nationalist appeals, even before the first Chechen war, were designed to overcome Chechnya's particularly divisive kinship structures (for example, in comparison with Dagestan's *tuhums*, that for the last 500 years have been transcended by traditional political structures known as *djamaats*), Robert Bruce Ware, 'Kinship and Conflict in the Caucasus', *Analysis of Current Events*, 14:1 (Feb. 2002), 12–13.

[61] This is the view advanced by Zadvornov and Khalmukhamedov, 'Posle pobedy', 14.

27 January 1997 presidential elections, and on 12 May Russia signed a peace treaty with him in the Kremlin as Chechnya's legitimate leader. The two sides 'renounced forever the use of force' in their mutual relations and pledged to develop their relations on the basis of 'generally recognized principles and norms of international law'. Further treaties and agreements would regulate specific issues.[62] Yeltsin noted the 'historic significance' of the treaty as putting an end to 400 years of war between Russia and Chechnya, effectively granting the republic independence, although negotiations on Chechnya's final status were postponed to 2001 (to allow, in Yeltsin's earlier words, 'for the wounds to heal and for emotions to be replaced by common sense').[63] Changes to Chechnya's status require amendments to Russia's constitution, something that is extremely difficult to do, so an interim agreement of this kind was the best that could be hoped for in the circumstances.[64] Although at this meeting Maskhadov pledged that 'there would be no place for terrorists and kidnappers in Chechnya', he spectacularly failed to deal with both problems. Maskhadov's inability to assert not only his own authority but that of the presidency on Chechnya's feuding warlords condemned his country to yet another murderous conflict.

Maskhadov proved both to be a president and not to be one. Unlike Michael Collins in a comparable post-independence situation in Ireland, Maskhadov failed to rise above the conflicts in Chechen society to become a statesman of the Chechen state. While willing to negotiate with Russia, his room for manoeuvre against unremitting domestic secessionists like Basaev and Salman Raduev was limited. His understandable but ultimately misplaced fear of a Chechen civil war led him to make endless concessions to his former comrades in arms, but he failed to represent the aspirations of the mass of the Chechen people for peace and order or to act as a responsible interlocutor with the Russian state. The new Chechen élite based itself on the victorious war party rather than working with 'centrist political forces and the modernized part of the population that was loyal to Russia'.[65] At the moment of grave crisis, when Chechen fighters under the leadership of Basaev invaded the neigbouring Russian republic of Dagestan in early August 1999, instead of confronting the rebel leaders (Russia made clear its support for him if he did so) he abnegated responsibility. His failure to sustain the

[62] 'Treaty on Peace and the Principles of Mutual Relations between the Russian Federation and the Chechen Republic of Ichkeria', reproduced in Otto Latsis, 'Dogovor s Chechnei: kto pobedil, kto proigral?', *Izvestiya*, 14 May 1997. [63] Aron, *Yeltsin*, 666.
[64] On the political and constitutional difficulties involved in changing Chechnya's status, see Edward W. Walker, *No Peace, No War in the Caucasus: Secessionist Conflicts in Chechnya, Abkhazia and Nagorno-Karabakh*, Harvard University, John F. Kennedy School of Government, Strengthening Democratic Institutions Project (Feb. 1998), 3–11; see also Walker's article, 'Constitutional Obstacles to Peace in Chechnya', *East European Constitutional Review*, 6:1 (Winter 1997), 55–60. [65] Tishkov, *Puti mira na Severnom Kavkaze*, 33.

state-building endeavour lost him much of the residual legitimacy that he may have enjoyed. It is for this reason that Russia during the second war was so reluctant to accept him as a legitimate interlocutor in political negotiations.

The Chechen national movement could not be contained within the borders of the Chechen state. This expansiveness was fuelled in part by traditional pan-Caucasianism (with dreams during the Russian Civil War of establishing a single republic from the Caspian to the Black seas), and in part by Islamic universalism, reinforced by the declaration of the struggle against Russia as a 'jihad'.[66] The role of Islam as the ideology of the nascent Chechen state is highly controversial. Dudaev was suspicious of Islamism: to the end he remained loyal to the national rather than the Islamic ideal.[67] Up to 1996 Basaev and most of his colleagues were largely secular in orientation. There were Islamic movements dating from the late 1980s, such as Beslan Gantamirov's party 'Islamic Path' that argued that only through independence could the republic return to true Islam, but on the whole it was not Islam that fuelled the Chechen revolution but a vapid nationalism that later required Islam to sustain the national revolution.[68] Islam became a tool in intra-Chechen struggles rather than the legitimating ideology of Chechen secessionism. Indeed, Islamic universalism as espoused by Basaev, Khattab, and others was antithetical to Chechen state-building endeavours. The failure of the outside world to recognize Chechen independence, something that would have required the maintenance of secular legality, prompted Dudaev during the first war to turn to the Islamic world for support. With material and spiritual support streaming in from a number of Middle and Near Eastern states (above all Saudi Arabia), Dudaev's options became increasingly narrow. He was forced to compromise and lost his traditional secular (Soviet) approach to religious affairs.[69]

With a bitterly divided and archaized society emerging from the war, Islam was the only supra-clan (*teip*) unifying principle in the new state. The liberal intelligentsia and other representatives of civil society had long fled, the Russian workers had gone, and all the institutions of a secular–legal

---

[66] For a full discussion of the role of Islam in the Caucasus, see Aleksei Malashenko, *Islamskie orientiry Severnogo Kavkaza*, Moscow Carnegie Center (Moscow, Gendal'f, 2001).

[67] In 1992 Dudaev had described Chechnya as 'a secular constitutional state with equal rights, duties and possibilities for all citizens', *Nezavisimaya gazeta*, 18 Feb. 1992. On the eve of the 1994 war at a council of elders Dudaev criticized attempts to introduce *sharia* law: 'I respect your consistency, but I consider it premature. If today we announce rule by *sharia* law, then tomorrow you will call on me to cut off the heads and hands of offenders, not realizing that the day after very few of you will keep your heads and hands', Abubakarov, 'Mezhdu avtoritarnostyu i anarkhiei', 193. Prophetic words indeed! See also Igor' Rotar', *Pod zelënym znamenem islama: islamskie radikaly v Rossii i SNG* (Moscow, AIRO-XX, 2001), 30–1.

[68] For a perceptive analysis of the issue, see A. D. Savateev, 'Islam i politika v Chechenskoi respublike', *Obshchestvennye nauki i sovremennost'*, 2 (2000), 84–95.

[69] On the change in his views and options, see *NG-Religii*, 23 Jan. 1998, 4.

order had been destroyed. As Savateev puts it, 'Islam became the main form of self-identification of Chechens in the post-Soviet period and soon became the symbol of opposition to the contemporary Russian state and Christian civilization as a whole'.[70] Despite the fact that Chechens have traditionally not been very strict Moslems, Islamic law was imposed immediately after the victory of 1996, and on 5 November 1997 Chechnya was declared an Islamic Republic. On 3 February 1999 Maskhadov decreed a constitutional reform that introduced *sharia* law as the basis of governance in Chechnya, while at the same time allowing the opposition field commanders to establish a *Shura*, effectively an alternative legislative body. Even before that as noted *sharia* law had been practised, but tempered by the influence of *adat* (customary) law, together with the secular democratic norms that had emerged out of the collapse of the Soviet Union. Islamic law only gradually gained precedence, and the first death penalty imposed according to the new code was fulfilled on 23 April 1997, and on 3 September of that year the first public executions took place. Maskhadov desperately sought to ensure control over his interpretation of *sharia* law, while the field commanders sought to establish their own, subordinate to their *Shura*. All of this was taking place in a society where there was not a single person with higher education in *sharia* law. The Islamification of Chechnya was thus a highly politicized process, reflecting domestic political struggles, social dislocation, and foreign dependency.

The rise of Wahhabism in Chechnya and neighbouring Dagestan is perhaps the most controversial aspect of Chechnya's failed attempt at state-building. The first Wahhabis emerged in Dagestan in 1988, but thereafter the movement spread rapidly as the idiom of political protest and resistance to social corruption. In July 1998 three villages in the Buinaksk district of Dagestan proclaimed themselves Islamic territory, based on *sharia* law. The opposition there had thus appropriated the mantle of Islam, just as the opposition to Maskhadov had done in Chechnya. In contrast to Chechnya's traditional Sufi form of Islam that was non-hierarchical and deeply rooted in village life and customs, Wahhabism represented a militant ascetic form of Islamic reformation, challenging both the traditional Islamic authorities in Chechnya and the relatively relaxed social norms that, for example, did not prevent the use of alcohol and smoking. Although Maskhadov banned the Wahhabis from Chechnya on 16 July 1998, their influence remained unchecked and continued to be espoused by the former Chechen foreign minister Movladi Udugov, the former acting president Zelimkhan Yandarbiev, and the warlords Basaev and Khattab. The Saudi-backed Wahhabi movement encountered, however, much popular resistance, being dubbed

---

[70] Savateev, 'Islam i politika', 86.

'Arabization'. As one commentator noted, 'In seventy years they couldn't turn us into Russians, and they won't be able to turn us into Arabs now.'[71]

THE SECOND CHECHEN WAR AND BEYOND, 1999–

Renewed Russian intervention in Chechnya in late 1999 demonstrated that Russia's 'strategic retreat' from the Caucasus had only been temporary.[72] The attempt to export the Chechen revolution by 'Islamic' militants through the invasion of Dagestan in August and then again in September 1999 prompted Russia to act, even though according to the former prime minister Stepashin (May–August 1999) preparations for some sort of military operation had been in train since earlier that year in anticipation of the need to rein in Chechen lawlessness.[74] It was not accidental that the Chechen warlords were not content with the struggle for the independence of Chechnya and went further. Derluguian vividly expresses the problem:

Practically all Chechen military leaders, with the stubbornly noble exception of President Maskhadov, are on record openly threatening the populations of Russia with terrorism and (in the case of Shamil Basayev in 1995) the 'hypocritical' West… As to Chechen rationale and motives, it is apparent that Basayev, Khattab and Udugov could be carried away by their and their retainers' restless machismo and amateurish ideological fantasies.[73]

The collapse of the Soviet Union had opened up a power vacuum throughout the Caucasian and Central Asian region, while Russia proved hesitant to assert itself. The militant warlords in Chechnya sought to take advantage of Russian weakness to separate more territory from Russia and to create 'an Islamic republic from the Black to the Caspian seas'.[75] In response, Russia argued that it was obliged to act within the terms of the 'Code of Conduct on Politico-Military Aspects of Security' that was signed at the OSCE summit in Budapest in December 1994. Paragraph 6 states that 'participating states will take appropriate measures to prevent and combat terrorism in all its forms', while paragraph 25 states that 'the participating states will not tolerate or support forces that are not accountable to or controlled by their constitutionally established authorities'.[76] The applicability of both these

[71] *Nezavisimaya gazeta*, 27 Jan. 1999.

[72] In addition to Baev's comment (above), other commentators had also noted a 'broader disengagement of Russia from the Caucasus states'; this quotation comes from Dov Lynch, *The Conflict in Abkhazia: Dilemmas in Russian 'Peacekeeping' Policy* (London, The Royal Institute of International Affairs, 1998), 44.

[73] Georgi Derluguian, *Reflections on Putin's Rise to Power*, Davis Centre for Russian Studies, Harvard University, Program on New Approaches to Russian Security, Policy Memo Series No. 104 (January 2000), 1–2.   [74] *Nezavisumaa gazeta* 14 Jan. 2000.

[75] S. Shermatova, 'Tak nazyvaemye vakhkhabity', in Furman, *Chechnya i Rossiya*, 419.

[76] Quoted in William Church, 'Moscow's Actions: Rationale Deserve Reappraisal', *Defense News*, 20 March 2000.

provisions to Chechnya are clear. By 1999, as William Church puts it, 'Russia was faced with an autonomous state within its political control that had disintegrated into warlord factions, and which invaded a neighbouring state'.[77] Anatol Lieven argues that 'Russia's legal right to prosecute this [the second Chechen] war is incontestable': Chechnya is an internationally recognized part of Russian territory; and when given the chance of self-rule from 1996 'the government there proved incapable of controlling its own territory'.[78] It was this combination of sovereignty and security concerns that Putin drew on to justify his policy.[79]

Although Russia's intervention in Chechnya in September 1999 violated the terms of the 1996 Khasavyurt agreement and the treaty of May 1997, the maintenance of some order in the region was, many argued, not only Russia's right but its duty. This was reflected in the high degree of public support for the second war.[80] This support was due to the perception that Chechnya constituted a real threat to regional security in the Northern Caucasus and for stability in Russia itself. Any influence that oil politics may have had in the first war was now mitigated by the completion of the bypass pipeline in April 2000. A war in self-defence was thus perceived as a 'just cause'. The Chechen military activities in Dagestan further demonstrated that there was no other 'last resort' solution. The 'legitimate authority' of the presidential candidate Vladimir Putin to have Russian troops intervene in Chechnya was not challenged either, contrary to the first war when Boris Yeltsin encountered strong criticism from some generals and the political establishment. Only in May 2001 was a revised Law on the State of Emergency adopted that could be used to provide a legal framework for military operations within Russia itself. The principles of 'reasonable chance

---

[77] Church, 'Moscow's Actions'.

[78] Anatol Lieven, 'Morality and Reality in Approaches to War Crimes: The Case of Chechnya', *East European Constitutional Review*, 10:2/3 (Spring/Summer 2001), 72.

[79] For example, in an interview with the Polish paper *Gazeta Wyborcja* and the Polish television station TVP on 14 Jan. 2002 Putin noted that in Chechnya 'a strange symbiosis of separatism and international terrorism took place, involved with extreme manifestations of Islamic fundamentalism', 24 Dec. 2001, http://www.president.kremlin.ru/events/433.html

[80] Emil' Pain suggests that part of the reason for strong support for the war was the manipulation of mass consciencesness, 'Vtoraya Chechenskaya voina i ee posledstviya', in Nikolai Petrov (ed.), *Regiony Rossii v 1999g.: Ezhegodnoe prilozhenie k "Politicheskomu al'manakhu Rossii"*, Moscow Carnegie Center (Moscow, Gendal'f, 2001), 280–94. Although the overwhelming majority of the Russian population initially supported the second Chechen war, with opinion polls showing a steady 70-odd per cent in favour, there are certain ambiguities. In February 2000, for example, 48 per cent supported the ending of hostilities and the resolution of the Chechen problem by negotiation if Putin proposed such a course of action, while 42 per cent said they would not. A poll in late December 1999 revealed that even among the supporters of the war a large majority, 59 per cent, would accept an independent Chechnya, and another 21 per cent would be 'happy for this to occur'. Poll conducted by VTsIOM. Henry E. Hale, *Is Russian Nationalism on the Rise?*, Program on New Approaches to Russian Security, Davis Center for Russian Studies, Harvard University, Policy Memo Series, No. 110 (Feb. 2000), 1.

of success' and 'proportionality' could also be considered as better respected than in the first war: Chechnya was a far greater security threat in 1999 than in 1994, which increased the potential benefits of a military operation as compared to its costs. Despite the failure of the military reform policies of Yeltsin, the Russian military were still better prepared to confront a guerrilla war than in 1994 and to make use of their vast superiority in military technology and manpower.

Respect for the *jus in bello* principles remained no less a problem than in the first war. The war in Chechnya was an internal war 'where its own citizens were mixed in with the Chechen warlords'.[81] The mission statement of the Russian armed forces that their task was to 'restore constitutional order' was accurate: the methods used, however, were far from commensurate with this aim. The problem, in the words of Lord David Russell-Johnston, president of the Parliamentary Assembly of the Council of Europe (PACE), is the way that the civilian population suffered from 'the disproportionate and indiscriminate' use of force by Russian troops. As he noted, the Council of Europe 'was set up to defend human rights, democracy and the rule of law. This is a mandate that leaves very little room for *realpolitik*'.[82] In the event, Russia's voting rights in the Parliamentary Assembly were suspended between April 2000 and January 2001. The Council of Europe went beyond an exclusive criticism of Russia's lack of compliance with international humanitarian law when it stressed the need for a dialogue between the warring parties. It operated within the framework of two key principles: the territorial integrity of the Russian Federation; and open dialogue with all parties to the conflict.[83] As long as Russia continued to condemn the insurgent Chechen leadership as terrorists it was difficult to see how such a dialogue could be achieved.

Kadyrov, the mufti of Chechnya and the main representative of traditional Sufism (and thus hostile to Wahhabism), assumed the leadership of the Russian-sponsored administration of Chechnya on 20 June 2000. The failure to check Wahhabism was one reason why he broke with Maskhadov. Kadyrov accused Basaev and Khattab of religious heresy for advocating Wahhabism in Chechnya.[84] He argued that there could not be any order in Chechnya without direct rule imposed by the federal authorities.[85]

[81] Church, 'Moscow's Actions'.

[82] David Russell-Johnston, 'Human Rights for the Chechens, Too', *International Herald Tribune*, 14 April 2000.

[83] The Council of Europe established a Joint Working Group on Chechnya, consisting of Russian and other deputies of PACE, chaired by Lord Judd. On 27 September 2001 they issued a report condemning Russia for continued humanitarian abuses, but at the same time condemned Maskhadov for withdrawing his representatives from PACE consultations. The Jamestown Foundation, *Chechnya Weekly*, 2 Oct. 2001.

[84] In July 2000 he banned the Wahhabi movement in the republic. Jamestown Foundation, *Monitor*, 26 July 2000.   [85] Zadvornov and Khalmukhamedov, 'Posle pobedy', 14.

Long-term alternatives were also discussed. Many at that time argued that a key element of any future settlement would be the development of Chechnya's rich tradition of local self-government. Khasbulatov, the former speaker of the dissolved Russian Supreme Soviet, found himself a new role. In April 2000 he was named chairman of the newly created Public Council for the North Caucasus, a body established to build consensus for a peaceful resolution of the Chechen and broader North Caucasian problems.[86] His appointment suggested that some of the divisions of the Yeltsin era were being healed. With the election of Aslanbek Aslakhanov, the head of Chechnya's Association of Law Enforcement Workers and someone who had never advocated Chechen independence, on 20 August 2000 as a parliamentary deputy to the Russian State Duma, it appeared that a section of Chechnya's political élite was gradually being reintegrated into the Russian political community. In the Duma Aslakhanov lost no opportunity to condemn the arbitrary detention, beating and torture of Chechen civilians.[87] Some Russian scholars, however, were pessimistic about the possibilities of integration, and called for a more radical solution. As Dmitrii Furman, a senior scholar at the Russian Academy of Sciences Institute of Europe, put it, Moscow's approach to both Chechnya and the Chechens left him unable to 'imagine a peaceful integration of Chechens into Russian society'. Taking the negative impact of a protracted war on Russia's political culture into consideration, he concluded that Russian democracy was impossible without Chechen independence.[88] An alternative view is that Chechnya is the exception, and that Russia's observance of human rights standards is increasingly in conformity with international norms. The Western conduct of war, it is argued, has typically been no less savage than Russia's in Chechnya.[89]

Following the attack on the World Trade Center and the Pentagon on 11 September 2001 the Putin government joined the 'coalition against terrorism'. Russia's attempts since 1999 to portray its renewed intervention in Chechnya as part of the global anti-terrorist struggle became rather more credible.[90] Threats to Russia appeared to come less from states but from a range of transnational actors. Putin at this time played down sovereignty questions and insisted that 'it is not an issue of Chechnya's membership, or non-membership, of the Russian Federation'; of primary concern was that Chechnya had become an 'irresponsible quasi-state' that became 'a gangster

[86] *Nezavisimaya gazeta*, 18 April 2000.
[87] e.g. on 19 October, RFE/RL, *Newsline*, 20 Oct. 2000.
[88] Cited by Paul Goble, 'On Equal Terms', RFE/RL, *Newsline*, 14 March 2000. Furman reiterated these views in an interview with the present author on 26 June 2002.
[89] Both these arguments are made by Eric A. Heinze and Douglas A. Borer, 'The Chechen Exception: Rethinking Russia's Human Rights Policy', *Politics*, 22:2 (2002), 86–94.
[90] Fiona Hill, *'Extremists and Bandits': How Russia Views the War Against Terrorism*, Policy Memo No. 246, Program on New Approaches to Russian security, CSIS, Washington DC, 2002.

enclave while the ideological vacuum was quickly filled by fundamentalist organizations'.[91] The official emphasis on security rather than sovereignty distinguished Chechnya from anti-colonial struggles like that of Algeria against France.[92] In his speech of 24 September 2001 Putin unexpectedly called on Chechen rebels to lay down their arms within two days and start negotiations with his envoy to the South Russia Federal District, General Viktor Kazantsev. Putin's desultory search for a political solution to the conflict[93] was hampered by a fundamental lack of consensus within the Russian policy community (especially between the military and civilian branches)[94] and, above all, by divisions *within* the Chechen insurgency. It was clear that Maskhadov and field commander Ruslan Gelaev had a secular European orientation, while the 'fundamentalists' Basaev and Khattab had close links with Osama bin Laden.[95] While Maskhadov sought to establish a secular state, independent of Russia but associated with it economically and militarily, the Basaev wing sought to create an Islamic state completely independent of Russia and oriented towards the Islamic world. Divisions within Chechnya, Russia, and the international community all hampered the resolution of the conflict.

CONCLUSION

The year 1991 was for the Soviet Union what Robert Jackson calls 'the Grotian moment', the reshuffling of the title to sovereignty.[96] Bartkus has

[91] From an interview in *Focus*, 21 September 2001, cited in Hughes, 'Chechnya: the Causes of a Protracted Post-Soviet Conflict', 39.

[92] Although journalists like Pavel Felgenhauer drew the comparison with Algeria (e.g. *Moskovskie novosti*, 24 April 2002), others insisted that 'Chechnya's separation from Russia would not only provoke the deterioration of the situation throughout Eurasia, but would in practice lead to geopolitical catastrophe', Sergei Mikhailov, 'V Chechne reshaetsya sud'ba Rossii', *Argumenty i fakty*, 12 (2000), 6.

[93] Two-hour talks were held between Kazantsev, and Maskhadov's representative, Akhmed Zakaev, at Moscow airport (Sheremetevo 2) on 18 Nov. 2001, in the presence of the president of the Liberal Party of Turkey, but the stiff preconditions set by the Russian side (effectively, Chechen disarmament) precluded serious progress at this time.

[94] On military concerns, see Roy Allison, 'The Chechnia Conflict: Military and Security Policy Implications', in Roy Allison and Christoph Bluth (eds.), *Security Dilemmas in Russia and Eurasia* (London, Macmillan, 2001), 128–46. In November 1999 several Russian generals threatened to resign if a negotiated solution was attempted or if there was excessive political interference in the conduct of the second Chechen war, *Moskovskii komsomolets*, 5 Nov. 1999. For an overview of the military perspective on the wars and of the moral compass of Russia's officer class at its best (i.e. of the non-corrupt elements), see Gennadii Troshev, *Moya voina: Chechenskii dnevnik okopnogo generala* (Moscow, Vagrius, 2001).

[95] A point made by Anna Politkovskaya in *Obshchaya gazeta*, 71, 2 October 2001, cited in RFE/RL, *Newsline*, 3 Oct. 2001. For details of a videocassette showing the links between Khattab and Osama bin Laden, see The Jamestown Foundation, *Monitor*, 25 Jan. 2002. These links are not surprising since Chechen fighters had long-standing ties with the Afghan *mujahadeen*. The death of Khattab in early 2002 strengthened Maskhadov's hand.

[96] Robert Jackson, 'Sovereignty in World Politics: a Glance at the Conceptual and Historical Landscape', *Political Studies*, 47, Special Issue, *Sovereignty at the Millenium* (1999), 434.

theorized these liminal periods in the constitution of states as the 'opportune moment' when the weakening of central government (or foreign intervention) raises the prospects for success of a bid for independence.[97] In both the former USSR and Yugoslavia, however, the Grotian moment was limited to existing Union republics, and despite numerous wars of secession the new borders have been maintained. In other words, the constitutional provisions of the antecedent state set the bounds for the recognition of new states. The Chechen secession bid was an attempt to expand the Grotian consensus without a basis in 'just cause', as described above. Outside the colonial context, international law and practice does not recognise the unilateral right to secession under whatever conditions and through any procedure, however democratic (like a referendum). In addition, just as the 'opportune moment' of 1917–18, when the collapse of Tsarism prompted independence bids by many of the nations of the Russian empire, came to an end with the restoration of state power under the Bolsheviks so, too, this window of opportunity in post-communist Russia appeared over by the late 1990s. Above all, an examination of the ethics of secession from the perspective of just war theory does not provide normative support for the Chechen secession bid.

Choice theories argue that a territorially concentrated group has a legitimate case for seeking secession if a majority express such a clear preference in a referendum or plebiscite. In Chechnya in the early 1990s there was no such clear moment of self-realization. At the heart of choice theory is an individualistic understanding of the democratic right of individuals to chose the institutional framework of the society in which they wish to live. As we argued above, this tends to ignore the ethnic or ascriptive character of most secessionist movements, a feature that was strongly in evidence in the Chechen case. Just cause theories have greater relevance to Chechnya, since clearly the region had suffered a persistent history of injustice. As with Locke's theory of revolution, secession can be justified if it seeks to remedy an injustice. Again, however, it was far from clear whether the Chechen secession bid, viewed from the perspective of the attempt to enhance human rights and to achieve a greater degree of justice, falls into this category. A third category of theories of secession is explicitly grounded on ideas of national self-determination, accepting the importance of notions of cultural and national identity. However, the problem of how to guarantee the rights of minorities within the seceding community, and the general problem of ensuring that the human and civic rights of all the citizens of the seceding community are protected, are left undeveloped. In addition, we have suggested that the seceding community in certain circumstances should take into account

---

[97] Viva Ona Bartkus, *The Dynamics of Secession* (Cambridge, Cambridge University Press, 1999), '"Opportune Moments": A Reduction in the Costs of Secession', 145–66.

the interests of the community from which it seeks to secede. In the Russian case of the early 1990s this is particularly important. For the first time in decades, if not centuries, Russia itself was trying to democratize on a civic and federal basis, and the successful secession of one area could have acted as the catalyst for the disintegration of the state leading to Yugoslav-style wars and ethnic cleansing.

While Russia may have had a 'just cause' in intervening militarily in Chechnya in 1994, this does not mean that it fought a just war. The launching of the war failed to respect the other *jus ad bellum* principles of 'last resort', 'legitimate authority', 'proportionality', and 'reasonable chance of success'. Moreover, the conduct of the war was not in line with the *jus in bello* principles of 'proportionality' and 'discrimination'. The *jus ad bellum* principles were far better respected in the second Chechen war from September 1999. But the justice of the war was likewise at stake in the criticism by Western governments and the Council of Europe for the numerous breaches of humanitarian law (*jus in bello*).

The Chechen case demonstrates that the nature of leadership is critical in determining the level of violence in new republics and their secessionist regions. The nationalistic leadership that came to power in the Chechen revolution of 1991 resulted in a violent outcome in Chechnya's transition to a post-Soviet order. The case also vividly demonstrates the limited impact that international agencies and foreign governments can play in such secessionist crises, although the role of multilateral agencies and the international community was not entirely negligible (above all, the Council of Europe). The large corpus of mediation theory, where a third party seeks to provide a forum for the non-violent reconciliation of warring parties, has had little impact on the course of this intractable conflict. The Chechen wars demonstrated the high costs of separatism and partition through wars of secession,[98] and appears to vindicate the case of those who argue against trying to resolve ethnic conflicts by partitioning states.[99]

Was there a way of squaring the circle: of accommodating Chechen demands while maintaining the integrity of the Russian state and its nascent democracy? Do you 'appease', and if so, are you on the 'slippery slope' to independence; or can timely concessions, however asymmetrical these may render a federal system, avert more radical separatist demands?[100] A further

---

[98] Cf. Metta Spencer (ed.), *Separatism: Democracy and Disintegration* (Lanham, Md., Rowman & Littlefield, 1998).

[99] e.g. Robert K. Schaeffer, *Severed States: Dilemmas of Democracy in a Divided World* (Lanham, Md., Rowman & Littlefield, 1999).

[100] The question of why the extension of autonomy in some circumstances blunts the drive for secession while in others only whets the appetite of secessionist movements is at the core of Bartkus's conceptual model in her *The Dynamics of Secession*.

question then arises: where is the line to be drawn between a 'distinct community' and a state? Our discussion of the normative bases of secessionism suggests that there is no basic collective right to exit pre-existing political communities except in exceptional circumstances. If the threshold for secession is set too low, law would lose universal jurisdiction and the revolving door of entry and exit into the political community would open on to anarchy. Our application of theories of the ethics of secession and just war theory to the two Chechen wars, further, suggests that the search for an appropriate institutional solution is not facilitated by the use of force. The combatants dug in for the long haul in a war that Russia could neither win outright (given the nature of Chechen resistance), nor lose (given adequate resources and commitment). The only way out was some sort of negotiated settlement. The scale of violence during the two wars clearly made the political integration of Chechnya into Russia more difficult. But this does not mean, as argued by Furman, that independence for Chechnya is the only reasonable alternative. It is in principle possible to design an institutional arrangement where the linkage between Russia and Chechnya is limited to a restricted number of competencies. Self-government in the domestic field may be combined with a separate international legal personality, which then finds an expression in international treaty-making power and specific forms of diplomatic representation.[101] Comparative federalism can provide a wealth of concrete experiences in such areas.[102] Post-communist Russian

[101] These are precisely the ideas that were hammered out in indirect talks in Liechtenstein on 16–19 August 2002 between former State Duma speaker and Security Council secretary Ivan Rybkin, former speaker of the Supreme Soviet Ruslan Khasbulatov, Duma deputies Aslanbek Aslakhanov and Yurii Shchekochikhin (also a journalist with *Novaya gazeta*), and Maskhadov's representative, deputy prime minister Akhmed Zakaev. The discussions brought together a plan drafted by Khasbulatov, that was highly critical of Maskhadov but sought to give Chechnya 'special status' allowing it to conduct its own domestic and foreign policy, and a plan drafted by Zbigniew Brzezinski, to produce the Liechtenstein plan. Russia's territorial integrity was to be preserved but Chechnya was to be granted wide powers of self-determination and autonomy. No agreement was reached on whether the model of Chechen autonomy could be based on that granted to Tatarstan, and on the deployment of Russian troops on Chechnya's Southern border. Concurrently, Maskhadov's special negotiator Kazbek Makhashev appeared to have started talking directly with the Russians and to have accepted the need for the introduction of direct Russian presidential rule. By then both the Chechen and Russian sides had clearly wearied of the war. In a VTsIOM poll of 29 Aug. 2002 31 per cent of respondents in a Russia-wide poll considered the continuation of the war necessary, while 59 per cent favoured peace negotiations, results cited in *Chechnya Weekly*, 9 Sept. 2002.

[102] See Uwe Leonardy, 'Treaty-Making Powers and Foreign Relations of Federated Entities, in Bruno Coppieters, David Darchiashvili, and Natella Akaba (eds.), *Federal Practice: Exploring Alternatives for Georgia and Abkhazia* (Brussels, VUB University Press, 2000); 151–68; and Gocha Lordkipanidze, 'Segmentation and Fragmentation: Proposals for a Federalisation of Foreign Policy in Georgia', ibid. 169–78. Also on http://poli.vub.ac.be/; Russian version with same authors published as *Praktika federalizma: poiski alternativ dlya Gruzii i Abkhazii* (Moscow, Ves Mir, 1999).

experience also suggests that there is considerable scope for achieving tailored institutional arrangements.[103] Putin's state-gathering exercise has further demonstrated that there were limits to the development of autonomous jurisprudence (for example, restricted to civil matters), but even he was unable to reverse the development of asymmetrical federalism or to deprive the republics of their competencies. Negotiators of a peace settlement for Chechnya will have to engage in the difficult exercise of finding an institutional formula that acknowledges the claims of Chechnya's titular nationality to statehood while stopping short of recognizing its full sovereign independence.

[103] For a discussion of the context and implications of the 17 June 1996 Russian law 'On National-Cultural Autonomies', see Bill Bowring, 'Austro-Marxism's Last Laugh?: the Struggle for Recognition of National-Cultural Autonomy for Rossians and Russians', *Europe-Asia Studies*, 54:2 (2002), 229–50. The extra-territorial approach had been advocated by the Austro-Marxists Otto Bauer and Karl Renner, but had been opposed by Lenin and other early Soviet leaders who had favoured territorial autonomy. According to the extra-territorial perspective, individuals can enjoy certain national rights regardless of where they live, and thus the need to have a certain territorial concentration became redundant. The attractiveness of such an arrangement for widely dispersed groups like the Jews was obvious in the Russian and Austro-Hungarian empires, but the very pervasiveness of such a scheme alarmed Lenin, who considered it administratively disruptive as well as undermining working class unity. Discussions about whether to grant extraterritorial cultural autonomy to Russia's one million Roma reflects the continued search for solutions to the problem. See Paul Goble, 'A New Kind of Autonomy', RFE/RL, *Newsline*, 5 May 2000, 14–16.

9

War and Secession: A Moral Analysis of the Georgian–Abkhaz Conflict

Bruno Coppieters

INTRODUCTION

The Soviet Union was highly centralized at the political and partly decentralized at the administrative levels. The Communist Party controlled every level of authority, and the principle of the separation of powers was rejected as a 'bourgeois ideology'. The Moscow leadership, however, had made serious attempts to accommodate demands for national self-determination.[1] Soviet federalism combined the objective of political control by the Communist leadership with an ethno-territorial form of administrative decentralization. A multi-tiered form of government allowed the major nationalities to exercise a certain degree of self-administration over a particular territory and to be recognized as its 'titular nation'. This was done according to a hierarchical pattern, whereby nationalities were ranked according to a number of criteria such as population size and geographical location. The political leverage of a national group inside the Communist leadership could also play a role. Union republics had the highest political status, which formally included sovereignty and the right to secession. They were followed by autonomous republics, which had a constitution and certain other characteristics of partial statehood but did not possess sovereignty or the right to secession. Autonomous regions came even lower in the hierarchy.

Soviet federalism was thus based on three contradictory ways of applying constitutional principles. It formally rejected the principle of a 'horizontal'

I would like to thank Boris Kashnikov, Catherine Guicherd, George Hewitt, Jonathan Cohen, Thomas Markert, Michael Lobzhanidze, Craig Oliphant, Theodore Hanf, Rachel Clogg, Viacheslav Chirikba, Ghia Nodia, Tamara Kovziridze, Irakli Laitadze, Carl Ceulemans and Alexei Zverev for their comments on a first draft of this chapter.

[1] On Soviet nationality policies and their consequences for the break-up of the Soviet Union see Robert J. Kaiser, *The Geography of Nationalism in Russia and the USSR* (Princeton, Princeton University Press, 1994) and Valery Tishkov, *Ethnicity, Nationalism and Conflict in and after the Soviet Union* (London, Sage, 1997).

division of power between the legislative, the executive, and the judiciary, but it formally accepted federalism, which is based on the principle of a 'vertical' division of competences and where areas of government are distributed in a multi-tiered fashion. It acknowledged the nationalities' right to self-determination, but had their political status determined autocratically by the Communist leadership. Finally, it regarded sovereignty as being indivisible— a concept reflected in the one-party system—but it constitutionally entrenched the sovereignty of the Union republics, up to and including their right to secession, in parallel with the sovereignty of the Soviet state.[2] All three contradictions reflected particular forms of discrimination: the unequal distribution of powers among the various titular nations and their political units, in a federal system of administrative decentralization, led to inequality among the various nationalities when it came to having their right to self-determination acknowledged at the formal constitutional level, particularly as regards sovereignty and the right to secession.

These contradictions did not lead to open conflict as long as the Communist Party was able to impose its authority as an undisputed arbiter in nationality conflicts. But even then there were numerous attempts by national leaderships to redress these perceived injustices and to upgrade their own political status using official channels. This was the case for instance for the Tatars and the Abkhazians throughout Soviet history. The democratization of the Soviet regime after 1987 led to radical claims and popular mobilization. From 1988 on, the Armenians of Nagorno-Karabakh, an autonomous region of Azerbaijan mainly populated by Armenians, strove in vain to 'correct' the boundaries between Armenia and Azerbaijan and to have their territory included in Armenia. Once the power of the Communist Party began to wane, the lack of legitimacy of the existing distribution of competences led to the dismantling of the Soviet federal system.

The acquisition of independence by all the Union republics did not lead to major confrontations between republics of equal rank. Their integration into the world community and active participation in a number of intergovernmental security organizations—such as the Conference on Security and Cooperation in Europe (CSCE)—facilitated diplomatic solutions to disputed questions of territorial borders, populations and minority rights. The only exception was the escalation of the conflict between Armenia and Azerbaijan over Nagorno-Karabakh. The situation between political units of unequal rank, however, was very different. In this case, the dissolution

---

[2] The sovereignty of the Soviet state was enshrined in Article 75 ('The sovereignty of the USSR extends throughout its territory') and the sovereignty of the Union republics in Article 76: 'A Union Republic is a sovereign Soviet socialist state that has united with other Soviet Republics in the Union of Soviet Socialist Republics'. *Constitution (Fundamental Law) of the Union of Soviet Socialist Republics* (Moscow, Novosti Press Agency Publishing House, 1977), 59.

process led to numerous secessionist or irredentist claims and—in the cases
of the Caucasus and Moldova—to violent conflicts. This is well illustrated
by the relations between Georgia and Abkhazia.[3]

In the Soviet federal system Georgia was a Union republic, with a popu-
lation of about 5.4 million, while at the time of the last census (1989) the
Georgian titular nationality represented some 70 per cent of the population.
Other nationalities include Armenians, Azeris, Russians, Ossetians, and
Abkhazians. Abkhazia was an autonomous republic with a population of
526,061, of which the Abkhaz titular nation accounted for roughly 18 per cent.
Other nationalities included Georgians (about 46 per cent—this percentage
includes sub-ethnic groups such as Mingrelians and Svans), Armenians,
Russians, and Greeks. Relations between the Georgians and Abkhazians
were characterized by conflict throughout the whole of the twentieth century. This was particularly the case during the brief period of Georgian
independence, 1918–21.

Ethnonational conflicts were repressed by the imposition of the Soviet
regime. Abkhazia then became subordinated to the Georgian Union republic. This process of subordination was carried out in a series of constitutional steps during the 1920s. In the 1930s and 1940s, Stalin's policies of
terror left no room for the public expression of national discontent. From

[3] On the history of Georgian–Abkhaz relations see Stanislav Lakoba, *Ocherki politicheskoi istorii Abkhazii* (Sukhum, Alashara, 1990), and *Abkhazia: Posle dvukh okkupatsii* (Gagra, Assotsiatsiya 'Intelligentsia Abkhazii', 1994); Darrell Slider, 'Georgia', in Glenn Eldon Curtis (ed.), *Armenia, Azerbaijan and Georgia: Country Studies* (Washington, DC, Library of Congress, 1995), 149–230; Giorgi Zhorzholiani, Solomon Lekishvili, Levan Toidze, and Edisher Khoshtaria-Brosset, *Historic, Political and Legal Aspects of the Conflict in Abkhazia* (Tbilisi, Samshoblo Publishers, 1995); Levan Toidze, *K voprosy o politicheskom statuse Abkhazii. Stranitsy istorii 1921–1931 gg.* (Tbilisi, Izdatelstvo Samshoblo, 1996); Jürgen Gerber, *Georgien: Nationale Opposition und kommunistische Herrschaft seit 1956* (Baden-Baden, Nomos Verlag, 1997); Naira Gelaschwili, *Georgien: Ein Paradies in Trümmern* (Berlin, Aufbau Taschenbuch Verlag, 1993); Svetlana Chervonnaya, *Conflict in the Caucasus: Georgia, Abkhazia and the Russian Shadow* (London, Gothic Image, 1994); Avtandil Menteshashvili, *Istoricheskie predposylki sovremennogo separatizma v Gruzii* (Tbilisi, Tipografiya Tbiliskogo Gosudarstvennogo Universiteta, 1998); Bruno Coppieters, Ghia Nodia, and Yuri Anchabadze (eds.), *Georgians and Abkhazians: The Search for a Peace Settlement* (Cologne, Sonderveröffentlichung des Bundesinstituts für Ostwissenschaftliche und internationale Studien, 1998); Bruno Coppieters, David Darchiashvili, and Natella Akaba, *Federal Practice: Exploring Alternatives for Georgia and Abkhazia* (Brussels, VUB University Press, 2000); Ghia Nodia, 'Trying to Build (Democratic) State Institutions in Independent Georgia', in Gerhard Mangott (ed.), *Brennpunkt Kaukasus: Aufbruch trotz Krieg, Vertreibung und Willkürherrschaft?* (Vienna, Braumüller, 1999), 105–37; Jonathan Cohen (ed.), *A Question of Sovereignty: The Georgia–Abkhazia Peace Process*, Accord: An International Review of Peace Initiatives, 7 (1999); George Hewitt (ed.), *The Abkhazians* (Richmond, Surrey, Curzon, 1999); Edmund Herzig, *The New Caucasus: Armenia, Azerbaijan and Georgia* (London and New York, Pinter, 1999); Georgii Zhorzholiani, *Istoricheskie i politicheskie korni konflikta v Abkhazii/Gruzia* (Tbilisi, Metsniereba, 2000); Svante Cornell, *Small Nations and Great Powers: A Study of Ethnopolitical Conflict in the Caucasus* (Richmond, Surrey, Curzon, 2001); Bruno Coppieters, *Federalism and Conflict in the Caucasus* (London, The Royal Institute of International Affairs, 2001).

the Georgian and Abkhaz perspective, this period was the darkest of the twentieth century. The Soviet repression was extremely harsh in Georgia, as it was
elsewhere in the Soviet Union, but the Abkhazians had additionally to endure
an attempt to obliterate their national culture. Policies of forced
Georgianization were imposed by the Soviet regime, which made it difficult
from an Abkhaz perspective to differentiate between the injustices imposed by
the Soviet and by the Georgian authorities. The Abkhazians escaped, however,
sharing the fate of the Chechens and other nations from the Caucasus, who
were deported to Central Asia. A fear of forced Georgianization and oppression has since those days fuelled Abkhaz nationalism. After Stalin's death in
1953, the question of political status erupted again. Abkhaz intellectuals and
prominent party members drafted numerous appeals to the Moscow leadership, asking to secede from the Georgian republic and either to constitute a
Union republic or to be integrated into Russia. The striving of the Abkhaz
leadership for equal formal status with the Georgian Union republic had great
political significance. They hoped that Abkhazia would then be treated by
Moscow just like the other Union republics, as an equal among equals.
Abolition of their subordination to Tbilisi would protect them from the
Georgianization of their republic. Enhancing the status of the 'titular nation'
would consolidate the privileged status of the Abkhaz élite and would also
improve the status of all ethnic Abkhazians in education and cultural life.

Georgia's declaration of independence in April 1991 was perceived by the
Abkhaz community as a threat. The stated intention of the Georgian leadership to challenge the privileges of the titular nations of the autonomous
entities in Georgia were taken very seriously in Abkhazia. These fears were
reinforced by the violent conflict that had broken out in the Autonomous
Region of South Ossetia. The Ossetian national movement was striving for
the unification of their region—situated in the Georgian Republic—with the
Autonomous Republic of North Ossetia, which is in the Russian Federation.
By contrast, the Georgian national movement claimed that Georgians in
South Ossetia were being discriminated against in education and employment, and that the Georgian language was being excluded from the civil service. The movement appealed for the abolition of the autonomous status of
South Ossetia, a call which was endorsed by the Georgian parliament on 11
December 1990. The armed conflict was halted only in June 1992. The fear
that the Georgian nationalists would also challenge the political privileges of
the Abkhaz titular nation in Abkhazia itself was an additional reason for the
latter to strive for equal status with the Georgian state.

In 1991, the Abkhaz leadership accepted a proposal of the newly elected
Georgian president, Zviad Gamsakhurdia, to distribute the seats in the
Abkhaz parliament among the nationalities according to proportions
agreed beforehand. According to the rules agreed for the elections of

autumn 1991, the Abkhaz members of parliament would be granted overrepresentation in the legislature, in line with previous Soviet practice. Abkhazia was divided into 65 electoral districts. Each of them was reserved for one of the three national groups: Georgian, Abkhaz, or 'others'. As a result of the elections, the 11 representatives of the other nationalities could choose either to side with the Georgians or the Abkhazians. The Abkhazians could mobilize a small majority of 33 seats, to 31 for the Georgians. This compromise solution failed to resolve the conflict between the two main communities in Abkhazia.

In winter 1991–2, a *coup d'état* against the Georgian president Zviad Gamsakhurdia brought to power a Military Council, which in March 1992 was renamed State Council and brought under the leadership of Eduard Shevardnadze. It abolished the 1978 Georgian Constitution and replaced it by the pre-Soviet Constitution of 1921, where the autonomous status of Abkhazia was only mentioned, not specified in terms defining either its legal status or powers. The autonomous areas were not involved in the decision. As a countermove, the Abkhazians reinstated a draft constitution prepared in 1925, although never adopted, that declared Abkhazia to be a sovereign state. This was approved by the Abkhaz parliament by a very slim majority, and went against the compromise solution reached with the Georgian authorities concerning two-thirds majorities for constitutional changes. The loss of control over Abkhazia was a threat to the Shevardnadze leadership, which also had to confront armed opposition from supporters of the deposed president, Gamsakhurdia. In August 1992, Georgian troops entered Abkhazia, their official purpose being the protection of rail communications along the Black Sea coast. The intervention failed. The Abkhaz units fought back, receiving informal support from Russian military forces stationed in the region and from volunteers from the North Caucasus, particularly Chechnya. The Georgian troops were ousted from Abkhazia in autumn 1993, and this was immediately followed by a rapid exodus of more than 200,000 people, including the vast majority of the Georgian population.

Negotiations on a peace settlement began, with mediation by the UN and with the Russian Federation as a facilitator. Discussions on the political status of Abkhazia were reopened. Unlike the leaders of Chechnya and Nagorno-Karabakh, the Abkhaz leadership did not strive openly for independence. It took a more gradual approach, proposing the establishment of confederal links with Georgia, reflecting an equal right to national self-determination and sovereign status. The Georgian authorities refused to accept such a status, as it would imply recognition of Abkhazia's right of secession. According to the Abkhaz leadership, their refusal to grant a right of return to the whole Georgian population from Abkhazia was the price the Georgian authorities had to pay for their refusal to recognize Abkhazia's sovereignty. The discussions on political status made no progress in the ensuing years. In 1999, Abkhazia declared its independence. This has not been recognized by any government in the world.

The aim of the present analysis is to explore the accuracy of the justifications given by both sides for their involvement in the 1992–3 war and of their claims concerning the secession of Abkhazia. The questions of war and independence are closely interrelated. The war is generally viewed as a turning-point in the history of Georgian–Abkhaz relations. From the Georgian perspective, their military defeat was the result of Russian support for Abkhaz secessionist forces. The Georgian–Abkhaz conflict and the Abkhaz demand for independence are thus perceived as part of the Georgian struggle for emancipation from Russian imperial rule. From the Abkhaz perspective, the victory of the Abkhaz forces over the invading troops was the culmination of a century-long struggle against Georgian colonization. The Abkhaz authorities have pursued the political negotiations since the war with the firm position that there is no possibility of returning to a *status quo ante*. In their view, their military victory should result in international recognition of Abkhaz sovereignty and independence.

The fact that the questions of war and independence are closely interrelated does not mean that they should not be analysed separately. This chapter defends the thesis that disproving the various Georgian justifications for their war aims does not mean that the Abkhaz claim to independence is justified. In just war theory, the relationship between war and justice is assessed by a highly differentiated set of criteria referring to moral constraints on starting military operations (*jus ad bellum*) and on the military operations themselves (*jus in bello*). In the following, we will explore how these criteria may also be used to determine to what extent unilateral secession is morally justified. In particular, we will apply these criteria both to the analysis of the 1992–3 war and to the question of whether Abkhazia's demand to have its independence recognized is justified. The *jus ad bellum* criteria of just cause, legitimate authority, right intentions, last resort, proportionality, and chance of success will first have to be reinterpreted in order to assess the justification for independence.

Structural affinities between the moral analysis of the use of force and that of unilateral forms of secession make it possible to apply the criteria derived from the just war tradition to cases of secession. First, the two ethical approaches deal with exceptions to general rules. One of the main functions of the state is to protect its citizens by preserving peace at the domestic and international levels. This should preferably be done by peaceful means. The legitimate use of force with the aim of restoring peace or redressing injustice is an exception to this rule. Unilateral forms of secession go against the principle of territorial integrity of states and can likewise only be justified as resulting from the application of clear principles to exceptional circumstances.[4] Second, the use of force and attempts to secede can be analysed as unilateral acts intended to impose one's own will on a political adversary. In both cases, negotiations are considered inappropriate to prevent or to redress extreme forms of injustice. These structural similarities between acts of war and acts of unilateral secession make it understandable that unilateral acts of secession are generally accompanied by the use of force.

The use of this particular theoretical framework in the ethics of war and secession is not based on the presupposition that the parties in conflict share its principles when making their decisions. It is quite possible that they do not consider that moral considerations have any role to play in a situation where they consider the survival of their nation to be at stake. But it can be demonstrated that they explicitly invoked all individual *jus ad bellum* principles described below in their legitimation of the use of force or of their position on the secession of Abkhazia.[5]

WAR AND JUSTICE: THE GEORGIAN PERSPECTIVE

Just war theory requires the individual just war principles to be applied to a war setting as if they were all independent of one another.[6] A war can only be considered just if all the principles are respected or if there are good reasons why some of the principles are overruled. If not, the war has to be characterized as unjust. The distinction between the *jus ad bellum* and *jus in bello* principles means that a war may be considered just in respect of one set of principles but not the other. The moral analysis proceeds serially: all the historical aspects of the military intervention are analysed in turn. The testing of each principle individually means that each time we have to focus on certain historical aspects and leave aside the others for the time being. Such a sequential, contextualizing procedure makes it possible to arrive at an overall judgement on whether or not the war is a just one. As justice and injustice are questions of degree, we also—in order to reach a differentiated historical and moral analysis of the Georgian military intervention in Abkhazia—have to assess to what extent each belligerent had justice on its side.

Redressing or preventing serious injustice constitutes a *just cause*. Was the decision in August 1992 by the Praesidium of the State Council—to send

---

[4] A distinction has to be made in this context between unilateral and mutually agreed forms of secession. When a legal procedure on secession is mutually agreed by the government and a secessionist party, it is far easier to respect the interests of all parties according to the rules of justice.

[5] In both cases, the Georgian and Abkhaz leaders claimed that they had a just cause to defend, the legitimate authority to act, that they pursued right intentions and that their actions were in accordance with the principles of last resort, proportionality and likelihood of success.

[6] Nick Fotion and Bruno Coppieters, 'Concluding Comments' in Bruno Coppieters and Nick Fotion (eds.), *Moral Constraints on War: Principles and Cases* (Lanham, Md., Lexington Books, 2002), 298–9.

troops to Abkhazia—based on such a cause? The Georgian authorities are convinced that it was. They have justified their military action by the need to restore law and order and to defeat the military forces supporting the over-thrown president Zviad Gamsakhurdia.[7] The disruption of the strategic railway lines linking Georgia with Russia and Armenia was seen as sufficient ground for using military force. In their view, the use of force should be considered not as initiating a war, but as a police operation on Georgian ter-ritory. When crossing the borders of the Abkhaz Autonomous Republic, Georgian troops claim to have been attacked by Abkhaz military forces. From that moment on, Georgian actions, they claim, took on a defensive character. The Georgian troops advanced deep into Abkhaz territory, occupying the capital Sukhum(i).[8] From their point of view, this military deployment was a legitimate response to the aggression by the Abkhaz side and the latter's attempt to violate the territorial integrity of the Georgian Republic.

The Georgian authorities have thus advanced two different kinds of 'just causes' to justify their military intervention. The chronological sequence of the two stages is particularly important here. In the first stage, the military operations, they claim, were not directly linked to the fact that the Abkhazians were striving for secession but to the disruption of law and order on Abkhaz territory, while in the second stage the intervention was purely defensive. It may be questioned whether there is any historical evidence to support such a distinction between a first and second stage in the intervention, which it is claimed were based on distinct just causes for military action.

It is true that the disruption of strategic communication constituted a serious breach of the rule of law. But this does not mean that the sending of troops to Abkhazia could be considered a legitimate step. The breakdown in law and order was a general feature of social order in the whole of Georgia, and not particular to Abkhazia. Some observers even state that there was no problem with the railway service in Abkhazia itself. The disruption would have been entirely confined to the Georgian region of Mingrelia that neigh-bours Abkhazia.[9] The consequences of military operations in an escalating domestic political conflict are, furthermore, of such gravity—taking into account the number of potential victims and the scope of the potential material destruction in a civil war—that under no circumstances could they have been justified by the disruption of the railway system. This is most probably also the opinion of the Georgian authorities, when they argue that the first stage of the military intervention in Abkhazia should be regarded as

[7] On the Georgian official justification of the military intervention in Abkhazia see Zhorzholiani et al., *Historic, Political and Legal Aspects of the Conflict in Abkhazia*, 36–8.

[8] Georgian authors would generally use the transliteration 'Sukhumi' in English texts, whereas Abkhaz scholars would drop the 'i' and write 'Sukhum'. I refer to 'Sukhum(i)' in order to avoid choosing between the Georgian and the Abkhaz preferences.

[9] George Hewitt, personal communication 7 Nov. 2001.

a kind of police operation and not as the initiation of a war. In their view, the war started with Abkhaz attacks on Georgian troops. Such an interpretation of historical events, even if we accept it at face value, does not justify the ensuing deployment of Georgian troops in Abkhazia or the occupation of its capital Sukhum(i). Once it was made clear that the Abkhaz leadership considered the military intervention to be an act of war, and was using military force to repel what it viewed as an invasion, the Georgian authorities should have ordered the immediate withdrawal of their forces. Being attacked by Abkhaz forces may have been considered unjust by the Georgian side, but the scale of this injustice did not constitute a sufficient reason—in other words, it was not a just cause—for starting a full-scale war in Abkhazia. It may thus be concluded that the Georgian authorities did not act in accordance with the *just cause principle* when starting the military operations in August 1992.

The second principle that has to be assessed is the *principle of right intentions*. To what extent did the Georgian authorities genuinely intend to pursue what they considered to be a just cause? Central to the testing of the *principle of right intentions* is the historical demonstration that there was in reality a predominant and genuine intention of attaining a just cause. Even in cases where there was no objectively just cause for using force, it remains possible that the intention of winning a struggle that is perceived as just was present, and perhaps even triggered the decision. The previous just cause analysis did not consider the various motives that might have led the Georgian authorities to initiate the military hostilities. Among the various intentions that may have been present we can distinguish between:

1. The intention of securing the railway communications on Abkhaz territory.
2. The intention of weakening the Zviadist forces present in Abkhazia and achieving a conclusive victory in the civil war between the Georgian factions.
3. The intention of crushing Abkhaz nationalism, thereby making any further attempt at secession impossible.
4. The intention of enhancing the legitimacy of the new government through a full-scale war against the Abkhaz community.

In considering the deliberations of the Praesidium of the State Council that preceded the decision to wage war, academic literature supports an interpretation in which all four motives are taken into account. But it would be difficult to determine their order of importance. We also have to bear in mind that the various members of the Praesidium had different motives. The intentions of Eduard Shevardnadze were not necessarily those of Tengiz Kitovani, the leader of the paramilitary National Guard and Minister for Defence in the Presidium of the State Council. It is necessary, however, to set these distinctions aside for a normative analysis. The principle of right intentions does not concern private individuals but a public authority. We have therefore to consider the Praesidium as a collective actor.

We would offer the following interpretation of events: as we have seen above, the disruption of railway communications in Abkhazia constituted a serious threat to the new Georgian authorities (intention 1). In order to secure their own survival, the latter had to crush the supporters of the deposed president Gamsakhurdia and to achieve a decisive victory in the civil war between Georgian factions (intention 2). But the possibility of gaining the upper hand in this intra-communal conflict simultaneously gave them an opportunity to achieve the same thing in the inter-communal conflict with the Abkhaz community. Since their accession to power, the new Georgian authorities had been unable to halt the escalation of the political conflict between the two main communities in Abkhazia. On both sides, the population had begun to arm. Sending Georgian military forces to Abkhazia would provide an opportunity for deciding, once and for all, the question of the possible secession of Abkhazia (intention 3). Gamsakhurdia had been elected in May 1991 by over 86 per cent of the population. This support was largely due to his radical nationalistic discourse. Those who had deposed him by force then had to prove that they were no less 'patriotic' than he was. A war against the Abkhaz nationalist movement would rally support for the new authorities among the Georgian population (intention 4).

According to the official Georgian interpretation of events, the Praesidium of the State Council had 'right intentions' in deciding to send troops to intervene in Abkhazia. The distinction between two stages in the escalation towards war (a police operation in the first stage and a defensive war against 'aggressive separatism' in the second) means that there would also have been two distinct intentions, which would have been predominant at different moments. According to this interpretation, there would have been an objective just cause, and subjectively right intentions, twice over. There is, however, no convincing historical evidence that there actually were two different stages in the escalation, driven by completely distinct intentions. Historical literature does not take this justification seriously.[10] It thus cannot be proven that the Georgian authorities had right intentions.

[10] An alternative historical interpretation of the intentions of the Georgian authorities is to be found in Ghia Nodia, 'The Conflict in Abkhazia: National Projects and Political Circumstances', in Coppieters, Nodia, and Anchabadze, *Georgians and Abkhazians*, 34–6. Nodia's interpretation of events is based on a distinction between the intentions of Shevardnadze and those of the Georgian paramilitary commanders. He regards Shevardnadze's intentions as subjectively right. Nodia's interpretation does not contradict the one presented in this chapter. In testing the right intentions principle I set this distinction aside, analysing the Georgian military policies as those of a collective player. A distinction between the various players in the Praesidium of the State Council is made in testing the *principle of legitimate authority*.

The third principle that has to be tested is the *principle of legitimate authority*. Did the Praesidium of the State Council have the moral authority to wage war? Such a moral authority is to be derived from various factors, such as the way in which the new regime had come to power, the democratic legitimacy of the political leadership, and its commitment to the rule of law and to the common good of the whole population living on its territory. All four of these criteria—that have been invoked by the Georgian authorities themselves when legitimizing their authority—have to be examined.

The overthrow of the elected president Gamsakhurdia was justified by the coup leaders as a revolt against an unjust regime. After the flight of Gamsakhurdia from Tbilisi on 6 January 1992, the coup leaders had invited the previous leader of the Georgian Communist Party and former Soviet Minister for Foreign Affairs, Eduard Shevardnadze, to return to his home country and take the leadership of the new government. Shevardnadze returned from Moscow to Tbilisi in March 1992. They felt that in these circumstances he was the only person who would be able to restore confidence in Georgia's new leadership among domestic and international public opinion. This calculation proved to be correct. Western governments, who had refused to establish diplomatic relations with Georgia as long as the Soviet Union existed and Gamsakhurdia was in power, were quick to give full support to the person they regarded as one of the main architects of the peaceful reordering of Europe. They expected that Shevardnadze would have a moderating effect on Georgian nationalism. Moreover, they were prepared to overlook the fact that Shevardnadze had to ally himself with paramilitary forces, whose involvement in criminal activities was widely known. The international community was convinced that Shevardnadze would bring about stabilization and democratization. In July 1992 Georgia was accepted as a full member of the United Nations. It may be concluded that the new Georgian regime of August 1992 lacked the formal characteristics of a democratic government, and was largely dependent on the support of paramilitary forces which had no democratic legitimacy, but that the personal leadership of Shevardnadze seemed to offer reasonable chances for the democratization of the regime and the re-establishment of the rule of law.[11]

More problematic, however, was the commitment of the new Georgian government to the common good of the whole population living on its territory. During Soviet times, Shevardnadze had been successful in consolidating the political privileges and hegemonic position of the Georgian titular nationality in his multinational country. At that time, however, he was also opposed to the radical nationalism of dissidents under the communist regime, such as Gamsakhurdia. After his return to Tbilisi, Shevardnadze managed to

---

[11] Democratic elections were held in Georgia on 11 Oct. 1992.

achieve a cease-fire in the conflict with the authorities of South Ossetia. But he remained entirely dependent on radical nationalist forces when starting and waging the war in Abkhazia. This dependence was to undermine the moral authority of his government. It has also been said—by Shevardnadze himself, among others—that by deploying his troops deep into Abkhaz territory and occupying the Abkhaz capital Sukhum(i) Kitovani had exceeded the order to protect only the railway links. Shevardnadze apparently felt obliged to support the war and grant it his formal authority rather than oppose it openly. If he had left the government—so the argument goes—he would have risked the complete disintegration of the Georgian state. Such an interpretation means that it is preferable to have no legitimate state authority than no state authority at all. This choice may be justified. Shevardnadze's choice may have been a responsible one, as it is difficult to estimate what the consequences of his dismissal would have been. Georgian authors critical of Georgian policies towards Abkhazia are divided on the question of which decision Shevardnadze should have taken at that particular moment.[12] But this difficult moral choice also fully confirms the lack of legitimate authority for the Georgian decision to use force.

According to Shevardnadze's account, before the war he informed the Abkhaz leader Vladislav Ardzinba by phone of his intention to deploy Georgian forces along the Abkhaz railways. This would confirm his respect for the vertical distribution of authority between the central and the local governments. But the Abkhaz authorities have strongly denied that Ardzinba would ever have approved of this deployment—and indeed, such approval would have been most surprising. It was quite obvious that an incursion by Georgian military forces into a region where the political conflict between the Abkhaz and Georgian communities had been escalating for years would be perceived by the Abkhaz side as a serious threat. Even if Shevardnadze's account was true, and he was indeed the victim of an Abkhaz 'provocation', as stated by the Georgian authorities, it still would not justify the deployment of Georgian troops throughout the territory of Abkhazia. As stated above, the duty of the Georgian troops would have been to retreat after the initial

---

[12] Back in August 1992, Naira Gelashwili had already defended the position that Shevardnadze would have to resign in order to avoid taking formal responsibility for launching the civil war in Abkhazia: 'Back in Tbilisi, on 19 August I was called to see Shevardnadze. He was severely shaken by the unexpected disaster. I found it very difficult to tell him what I thought, which was that he should resign, otherwise he would bear formal responsibility for the bloodshed and chaos. If he resigned, the Ministry of Defence and Kitovani would have to bear this responsiblity, and that might restrain them. For me it was crucial that he should be spared the burden of being responsible for the deaths of so many people.' Gelaschwili, *Georgien: Ein Paradies in Trümmern*, 163. Ghia Nodia, on the contrary, considers that a decision to resign would at that point have been 'extremely irresponsible'. Nodia, 'The Conflict in Abkhazia', 35. On Nodia's analysis see also my contribution 'Shades of Grey: Intentions, Motives and Moral Responsibility in the Georgian–Abkhaz Conflict', in Coppieters, Nodia, and Anchabadze, *Georgians and Abkhazians*, 143–67.

clashes, instead of engaging in a civil war with the Abkhazians. The term 'provocation', moreover, is quite inappropriate to justify the actions of the government of a sovereign state. Explaining and excusing one's behaviour as the result of an irresistible reaction to a 'provocation' is commonly done by thugs, but is not to be expected of governments. In order to qualify as a legitimate authority, such a government has to be capable of exercising self-restraint in the use of force. Its inability to do so further demonstrates that the Georgian authorities failed to respect the *principle of legitimate authority*.

According to the *principle of last resort*, the use of force is morally authorized only on condition that all reasonable steps have been taken to avoid a military confrontation. This condition was not respected either. In 1991 the Gamsakhurdia government had made an attempt to avert confrontation by negotiating a compromise solution on the ethnic make-up of the Abkhaz parliament. The failure of the two communities to share power was largely due to the unwillingness of the Abkhaz authorities either to allow representatives of the Georgian community to participate in the government of the autonomous republic or to respect the agreement that no substantial changes would be introduced into the Abkhaz Constitution without a two-thirds majority in parliament. But the lack of commitment on the Abkhaz side to sharing power with the Georgian community, and their violation of the agreements made, do not mean that no further attempts should have been made by the Georgian authorities to negotiate a compromise.

Before the arrival of the Georgian troops, the Abkhaz parliament had been about to discuss a proposal for the distribution of power between Georgia and Abkhazia according to a confederal framework. Such a proposal would clearly have been unacceptable to the Georgian authorities. It was based on the recognition of Abkhazia's external sovereignty and statehood, and it did not take into account the interests of the non-Abkhaz and particularly of the Georgian population of Abkhazia. It could, however, have been one of the documents to be tabled for discussion. It would then probably have taken time for the negotiations to achieve positive results, but the many hurdles to be overcome do not excuse the Georgian authorities' lack of commitment to the search for a peaceful outcome to the conflict. The Georgian authorities did not take the *principle of last resort* seriously. Their unwillingness to compromise was clearly illustrated by Shevardnadze during the war, when he declared—in an address to the Georgian parliament in November 1992—that the electoral law negotiated by his predecessor, which introduced ethnic quotas into the distribution of parliamentary seats in the Abkhaz legislature, should be seen as a form of 'de jure apartheid' and 'the establishment of an ethno-dictatorship'.[13]

---

[13] See Chervonnaya, *Conflict in the Caucasus*, 91. See also Coppieters, *Federalism and Conflict in the Caucasus*, 24–5.

According to the *principle of proportionality*, the anticipated cost of fighting a war should not be out of line with the benefits to be expected from the attainment of its just cause. No such benefits were to be expected from a war in Abkhazia. To begin with, the Georgian authorities had no just cause which could justify the high cost of an armed confrontation. Of course, the Georgian authorities could expect that their military presence would expel the Zviadist forces from Abkhazia. But such benefits were far from sufficient to be in line with the *principle of proportionality*. Moreover, comparable benefits at far less cost could have been expected through a request for Russian military support against the Zviadists. The policies of Zviad Gamsakhurdia during his brief term in office had in fact become a heavy burden on the Moscow authorities, who were keen to prevent him returning to power. Of course, the Georgian authorities would have had to make far-reaching compromises, such as accepting the Russian military presence on Georgian territory and participation in the Commonwealth of Independent States, but these compromises would have been far less costly than the consequences to be anticipated from a war against Abkhazia. Better cooperation with Moscow would moreover have opened up the prospect of a more neutral role for Russia in the Georgian–Abkhaz conflict. It is true that compromise solutions of this nature run counter to the basic principles of Georgian nationalism, which aims at emancipation from Russian dominance. But Georgia found itself in such a difficult situation after its defeat in Abkhazia in October 1993 that it was forced to make all the compromises described above in order to secure Russian support against the Zviadist forces, which were threatening the strategically important town of Kutaisi. The danger was averted with Russian help, but Georgia then had to make concessions to Moscow under far less favourable conditions than in 1992. The war could probably have been avoided if it had made those and other compromises earlier.

The last principle to be assessed concerning Georgia's *jus ad bellum* is the *principle of likelihood of success*. This principle, like the previous one, deals with the consequences of initiating a war and has therefore a strong prudential character. Was there a strong probability that the Georgian authorities would be outstripped militarily, so that it would have been more prudent for them to abstain from the use of force? It is indeed morally unjustified to start a war if there is no realistic chance of gaining the upper hand. This possibility was rejected at the time by the Georgian authorities. They were convinced that the overwhelming numerical superiority of the Georgians over the Abkhaz community ruled out any possibility of defeat. This calculation, however, omitted to take into account the lack of military preparedness of the Georgian troops and possible support for the Abkhaz cause from the non-Georgian population of Abkhazia, from the Northern Caucasus and from the Russian military forces stationed in the region. This lack of understanding of the military and political relationships between the forces meant that the Georgian authorities were no more able to respect the moral *principle of likelihood of success* than any other *jus ad bellum* principle.

During the 1992–3 war, the Georgian side likewise failed to respect the two *jus in bello* principles of *proportionality* and *discrimination*. The *principle of proportionality* has to do with the moral costs and benefits of military operations. Owing to their lack of military preparedness and lack of coordination, the Georgian troops engaged in battles where the costs to both sides in human lives and material destruction were too high.[14] Nor did they respect the *principle of discrimination* and distinguish between combatants and non-combatants, as was shown by a UN assessment mission at the end of the war.[15] The Georgian troops even committed atrocities against the civilian population of their own community.

WAR AND JUSTICE: THE ABKHAZ PERSPECTIVE

The fact that one of the warring parties did not fight a 'just war' does not mean that the war fought by the other party has to be called just. In this case too, every single *jus ad bellum* and *jus in bello* principle has to be applied to the circumstances of the war before an overall judgement can be reached. The defence of a territory and its population against foreign aggression is a classic case of a just cause. But the concept of territory is traditionally understood as the territory of a sovereign state. In the case of the Georgian military intervention, it would be impossible to consider crossing the border into Abkhazia as 'foreign' aggression or as a violation of the principle of territorial sovereignty, to the extent that Abkhazia was an autonomous republic which was part of the Georgian republic. The Georgian intervention was, moreover, intervention by the federal authorities in an internal political conflict between the two main national communities in the federated state of Abkhazia on the side of the Georgian community. The Georgian intervention by paramilitary troops could, however, be regarded as a direct threat to the physical survival of the Abkhaz community. In this sense, the ethical *just cause principle* does apply, even though the concept of a political community does not have the same meaning as a sovereign state.

[14] See Dodge Billingsley, 'Military Aspects of the War: the Turning Point', in Hewitt, *The Abkhazians*, 147–56.

[15] See the 'Report of the Secretary-General's Fact-Finding Mission to Investigate Human Rights Violations in Abkhazia, Republic of Georgia', UN Document S/26795, 17 Nov. 1993. The report of the mission, which visited the area from 22 to 30 October 1993, lists the following categories of human-rights violations committed by both sides in the conflict: extra-judicial executions; torture and ill-treatment, including rape; violations of property rights including looting and the burning of houses and apartments; forced deportations.

Nor does the fact that the Abkhaz political community was defined in ethnic rather than in civic or territorial terms alter anything in this respect.

The *principle of proportionality* may likewise be considered to have been
respected by the Abkhaz side. In the circumstances of a civil war with the
Georgian community, the small Abkhaz community had serious reasons for
considering its physical survival as being threatened, and this justifies the
cost of a military response.

Concerning the *principle of likelihood of success*, both sides were utterly
unprepared for war at the organizational level. The Abkhazians were unable
to assess before August 1992 the range of external support they would
receive from the Russian military and from allied paramilitary forces in the
Northern Caucasus.

Far more problematic in this context—and no less important in a moral
assessment of the Abkhaz authorities' war policies than the previous three
principles—was the application of the *principle of last resort*. Confronted
with the Georgian intervention, the Abkhaz side did not have the possibility
of entering into political negotiations with Tbilisi. Seen from this perspective,
it respected the *principle of last resort*. But in this context it has to be added
that the Abkhaz authorities had not previously made any serious attempt to
de-escalate the conflict. Quite the reverse: they had unilaterally carried out a
series of constitutional reforms, which went against the existing formal constitutional procedures and were made without the political participation of
the—large—Georgian community. These Abkhaz policies mirrored the
Georgian policies of making unilateral changes at the constitutional level
which went against a federal division of power between the centre and the
autonomous federated entities, and which were made without political participation by any of the minorities. In the escalation of the conflict from a
political to a military one, both parties may therefore be said to have violated
the *principle of last resort* to the extent that—with the sole exception of the
electoral law of 1991—they made no serious attempt to resolve their political differences through negotiation or compromise. But this does not mean
that Georgian and Abkhaz sides shared an equivalent responsibility for
starting the August 1992 civil war. A more differentiated analysis is needed
in this case. The Georgian leadership bears the full burden of responsibility
for the initiation of the hostilities, as it left the Abkhaz leadership with no
reasonable choice other than military self-defence.

The Abkhaz intention to defend their community and to uphold the
political status they had acquired during Soviet times was decisive in their
decision to repel the Georgian intervention by force. It was linked to their
struggle in the just cause of self-defence against aggression, as defined
above, and may therefore be considered right. It may be questioned, however, whether no other intentions were present which went beyond the aim

of self-defence and which were not linked to winning a just cause. It may also be asked to what extent such intentions were not more prominent than the cause of self-defence, which would go against the *principle of right intentions*. Three intentions have to be considered in the Abkhaz decision to use force in self-defence:

1. The intention of defending the Abkhaz community against physical threats and loss of political and social rights.
2. The intention of increasing the legitimacy of the Abkhaz authorities among the Abkhaz and other non-Georgian communities in Abkhazia through military mobilization, in line with the vision of the nineteenth-century military historian, Heinrich von Treitschke, that it is war that 'turns a people into a nation'.[16]
3. The intention of achieving sovereign or even independent status through the use of force.

The moral legitimacy of the first intention has been analysed above. This intention was to struggle for a cause which may be considered just. The objective of increasing the legitimacy of a government or achieving sovereign status through war should not, however, be dismissed. The authorities effectively used the popular mobilization for self-defence as a means to these two ends. This would go against the *principle of right intentions* if it could be proven that they were more prominent than the intention of defending the Abkhaz community. Such an accusation has been levelled against them by Shevardnadze, when he condemned the Abkhaz authorities for having waged a war of 'aggressive separatism'. There is, however, no historical evidence to support such a claim. The Abkhaz authorities had a legitimate right to use force in self-defence, and it cannot be proven that this motive was only a secondary one. It is not only possible but also highly probable that all three intentions were present in the discussions on the use of force by the Abkhaz side, but insofar as the first one was prominent in the mobilization of military forces, the *principle of right intentions* may be said to have been respected.

It may be concluded that the Georgian authorities failed to respect any of the just war principles, whereas the Abkhaz authorities largely went against the *principles of last resort* and *legitimate authority*. When confronted by the threat of a military occupation by Georgian paramilitary forces they had no reasonable alternative but to defend their national community by military means. An analysis of the escalation process which led to the war also makes it clear that the Abkhaz authorities failed to take all necessary steps to avoid

---

[16] Quoted in Susan-Mary Grant, 'Making History: Myth and the Construction of American Nationhood', in George Schöpflin and Geoffrey Hosking (eds.), *Myths and Nationhood* (London, C. Hurst and Co., 1997), 101.

the use of force. The Abkhaz government never developed a policy that went beyond ethnic antagonism to the Georgian population. The other nationalities were at most regarded as allies in the struggle against the Georgian occupier. The Abkhaz national project did not include a view of statehood that would be responsive to the interests of all the inhabitants of Abkhazia. This has direct implications for an assessment of their present claims to sovereignty and independence.

THE ABKHAZ CLAIM TO INDEPENDENCE

The various just war principles need to be reinterpreted in order to be applied to secessionist conflicts and claims to independence. In this moral context, the *just cause principle* means that unilateral secession is a necessary means to redress or to prevent a grave injustice. This may be the denial of the right to national self-determination through military occupation, colonization, oppression, or exploitation. Respect for the *principle of last resort* means in this context that no alternatives are available, such as minority rights or federalism, or the possibility of achieving independence according to mutually agreed procedures. The application of the *principle of legitimate authority* requires the seceding state to affirm the principle of popular representation, the rule of law, democracy and minority rights. The *principle of right intentions* prescribes in this context that the primary intention of the decision to unilateral secession must be to redress or to prevent a severe injustice. According to the *principle of proportionality*, the total cost of unilateral secession must not be out of line with the benefits to be expected from this measure. Applying the *chance of success principle* makes it necessary to assess to what extent the seceding state can have a reasonable expectation of being internationally recognized.

Various arguments have been put forward by the Abkhaz authorities to strengthen their claim to sovereignty and equal status with Georgia in a confederal framework and (since 1999) their claim to independence.[17] They argue that Abkhazia has three basic characteristics of *de facto* statehood: a reasonably well-defined territory, a permanent population, and a stable government. In their view, the existence of Abkhazia as a state is not at stake in the discussion on recognition. The normative discussion on Abkhazia's statehood should thus be limited to the legal and moral obligation for the international community to recognize the legitimacy of the Abkhaz claims.

---

[17] The following presentation of Abkhaz and Georgian views is largely based on the presentations made by governmental delegations from Georgia and Abkhazia to the seminar 'State-Legal Aspects of the Settlement of the Georgian-Abkhazian Conflict', a seminar organized by the Venice Commission of the Council of Europe held at Pitsunda, Abkhazia, 12–13 Feb. 2001. I participated in this meeting in the capacity of an expert for the Venice Commission.

In this respect, it can be observed that all the arguments used by the Abkhaz authorities to support their claims are in one way or another linked to one of the traditional just war principles. This does not mean that they are all related to the experience of the war. This is the case, for instance, with various historical arguments in line with the *just cause principle* or the *principle of legitimate authority*. Countering the Georgian claim that Abkhazia was always a part of the Georgian political realm, Abkhaz historians defend the thesis that Abkhazia experienced 1,200 years of statehood.[18] When unified with Georgia under tsarist rule, the region, they claim, was forcibly colonized by Georgians.

Abkhaz historians further dispute the view that Abkhazia failed to establish its independence after the demise of the tsarist empire and before the establishment of Soviet power in the region. They underline the numerous attempts by the Abkhaz national movements to emancipate themselves from Georgia. In addition, Abkhaz historians regard the Soviet federal policies, which subordinated Abkhazia to Georgia, as fundamentally unjust. The fact that these policies had been implemented by Stalin, a Georgian national, in their view confirms that these policies suited Georgian imperial interests. They criticize the international community's interpretation of the Soviet constitution, according to which only Union republics would have had the right to secession. In their view, the attempts to reform the Soviet federal state at the end of the 1980s included a Soviet law 'On the Procedure for the Resolution of Questions Involved in the Withdrawal of a Union Republic from the Union of Soviet Socialist Republics (USSR)', which gave the population of autonomous republics and other autonomous entities the option of 'taking an independent decision on the question of whether to stay in the USSR or the seceding Union republic, and also of posing, independently, the question of its legal status as regards statehood'.[19] According to the Abkhaz interpretation, the unilateral secession of the Georgian republic from the Soviet Union presented Abkhazia with such an option. The people of Abkhazia, they claimed, had opted for sovereignty and the right to secede. The Georgian military intervention in August 1992 was, in their view, an attempt to wipe out these achievements. In this narrative, the arguments concerning the history of Abkhaz independent statehood and the Soviet federal system are in line with the *principle of legitimate authority*, whereas the references to previous injustices such as colonisation and oppression by an imperial power are in line with the *just cause principle*.

---

[18] Viacheslav Chirikba, 'Georgia and Abkhazia: Proposals for a Constitutional Model', in Coppieters, Darchiashvili, and Akaba, *Federal Practice*, 247.

[19] Article 3 of the USSR law 'O poryadke resheniya voprosov, sviazannykh c vykhodom soyuznoi respubliki iz SSR', published in *Izvestia*, 6 April 1990. The law was signed by Mikhail Gorbachev, President of the USSR, on 3 April 1990.

This interpretation of Abkhazia's political history is challenged by Georgian authors. They likewise use historical arguments in line with the *just cause* and *legitimate authority principles*. At no time, they say, had Abkhazia established its statehood independently of the Georgian political realm. Georgian authors deny the existence of Georgian colonization of the Abkhaz region, considering their own presence there as having continued from time immemorial or as the natural result of migratory flows. They do not deny that the Abkhazians have been unjustly treated in modern history, but consider that this has also been the case for the Georgian nation. Such injustices were the doing not of the Georgian, but of the tsarist and Soviet authorities. As they see it, the subordination of Abkhazia to Georgia in the Soviet constitutional set-up was not unjust, as Abkhazia would never have attained independent statehood anyhow, so its lack of sovereignty is in line with history. They further deny the constitutional validity of the Soviet law on secession of April 1990 which gave autonomous entities in Georgia and other Union republics the right to choose their international status independently. This law was intended to deter Union republics from seceding from the Soviet Union, since the exercise of this constitutional right would now threaten to provoke the disintegration of their state.

In these contradictory narratives, history is used to defend particular political objectives. It is difficult to base political choices, such as the recognition of states, on such a type of knowledge. Historical injustices must undoubtedly be taken into account in discussing opposing claims, but the history of nations remains permanently open to contradictory interpretations. It cannot be expected that one single narrative will guide the political act of international recognition. In the event of the disintegration of federations, such as the Soviet Union or Yugoslavia, international recognition has largely been granted on the basis of an interpretation of their constitutions. This was practised out of necessity, irrespective of the historical origin and the moral legitimacy of the Soviet and Yugoslav constitutions. This does not mean that the normative discussion on secession should be entirely subordinated to the factual existence of constitutional rules. In the following, we will analyse both claims from the perspective of political ethics and will apply the various criteria to be found in just war theory to the ethics of secession.

It has been demonstrated above that the Abkhaz and Georgian historical narratives implicitly make use of the principles of *just cause* and *legitimate authority*. It can also be demonstrated that they also use other *jus ad bellum* principles such as *proportionality, likelihood of success, last resort*, and *right intentions* in framing their historical arguments for or against the right of secession of Abkhazia. These criteria have to be made explicit and redefined for that purpose: the *just cause principle* prescribes in this context that severe forms of injustice must be prevented. This particularly concerns the risk of a repetition of the Georgian armed incursion into Abkhazia in August 1992. But a unilateral declaration of independence—which, as a unilateral action, creates new forms of conflict and injustice (affecting minorities, the rump state and the international community)—can only be used as solution of last resort. As will be argued below, a federal arrangement is a preferable option. A unilateral declaration of independence may only be considered a just means of attaining a just cause if no reasonable alternative is available. The Abkhaz authorities themselves seemed to agree with this reasoning in the past, by postponing their decision to proclaim independence unilaterally until 1999. They then claimed that their previous proposals for a confederal arrangement had not been taken seriously by the Georgian government and that they were still awaiting a response.[20]

Among the various alternatives, a federal framework has a number of advantages. It would facilitate an accommodation between the competing claims for self-determination of the two main communities in Abkhazia itself. Democratic federations can prevent the type of subordination between the federal centre and the federated units that prevailed in the Soviet Union. A federal order would moreover acknowledge the legitimate need of the international community for a restrictive approach to the question of recognition of sovereign status, in order to preserve its efficiency as the cornerstone of international order. Strong international guarantees for the peaceful coexistence of the Georgian and Abkhaz national communities may furthermore be envisaged in a federal framework. These security guarantees would not be necessarily as far-reaching as those that can be provided by the institution of international sovereignty, but should be sufficient to avoid a repetition of the 1992 intervention. Through a federalization of the foreign competences of the Common State of Georgia and Abkhazia, Sukhum(i) could wield its internal competences in the international arena as a subject of international law. Its limited international personality and treaty-making power, enshrined in the constitution, would, however, have to be recognized by the international community.[21]

Should a federation prove unable to resolve the national conflict between Georgians and Abkhazians, it could still have the advantage of regulating them in a peaceful way. A federation has to be regarded as an open system,

[20] Interview with the Abkhaz Minister for Foreign Affairs Sergei Shamba, 9 Nov. 2000.
[21] See Bruno Coppieters, Tamara Kovziridze and Uwe Leonardy, 'Federalization of Foreign Relations: Discussing Alternatives for the Georgian–Abkhaz Conflict,' published as Working Paper No. 2 from the *Caspian Studies Program's Working Paper Series*, Harvard University, 2003. On the normative preference for federal status see Bruno Coppieters, 'Ethno-Federalism and Civic State-Building Policies: Perspectives on the Georgian–Abkhaz Conflict', in *Regional & Federal Studies*, 11:2 (Summer 2001), 69–93.

open to transformation, where the creation of confederal relations between
federated entities, or even full independence, may be a legitimate outcome,
provided that procedural rules are designed that are commonly accepted by
all parties. A federal arrangement or peace settlement where the option of
secession is not a priori excluded, but is regulated according to general rules,
increases its democratic legitimacy for all parties involved. The possibility
that constitutional procedures on secession may be jointly accepted by those
who are striving for secession and by those who are opposing it has been
demonstrated by the positive reactions from pro- and anti-secessionist
movements alike to the Good Friday Agreement on Northern Ireland, in
April 1998,[22] and to the opinion of the Supreme Court of Canada concerning the secession of Quebec, in August 1998.[23]

The above analysis of the events leading to the 1992 war has demonstrated that the Abkhaz authorities did not act according to the *principle of
last resort*. Neither before nor after the war did they seriously address questions such as international guarantees, power-sharing or minority rights
within a federal framework.[24] It is true that the Georgian authorities likewise remained largely silent on such matters, despite their declared readiness to federalize relations between Georgia and Abkhazia. Their proposals
have been confined to a distribution of competences between Georgia and
Abkhazia, leaving open the question of to what extent Abkhazians will participate in the exercise of government in Abkhazia itself. Nor do the
Georgian proposals deal with such central issues as possible conflicts
between federal institutions over their respective areas of competence, or
the key question of how military intervention by the federal government in
a political conflict between national communities in Abkhazia can be ruled
out. The stalemate in the negotiations has led to a situation where each
party now provides its own interpretation of the *principle of last resort*. Each
points to the unwillingness of the other to compromise in order to advance
more radical solutions. Shevardnadze has made repeated appeals for a military enforcement of a peace settlement with the help of Russian or NATO
troops. For Tamaz Nadareishvili, the Georgian chairman of the so-called

---

[22] The Good Friday Agreement recognizes 'the legitimacy of whatever choice is freely exercised by a majority of the people of Northern Ireland with regard to its status, whether they
prefer to continue to support the Union with Great Britain or a sovereign united Ireland'. The
full text of the agreement is to be found on http://www.irelandstory.com/today/good_friday/
full_text.html.

[23] According to the opinion of the Supreme Court of Canada of August 1998 there is no
right, under international law or under the constitution of Canada, for Quebec to secede unilaterally. A clear majority in Quebec in favour of secession would, however, under certain conditions—such as a referendum on a clear and unambiguous question—create an obligation for
the federal government to negotiate the secession of Quebec.

[24] Alternative proposals have been designed by Abkhaz scholars such as Viacheslav Chirikba
(see Chirikba, 'Georgia and Abkhazia: Proposals for a Constitutional Model', 233–78).

'Abkhaz parliament-in-exile', force has to be used against the breakaway state, with or without external support. The Abkhaz leadership has likewise declared that negotiations on political status have been fruitless and that unilateral secession by Abkhazia should now be accepted as a last resort. As neither the Abkhaz nor the Georgian authorities demonstrate a clear willingness to compromise or to develop practical models of conflict settlement, neither of these 'last resort' solutions can be considered legitimate.

The claim by the Abkhaz authorities that they have the *legitimate authority* to take the step of declaring unilateral secession is seriously flawed. Their implementation of the principle of national self-determination is restricted to Abkhazia's 'titular nation'. The Russian and Armenian nationalities are seen only as passive supporters of the Abkhaz leadership. There is no blueprint for the inclusion of the large Georgian population in the future of Abkhazia. In addition, the perception that their presence is primarily a result of colonization makes inclusive nation-building policy even more difficult. The Abkhaz authorities have the greatest difficulty in bringing their policies into line with international human rights standards. The return of the refugee population is seen as a serious threat to the political privileges of the Abkhaz titular nation, and only a minority—primarily the inhabitants of the Gali region—have been allowed go back to their homes. The lack of prospects for the return of refugees led to the condemnation of the ethnic cleansing by the Abkhaz authorities in the final documents of summits of the Organization for Security and Cooperation in Europe (OSCE).[25] There have been some attempts to foster the Mingrelian identity of the Georgian population of the Gali region; for example, a newspaper in the Mingrelian language was published in the summer of 1995 with the support of the Abkhaz authorities.[26] Such attempts to take a more inclusive view of Abkhaz citizenship by strengthening the cultural identity of the local population have not, however, been pursued with great determination, and they have failed to arouse political allegiance to the Abkhaz authorities among the Mingrelians.

According to the Abkhaz constitution, the source of sovereignty is located in the population living on Abkhaz territory.[27] As far as the notion of popular sovereignty is concerned, no distinction is made here between ethnic groups. Despite this constitutional provision, however, in October 1999 the Abkhaz authorities organized a referendum on independence that failed to

[25] The final declarations of the OSCE summits in December 1994 (Budapest), December 1996 (Lisbon) and November 1999 (Istanbul) are to be found on the OSCE website http://www.osce.org/
[26] See George Hewitt, 'Abkhazia, Georgia and the Circassians (NW Caucasus)', *Central Asian Survey*, 18:4 (1999), 477.
[27] The text of the Abkhaz constitution can be found on http://www.abkhazia.org/

take into account the part of the population of Abkhazia that had to flee as a result of the war. Moreover, the discussions preceding the referendum left no room for pluralism or open debate. It may be concluded that the principles of popular representation, of the rule of law, of democracy and minority rights have not been respected in Abkhazia's unilateral declaration of independence.

The lack of prospects for the integration of national minorities is also central to the testing of the *principle of proportionality*. According to the Abkhaz authorities, international recognition of Abkhaz independence would increase the possibilities for the Georgian refugees to return. They consider that a massive return of refugees would at present constitute a threat, but that recognition would in principle give sufficient security guarantees to Abkhazia to permit such a return. This argument, too, is seriously flawed. It is unclear how participation by the large Georgian population in political life in Abkhazia would be facilitated by independence. The problem of power-sharing remains no less acute in a sovereign state than in a federated one. Thus, where the problem of the coexistence of the various communities is concerned, no substantial benefits are to be expected from secession for any of them.

The Georgian authorities deny that the Abkhaz authorities have right intentions in pursuing the cause of secession. They argue that there is no valid reason to strive for secession from a state that has granted so many rights and privileges to the Abkhaz nation. The 'real' intentions of the Abkhaz, they claim, lie rather in an attempt to revive the Soviet state and to serve Russian imperial interests. According to other interpretations of Abkhaz policies, secession reflects the interests of the local *nomenklatura*. Such views—which are widespread in the Georgian media—are only partly correct. The Abkhaz authorities have indeed built their policies of secession on the idea that Russia has the will and the capacity to reinforce the Abkhaz position in the conflict, even if it does not support the option of independence. Contrary to the Georgian view of Russia's imperial role—that is, that its foreign policies are based on the principle of 'divide and rule'—the Abkhaz authorities expect their northern neighbour to play a stabilizing role. They try to convince the Moscow authorities that sovereignty would be a prerequisite for such stabilization. International sovereignty could either find an expression in independence or in the status of an associated state with the Russian Federation.

The interests of the Abkhaz leadership would in many respects be better served by independence than by federated status for their state. Independence gives access to a large number of resources that cannot be accessible to the same extent to non-sovereign entities. As members of international economic organizations, they may obtain easier access to grants and loans than federated states. They would also have exclusive access to international security organizations, which are barred to non-sovereign entities.

The nationalist view of emancipation from foreign oppression has been decisive in the mass mobilization of the Abkhaz community. Support for independence in the referendum of October 1999 has largely been a question of loyalty to the national community and to the authorities. For those who supported the decision, the primary intention was to consolidate the just cause of self-defence. The absence of public debate and democratic procedures rendered it impossible for voters to assess the viability of alternative options. But the *principle of right intentions* was respected to the extent that this principle assesses not the rightness of the Abkhaz cause but the rightness of the—subjective—Abkhaz intentions.

A further condition for unilateral secession to be considered legitimate is that it should have a reasonable chance of succeeding (*the likelihood of success principle*). This possibility has to be regarded as very slim. The international community—including the Russian Federation—has no interest in creating a precedent for other secessionist movements. The decision not to pursue negotiations on the federalization of Abkhazia and Georgia also has dramatic economic and social consequences for the Abkhaz population. Investment is hardly possible in an insecure environment. International development agencies are unable to provide reconstruction funds as long as such support may be interpreted as a form of recognition for Abkhazia's independence.

CONCLUSIONS

The present paper has defended the thesis that rejecting the various Georgian justifications for their war aims does not mean that the Abkhaz claim to independence is justified. Independent status is not a necessary consequence of the application of the *just cause principle* to the Georgian–Abkhaz ethnonational conflict. Federalization could—according to the *principle of last resort*—redress and prevent the various types of injustice suffered in the past. Unilateral secession has been justified in Abkhazia as the exercise of the right to national self-determination by a relatively small part of the population, which goes against the *principle of legitimate authority*. The unilateral declaration of secession has made it even more difficult to acknowledge the right to return of the Georgian population of Abkhazia. Its political and social costs far outweigh its benefits, which goes against the *proportionality principle*. There is no reasonable chance that the international community will recognize Abkhazia's unilateral declaration of independence, which means that the *principle of likelihood of success* is not respected either. The decision, however, is in line with the *principle of right intentions* to the extent that this principle refers exclusively to subjective intentions.

A legitimate outcome to this ethnonational conflict does not depend on the Abkhaz side alone. It has been argued in this chapter that the Georgian authorities carry by far a greater share of responsibility for the launching of military intervention in 1992. Their refusal to acknowledge their responsibility casts a heavy shadow over the political negotiations. They have further failed to produce a blueprint for a federal state which would provide for shared rule by all nationalities in Abkhazia. The refusal of the Abkhaz authorities to start negotiations on the political status of Abkhazia within the framework of a common state, however, makes it impossible to judge to what extent the Georgian authorities are ready to explore alternatives to war and secession, and to base the future governance of their common state on the principles of shared rule and federalism.

The consequences of these policies may be fateful for Georgia and Abkhazia.[28] A new war is not excluded. The government of Shevardnadze has been largely delegitimized since the second half of the 1990s by the scale of its economic mismanagement and corruption and the lack of prospects for an end to the Abkhaz conflict. The Abkhaz leadership has likewise lost much of its popularity since the end of the war. The lack of economic prospects is forcing large numbers of young people to emigrate from Abkhazia. Georgia's failure to consolidate its statehood and the depopulation of Abkhazia may be the most obvious consequences of the general lack of adequate moral principles in dealing with the question of secession and the use of force, the lack of creative imagination in designing institutional solutions, and the lack of political will in making radical compromises.

[28] On the following see Bruno Coppieters, 'Tempting the Fates. Abkhazia and Georgia play a Dangerous Waiting Game', *Armenian International Magazine*, March 2001, 68–9.

10

A Case of Ambiguity: Unravelling Dichotomies in Quebec Secessionist Discourse

Ronald Rudin

The last decade of the twentieth century saw the proliferation of movements dedicated to the creation of new states, a process that was given a significant boost by the collapse of the Soviet Union. This outbreak of secessionist movements has generated a considerable literature by scholars in such fields as political science and philosophy who have invested much energy in trying to sift out claims that seemed reasonable from those which were not. In the process, these scholars have tried to develop an overarching normative framework in which to understand secessionist demands.

In order to develop such a framework, authors of varying perspectives have looked for case studies that illustrate the limits within which movements for national self-determination (defined very broadly) might be deemed 'justified', and among the cases most frequently referred to is that of Quebec, a Canadian province that has been home to a well-organized movement for sovereignty (the term secession is rarely used in Quebec) since the 1960s. The Quebec experience was featured in the subtitle of one of the more important books on the subject published during the 1990s, Allen Buchanan's *Secession: The Morality of Political Divorce from Fort Sumter to Lithuania and Quebec.*[1] The Quebec case also figured prominently in Michael Keating's, *Nations Against the State: The New Politics of Nationalism in Quebec, Catalonia and Scotland,*[2] and in Michael Ignatieff's *Blood and Belonging: Journeys into the New Nationalism.*[3] Quebec has also been given a prominent place in *National Self-Determination and Secession,* a

[1] Allen Buchanan, *Secession: The Morality of Political Divorce from Fort Sumter to Lithuania and Quebec* (Boulder, Colo., Westview Press, 1991).
[2] Michael Keating, *Nations Against the State: The New Politics of Nationalism in Quebec, Catalonia and Scotland* (London, Macmillan, 1996).
[3] Michael Ignatieff, *Blood and Belonging: Journeys into the New Nationalism* (New York, Farrar, Strauss and Giroux, 1993).

collection of essays edited by Margaret Moore.[4] While these essays touched upon numerous high-profile cases such as Bosnia and Croatia, Quebec constituted the single case study that received the largest number of index references.

At first glance, it is difficult to understand the particular attraction that Quebec has held for these scholars. After all, this secessionist movement has not been marked by either the violence or the inflammatory language that can be found in relation to other movements. Nevertheless, the Quebec case has proved attractive, perhaps in part for both its novelty in the context of North America and its apparent accessibility to scholars, many of whom are Canadians or Americans who might feel more comfortable referring to an example close to home than to ones far away. On another level, however, the Quebec experience has been interesting because it offers support for various approaches to the highly charged question of what constitutes an appropriate justification for secession.

In the sections that follow, we will see that nationalist discourse in Quebec, strongly supported by different understandings of Quebec history, has provided evidence for a variety of perspectives upon sovereignty. The Quebec case provides evidence for arguments based on an ethnic understanding of nationalism, for others grounded on a civic definition of the Quebec 'nation', and for still other perspectives that fall between those extremes. The Quebec case also demonstrates that shifts may take place in the nationalist discourse at different stages in the debate on secession, moving between the predominance of ethnic arguments towards a greater emphasis on civic arguments. Minority rights are another prominent theme in normative debates on the right to secession in general, and in Quebec politics in particular. There is also evidence in the Quebec experience of arguments for sovereignty couched in terms of 'just cause'—such as those justified in terms of threats to the French language or discriminatory redistribution— and others based on the right of a people to self-determination. Even the definition of sovereignty has been employed by different advocates in diverse ways: some arguing that Quebec's interests require a complete break with the rest of Canada, while others argue for Quebec's sovereignty in most domains, tempered by shared jurisdiction with the Canadian government over the remaining areas. These political debates refer to the application of the principle of 'last resort', as applied to normative studies on secession. This chapter will argue that there has been nothing straightforward about discourses over sovereignty in Quebec, and this is one reason why the case has proven so attractive to scholars of different viewpoints since each could find material that seemed to support their perspective.

[4] Margaret Moore (ed.), *National Self-Determination and Secession* (Oxford, Oxford University Press, 1998).

THE AMBIGUITY OF SOVEREIGNIST DISCOURSE
IN QUEBEC

Since the emergence in the 1960s of a well-organized movement to redefine Quebec's position within the Canadian federation, two different understandings of sovereignty have been at odds with one another. Each of these views received dramatic public airing in the aftermath of the two referenda that were held in the late twentieth century. While the propositions that may have led to Quebec's exit from the Canadian federation were rejected on each occasion, the leaders of the government in each instance presented projects that were grounded in different conceptions of Quebec's past, present and future.

The first referendum was held in 1980 during the first term in power of the Parti Québécois (PQ), the mainstream political party that had been advocating a redefinition of Quebec's relation with the rest of Canada since its creation in 1968. The founder of the party, René Lévesque, had been a cabinet minister in the Liberal government of the early 1960s that had introduced a series of reforms which are referred to collectively as having constituted a 'Quiet Revolution'. Those reforms were revolutionary in the sense that they led to the construction in Quebec of a state prepared to intervene into all aspects of people's lives. While this process had taken place earlier in other Canadian provinces, it came relatively late in Quebec because various state functions had traditionally been handled either by the Catholic church, which had held a central role in the provision of services in Quebec society since the establishment of a French colony on the banks of the St Lawrence in the late seventeenth century, or by private businesses run by English-speakers, who amassed considerable influence when Quebec passed into British control in 1763.

By the mid-nineteenth century, the division of power in Quebec society between a French-led church and an English-led business community was symbolized in Montreal by the construction at opposite ends of Place d'Armes, one of the city's more imposing squares, of Notre-Dame Basilica, the principal church in the city, and of the head office of the Bank of Montreal, the most important bank in British North America. In 1867, upon the uniting of most of the British North American colonies to create Canada, the distribution of power between the federal and provincial governments further reflected some of the divisions evident at Place d'Armes. The federal, or central government was given control over the construction of a transcontinental economy, while the provincial governments were given responsibility for such activities as the provision of education and social services. Allocating these powers to the provinces was, to a considerable extent, designed to secure the support of the project by Quebec's Catholic hierarchy, which wanted to be sure that there would be no interference in its sphere by the English-speaking Protestants who would dominate the new country both economically and numerically. The church leaders assumed, rightly as it turned out, that a Quebec government with responsibility for administering the province's schools and social affairs would leave the church alone to deal with education and other matters as it had done prior to 1867.

Over the century that followed, the machinery of the Quebec government remained rather small in comparison to that of other Canadian provinces. This underdevelopment of the state did not trouble many French-speaking leaders as long as they accepted the premise that their people did not wield very much power and that this inferior status was not likely to change in the foreseeable future. The levers of economic power were firmly in the hands of English-speakers, either Canadian or American, a situation that did not terribly bother the leaders of the Catholic church who ran the province's schools and social services and who exercised considerable control over one of the major trade unions in the province as well as a large network of credit unions. The church encouraged French-speakers to accept their lot as second-class economic citizens at the same time that it denied them the tools that might have helped them improve their status.

In the aftermath of World War II, however, the willingness of Quebecers to tolerate this state of affairs started to evaporate. Beginning with the war and continuing throughout the 1940s and 1950s, North America experienced an unprecedented economic boom, which had a profound impact upon Quebec. With declining rates of unemployment and rising wages, the per capita incomes of Quebecers expanded rapidly, in the process integrating French-speakers into the consumer culture that was taking root across the continent. While the objective circumstances of French-speaking Quebecers improved, they became increasingly troubled by their second-class economic status as success came to be defined almost exclusively in material terms, thus raising questions about the appropriateness of the control by English-run businesses over such natural resources as hydro-electricity, or the similar control over education exercised by the church.

Ultimately, this post-war questioning of the distribution of power in Quebec society manifested itself in 1960 with the election of a Liberal government, which replaced the *Union nationale* regime that had sustained the status quo since the 1930s. In fairly short order, the apparatus of the state was reconstructed by a broad-based coalition that included René Lévesque who, although new to partisan politics, was given responsibility for the nationalisation of the province's hydro-electric industry, whose control by English-speaking business interests had long symbolized the economic inferiority of French-speakers in a province where they constituted roughly 80 per cent of the population. At roughly the same time, there was also the 'nationalization' of education through the creation of a Ministry of Education to look after what would now be a truly state-run system.

It did not take long, however, for some members of the Liberal government to realize that the grandiose plans to build an interventionist state would require a renegotiation of the distribution of powers between the Quebec and federal governments. There were certain jurisdictions that leaders such as Lévesque felt needed to be under Quebec's control, if a state were to be constructed that might advance the interests of the French-speaking majority. Moreover, the unequal distribution of the powers of taxation between the two levels of government required renegotiation, if Quebec were to have the means to finance its ambitious programmes. With the rise to power of Pierre Elliott Trudeau as prime minister of Canada in 1968, elected with a mandate from the rest of Canada to hold the line on Quebec's increasingly insistent demands for greater autonomy, it appeared that the Quiet Revolution had gone as far as it could within the existing constitutional structure. In that context, Lévesque left the Liberal Party to form a new one, the Parti Québécois, committed to what he called sovereignty—association.

In defining his option in such a manner, Lévesque was pointing to one of the distinguishing characteristics of secessionist thought in Quebec, namely its ambiguity as to how radical any future break with the rest of Canada might be. For his part, Lévesque made it clear that he was not interested in separation, and so refused to be labelled, as his opponents such as Trudeau would have liked, with the term 'separatist'. Instead, he opted for the term 'sovereignist', in the process speaking both about the achievement of a degree of autonomy and the negotiation of a new relationship between two 'people' on a basis of equality. Of course, there was considerable ambiguity as to how the 'people' of Quebec were to be defined given the fact that while Quebec was primarily a French-speaking territory, it was also one that was home to a significant minority which did not have French as its mother tongue.

Going back to the mid-nineteenth century, roughly 20 per cent of Quebec's population had been made up of residents who did not have French as their mother tongue. In the aftermath of the British conquest of Quebec in the late eighteenth and up to the start of the twentieth century, in the absence of the arrival of French-speaking immigrants, nearly all of those who came to Quebec arrived from the American colonies (later states), England, Scotland, or Ireland speaking English. However, in the twentieth century immigration patterns changed and up to the Quiet Revolution newcomers tended to come from eastern or southern Europe, arriving in Quebec with neither English nor French as their mother tongue. In spite of the numerical superiority of French-speakers in Quebec, the power of the English language in North America was such that nearly all of these immigrants passed English along as the language to be used by the next generation, thus raising fears among many leaders of French-speaking Quebec that their numerical superiority was in danger.

This fear played a role in the emergence of sovereignist activity as the federal government's control over immigration and its disapproval of efforts on
the part of Quebec to protect its French-speaking character were viewed with
considerable concern. For Lévesque's part, however, there was a fine line to be
walked between the defence of the interests of the French-speaking majority
and the protection of the interests of the province's various minorities. He
thought of Quebecers as a 'people', whose French roots had the effect of
marginalizing those who were not French-speakers. As he put it, in a book
written to explain his new political option for Quebec, 'We are heirs to that
fantastic adventure—that early America was almost entirely French. We are,
even more intimately, heirs to the group obstinacy which has kept alive that
portion of French America we call *Québec.*' At the same time, however, he
indicated a certain territorial understanding of nationalism when he observed
that it was crucial to respect the collective rights 'which our English-speaking
citizens have acquired so that they might continue to exist as a cultural community in an independent Quebec. For better or worse, our respect of their
rights is a crucial test of our maturity'.[5] As for the native people of Quebec,
Lévesque observed, 'It is necessary that we establish good relations so that we
might have a harmonious coexistence. We must put an end to the attitude
towards development of the territory of Quebec which fails to take into
account the interests and way of life of these [indigenous] people'.[6]

In essence, Lévesque's thinking about Quebec reflected elements of both
ethnic and civic understandings of the nation: on the one hand viewing
French-speakers as a conquered people who now were on the road to
having their moment in the sun; and on the other viewing all Quebecers as
residents of an emerging modern state, in the process marginalising the
rhetoric of an oppressed past. With the sidelining of this older ethnic understanding of nationalism, Quebec's sovereignty became the 'normal' destiny
for a people, a free choice, instead of a necessity dictated by evidence of
mistreatment. Indeed, Lévesque's thinking in this regard was strongly supported by Quebec historical writing of the 1970s, which departed from a
long-standing preoccupation with the inferiority of French-speakers
(now in need of liberation) and rather turned to the depiction of Quebec as
a territory inhabited by people of various backgrounds, collectively moving
forward in the world.[7]

This ambiguity in the thinking within Lévesque's political party became
particularly clear for all to see following its rise to power in 1976. The first

[5] *Le Journal de Montréal*, 4 March 1971. I have translated this and all subsequent passages,
which were originally in French.
[6] Speech in Quebec National Assembly (originally in French), 19 March 1985.
[7] I have discussed this change in Quebec historical writing in my *Making History in
Twentieth Century Quebec* (Toronto, University of Toronto Press, 1997).

piece of legislation passed by Lévesque's government, Bill 101, was called the 'Charter of the French Language'. As this title suggests, it was primarily designed to defend the interests of French-speakers, building upon legislation passed by the previous Liberal government that restricted access to English schools (so as to stem the anglicization of newcomers) and which made French the language of business in the province (so as to convince the same newcomers that there were economic reasons for functioning in French in spite of the power of English in the North American economy). At the same time, however, there were aspects of Bill 101 that recognized the responsibility of the state to all its citizens, establishing in law the right of those who already were established in Quebec to educate their children in English. Once more, there were reflections here of both ethnic and territorial understandings of nationalism.[8]

In the end, however, the clearest sign of Lévesque's mixed message came with the holding of a referendum in 1980 in which the population was asked if the government should begin the process of negotiating a new relationship with the rest of Canada. The very nature of the question indicated something considerably short of a move towards independence, and even though there were moments of overheated rhetoric during the referendum campaign that suggested that Lévesque was only interested in advancing the interests of the French-speaking majority, the most telling moment of the whole affair came on the evening of the overwhelming defeat for the government whose option received only 40 per cent of the vote. The non-francophone population voted almost unanimously against the proposition, largely viewing sovereignty as a 'French' option that held no attraction for them. French-speakers themselves were evenly divided, with perhaps a small majority voting yes. Had Lévesque held a strongly ethnic understanding of nationalism, he might have reacted with some anger to the fact that 'they' had prevented 'us' from achieving sovereignty. Instead, he greeted his disappointed supporters on the night of the referendum without rancour, but with the hope that there might be another, more successful referendum. In accepting the verdict of the people, Lévesque left his supporters with the words, 'À la prochaine fois!' ('Until the next time!')

Lévesque's point of view was not shared by all in his party, with the result that he had to contend, both before and after the referendum, with individuals who had little enthusiasm for either sovereignty—association or a somewhat territorial understanding of nationalism. From its very inception, the Parti Québécois has been a coalition of individuals with varying points of view, and there had always been a strain that wanted the complete

[8] I made this point at some length in 'Collective Rights, the English-Speaking Minority and the Quebec Government, 1867–1988', in David Schneiderman (ed.), *Language and the State: The Law and the Politics of Identity* (Montreal, Editions Yvon Blais, 1991).

severing of ties with the rest of Canada as the best guarantee for the well-being of French-speakers in Quebec. Here was the conception of an ethnic-ally defined people who required separation as a just means of precluding their cultural annihilation. Historiographically, this point of view was grounded in a long tradition of writing that focused upon the misfortunes of French-speakers, most of whose problems stemmed from the conquest by the British in the eighteenth century.[9] Needless to say, there was little in this conception that reflected a civic understanding of nationalism. Over the last third of the twentieth century, the person who most consistently advanced this alternative vision within the PQ was Jacques Parizeau, who served as finance minister under Lévesque from 1976 to 1984, at which time he quit to protest against his leader's willingness to seek a new relationship with the rest of Canada, instead of pushing more forcefully for independence.

Parizeau's more militant stance had a certain following in the late 1980s and early 1990s in the wake of a series of constitutional developments that threw into doubt the role of the Quebec state as protector of the nation. In 1981 the federal government, led by prime minister Trudeau, and all the provinces except Quebec agreed to a new constitution that threatened to limit the power of the Quebec government in terms of such matters as the enactment of legislation protecting the French language. This new constitution took effect in 1982 without the approval of Quebec, although this failure to express approval made the stipulations of the new constitution no less binding. A broad consensus emerged among French-speakers that no Quebec government should agree to a constitution that was imposed upon them by English Canada. Accordingly, support for the Parti Québécois remained strong, fuelled to a considerable degree by the continuing sense of ethnic injustice stemming from the constitutional question.

For Trudeau, who retired from public life in 1984, the constitution was the crowning point of a career that had been committed to a territorial understanding of nationalism, and which had been opposed to those who even flirted with a more ethnic point of view. Within Quebec, however, the imposition of the new constitution resulted in the evaporation of support for Lévesque's rather cautious approach towards independence, with the result that he retired, as did Trudeau, in 1984. The party now turned towards more militant figures such as Parizeau, who ultimately became leader in 1988. Parizeau minced few words in the late 1980s and early 1990s as he led the PQ, which was then in opposition within the Quebec National

---

[9] Although professional historians have largely abandoned this Conquest-driven view of the past, it retains an important place in the collective memory of Quebecers. See Jocelyn Létourneau, 'La production historienne courante portant sur le Québec et ses rapports avec la construction des figures identitaires d'une communauté communicationnelle', *Recherches sociographiques*, 36 (1995), 9–45.

Assembly. Without the burden of power, he spoke out frequently about the dangers that the new constitutional regime created for Quebec, focusing upon the dangers to the French language with little evident concern about the role of the 'other' citizens of Quebec.[10] Moreover, in light of the failure of various efforts to bring Quebec into the constitutional fold, Parizeau called for the independence of Quebec, pushing Lévesque's idea of association to the side.[11] When Parizeau became prime minister of Quebec, following an election in 1994, he quickly moved for the holding of a second referendum on independence, one that he hoped to fight on the separation of Quebec from the rest of Canada without muddying the waters, as had Lévesque in 1980, by reference to some future partnership with the rest of the country. In the end, Parizeau was forced to accept a referendum question much like the earlier one in order to broaden his base of support, a tactic that almost resulted in victory when 49.4 per cent of the population voted 'yes' in 1995.

In the end, however, the most revealing part of the 1995 referendum campaign came following the counting of the votes that indicated that non-francophones had once again voted almost unanimously 'no'. However, with a much larger 'yes' vote than in 1980, Parizeau could see that there had been a significant majority within the French-speaking population, which probably voted 60 per cent in favour of beginning the process of separation. On the night of the referendum, when these results became known, Parizeau, who had never concealed his inclination towards an ethnic understanding of nationalism, spoke out in bitterness against the role of 'outsiders' who had stolen victory from the 'real' citizens of Quebec: 'Friends, we have lost, but not by a lot. It was successful in one sense. Let's stop talking about the francophones of Quebec. Let's talk about us. Sixty per cent of us have voted in favour. It's true we have been defeated, but basically by what? By money and the ethnic vote.' In his insistence that the term francophone was irrelevant, Parizeau made it clear that when he referred to Quebecers, or 'us', he meant French-speakers; no qualifier was needed, because all other Quebecers were non-citizens. He further marginalized 'them' by the reference to 'money', a not very subtle way of linking the non-francophone population with the wealthy English-speakers who had dominated Quebec before the Quiet Revolution of the 1960s. In 1995 the average incomes of French-speakers were indistinguishable from those of non-francophones, but this made little difference to Parizeau who made his ethnic understanding of nationalism perfectly clear

---

[10] Kenneth McRoberts, *Quebec: Social Change and Political Crisis*, 3rd edn. (Toronto, McClelland and Stewart, 1993), 419.

[11] Parizeau's hand was particularly strengthened by the collapse in 1990 of the Meech Lake Accord, a package of amendments that would have given Quebec much of what it had wanted to allow its signature of the constitution. In the end, however, ratification of the agreement was blocked by several English-speaking provinces, thus providing grist for the sovereignist mill in general, and for the Parizeau perspective in particular.

for all to hear. Numerous commentators pointed to the rather obvious contrast between Lévesque's gracious acceptance of the verdict of all the citizens
of the territory of Quebec in 1980 and Parizeau's much less 'civic' reaction
fifteen years later.

On the day following the referendum and his 'ethnic' speech, Jacques
Parizeau resigned as prime minister of Quebec. Some have speculated that
he knew he was going to resign when he made the speech; others have suggested that he was urged to leave because of it. In any event, Parizeau was
replaced by Lucien Bouchard, who reflected the ambiguity between civic
and ethnic views of citizenship that had marked René Lévesque's years at the
helm. Nevertheless, Parizeau did not disappear from the scene, emerging
from time to time to criticize Bouchard for a failure to advance separation
and the interests of French-speakers more forcefully, in the process com-
promising the party's image by making it appear as if it were a political
party largely committed to an ethnic understanding of the nation. For his
part, Bouchard resigned as prime minister in 2001, fed up with the internal
divisions within his party, and in the process showing that ambiguities in
sovereignist thought were still alive and well at the start of the new century.

DICHOTOMOUS VIEWS OF THE QUEBEC EXPERIENCE

In light of the contested nature of sovereignist thinking in Quebec, this particular case has proven attractive to scholars with various perspectives upon
the circumstances that justify secession. Since there is sufficient evidence
from the Quebec experience to support various points of view, authors have
gravitated towards different aspects of the sovereignist movement, frequently
brushing the ambiguities aside. In particular, the subtleties have frequently
been lost in trying to classify the Quebec case as one in which either an
ethnic or civic understanding of nationalism has exclusively been present.

For his part, Allen Buchanan found a movement in Quebec designed
exclusively to defend the interests of an ethnic (or linguistic) group, and so
he referred to a movement for secession driven by the desire to achieve 'the
preservation of French Canadian culture'.[12] Starting from this premise,
Buchanan argued that there had to be a preponderance of evidence indicating that the needs of the aggrieved group really justified the dislocations
that might result from secession. Accordingly, he pondered whether French-
speakers were in fact culturally vulnerable and whether secession was likely
to reduce the risks to the continued survival of such a population. In the
end, Buchanan was unimpressed with claims structured along such lines,
finding it 'problematic to hold that those Francophone Canadians *who live*

---

[12] Buchanan, *Secession*, 52.

in Quebec are now victims of ethnic discrimination'.[13] Even if such discrimination did exist, Buchanan doubted that the problem was beyond resolution within the Canadian federation, and he was concerned about the impact of sovereignty upon non-francophones, particularly Native people who had competing claims of their own. In presenting the case in such terms, Buchanan ignored those Quebecers of the Lévesque persuasion who were prepared to accept something less than complete sovereignty and who had pitched their appeal, at least in part, on the basis of a free choice for all Quebecers regardless of linguistic background, instead of basing it upon the historic grievances of a cultural group.

Buchanan's perspective was echoed to a certain degree by Michael Ignatieff who, in his book on the rise of nationalist movements in the late twentieth century, showed a marked preference for the civic form of nationalism based upon 'a democratic set of procedures and values' over the ethnic form, which he saw predisposed to authoritarianism. Ignatieff recognized, unlike Buchanan, that 'modern Quebec nationalists are at pains to differentiate their conception of the nation from the ethnic idea that they associate with the catastrophe of Yugoslavia...A national state need not be an ethnic state'. Nevertheless, in the end, Ignatieff seemed to feel that the dominant strain of sovereignist thinking was that expressed by individuals such as Parizeau, and so he presumed that Quebec constituted a case in which secession was driven by an 'ethnic nationalism [which] flourished within a state [Canada] formally committed to civic democracy'.[14]

Starting from a completely different premise than either Buchanan or Ignatieff, Kai Nielsen came to the Quebec experience with the view that 'the presumptive right to secession, where the majority of its citizens clearly express their preference for it, should generally be taken to be unproblematic'. He found that the 'burden of proof' rested with those who wanted to contest the right of a population to secede rather than with the secessionists themselves.[15] Having provided this definition, Nielsen then proceeded to examine the case of Quebec where he found not the allegedly oppressed ethnic group that emerged in the hands of Buchanan, but rather a broad coalition of people united under the umbrella of a 'liberal [i.e. civic] nationalism which is non-exclusionist...It is quite independent of descent and ethnic background...Membership is defined in terms of participation in a common culture, in principle at least open to all, rather than on ethnic grounds'.[16]

While Buchanan may have chosen to ignore the Lévesque legacy in sovereignist thought, Nielsen turned a blind eye to the Parizeau perspective,

[13] Ibid. 161.   [14] Ignatieff, *Blood and Belonging*, 173, 8.
[15] Kai Nielsen, 'Liberal Nationalism and Secession', in Moore, *National Self-Determination and Secession*, 103.   [16] Ibid. 107.

insisting that attention be focused upon the fact that in Quebec the majority population has 'protect[ed] the historic rights of [its] national minorities to have schools, hospitals, and other public services in [its] own language and the right to use this language in parliament'.[17] This experience gave Nielsen the confidence that the interests of the minorities would be looked after in any sovereign Quebec. Echoing this point of view, David Miller used the term 'Québécois' to refer to all residents of Quebec, regardless of linguistic background, thus focusing upon a civic understanding of nationalism that made him confident that 'an independent Quebec would protect the private rights of its English-speaking minority at least as effectively as Canada has so far protected the rights of French-speakers'.[18]

BEYOND MANICHEAN VIEWS

It is not difficult to understand the marked preference by a wide range of scholars for the territorial form of nationalism over the ethnically defined version. How can one avoid condemnation of ethnic nationalism in the aftermath of the decade that gave meaning to the term 'ethnic cleansing'? It does not necessarily follow from this experience, however, that all forms of ethnic nationalism are 'bad', or that all forms of territorial nationalism are 'good', even though such prescriptive judgments have proven attractive to academics engaged in establishing a normative framework through which acceptable demands for self-determination can be distinguished from more dubious ones. Even more fundamentally, however, there is no obvious reason for giving substance to the rather simplistic dichotomy between definitions of nationhood grounded in ethnicity from those based upon more universal notions of citizenship, as if one form tended to exist to the exclusion of the other, a perspective advanced by some of the scholars discussed in the previous section.

This dichotomous view has been challenged by a number of scholars who have shown that ethnic and civic forms of nationalism can and do coexist alongside one another. For instance, Anthony D. Smith advanced such a perspective in his thought-provoking work, *The Ethnic Origins of Nations*. Smith took the view that all forms of nationalism have an ethnic base, in the process throwing into doubt the pertinence of classifying concrete cases unequivocally as either ethnic or territorial forms of nationalism. As he put it,

The upshot of our brief account of the formation of nations in the modern world is that all nations bear the impress of both territorial and ethnic principles and

---

[17] Kai Nielsen, 'Liberal Nationalism and Secession', in Moore, *National Self-Determination and Secession*, 107.

[18] David Miller, 'Secession and the Principle of Nationality', in Moore, *National Self-Determination and Secession*, 72.

components, and represent an uneasy confluence of a more recent 'civic' and a more ancient 'genealogical' model of social and cultural organization. No 'nation-to-be' can survive without a homeland or a myth of common origins and descent. Conversely no 'ethnie-aspiring-to-become-a-nation' can achieve its goals without realizing a common division of labour and territorial mobility, or the legal equality of common rights and duties for each member, that is citizenship. Of course, given nations will exhibit ethnic and territorial components in varying proportions at particular moments of their history.[19]

While Smith can be criticized for insisting, in an unnecessarily rigid fashion, that there must be an ethnic component to movements of civic nationalism, his conceptualization of the issue makes it possible to imagine movements for self-determination that defy simple identification as either ethnic or civic.

A Manichean approach to the issue was also rejected by Rogers Brubaker, most notably in his comparative study of the underpinnings of citizenship in France and Germany. It would have been easy for Brubaker to simplify the two cases so as to present the former as representative of a civic understanding of nationhood, and the latter as the example *par excellence* of the ethnic version. In fact, however, he was careful to avoid simplistic and value-laden generalizations. As he put it,

The temptation to treat differences of degree as differences of kind, differences of contextual expression as differences of inner principle, is endemic to bipolar comparison…To characterise French and German traditions of citizenship and nationhood in terms of such ready-made conceptual pairs as universalism and particularism, cosmopolitanism and ethnocentrism, Enlightenment rationalism and Romantic irrationalism, is to pass from characterization to caricature.[20]

Accordingly, as Brubaker looked more closely at the French and German cases, he recognized that there were profound differences between the two without viewing them as representative of 'pure' and diametrically opposed notions of citizenship. He remarked:

In fact, traditions of nationhood have political [civic] and cultural [ethnic] components in both countries. These components have been closely integrated in France, where political unity has been understood as constitutive, cultural unity as expressive of nationhood. In the German tradition, in contrast, political and ethnocultural aspects of nationhood have stood in tension with one another, serving as the basis for competing notions of nationhood.[21]

In the considerable literature dealing with justifications for secession in Quebec, this more nuanced view has been advanced by such scholars as Margaret Moore who recognised 'the tension between the ethnic basis of the

[19] Anthony Smith, *The Ethnic Origins of Nations* (Oxford, Basil Blackwell, 1986), 149.
[20] Rogers Brubaker, *Citizenship and Nationhood in France and Germany* (Cambridge, Mass., Harvard University Press, 1992), 2. [21] Ibid. 10.

national movement and the territorial conception of citizenship'. Having questioned the dichotomy between ethnic and civic understandings of nationalism, Moore went on, however, to observe that 'the nationalist movement bases its claim to recognition on its distinct ethnic claim and yet, claims that borders must be determined on the basis of the administrative unit (the province) in the Canadian federation'.[22] Referring to a single nationalist movement speaking presumably with one voice, she elided the fundamental tension between the Lévesque and Parizeau understandings of the movement. Indeed, in the former case, there was an effort to articulate a justification grounded in a civic definition of the nation, so that the use of existing borders would create little problem.

For his part, Michael Keating has gone even further in moving beyond the simplistic use of dichotomies in sketching the nationalist underpinnings of sovereignist thought in Quebec. Keating observed, at one point in his comparative study of secessionist movements in Quebec, Catalonia, and Scotland, that 'while civic nationalism is the official doctrine of the political class and most intellectuals [in Quebec], it still competes with an ethnically based form'.[23] In this statement, he minimized the strength of ethnic nationalism within the political class, a point that he made even more forthrightly in arguing that 'the nation-building project is increasingly posed in civic terms, embracing the whole of society, rather than as the demand of one ethnically-defined section'.[24] In the end, the dominance of a civic view of the nation led Keating to view Quebec's demands for greater autonomy sympathetically, reserving his criticism for the rest of Canada which had yet to respond constructively to Quebec's proposals for the reshaping of the Canadian federation.[25]

FURTHER AMBIGUITIES

While some scholars have begun to wrestle with the ambiguities embedded in the nationalist discourse connected with the sovereignist movement in Quebec, relatively little attention has been paid to other ambiguities that form a central element of that movement. The conflict that has long brewed within the Parti Québécois between the Lévesque and Parizeau perspectives extends beyond different understandings of the nation to include such questions as the grounds that justify sovereignty in Quebec. While Buchanan presumed that Quebec constitutes a case in which a 'just cause' has been advanced by a particular linguistic group, Nielsen argued that the Quebec movement has promoted sovereignty as a 'free choice' by members of a broadly defined nation. However, neither author considered sufficiently

---

[22] Moore, 'The Self-Determination Principle and the Ethics of Separation', in Moore, *National Self-Determination and Secession*, 139.
[23] Keating, *Nations Against the State*, 73.   [24] Ibid. 106.   [25] Ibid. 227.

that the Quebec movement for sovereignty has seen claims of mistreatment emanating from a particular segment (albeit the majority one) of society interwoven with others grounded in a broader conception of the democratic right of a people to chart its future.

On another level, the Lévesque–Parizeau debate speaks to the issue of the very meaning of sovereignty, thus pointing to a further ambiguity in the Quebec context. Once again, there is relatively little reflection in the literature discussed above as to how sovereignty is to be defined, this in spite of the substantial and often conflicting formulations regarding the precise status that Quebec might occupy, were it to secede from Canada. In Lévesque's formulation, grounded as it was in a civic understanding of the nation, sovereignty was inextricably tied to the creation of a new association with the rest of Canada. Such an association was desirable from Lévesque's perspective since he did not begin from the premise that his people had been so badly mistreated that distancing themselves from English Canada was crucial to their survival.

Even before the creation of the Parti Québécois in 1968, Lévesque headed the Mouvement souveraineté-association whose name spoke to the option to be advanced. While advocates of a cleaner break from Canada joined the Parti Québécois (which took on the platform of the earlier Mouvement), they were never completely comfortable with their leader's insistence upon a renegotiated contract with the rest of the country. Over time, various leading members of the party drifted away in order to advance a perspective upon sovereignty that was more focused upon securing independence. Ties to the rest of Canada were viewed as desirable, although they did not constitute a pre-requisite to leaving the federation. The most important of these dissidents was Jacques Parizeau, who ultimately returned to push the party in the direction favoured by individuals whose ethnic understanding of the nation required a more radical break with the rest of Canada, lest an endangered people cease to exist.

As we saw earlier, Parizeau's petulant reply to those who had voted against sovereignty in 1995 led to his resignation and the rise to power of a new leader, Lucien Bouchard, who was more in the Lévesque mould. Only a few years later, Bouchard himself resigned, frustrated with the continuing conflicts within the party that reflected different understandings of the nation, of the justification for secession, and of the meaning of sovereignty. In the end, the Quebec case stands out, not because it has led to the outbreak of violence, but rather because it embodies various streams of thought. Some scholars have already begun to unravel the ambiguities arising from conflicting definitions of the nation, but further unravelling remains to be done on a wide array of issues.

11

A Unified China or an Independent Taiwan? A Normative Assessment of the Cross-Strait Conflict

Xiaokun Song

In recent years political philosophers have endeavoured to establish norms in order to regulate the upsurge in nationalist movements in the world today. Based on their different perceptions of the relationship between the right to self-determination and the right to secession, participants in this discussion can be divided into two camps.[1] The first defends a 'permissive' right to secession, according to which secession is a way of achieving national self-determination. The right to secession, as part of the right to national self-determination, is an *a priori* basic right rooted in liberal democratic theory; a sufficient condition for a territorially concentrated group to exercise such a right is a majority desire to do so. Since the right is a given, it can be invoked unilaterally by the party enjoying the right. But in practice the right is subject to moral conditions. How a group exercises its right to self-determination, that is, whether it adheres to or abuses the liberal

Note on transcription of Chinese: as Taiwan and mainland China use two different types of transcription, being Wade-Giles transcription and *hanyu pinyin* transcription respectively, the present article will adopt both transcriptions depending on the context. In the main text, for the transcription of a concept or an expression, quotation, and personal or place names in mainland China, the *hanyu pinyin* transcription is used while for personal, place and institution names in Taiwan, Wade-Giles transcription is used. In the footnotes, for the transcription of article and book titles, names of authors, editors and publishing houses, *hanyu pinyin* transcription is used.

[1] Different authors have categorized and labelled the arguments according to their own understanding. Margaret Moore and Wayne Norman distinguish three schools: choice theories, just cause theories, and national self-determination theories; Allen Buchanan and Daniel Philpott categorize the debates as the remedial right only (constrictive) theory versus the non-remedial, plebiscitary right (permissive) theory; then for Michael Freeman, the debates consist of three camps, these being communitarianism, liberal democracy, and liberal realism, respectively. In my view, the fundamental distinction is the authors' philosophical interpretation of the relationship between the right to self-determination and the right to secession. Their normative arguments on the right to secession can thus be divided into the *a priori* and *a posteriori* camps, as elaborated in the main text.

principles, becomes one of the criteria for judging the legitimacy of secessionist movements.[2]

The second camp, supporting a more 'restricted' view of the right to secession, argues that as the breaking up of an existing state and the creation of new ones are no simple matters, the attainment and exercise of the right to secession require legitimization by strong moral arguments. A right to secession is derived from a number of different considerations. The right to self-determination is only one element in a wider normative discourse justifying secession. Other factors, such as discriminatory redistribution or oppression, are regarded as morally stronger arguments. Thus the right to secession is *a posteriori* and remedial in essence. The central question is whether and when such a right can be attained. Some scholars in this group suggest different sets of criteria to judge whether a group is entitled to the right to secession or not.[3]

Scholars from both camps attach equal importance to the notion of justice in their arguments. Emphasizing democratic and liberal values in the procedure of exercising the right to secession, the camp defending an *a priori* right to secession is not as permissive as it might at first sight appear: it holds that in concrete cases the promotion of the right should be qualified and circumscribed, and formal conditions need to be met in exercising the right.[4] Similarly, while strict when it comes to the moral justification for acquiring the right to secession, those holding an *a posteriori* view of the right do not rule out the possibility of exercising such a right. In circumstances where unjust annexation, oppression, or discriminatory redistribution have threatened the cultural identity and even the very existence of a community, the exercise of the right to self-determination up to and including the right of secession is justified. From this perspective, when evaluating the legitimacy of secession in concrete cases, the two approaches may very well reach the same verdict.

Scholars from the two camps share a consensus on two points. First, the debate on the ethics of self-determination should be contextualized. This means that the prerequisite for the construction of such a normative theory is 'a fuller understanding of the patterns of ethnic politics (which) can—and

[2] Harry Beran, 'A Liberal Theory of Secession', *Political Studies*, 32 (1984), 21–31; Kai Nielsen, 'Liberal Nationalism and Secession', in Margaret Moore (ed.), *National Self-Determination and Secession* (Oxford, Oxford University Press, 1998); Daniel Philpott, 'In Defense of Self-Determination', *Ethics*, 105 (1995), 352–85, and 'Self-Determination in Practice', in Moore, *National Self-Determination and Secession*, 79–102.

[3] Lee C. Buchheit, *Secession: the Legitimacy of Self-determination* (New Haven and London, Yale University Press, 1978); Allen Buchanan, *Secession: The Morality of Political Divorce from Fort Sumter to Lithuania and Quebec* (Boulder, Colo., San Francisco, and Oxford, Westview Press, 1991); Lea Brilmayer, 'Secession and Self-determination: A Territorial Interpretation', *Yale Journal of International Law*, 16 (1991), 177–202.

[4] Philpott, 'In Defense of Self-Determination'.

assuredly should—inform emerging debates about self-determination in politics, philosophy, and law'.[5] It also means that, in analysing an actual secessionist movement, there is no fixed set of norms with which to evaluate its political legitimacy. The application of a normative theory of secession to empirical analysis should be case-sensitive. Second, while the liberal value of the principle of national self-determination is confirmed, one must be aware that there exists a wide range of political structures within which the community can fulfil its aspiration to political self-determination. Not all secessionist movements set independence as their ultimate goal. Those who do may change their political agenda as the circumstances change. A normative analysis of secessionist movements should not only enable us to make a moral judgement on the conflicting political claims involved, it should also cast light for further exploration of the best political structure to implement the principle of national self-determination for each community. In this sense, independence might not, in some cases, be the ideal form of nation-building.

The purpose of this chapter is to apply the existing conceptual distinctions and theoretical debates on the right to secession to the case of Taiwan and to the changing pattern of conflict. Basically, there are two main forms of ethnically induced territorial adjustment: secessions and irredentas. As Donald Horowitz defines the two terms, 'secession involves the withdrawal of a group and its territory from the authority of a state of which it is a part. Irredentism entails the retrieval of ethnically kindred people and their territory across an international boundary, joining them and it to the retrieving state.'[6] It is not possible to apply the concept of irredentism in the context of Taiwan, as the borders between Taiwan and Mainland China are not international borders. Cross-Strait relations fall firmly in the interstices of domestic and international politics.

The concept of reunification, however, may be applied. The cross-Strait conflict patterns since 1945 have evolved from reunification versus reunification to reunification versus secession. From 1949 to 1987, the People's Republic of China (PRC) aimed to 'liberate Taiwan' whereas the Republic of China (ROC) strove to 'take back mainland China'. Since then, from 1987 to the present day, the PRC has continued its project of reunification, but the major political players in Taiwan have been engaged in the construction of Taiwan as a sovereign state. The search for independent statehood in Taiwan should be understood in the context of Taiwan's particular international

---

[5] And on this score, Horowitz criticizes the fact that 'the theories have been cascading more quickly than has understanding of patterns of ethnic conflict in general or of ethno-territorial movements in particular'. Donald Horowitz, 'Self-Determination: Politics, Philosophy, and Law', in Moore (ed.), *National Self-Determination and Secession*, 182.   [6] Ibid. 183.

status: despite its claim to have the principal attributes of a state—namely, a defined territory, a permanent population and an effective government— Taiwan is not recognized as a nation-state by the international community and it is denied access to participation in international organizations, notably the United Nations (UN). Two central concepts, sovereignty and self-determination, are introduced to clarify what secession means in the case of Taiwan. Subsequently, I will apply the normative framework for the right to secession proposed by Alexis Heraclides to the case of Taiwan, and assess the legitimacy of the demand to exercise such a right.[7] Heraclides' normative framework is adopted for analysing the legitimacy of Taiwan independence because it has incorporated nearly all the qualifications and conditions listed by supporters of both camps. Finally, I will conclude my analysis with some tentative remarks in respect of the future development of cross-Strait relations.

CHANGING STRATEGIES

The so-called 'Taiwan question' dates back to 1949 when the Kuomintang (KMT) regime retreated to Taiwan after its defeat in the Civil War against the communist revolutionaries. While the Chinese Communist Party (CCP) pro-claimed the PRC in mainland China on 1 October 1949, the KMT established its government in exile in Taipei. Over the past fifty years, the conflict pattern across the Taiwan Strait has evolved from reunification (the PRC) versus reunification (the ROC) to reunification (the PRC) versus secession (Taiwan). It is only since the late 1980s that the idea of a sovereign Taiwan has become popular, albeit at the expense of the KMT's appeal for reunification.

The PRC's stand on the Taiwan issue has been quite consistent since 1949.[8] The official view is that there is only one China, the PRC, and that Taiwan is 'an inalienable part of China'. Before 1979, Beijing tried to 'liberate Taiwan' militarily, but without success. Since 1979, the Beijing government has changed its strategy for bringing about reunification. The framework for peaceful reunification proposed by the PRC is the 'one country, two systems' policy under the 'One China' principle. This is basically a formula for regional autonomy within a unitary state. According to this policy, Taiwan and the Mainland would be unified as One China, each maintaining its own economic, legal, and social systems. Moreover, Taiwan would be granted a high degree of political autonomy, to the extent that it would even be

---

[7] Alexis Heraclides, 'Ethnicity, Secessionist Conflict, and the International Society: towards Normative Paradigm Shift' in *Nations and Nationalism*, 3:4 (1997), 493–520.

[8] Before the CCP came to power, it had been quite flexible regarding the recovery of the lost Chinese territories, i.e. Taiwan, Korea, Tibet, Mongolia, and Manchuria. It had suggested a federal structure for accommodating the different peoples in a unified China.

allowed to keep its own army and flag. But the PRC has no intention of renouncing the right to use force as a last resort in order to bring about reunification. Meanwhile, the PRC guards with caution against any move from Taiwan in the direction of independence, in the form of either the pragmatic foreign policy pursued by the government or the activities of the Taiwan Independence Movement.

While Beijing strongly urges unification, a chronological examination of politics of nationalism on Taiwan in respect of the cross-Strait relationship reveals a fundamental change in the Taiwan authorities' position: they have moved away from the idea of unification during the era of Chiang Kai-shek and Chiang Ching-kuo to that of a sovereign Taiwan under Lee Teng-hui's rule. To cite Horowitz again, 'whether and when a secessionist movement will emerge is determined mainly by domestic politics, by the relations of groups and regions within the state'.[9]

During the period 1949–87, the basic assumption underlying the KMT's nationalist doctrine was clear: there is only one China and Taiwan is a part of China; though temporarily presiding over only Taiwan, the ROC will recover its lost territory in due course under the leadership of the sole legitimate government, the KMT. This basic assumption determined, to a very large extent, the KMT's domestic and foreign policies. At the domestic level, the nation-building project aimed to legitimize the ROC's claim to the whole of China and to promote Chinese identity among the population on Taiwan. With this in mind, after its flight from the mainland the KMT launched three cultural movements and implemented a series of cultural policies in spheres such as education, the media, and social science research.[10] The process of sinicization resulted in the oppression of the native Taiwanese culture and the establishment of a Chinese cultural hegemony. The cultural predominance of the Mainlanders (those who arrived in Taiwan between 1945 and 1949), mainly due to the language factor, provided them with easier access to political and economic resources in the society.[11] Despite the

---

[9] Donald Horowitz, *Ethnic Groups in Conflict* (Berkeley, University of California Press, 1985), 230.

[10] For example, Mandarin was imposed as the official language and a ban placed on the use of dialects and Japanese. Culture was nationalized in the sense that it became an object of discourse in the political sense. The objectification of culture has a biased implication for the construction of knowledge, as in the rewriting of history and the undertaking of archaeological research.

[11] The biased distribution of social resources based on (sub-) ethnic cleavages manifests itself mainly in the political dimension, especially the power distribution at the level of central politics, and not so much in the societal or economic dimensions. See the tables and analysis of the ethnic composition of the political and military élite in Taiwan in Shi Zhengfeng, 'Taiwan zhuqun jiegou yu zhengzhi quanli zhi fenpei' (Ethnic Composition and the Distribution of Political Power in Taiwan), in *Taiwan zhengshi jianguo (Political Constructs in Taiwan)* (Taipei, Avanguard Publisher, 1999), 127–72. See also Wu Naide, 'Shengji yishi, zhengzhi zhichi he guojia rentong' (The Question of Provincial Origin, Political Support and

cultural affinities and blood ties the local population shared with mainland China, a growing awareness of their differences and increasing tension divided the population along the Mainlander/Taiwanese line. Consequently, in 1946–7 the tension between Mainlanders and Taiwanese led to a Home-Rule movement. This movement, initiated by the local élite, strove for autonomy for the Taiwanese under the rule of the KMT, and was soon crushed by the KMT's ruthless repression (the February 28th Incident in 1947). Immediately afterwards, martial law was declared (it was to last for 38 years) and the whole of Taiwan was turned into a police state. Any activities or speech relating to Taiwan autonomy or independence were forbidden. Under this repressive control, the leadership of the Home-Rule movement that had survived the February 28th Incident resorted to attempting to gain independence for Taiwan, but could only carry on the struggle overseas.

At the international level, the KMT persisted with its claim to be the only legitimate government of China. In the early 1970s, as more and more countries came to recognize the PRC, the ROC responded by cutting off diplomatic ties with those countries that had established formal links with the PRC. In 1971, when the UN allowed the PRC to take the China seat at the UN, the KMT regime decided to 'withdraw' from the UN in protest before it was expelled.[12] The KMT's pursuit of the One China policy gradually led Taiwan into diplomatic isolation.

Political changes began in the 1980s when Chiang Ching-kuo initiated the process of indigenization and gradually transformed the authoritarian regime from within the system. A hallmark of the change in the political landscape was the lifting of the 38-year-old martial law, and of the ban on opposition political parties and the freedom of the press, in 1987. The first opposition party, the Democratic Progressive Party (DPP), founded the year before (1986), was thus legalized. The democratization of Taiwan has provided an environment where sensitive issues can be freely and openly discussed. By the same token, democratization has ensured that policy-makers are susceptible to popular pressures. National identity (Taiwanese versus Chinese) and the Taiwan–China relationship have become the most salient issues.

Real changes in the KMT's nationalist doctrine came later, in the era of Lee Teng-hui. On the one hand, under Lee the KMT was still, in principle, committed to the idea of a unified China, as is illustrated by the founding of new governmental institutions and the issuing of the Guidelines for Unification.[13]

National Identity), in Zhang Maogui (ed.), *Zhuqun guanxi yu gujia rentong (Ethnic Relations and National Identity)* (Taipei, Institute for National Policy Research, 1993), 27–51.

[12] The PRC attained its right of representation in the UN and was installed as one of the five permanent members of the Security Council in accordance with UNGA resolution XXVI of 1971.

[13] Both the National Unification Committee (NUC) and the semi-official Strait Exchange Foundation (SEF) were created in 1991 to promote unification. The NUC is under the direct

On the other hand, while still claiming adherence to the idea of unification, Taipei has gradually changed its perception of the cross-Strait relationship. Most noticeably, in 1991 the Taipei government formally abandoned the ROC's claim to sovereignty over the mainland. This step undoubtedly paved the way for Lee Teng-hui to advance a new definition of the cross-Strait relationship as a 'special state-to-state' one. While redefining the cross-Strait relationship, Lee also advocated the idea of the 'living community of Taiwan' (*shengming gonggongti*), or of the 'New Taiwanese' (*xin Taiwan ren*), in an attempt to construct a new 'imagined community' on Taiwan that was different from the previous official nationalist view.[14] This changed official view on the cross-Strait relationship has led to a reorientation and readjustment in foreign policy. The diplomatic priority now was to broaden Taiwan's space for participation in the international system in some meaningful way which might lead to the full recognition of its independence by the international community.

The evolving pattern of conflict across the Taiwan Strait is clear. Before the late 1980s, both the CCP and the KMT insisted on the unity of all China including Taiwan, the only difference between them being over which government was entitled to govern and to represent that China. Since the 1990s, and especially since Lee Teng-hui's redefinition of the cross-Strait relationship as a 'special state-to-state' one, the Taiwan authorities have placed sovereignty at the centre of the contest. The nature of the conflict has changed.

SELF-DETERMINATION AND SOVEREIGNTY

Two concepts, self-determination and sovereignty, may help us to understand better what secession means in the context of Taiwan. The concept of self-determination has been identified as being composed of two parts: (1) the principle of *external* self-determination, whereby a group of people are entitled to pursue their political, cultural and economic aspirations without interference or coercion from outside states, and (2) the principle of *internal* self-determination, which encompasses the right of various segments of a population to influence the constitutional and political structure of the system under which they live.[15] The practice of both external and internal principles of self-determination prompts the question of political legitimacy. Inherent in the notions of democracy and popular sovereignty is the universal acceptance that any population has the right to choose and

---

leadership of the President. The SEF has so far functioned as the second channel for cross-Strait negotiation.

[14] Lee Teng-hui, 'Understanding Taiwan', in *Foreign Affairs*, 78:6 (1999), 9–14.

[15] Buchheit, *Secession*, 14.

decide on how it is ruled, that a government is legitimate only with the consent of the people; hence the right to internal self-determination. As it involves the formation of a state, the right to external self-determination seems to be the equivalent of what would be called a right of secession, and the exercising of such a right remains highly controversial.

Today the people of Taiwan appoint their government in elections that are held according to the usual democratic standards and are considered free and fair. As a result, the government is representative and the policies it pursues in various fields are approved democratically. This is internal self-determination in action for the people of Taiwan. And yet, although Taiwan has developed extensive external links with most countries and regions in the world but is not recognized as an independent state, it has been denied the right to external self-determination. When the first opposition party, the DPP, was founded in 1986, the principle of self-determination was written into its charter. In the paragraph dealing with foreign affairs it was stated that Taiwan's future was to be freely decided upon by its whole population. But for the two factions in the DPP—the moderate Formosa faction (*meilidao*) and the more radical New Wave faction (*xinchaoliu*)—the principle of self-determination meant different things. For the members of the New Wave, this principle was a roundabout way of advocating independence. The proclamation and attainment of *de jure* independence was the necessary condition for introducing democracy into Taiwan. For the members of the Formosa faction, on the other hand, the significance of the principle of self-determination remained mainly internal: it meant that the whole of the Taiwan population was to be responsible for the political, social, and economic evolution of the land they inhabited.[16] With the growing importance of the radical faction, the demand for independence was explicitly written into the party's charter in 1991.

To understand the conflicting claims over the status of Taiwan, it is necessary to start with the concept of 'sovereignty'. Sovereignty has meant different things at different times. As Stephen D. Krasner points out in *Sovereignty: Organized Hypocrisy*, this term has been used over time in four different senses: international legal sovereignty, Westphalian sovereignty, domestic sovereignty, and interdependence sovereignty. International legal sovereignty refers to the mutual recognition between territorial entities with formal legal independence. Westphalian sovereignty refers to the ability of a polity to exercise exclusive control within a given territory. All external players are excluded from its structures of authority. These first two senses of sovereignty are concerned with the issue of authority, whereas the other two senses mainly involve the issue of administration. Domestic sovereignty

[16] Samia Ferhat-Dana, 'The Democratic Progressive Party and Independence', *China Perspectives*, 19 (1998), 32.

refers to the formal organization of political authority and the ability of public authorities to exercise effective control within the borders of their own
polity. Interdependence sovereignty refers to the ability of public authorities
to regulate cross-border movements such as the flow of people and capital.[17]

However, the term 'sovereignty' has often been used narrowly in its
domestic and interdependence senses. In recent years, some analysts have
argued that sovereignty is being eroded. Such erosion (the diminishing
function of the state as a result of phenomena such as economic globalization and regional integration), they say, is taking place simultaneously on
two levels: both supra-state and sub-state.[18] But what we are actually witnessing is the erosion of sovereignty in the domestic and interdependence
senses. Sovereignty in the international legal and Westphalian senses
remains the cornerstone for the establishment of norms of international
order, and determines the foreign policy and behaviour of a state.

When the ROC on Taiwan proclaims itself to be sovereign, this may refer
to the fact that it enjoys the Westphalian sense of sovereignty as the government exerts effective and exclusive control over the territory. But as it is not
recognized as an independent state by most countries in the world, and is
denied access to international organizations, the ROC on Taiwan does not
have sovereignty in the international legal sense. It is a non-recognized
state.[19] The PRC has not been able to rule Taiwan since the date of its foundation. One of the justifications given for its claim to sovereignty of Taiwan
stems from the international community's recognition of such a claim. The
PRC thus claims sovereignty over Taiwan in an international and legal—but
de facto not Westphalian—sense. This analytic differentiation of what each
party really has in respect of sovereignty over Taiwan will be very important
later when we come to the territorial dimension in our normative discussion of the legitimacy of the Taiwan secessionist movement.

It is important, however, to note that the distinction between the four
senses of sovereignty is used mainly for analytical purposes. In political practice, the claimant of sovereignty tends to regard it as the absolute and indivisible 'soul' of a state. That explains why, whenever there is a dispute over
sovereignty, the conflict is easily reduced to a zero-sum game. The collective

---

[17] Stephen D. Krasner, *Sovereignty: Organised Hypocrisy* (Princeton, Princeton University
Press, 1999).

[18] Gidon Gottlieb, *Nation Against State: A New Approach to Ethnic Conflicts and the Decline
of Sovereignty* (New York, Council of Foreign Relations Press, 1993), 14–24.

[19] Having the status of a non-recognized state does not necessarily hinder a state's commercial conduct, or even diplomatic discourse, as revealed by the experience of Taiwan. But
when recognition as a state is a widely understood construction in our contemporary world,
from the sociological and cognitive perspectives, the absence of it does challenge the legitimacy
of the ruler and cause confusion among the population concerning its national identity.
Research has shown that Taiwan society today is indeed experiencing a national identity crisis.

non-recognition of Taiwan as a state makes clear the international community's consent to the PRC's One China principle, thus lending support to its non-negotiable position on the issue of Taiwan independence.

The two key concepts, 'self-determination' and 'sovereignty', reveal that, analytically, secession in Taiwan is in its essence a struggle for external self-determination and sovereignty in the international/legal sense. The issue at the heart of the contest is the recognition of its status as an independent and sovereign state by the international community.

NORMATIVE ASSESSMENT OF THE CASE

Against this historical background, I will now turn to the main purpose of the chapter, which is to make a normative assessment of the political status of Taiwan. As regards the existing variants of normative approaches, I argue that each of them, when applied on its own—whether the *a priori* approach or the *a posteriori* one—fails to take all aspects of a concrete case into account. In this sense, I find the framework proposed by Alex Heraclides a more comprehensive one. The six conditions in his framework have, in my opinion, covered most variants of the criteria in the existing literature. With only some minor changes to his framework, a total of seven conditions are suggested:

- Prerequisites (past and present conditions):
  1. A sizeable self-defined community or society that overwhelmingly supports the breakaway.
  2. The community has a legitimate claim to the territory it wishes to occupy after the breakaway.
  3. Systematic discrimination, exploitation and injustice.
  4. Cultural domination against the community or society seeking separation.

- Necessary and pivotal prerequisite (continuing conflict):
  5. State intransigence: repudiation of peace talks, no accommodation by meaningful autonomous rule and/or repression *manu militari*.

- Supplementary reinforcing factors (future prospects):
  6. Conflict settlement and regional stability following the breakaway.
  7. Respect for the human rights of minority cultures in the new state.

According to this framework, a normative analysis of a secessionist movement is highly path-dependent. It takes into account the passage of time in the secessionist movement. In the ensuing paragraphs, following the elaboration of each condition, an analysis of the relevant aspect in the case of Taiwan will be made. In the elaboration of each criterion, I will refer to other authors who share similar arguments. To be sure, confined to the context of our case, some conditions may not prove relevant to this analysis. We may not, even, expect to reach a simple verdict by the end of our normative analysis, for 'we must accept that the different criteria may pull in opposite directions, and so to reach a verdict on any concrete case we are likely to have to balance conflicting claims'.[20] But it is surely possible to come to a conclusion concerning the question of whether Taiwan has a unilateral right of secession.

(1) A sizeable self-defined community or society that supports the breakaway

A discussion on the right to self-determination invariably starts with the notion of the 'self': who constitute the 'self' that is entitled to claim the right to self-determination? Different expressions such as 'national self-determination' or 'self-determination of peoples' seemingly presuppose the existence of such a nation or people, whereas in fact 'the people' or 'the nation' remain to be delimited.[21] Two distinct concepts of the 'self' have predominated in both international law and political science in different historical periods. From the nineteenth century to the first half of the twentieth, particularly in the Bolshevik and the Wilsonian periods, the right to self-determination was perceived primarily in ethnic terms. An ethnic or national community constituted a people entitled to political self-determination. In the 1930s, in Eastern and Central Europe, a primarily ethnic interpretation of self-determination facilitated the abuse of this principle by Nazi Germany. Nazism discredited the idea of the ethno-nationalist self. This is one reason why self-determination was not defined according to the ethnic criterion after World War II. In the process of decolonization, the principle of self-determination was not applied to ethnic or national groups, but to multi-ethnic peoples under colonial rule. These two concepts of the 'self', based on either ethnicity or territorial proximity, are still very much alive today in the popular understanding of the right to self-determination. The adoption of a different concept of the 'self' has different implications for the drawing of political boundaries.[22]

So what kind of group may legitimately invoke the principle of self-determination? To identify such a group, one needs to examine it from both

[20] David Miller, 'Secession and the Principle of Nationality', in Moore, *National Self-Determination and Secession*, 65.

[21] In the often quoted remark of Sir Ivor Jennings: 'On the surface it seemed reasonable: let the people decide. It was in fact ridiculous because the people cannot decide until somebody decides who are the people.' Buchheit, *Secession*, 9.

[22] In a way, the two conceptions of the 'self' correspond to the distinction between ethnic and civic nationalism in the studies on nationalism. Civic nationalism emphasizes the voluntary basis for the formation of nation, while ethnic nationalism presupposes the primordial nature of the nation.

the subjective and objective angles. On the one hand, the members of the group should share a sense of 'we-group consciousness' that distinguishes them from their neighbours, and this group consciousness should seek expression in political forms of self-government. Besides shared beliefs and mutual commitments, some objective characteristics further distinguish such a group from the ambient population. These characteristics may be of a religious, historical, geographic, ethnic, linguistic, or racial nature. Of the two sets of criteria, the subjective one is the more easily identified, because the objective characteristics of a group may be subject to various interpretations which will lend support to conflicting claims regarding the group's identity. Furthermore, mobilized majority support based on the in-group consciousness is needed for such a group to claim the right to self-determination.

Taiwan has a population of 22 million people, divided into three (sub-) ethnic groups—native Taiwanese, Mainlanders, and Aborigines. According to the 1990 census, approximately 85 per cent are native Taiwanese, 14 per cent are Mainlanders and just over 1 per cent are Aborigines. One important criterion for differentiating between the ethnic groups is the date of their settlement in Taiwan. The Aborigines and their descendants, who are of Malay-Polynesian origin, are the original inhabitants of Taiwan. The native Taiwanese and their offspring are those who emigrated from mainland China before World War II. This category is further subdivided into two groups, mainly according to linguistic difference: the Hoklos, people originally from the provinces of Fujian and Guangdong who started immigrating to Taiwan in the seventeenth century, and who speak a Fujian dialect known as Hoklo, and the Hakkas, who also originated mainly from the same two provinces from the eighteenth century onwards and speak another dialect—Hakka.[23] The Mandarin-speaking Mainlanders comprise the troops and followers of the KMT who retreated to Taiwan between 1945 and 1949 following the KMT's defeat in the Civil War, and their descendants—Mandarin being the official language in China.

In Chinese literature on Taiwan studies, one label for the native Taiwanese is *benshengren* (literally meaning 'folks of this province'), in contrast to *waishengren* ('folks from other provinces') for the Mainlanders. It is important to note that

---

[23] The common use of 'dialect' is adopted here. However, since in the minds of many people the term 'dialect' tends to denote a subordinate form of a dominant language with only some variations in pronunciation and vocabulary, we would like to point out that here 'dialect' can be used as an equivalent of 'language'. In fact, the question whether a dialect is a limited deviation of a dominant language and should not be regarded as a language itself is the subject of heated debate even among linguists. Furthermore, in Taiwan some socio-linguists argue that Hoklo, Hakka, and Mandarin are 'three branches off the main trunk of the Chinese language'. For a more detailed study of the relationship between the ethnic groups and their dialects in Taiwan, see Shi Zhengfeng, 'Ethnic Differentiation in Taiwan', *Journal of Law and Political Science (Taiwan)*, 3 (1995), 141–66.

the term 'Taiwanese' has had different connotations for different commentators in the past fifty years. This changing connotation of the word 'Taiwanese' is a good illustration of the complexity of Taiwan's debate on national identity.

On Taiwan itself, there are four main interpretations of who the Taiwanese are. First, used in a common way, the population of Hoklo origin are often regarded by themselves and the rest of the population as Taiwanese, and their dialect is labelled 'Taiwanese' in Mandarin. Second, some advocates of Taiwan independence claim that the Taiwanese are a nation made up of the *benshengren*, that is, Hoklos and the Hakkas. They regard the KMT as an alien ruler, and the *waishengren* (the Mainlanders), who migrated to Taiwan after 1945, as not belonging to the Taiwan nation. National self-determination is meant only for the *bengshengren*.[24] A third view instead identifies the Taiwanese as a nation on a territorial basis, therefore including the whole population, and urges greater social integration.[25] And fourth, the official view before the 1990s was that the Taiwanese—the local population on Taiwan—were a part of the Chinese nation (the ROC). Since the 1990s, the third definition of Taiwanese—that the Taiwanese are a nation on a territorial and political basis—has become the dominant view among the élite.[26] The issue of national identity that used to divide the two major parties, the DPP and the KMT, began to disappear as both moved closer to the third definition of Taiwanese.

Across the Strait, to the PRC, Taiwanese refers simply to the residents of the 'renegade province', and they are Chinese by nationality as indicated by various objective criteria such as anthropological findings and historical documentation. That people in Taiwan constitute a part of the Chinese nation implicitly denies the Taiwanese the right to external self-determination. When it is claimed otherwise, this is perceived by the Beijing government as an illegitimate separatist attempt.

In Allan Wachman's view, in defining their national identity the people on Taiwan have conjured up rationales comprising two key ingredients: history and pragmatism. The history rationale runs that the joint history of

[24] Objective criteria—such as historical (the two centuries' frontier experience and the fifty years of common colonial experience), racial (mixed blood), and linguistic ones (two dialects)—were employed to demonstrate the distinctiveness of the Taiwan nation.

[25] This is the so-called 'thesis of non-differential identity' (*wu cabie rentong lun*) first advocated by the overseas Taiwan independence activists. According to this view, regardless of the date when one (or one's ancestors) settled down on Taiwan, and regardless of one's ethnic origin, as long as a person subjectively identifies himself/herself with the Taiwan nation, he/she will be a true member of the nation. See Huang Shaotang, 'Zhanhou Taiwan duli yundong yu Taiwan mingzuzhuyi de fazan (The Post-War Taiwan Independence Movement and the Evolution of Taiwan Nationalism)', in Shi Zhengfeng (ed.), *Taiwan minzuzhuyi (Taiwan Nationalism)* (Taipei, Avanguard Press, 1994), 195–227.

[26] The second and fourth views still remain valid for extreme advocates of independence and for supporters of unification, respectively.

Taiwan and China predetermines the future of Taiwan. Following their respective interpretations of the history of Taiwan—China relations, the extreme supporters of independence and unification defend their different positions: that either the absence of historical links justifies independence, or that the existence of extensive historical links makes unification inevitable. The pragmatists, in contrast, may support unification or independence, but require either outcome to be in keeping with the interests of the people who will live under it.[27]

Survey studies have confirmed Wachman's view. The extensive surveys conducted in the 1990s have shown that the national identity of Taiwan's population can be located on a pro-unification/pro status quo/pro-independence spectrum. Literature on survey studies has made a number of similar observations on the issue of national identity in Taiwan.[28] First, the population does not have a uniform national identity; there exist three main forms of identification: I am Taiwanese; I am Chinese; I am both Taiwanese and Chinese. To most of those questioned in the different surveys, the terms 'Chinese' and 'Taiwanese' can have at the same time national, ethnic and/or cultural connotations. Terms such as 'ambivalent national identity', 'crisis of national identity' appear frequently in newspapers and academic works.[29] Secondly, as discussion on national identity and Taiwan independence spread after democratization, since the 1990s there has been a steady increase in the number of people identifying themselves as Taiwan nationalists and supporting independence, in contrast to a decline in the number of people supporting unification with China. Despite the trend—and here we come to the third observation—the percentage of nationalists in Taiwan has never reached the halfway mark, even after the missile crisis in 1996.[30]

---

[27] Allan M. Wachman, *Taiwan: National Identity and Democratization* (New York, Sharpe Inc., 1994), 65; Rigger Shelly, 'Competing Conceptions of Taiwan's Identity: The Irresolvable Conflict in Cross-Strait Relations', *Contemporary China*, 6 (1997), 307–8.

[28] For detailed reading on recent survey studies of Taiwan national identity, see Robert Brown, 'National Identity and Ethnicity in Taiwan: Some Trends in the 1990s', in Stephane Corcuff (ed.), *Memories of the Future: National Identity Issues and the Search for a New Taiwan* (New York and London, M. E. Sharpe Inc., 2001), 144–59; Lin Jialong, 'Taiwan's Emerging Civic Nationalism: Origin and Implications', paper presented at the fourth annual North America Taiwan Studies Conference (NATSC) (June 1999); Wu Naide, 'Liberalism, Ethnic Identity and Taiwan Nationalism', *Taiwan Political Review*, 1 (1996), 5–39, and 'Shengji yishi, zhengzhi zhichi he guojia rentong' (The Question of Provincial Origin, Political Support and National Identity), in Zhang Maogui (ed.), *Zuqun guanxi yu guojia rentong (Ethnic Relations and National Identity)* (Taipei, Institute for National Policy Research, 1993), 27–51.

[29] See Lu Jianrong, *Fenlie de guozurentong 1975–1997 (Ambivalent National Identity)* (Taipei, Maitian Press, 1999).

[30] In 1996 the PRC fired missiles before Taiwan's first presidential election by universal suffrage. The missile test was intended to influence the electorate against the supporters of independence, but it backfired: support for Taiwan independence soared to a historic high of 46 per cent, and Lee Teng-hui was elected with a 54 per cent majority vote.

Most of the population is pragmatic about the final resolution of the cross-Strait relationship. Neither radical pro-unification nor pro-independence positions have majority support.

The democratization of political life has transformed the Taiwan population into a collective player entitled to internal self-determination. But the conflicting national identities suggest the absence of a majority will for political independence. At this moment, I conclude that the self as a collective player entitled to external self-determination is not present in Taiwan. Under such circumstances, the future development of national identity of the Taiwan people depends very much on the process of cross-Strait interaction, in which the political élites from both sides play the decisive role.

(2) Legitimate territorial claims

Territory is an essential and generally contested element in a secessionist crisis. In the case of internal self-determination, it involves delimiting domestic boundaries so that various autonomous or federal arrangements can be implemented. And in the case of external self-determination, secession, the creation of two new states by the act of separation, means redrawing state borders. Ideally, when the national boundary coincides with the territorial boundary, it is easy to determine the territory on which national self-determination should take place. In reality, however, ethnic diversity on the same territory is the norm for most cases of secession. In the process of decolonization, the method adopted is to draw the borders within which self-determination should take place on the basis of previous administrative units. This method, as argued by Horowitz and Moore, may be appropriate in states where the linguistic or ethnic groups are numerous and of equal strength. But when the national community striving for self-determination constitutes the majority within the previous administrative units, it would be problematic to draw the boundaries along previous administrative dividing lines as this could produce 'trapped minorities'. It might even be suspected that the demand to revive the borders of previous administrative units could be 'a way for the dominant nationality to increase its territory'.[31] Often it is quite clear to the parties in dispute which territory they are talking about. But the exact delimitation can still be a very important step in the negotiations when the parties agree to settle the conflict following a democratic procedure, i.e. through a referendum. In all cases, the parties in conflict have over time developed various arguments to strengthen their territorial claims. A normative assessment of a secessionist movement requires an evaluation of the validity of the conflicting territorial claims.

[31] Margaret Moore, 'The Territorial Dimension of Self-Determination', in her *National Self-Determination and Secession*, 138; see also Horowitz, 'Self-Determination: Politics, Philosophy, and Law', 192–3.

One simple and conclusive way to judge the legitimacy of a national community's territorial claim is the so-called 'stolen property [or] historical grievance version of the territoriality thesis', shared by both Lea Brilmayer and Allen Buchanan. According to this view, when a particular territory and the community inhabiting it have been incorporated into a larger unit by force at some point in their history, either by annexation or conquest, the community in question has a valid claim to the territory and a moral right to self-determination.[32]

Apart from the argument of unjust annexation, the parties in conflict have frequently appealed to historical, religious, or cultural arguments to support their territorial claims. In her article, Margaret Moore has examined these different types of argument and come to the conclusion that they are all inadequate because they are 'only acceptable to people who accept that particular version of history, or religion, or ethnic value'.[33] Discussing what counts as a valid territorial claim in the case for self-determination, David Miller maintains that if a community has over time cultivated and transformed the territory they inhabit through their physical and political activities, an attachment to the land is thus developed that cannot be matched by any rival claimants. This is particularly true in the case of a divided community where the mother state has not invested physical capital in that territory. Consequently, when the majority of the community inhabiting the territory share a distinct national identity, they have *prima facie* a good claim to self-determination.[34] It should be pointed out that when Miller argues in favour of the right to secession based on the principle of nationality, he emphasizes the importance of the need to seek other forms of constitutional accommodation within existing state borders, as outright secession might not produce a peaceful resolution of the conflict.

In our case, the territory in dispute has a clear geographical delimitation. The region known today as Taiwan comprises the island of Taiwan, the Pescadores (Peng-hu) Islands (numbering 64 in all), the Offshore Islands (the Quemoy and Matsu groups) and a handful of islands in the South China Sea. The island of Taiwan is geographically separated from mainland China by 100 miles of water. The PRC bases its territorial claim to Taiwan on historical and cultural links between Taiwan and the mainland, on the one hand, and on international law in respect of government succession, on the other hand. There is no denial of the extensive cultural, ethnic, historical, and religious links between Taiwan and mainland China, but there is no agreement on the political implications of these links. It is a fact that, technically

[32] Allen Buchanan, 'Towards a Theory of Secession', *Ethics*, 101 (1991), 322–42; Brilmayer, 'Secession and Self-Determination', 189.
[33] Moore, 'The Territorial Dimension of Self-Determination', 154.
[34] Miller, 'Secession and the Principle of Nationality', 68–9.

speaking, the Chinese Civil War has still not ended. Since it came to power in 1949, the Beijing government has not been able to rule Taiwan for a single day, and has invested no physical or political capital there. The use of historical and cultural links is therefore relevant but insufficient as a moral justification for the Beijing government's territorial claim over Taiwan. This means that other types of arguments and scientific disciplines have to be brought into our enquiry.

The PRC also advances its territorial claim to Taiwan on a legal basis. A White Paper released in 2000 and entitled 'The One China Principle and the Taiwan Issue' maintains that what happened on 1 October 1949 was a change of government by revolutionary means. The personality of the Chinese state remains unchanged even though the PRC replaced the ROC as the sole legal Chinese government and international representative. The changes in the government or internal policy of a state do not as a rule alter or affect the state's sovereignty, territorial integrity, or position in international law. As the succeeding government, the PRC is entitled to full sovereign control over the entire territory of China, Taiwan included.[35] The return of the sovereignty of Hong Kong and Macao to the PRC is provided as an illustration of government succession in contemporary China. It should be noted, however, that the international legitimization of the PRC as the sole government of China, on the basis of the principle of government succession, was not granted immediately in 1949 when the PRC was founded. Despite its defeat and the loss of control over mainland China, up until the 1970s the KMT government continued to be recognized as the legal Chinese government during its exile in Taiwan. It was not until 1971 that the UN ousted the ROC and installed the PRC in China's seat, in accordance with UN General Assembly Resolution 2758.

Some Taiwan scholars have attempted to refute the Beijing government's territorial claim to Taiwan from the angle of international law. Their main argument is that the PRC, founded in 1949, is in fact a new state and that what applies in this situation is the principle of state succession in international law.[36] Succession of states is one state replacing another state with respect to the territory, capacities, rights, and duties of the predecessor state. International law makes a clear distinction between state succession and the change of government within a state. Depending on the type of succession, a new state may succeed to all, none, or part of the preceding state's rights

---

[35] The Taiwan Affairs Office of the State Council and the Information Office of the State Council, *White Paper on 'The 'One China' Principle and the Taiwan Issue'*, 21 Feb. 2000.

[36] Qiu Hongda, 'Pingshu yige zhongguo baipishu (On the 'One China' White Paper)', *Journal Europe*, 24 February 2000; Xu Qingxiong, *Taiwan de guojia dingwei (Taiwan's Status as a State)*, Taipei, Xueying Cultural Publisher, 1995; Xu Qingxiong, 'Exploring Taiwan's International Status', paper presented at the 1996 Annual Conference of the Taiwan Legal Study Society, http://www.wufi.org.tw.

and responsibilities.[37] As these scholars see it, the PRC as a new state has taken control of only part of the ROC; this is therefore a case of partial state succession, that is, only the territory of mainland China, property located in this territory, and the rights and obligations of the ROC under contracts relating to the mainland, have been transferred to the PRC.

These scholars' argument of partial state succession is fundamentally flawed in its basic assumption that the PRC is a new state. It is a fact that China was split into two in 1949 as a result of the Civil War. But, contrary to what these Taiwanese scholars assume, the break-up did not automatically create two Chinese states. Both parties, the PRC and the ROC, were still very much engaged in the unfinished Civil War and, more importantly, neither of them claimed to be the government of a new state. What happened in 1949 was a change of regime, of government. China as a sovereign entity in international law did not change its legal personality. For both the PRC and the ROC there is but one sovereign China; their continued contention is over the legitimate and legal representation of its sovereignty.[38] The debate in the 26th session of the United Nations General Assembly in 1971, and Resolution 2758, passed by the General Assembly as a result, further illustrate that the contention between the PRC and the ROC since 1949 is not between two states, but between two governments within one state.[39] This is therefore a case of government succession. It is merely unfortunate that the PRC did not have the succession internationally recognized until 1971.[40]

(3) Systematic discrimination, exploitation and injustice, and (4) cultural domination

According to the scholars defending an *a posteriori* right of secession, systematic and deliberate discrimination perpetrated on one community by the state constitutes the basis of a strong *prima facie* right to secede. Discrimination can take place in economic and/or political fields. The best illustration is colonization, where the native people are deprived of their right

[37] In international law there exist three competing theories of state succession. The theories of universal succession, 'clean slate' and partial succession, respectively, provide for the new state to succeed to all, none or part of the preceding state's rights and responsibilities. The theory used in practice often depends on the type of succession or, in the case of international agreements, the type of treaty involved. For a more detailed account of the law of state succession, see Barry E. Carter and Phillip R. Trimble, *International Law* (Boston, Mass., Little Brown, 1995), 477–87.

[38] According to James Crawford (*The Creation of States in International Law* (Oxford, Clarendon Press, 1979), 151), 'a government is only recognised for what it claims to be. Statehood is a claim of right, and in the absence of any claim to secession the status of Taiwan can only be that of a part of the State of China under separate administration'.

[39] Had the PRC considered itself a new state, it would have applied for separate entry to the UN as a new state. In the early 1970s, the ROC also rejected the US's suggestion of 'one China, two seats'.

[40] In this case, recognition of the government is a vital condition. Recognition is essentially a political act, but it has importance legal consequences.

to equal economic redistribution and political participation. Another source of injustice is to be found in the circumstances where the culture of one community in a state is threatened owing to the cultural domination of another group. Economic and/or political discrimination violates basic individual rights, while cultural domination puts the individual's identity at stake when the specific cultural context that gives meaning to this identity is under threat. Evidence of discrimination and cultural domination alone cannot justify secession. The state's response to the injustice suffered by the secessionist group must also be taken into account. If the state lacks the will to undo the injustice by various forms of political accommodation, secession will be the community's last resort in order to defend its liberal rights and cultural survival.

Discrimination and cultural domination are not directly relevant to the analysis of PRC—Taiwan relations, because of the division that has existed between them since 1949 due to the Civil War. Nevertheless, they are significant in understanding the rise of the Taiwan Independence Movement in post-war Taiwan, both as explanatory factors and as legitimizing forces for political mobilization. As shown in the first section above, in the brief historical review of political developments on Taiwan after 1945, to legitimize its project of reunification the KMT regime had initiated its nation-building project on Taiwan, which had resulted in a Chinese cultural hegemony and the suppression of local culture. Furthermore, political discrimination denied the native Taiwanese (*benshengren*) access to the power structure, and especially to the centre of power. Consequently, the native élite mobilized the movement for autonomy and self-rule but was ruthlessly suppressed. The massacre of civilians participating in the 1947 protest and the imposition of martial law for 38 years dashed, in the view of the native élite, all hopes of resolving the problems of discrimination and cultural domination through political accommodation and reform. The advocates of autonomy opted for Taiwan independence. This movement is effectively a secessionist movement, which envisages a Taiwan independent from the ROC and the PRC.[41] The principle of Taiwanese self-determination was written into the DPP's political platform in 1991. The DPP leaders have built up their electoral support by highlighting the shared sense of suffering and deprivation among the native Taiwanese. Here we see clearly, in a case of discrimination and cultural domination, that the lack of political accommodation due to the central government's intransigence pushes the movement for self-determination further in the direction of independence.

As Taiwan evolves into a fully-fledged democracy, the issue of political discrimination has effectively been resolved by the so-called Taiwanization

[41] In the view of the radical supporters of Taiwan independence, after its defeat in the civil war, the territory of the ROC included only Quemoy (Jinmen), Matsu (Mazhu) and the offshore islands. The Republic of Taiwan on Taiwan Island should have been founded on the principle of self-determination.

or indigenization of the KMT's power structure, a competitive multi-party system and a fully functioning electoral system. Under Lee Teng-hui, the KMT shifted from an arch-unificationist position to a Taiwan-centred one. The relationship between the KMT and the DPP has gradually evolved from the stage of loyal opposition to a phase of both competition and cooperation. Given the prevailing status-quoism among the electorate regarding the issue of unification/independence, the mechanism of maximizing electoral gain in a competitive democratic system has pushed both the KMT and the DPP to adopt a more centralist and pragmatic policy.[42] By accommodating the conflicting political aspirations of the different social alignments in Taiwan, the process of democratization has succeeded in turning the previous intra-system conflict (the radical Taiwan Independence Movement versus the ROC) into inter-system competition. What has happened in Taiwan during the last two decades should be regarded as illuminating for future thinking on how to resolve the cross-Strait relations.

(5) State intransigence and (6) conflict settlement and regional stability following the break-away

Secession inevitably involves a change in the status quo, and any such change is a disturbance of sorts. From this perspective, the question of legitimacy should also be determined by pragmatic considerations: whether secession, or a continuation of the present union, would be more conducive to international peace and security. On a domestic level, disadvantages resulting from the break-up of the state—such as an economic setback or increased strategic vulnerability, depending on the economic significance and the strategic value of the seceding part—need to be taken into account. On an international level, the creation of new states may seriously alter the balance of power in the area, and this may provoke intervention or other hostile acts from third-party states affected by the change.

Security is probably the most volatile dimension in the cross-Strait relationship. The formula for reunifying Taiwan proposed by the Beijing government is the 'one country, two systems' policy. Within this framework, the most important principle is that there is only one sovereign China. Taiwan, as a part of China, will be granted the status of a special administrative region. The high degree of autonomy enjoyed by the region will preserve its own unique economic and social systems. Preferring a peaceful resolution to the cross-Strait impasse, the Beijing government nevertheless reserves the right to use force if necessary. But when and under what conditions is the use of force justified? To answer this question, one has to turn to just war theory for

---

[42] This is best illustrated by Chen Shui-pian's moderation of his pro-independence stance once he was elected president in 2000.

guidance. In the previous section dealing with territorial dimension, it has been argued that, from the legal perspective, the Beijing government is entitled to the territory of Taiwan by government succession, even though this succession was not internationally recognized until 1971. As the sole legal government of China, Taiwan included, the Beijing government can legitimately invoke the principle of territorial integrity when confronted with secessionist claims. It should, thus, be regarded as the legitimate authority defending a just cause.

Secession generally causes disruption at different levels and in different ways. The most violent form of disruption is armed conflict, which can result from the failure of the central government and the secessionist party to settle the conflict. Just war theory has always stressed that the use of force is legitimate only as a last resort. There is a responsibility on both sides to avoid an escalation of the conflict and to search for a settlement by political and peaceful means. If one party refuses political negotiation but favours military means instead, its political legitimacy will be in question, even if by other criteria it has a strong moral case for or against secession. This implies that all means of negotiation have to be exhausted before force may be used to prevent an unjust outcome. Thus far, Taiwan has not pursued a radical policy towards mainland China. This is also true of the Chen Shui-pian administration since his election to the presidency in March 2000. Although formerly an ardent supporter of Taiwan independence, Chen Shui-pian has considerably moderated his pro-independence stance since his presidential election campaign.

However, political negotiation has not been possible owing to the opposing perceptions of what is considered an acceptable basis for negotiation. For Taiwan, the ROC has to be recognized as equal in rights to the PRC prior to any form of political negotiation. For the PRC, the negotiations are to be conducted between two governments, not between two equal political entities. In its view, granting equal status to Taiwan would be tantamount to recognizing Taiwan as being a sovereign political entity, and would ultimately lead to its separation and independence. So far, there has been no direct political negotiation between the two governments.[43]

The PRC has insisted upon unification within a unitary state system, in which a high degree of autonomy is granted. The 'one country, two systems' model (as applied to Hong Kong) is itself a quite flexible formula, but the Taiwan side considers that the fundamental basis of this formula, namely the 'one China principle', should be one of the issues up for negotiation. Presently, Taiwan does not consider it a principle that it could accept. For

---

[43] The main agencies used by the two sides in approaching each other have been the quasi-official organizations, the Strait Exchange Foundation on the Taiwan side and the Association for Relations Across the Taiwan Strait in mainland China. These organizations deal with practical problems arising in people-to-people relations only; they are not authorized to discuss political differences between the sides.

the 'one country, two systems' formula to be effective, positive support from the Taiwan side would be required.

Some scholars have suggested that both sides should put aside the issue of sovereignty for the time being, in order to start negotiations.[44] Discussions on the question of sovereignty quickly reduce the negotiations to a zero sum game. Instead of searching for an ultimate settlement to the dispute over sovereignty, priority should, according to these scholars, be given to cooperation and confidence-building through integration on a functional level.[45] As the experience of the European Union has demonstrated, economic and social integration will pave the way for political integration.

Since the Taiwan government is not pushing for unilateral independence, the PRC has an interest in refraining from the use of military force. The use of military threats has various consequences. Military manoeuvres by the mainland authorities could lead effectively to a moderation of the position of the Taiwan government, but could also be counterproductive for the course of unification in other respects. Studies based on opinion polls have shown that the military exercises and missile tests conducted by the PRC both in July–August 1995 and March 1996 in Taiwan's offshore area provoked a negative reaction from the Taiwan public. The percentage of people identifying themselves with a Taiwanese nation doubled after the successive military exercises and missile tests.[46]

On the international level, the resolution of the Taiwan issue will have a profound impact on security in East Asia. In this respect, one cannot ignore the involvement of the United States in the Taiwan Strait. The US policy on Taiwan security, characterized by its ambiguity, remains one of the major flash-points in Sino–American relations. On the one hand, according to three US–PRC communiqués, the American government holds that, under the One China principle, unification is a domestic affair for China and should be achieved by the two peoples through exclusively peaceful means. On the other hand, the Taiwan Relations Act (TRA) provides the US with a framework for continuing extensive cooperation with Taiwan on a people-to-people basis. Moreover, by making the security of Taiwan a

[44] Li Yihu, 'Ruhe chujing liangan tongyi (How to Promote Cross-Strait Reunification)', Hong Kong, *China Review*, 3 (2000), 10–14.

[45] For example, some American scholars proposed the so-called 'interim agreement' as a possible procedure for unification. For an elaborate discussion on such an approach by Taiwanese scholars, see *Guoce zhuankan (Special Issue on State Policy)* vol. 11, at http://www.inprnet.org.tw. Other Taiwan scholars suggest that there should first be integration through extensive economic, cultural and people-to-people cross-Strait exchanges before unification. See Yung Wei, 'From "Multi-System Nations" to "Linkage Communities": A New Conceptual Scheme for the Integration of Divided Nations', in *Issues and Studies*, 33:10 (1997), 1–19.

[46] Robert Marsh, 'National Identity and Ethnicity in Taiwan: Some Trends in the 1990s', in Stephane Corcuff (ed.), *Memories of the Future: National Identity Issues and the Search for a New Taiwan* (Armonk, New York, M. E. Sharpe, 2002).

'grave concern' for the US national interest, the TRA makes it possible to sell arms to Taiwan and to justify its intervention in the area 'to resist any resort to force or other forms of coercion that would jeopardize the security, or the social or economic system, of the people on Taiwan'.[47]

During the PRC's 1996 missile test, the US dispatched two carrier battle groups to patrol the waters around Taiwan. Though the TRA gives the US the option of defending Taiwan, it does not necessarily commit it to doing so. The US as an external party should observe the principle of non-interference, although it might facilitate peaceful negotiation across the Taiwan Strait. It is the responsibility of the US not to complicate matters by giving further ambiguous signals to both sides. The discussion on incorporating Taiwan into the US Theater Missile Defence system and on an enhanced TRA actually militates against its proclaimed support for a peaceful settlement of the Taiwan problem.

(7) Respect for the human rights of minority cultures in the new state

Theorists in the normative debate on secession are fully aware that, in concrete cases, secession rarely creates an ethnically homogeneous state out of an ethnically heterogeneous parent state. New minorities emerging after the separation create the possibility of new ethnic conflicts and new secessionist drives.[48] In our normative assessment of a current secessionist movement, we need to estimate whether minority rights are likely to be better or worse protected after secession. To achieve self-determination through secession, the community should adhere to liberal democratic values.[49]

Given the fifty years of separate forms of political rule on Taiwan and mainland China, our question in this particular case should be posed from the opposite perspective: would liberal rights, including minority rights, be better protected if unification were to take place? The incompatibility of the political systems of Taiwan and mainland China has been perceived by the Taiwan people and authority as the biggest obstacle on the path to unification. Although the 'one country, two systems' policy guarantees the coexistence of two different economic, political and socio-economic systems in a unified China, the country would remain a unitary one. The autonomy promised to Taiwan, however extensive its range, would be devolved in a unitary system

---

[47] The text of the Taiwan Relations Act can be found on the Internet on http://ait.org.tw/ait/tra.html.

[48] Based on his extensive comparative studies on ethnic conflict, Horowitz ('Self-Determination: Politics, Philosophy, and Law', 191) has argued that secession nearly always intensifies conflicts between groups.

[49] Philpott, 'Self-determination in Practice', 38; Miller, 'Secession and the Principle of Nationality', 70–2; Heraclides, 'Ethnicity, Secessionist Conflict, and the International Society', 511.

where central government surrendered a certain degree of authority to regional territorial communities. From the Taiwanese perspective, this could always entail the risk of interference by the central government. The different political values and systems largely explain the difficulty of having the 'one country, two systems' policy accepted by the majority of the population in Taiwan, despite their rejection of a unilateral declaration of independence.

TENTATIVE CONCLUSIONS

Where do we find ourselves after the normative assessment of the dilemma, between independence and unification, in which Taiwan finds itself? As expected, no simple verdict can be reached as a result of our analysis. After all, the aim of such a normative assessment is a better understanding of the situation, both descriptively and normatively. Among the seven criteria applied in the analysis of Taiwan, a few points need highlighting. First, despite the suggestion of the political élite and some scholars that there is an emerging Taiwan nation that is consolidating itself, the question of the future of Taiwan is far from clear among the population. Ambivalence is the word that best captures their attitude and national identity. Second, on the issue of territorial sovereignty, the PRC can justifiably make its claim to Taiwan by evoking government succession. The existence of one sovereign China that encompasses Taiwan is acknowledged by the international community. Nevertheless, *de facto* the state of China is divided under two jurisdictions. To resolve this historical anomaly, the governments on both sides have the responsibility of taking the people's interests and regional security into account. The eventual resolution of the Taiwan issue is of great concern to the peoples on both sides. But what is even more important is that it should be achieved by peaceful means.

The future development of nationalism in Taiwan will be influenced by several factors. On the one hand, internally, continued participation in democratic governance will undoubtedly deepen the in-group sense of solidarity among the population. In this situation, the élite in Taiwan will play a significant role in the (trans)formation of national identity and in the debate on independence versus unification. Externally, if the PRC demonstrates its ability to come up with new concrete proposals and further demonstrates its willingness to resolve the differences through political negotiation, the Taiwanese population may become more open to the idea of unification. On the other hand, the extensive economic links that have developed across the Strait since the late 1980s may, in the opinion of some scholars, effectively evolve into integration on a functional level and may pave the way for political dialogue.[50]

---

[50] Yung Wei, 'From "Multi-System Nations" to "Linkage Communities" '.

Conclusion: Just War Theory and the Ethics of Secession

Bruno Coppieters

The introduction to this volume outlined four themes that are central to the ethics of secession. The themes focus, first, on normative issues, and in particular the tension between 'choice' theories and those based on remedial 'just cause' arguments; second, the problem of violence in secessionist struggles and the ensuing relationship between just war theory and the ethics of secession; third, the relationship between nationhood and citizenship, and in particular the problem of applying what has now become a conventional distinction between ethnic and civic representations of the political community; and, finally, the contentious issue of sovereignty and the way that it frames debates about self-determination. With each of these themes, the application of general moral principles to particular historical contexts opens up new avenues of research.

The first of these four themes—the discussion of a normative framework within which to judge demands for or opposition to secession—is the most prominent in the book. All the authors refer to previous attempts to apply general ethical criteria to concrete secessionist crises. They have given various names to the two main theoretical approaches to be found in the literature on the ethics of secession. Such a variety of names is also common in the literature itself, where alternative labels are used to distinguish between what are generally called the just cause and the choice approaches. Daniel Philpott writes about a 'constrictive' versus a 'permissive' view,[1] Allen Buchanan about a 'remedial right view' versus a 'plebiscitary right view',[2] and Kai Nielsen about a 'remedial right only theory' versus a 'primary right theory'.[3] The

I wish to thank Michel Huysseune, Richard Sakwa, Raymond Detrez, Gunter Lauwers, Xiaokun Song and Alexei Zverev for their comments on this comparative analysis.

[1] Daniel Philpott, 'Self-Determination in Practice', in Margaret Moore (ed.), *National Self-Determination and Secession* (Oxford, Oxford University Press, 1998), 80.

[2] Allen Buchanan, 'Democracy and Secession', ibid. 15.

[3] Kai Nielsen, 'Liberal Nationalism and Secession', ibid. 118. This latter distinction is also used by Buchanan in 'The International Institutional Dimension of Secession', in Percy B. Lehning (ed.), *Theories of Secession* (London, Routledge, 1998), 227–56.

authors of this volume adopt such names without substantially changing their meaning. Xiaokun Song introduces an alternative pair of labels. She focuses on the logical structure of the apprehension of reality using general normative principles and calls the choice approach—with its stress on the primacy of the principle of national self-determination over other concerns taken into account when secession is being considered—an 'a priori' view, and the just cause approach—with its concern for concrete historical analysis—an 'a posteriori' view.

The authors of this volume do not systematically analyse the general strengths and weaknesses of the just cause and choice approaches from a comparative perspective, as has been done in previous debates. They are concerned rather with making a well-founded judgement on their own particular cases. For this purpose, most of the contributions draw heavily on the just cause approach, but they also include other perspectives. In some cases, they prefer to build up their own systematic framework with a particular set of normative criteria. In her case study of Taiwan, Xiaokun Song uses a set of criteria established by Alexis Heraclides and Wayne Norman. Analysing the prospects of secession for Tatarstan, Alexei Zverev refers not only to Western contributions, such as those of Allen Buchanan or David Miller, but also to Russian scholars, such as the late Galina Starovoitova.

The debate between the just cause and the choice approaches may benefit in different ways from being contextualized. In the chapters on this theme, the authors aim to reach a better understanding of secessionist crises by increasing the number of disciplines involved in the study of them. Embedding just cause and choice principles in particular contexts makes it possible to go beyond the perspectives of philosophy and international law, and to include also research in history, international relations and comparative federalism. When particular secessionist cases are judged with the help of general principles, keen attention has to be paid to the moral value of historical and legal precedents. Such an approach also highlights the practical consequences of the application of general principles to the right to secession. Moreover, the design of institutional alternatives to secession—as prescribed by the last resort principle, which is central to the just cause and choice approaches to the ethics of secession—calls for a good knowledge of actual circumstances. Finally, a comparative approach involves an analysis not only of the meaning of general principles in concrete case-studies, but also of the extent to which a universal ethical theory of secession may benefit from a contextualization of its principles.

Similar benefits may be expected from a contextualization of the principles of just war theory in secessionist crises, which is the second theme of this book. Although at present they constitute two distinct and largely separate fields of research, the ethics of war and the ethics of secession are closely related. More than half of the chapters in our book deal with secessionist and irredentist movements that have attempted to impose their will unilaterally. Nationality conflicts in Northern Ireland, the former Yugoslavia and Chechnya became violent when one of the parties involved—or all of them—ceased to view these conflicts as capable of being regulated according to mutually acceptable rules. In Cyprus and Abkhazia, unilateral declarations of independence were the outcome of violent conflicts. In these five cases, a substantial part of the population was mobilized in support of the demand for secession or in opposition to it.

Unilateral declarations of secession tend to result in full-scale wars. The possibility of a military confrontation with mainland China largely explains why the Taiwan Independence Movement has exercised self-restraint in advancing its cause, and why only a relatively small minority of the population of the island would support a declaration of independence. In Corsica, a majority in the autonomist movement regards negotiations to achieve self-government for the island as the only viable option, and opposes the actions of small groups that advocate terrorist tactics to achieve independent statehood. Similarly, in the two remaining cases described in our volume—Quebec and Northern Italy—the option of unilateral secession has been discussed and, again, rejected. It is clearly the view of the Parti Québécois that the people of Quebec have an inherent right to secession which cannot be abrogated by any federal institution, whether the federal government, the federal parliament, or the supreme court. This does not mean, however, that it would necessarily exercise this right. In 1998, the Canadian Supreme Court addressed the question of whether or not the people of Quebec had a unilateral right to declare independence. It found that no such right existed, but it did prescribe a complex set of rules compelling the governments of both Canada and Quebec to engage in negotiations on secession if a majority in Quebec should express a wish for this in response to 'a clear question' put to the people in a referendum. But the failure of such negotiations could result in a unilateral declaration of secession, in which case the international community would have to adopt a position on the question of recognition. The Lega Nord issued a unilateral declaration of the independence of Padania on 15 September 1996. This declaration was characteristic of the Lega's 'politics of the virtual': the ritual enactment of the Padanian nation-to-be. Initiatives taken by the Lega in 1997 included a referendum on Padanian independence, elections for a Padanian parliament and the creation of a bogus northern state with its own parliament and government. While symbolically contesting the existence of the Italian state, these 'politics of the virtual' have never really attempted to replace Italian institutions by Padanian ones.[4]

[4] On the Lega's 'politics of the virtual' see Michel Huysseune, 'Conflicting Loyalties for Northern Italian Citizens: Padania versus Italy', paper presented at the workshop 'Loyalty and the Post-National State', Keele European Research Centre (Keele University, Britain), 5–6 June 1998.

The various ways in which nationhood and citizenship may be conceived have been introduced as the third theme of the book. A context-sensitive use of the civic/ethnic dichotomy is useful in analysing how secessionist movements define the holder of the right to national self-determination and the source of sovereignty. Such an analysis may be decisive in an assessment of the democratic legitimacy of secessionist claims, and more particularly of the respect shown for minorities. In a discussion on civic and ethnic forms of nationhood, answers have to be found to the questions 'Who are the people?' and 'Who is entitled to rule?' The holder of the right to self-determination is also entitled to either full or shared sovereignty—which leads us directly to the question of how to define sovereignty, the fourth and final theme of this volume.

The issue of sovereignty is addressed in all the contributions. The authors are concerned with exploring alternatives to secession. Each case discussed here thus sheds new light on the variety of ways in which domestic and international sovereignty can be (re)organized. Some cases also highlight the limits of institutional reform—some stemming from particular domestic constraints, others caused by the very nature of the international order. The principle of national self-determination is only partly compatible with the sovereignty of a multinational state, whereas sovereignty is still the cornerstone of the international order. Defence of sovereignty implies a defence of the principle of territorial integrity. It is clear that the principles of national self-determination and the inviolability of international borders are dynamic ones. The absolutization of either usually provokes violent conflicts. A contextualized approach to the meaning of sovereignty in a secessionist crisis has to reflect on how opposing demands—for national self-determination and territorial integrity—can be mediated by a concern to achieve and maintain a just and stable security system.

The question of the use of force in secessionist crises is addressed by Nathalie Tocci, Xiaokun Song, and Richard Sakwa with the help of just war theory, but they do not use this normative framework for assessing the legitimacy of the political objectives of the warring parties. Nonetheless, it is also possible, as demonstrated by the chapter on the Georgian–Abkhaz conflict, to analyse both the use of force in secessionist crises and the secessionist claims themselves using the set of criteria to be found in the *jus ad bellum* section of just war theory. These criteria refer to the principles of just cause, right intentions, legitimate authority, likelihood of success, proportionality, and last resort. This approach can be justified by the specific character of the ethics of war and secession (both ethical approaches deal with exceptions to general moral rules) and by the structural similarity between the use of force and a unilateral declaration of secession (in both acts, the aim is to impose one's political will on an adversary outside a commonly accepted legal framework).

In the following, we will use these criteria to compare the moral claims of the different movements striving for unilateral secession.[5]

The various criteria derived from a just cause, a choice, or some other perspective on the ethics of secession may be linked to those listed above. Moreover, the two other themes of this book—the normative value of the distinction between ethnic and civic forms of nationalism and the analysis of sovereignty—may also be analysed in a framework constructed using criteria drawn from just war theory. The oppression of a nation, illegal occupation of a territory, and discrimination are themes that can be subsumed under the just cause criterion. The need for a well-defined national identity and for an absolute majority of referendum votes in favour of independence— which is central to the choice approach in secession theory—may be examined in the light of the legitimate authority criterion. The same goes for the whole problematic issue of the distinction between a civic and an ethnic understanding of nationhood. A moral analysis of the interests and motives of secessionist and anti-secessionist forces can be subsumed under the criterion of right intentions.

It is not always possible for every single political question relating to secession to be subsumed under one single principle of just war theory. The principles have to be applied serially, but one needs to bear in mind that they are interconnected in such a way that the meaning of each cannot be assessed independently of the others.[6] Moral questions may be assessed from various perspectives. The problem of national self-determination involves the principles of just cause, legitimate authority and last resort. The issue of sovereignty may be analysed from the perspective of legitimate authority and last resort. The international community's concern to ensure a secure international environment may be addressed using the criteria of proportionality and likelihood of success. The rights of 'trapped' minorities may be analysed with the help of the legitimate authority and proportionality criteria.[7] Moreover, the application of just war principles to the ethics of secession requires a reinterpretation of their meaning. Below we will analyse each principle individually while defining its meaning in the context of the ethics of secession in individual, contextualized cases.

---

[5] A distinction has to be made in this context between unilateral and mutually agreed forms of secession. A procedure on secession mutually agreed by the government and a secessionist party makes it possible to respect the interests of all parties in accordance with the rules of justice.

[6] See Nick Fotion and Bruno Coppieters, 'Concluding Comments', in Bruno Coppieters and Nick Fotion, *Moral Constraints on War: Principles and Cases* (Lanham, Md., Lexington Books, 2002), 298–9.

[7] The correspondence between the ethics of war and the ethics of secession does not extend to the *jus in bello* principles of just war theory. The principles of 'proportionality in war' and 'discrimination' are used to make moral choices on the conduct of military operations. It would be difficult to compare military operations to a political process of secession.

JUST CAUSE

In the ethics of war, the just cause principle refers to the right to use military force to redress or prevent an injustice to one's own or another community.[8] The violation of a state's political sovereignty or territorial integrity, or massive human rights violations through genocide, may be regarded as typical cases of an injustice so great that it justifies military action. The use of force may be justified only by the need to remedy or prevent a serious injustice, and not by the need to create more justice in the world. In this respect, just war theory has far more affinity with the just cause approach to the ethics of secession than with the choice approach. The choice theory suggests that a 'distinct community', to use the term used by Viva Ona Bartkus,[9] has an a priori right to secede even if no antecedent wrong has been inflicted on it. As argued by Daniel Philpott and others, the rights of a community are viewed as being homologous to those of a person: just as an individual may or may not wish to participate in a political association, so too may a community exercise this right.[10] This argument in favour of the a priori right of every nation to constitute its own state— provided a number of specific conditions are fulfilled—is less about remedying or preventing an injustice than about cultural self-affirmation and the ability to shape one's own national identity.

According to the just cause approach of Allen Buchanan and Wayne Norman, 'the right to secede is only legitimate if it is necessary to remedy an injustice'.[11] The nature of these injustices may vary, ranging from infringement of political rights to the threat of cultural assimilation. Such a claim may be formulated in the language of national self-determination, but secession is not to be seen as a justified means of turning every people and every nation into a sovereign polity. A parallel may be drawn with just war theory, which considers the preservation of peace to be the general rule and the use of force an exceptional right. Similarly, the just cause approach in the ethics of secession regards the preservation of existing states—including the preservation of their sovereignty and right to territorial integrity—as the general rule, and unilateral secession an exceptional right. This view should not be viewed as conservative, insofar as the preservation of peace and the existing state order does not necessarily lead to a passive acceptance of injustices. It only means that there are other political ways of achieving a just peace. War

---

[8] See Carl Ceulemans, 'Just Cause', in Coppieters and Fotion, *Moral Constraints on War*, 25–39.
[9] Viva Ona Bartkus, *The Dynamics of Secession* (Cambridge, Cambridge University Press, 1999), 10–11.   [10] Philpott, 'Self-Determination in Practice', 79–102.
[11] Moore, 'Introduction' in her *National Self-Determination and Secession*, 6. Buchanan's argument is presented in full in his *Secession: The Morality of Political Divorce from Fort Sumter to Lithuania and Quebec* (Boulder, Colo., Westview Press, 1991).

and secession should not be seen as appropriate instruments for implementing more justice, but only for remedying or preventing injustice. The principle of national self-determination is a key element in such a perspective on the ethics of secession, but this does not mean that the fact that not every nation or every people is governed by its own state has to be seen as unjust.

Some of the present authors apply the various criteria central to the choice perspective to their particular case. Most, however, focus on the question of how much the claims of political movements striving for secession refer to forms of injustice. Different kinds of injustice are described in this volume, the most prominent being colonialism, the illegal occupation of a territory, national oppression, ethnic cleansing and the threat of genocide. Colonialism is the first form of injustice that could justify secession, and some supporters of independence in Abkhazia, Chechnya, Northern Ireland, and Corsica have advanced a claim to this effect. In none of these cases, however, does the concept of colonialism to be found in international legal doctrine—the one that would justify independence—apply. The problem, of course, is one of definition. The term 'internal colonization'—a concept without any legal meaning—is sometimes used in this context. From the perspective of historiography, it undoubtedly makes sense to go back to Russian, British or French colonial history in order to understand present-day politics in Chechnya, Northern Ireland or Corsica. In these contexts, the use of the term 'colonialism' to describe centre/periphery relations is not even disputed. As mentioned by Richard Kearney, in November 1998 the British prime minister, Tony Blair, declared in Dublin that Britain was overcoming its 'post-colonial malaise'. In the case of Georgia and Abkhazia, both were gradually absorbed into the colonial system of the Tsarist empire. However, none of the chapters, including those that refer to a colonial past, considers the term 'colonialism' as appropriate to describe present forms of injustice, or as justifying unilateral declarations of independence.

Forms of national oppression other than colonization are acknowledged in the chapters describing past relations between Georgia and Abkhazia, and Russia and Tatarstan, and between the various nationalities making up the Yugoslav federation. In these three cases, rigid hierarchical relations between national communities have been institutionalized. But this does not justify the creation of a separate sovereign state for the subordinated nationality. In Taiwan, all expressions of autochthonous culture were severely repressed by the anti-communist Kuomintang even before its final retreat to Taiwan. Martial law was introduced in 1947, and lasted for four decades. But such forms of discrimination took place along the Mainlander/Taiwanese line in domestic policies, and were easily remedied through political democratization after the lifting of martial law in 1986. They cannot therefore be used in an attempt to justify unilateral secession from the People's Republic of China.

In exceptional cases, a just cause approach may consider unilateral secession to be justified as a means of preventing a severe injustice. Serb nationalists in Croatia used this type of justification to defend their demands for secession. In their view, Serb-populated territories in Croatia could remain part of the country as long as it in turn remained part of Yugoslavia. The Chechen declaration of independence in 1991 was supported by similar arguments, with Dudayev stating that Chechnya could remain part of the USSR as a sovereign Union republic, but not part of an independent Russia, a rather peculiar position given the suffering imposed on Chechnya by the Soviet Union and the prospects of democratic federalism in the new Russia. In this case, the historical argument about the need to avoid a repetition of previous experiences of oppression itself helped provoke repression after 1994. The lack of problematization of the historical experiences of the Chechen, Russian, and 'Soviet' peoples allowed history itself to become part of the Chechen people's sad destiny after 1991.

Neither the Serb nor the Chechen case justifies the need for independent statehood as a pre-emptive move. According to just war theory, a pre-emptive strike has to be a response to a sufficient threat. Michael Walzer states as conditions that the potential aggressor should have a manifest intent to injure and should exhibit a significant degree of preparedness to execute this threat, so that waiting would increase the risk to the victim nation.[12] These particular conditions were not fulfilled in either case. It is certainly true that the fear of extinction had a basis in historical reality. Genocide attempts against the Chechen people had only been halted in the 1950s, after the death of Stalin. More recently, the 1994 and the 1999 Russian military operations against Chechen independence were characterized by open contempt for the discrimination principle, and neither of these interventions may be regarded as just. In Croatia in 1995, after the Krajina Serbs' attempt to secede, Croatia completed its military operations by a massive campaign of ethnic cleansing. In both the Chechen and Serb cases, war and repression followed rather than preceded the secessionist moves. Unilateral secession leads to an escalation of existing conflicts and cannot be justified by the violence that accompanies it. The remedial element was particularly anachronistic in the case of Chechnya, where the injustices imposed on the Chechen people in an earlier age were laid at the door of a regime that specifically repudiated them.

Force has also been used against populations in Abkhazia and Kosovo. In the latter case, it was justified by the central government as a pre-emptive move, designed to crush secession attempts. The Kosovar population had already organized a referendum on independence in 1991, leading to a declaration that remained unrecognized by other states except Albania, while

[12] See Ceulemans, 'Just Cause', 28.

the Abkhaz authorities had not yet taken such a step when Georgian troops intervened in Abkhazia in August 1992. Both of these conflicts ended in military defeat for the central government. In these cases, secession cannot be regarded as the natural outcome of an unjust war. The right of the Abkhazians and the Albanian Kosovars to defend themselves militarily against aggression does not necessarily include the right to set up their own state. In the case of Abkhazia, where military operations ended in 1993 and independence was declared in 1999, the *de facto* authorities waited for six years before formally abandoning the negotiations on a common federal state. In Cyprus—to take a third example—the repression of the Turkish minority led to outside intervention by Turkey, as an external guarantor of the 1960 Treaty, and to the division of the island in 1974. An independent Turkish Republic of Northern Cyprus was not declared until 1983, however. In all these cases, a declaration of independence would have needed to be justified by stronger arguments than the mere need for self-defence.

Secessionist movements in Abkhazia, Quebec, Corsica, Taiwan, Tatarstan, and even Northern Italy defend their case for sovereignty by pointing to the danger of the cultural assimilation of the weaker party. None of the studies in this volume supports the validity of such an argument, even if in some cases the legitimacy of such fears may be acknowledged. The endangering of a group's culture does not necessarily mean that sovereignty is the only institution capable of protecting it.

Certain claims advanced by secessionist movements are regarded by the authors as completely fallacious—as for instance the Lega Nord's presentation of the malfunctioning of the Italian state as a form of discrimination. In the Lega's view, the central state ('*Roma ladrone*') is dominated by Southern interests and favours transfers from the productive North to the South, which is accused of leading a parasitic existence. Michel Huysseune acknowledges the dysfunctional nature of many Italian state institutions, but refutes the thesis that this is because they are dominated by Southern Italian interests.

None of the injustices described in this volume can be regarded as serious enough to constitute a just cause for unilateral secession. But at the extreme, when the very existence of the seceding community is threatened by ethnic cleansing, a just cause for secession may exist. This does not apply to the Chechens in the post-Stalin era, still less in post-communist Russia—in the early 1990s the latter posed no aggressive or intentional threat to Chechnya's existence, either as a nation or a culture. This distinguishes Chechnya's case from that of Kosovo where, in 1998–9, such an aggressive and intentional threat did exist. But the just cause criterion is only one of six, each of which has to be met in turn. We still have to examine to what extent the other five criteria can justify the claim that independence for Kosovo is grounded in a remedial right to end a persistent and massive violation of human rights.

RIGHT INTENTIONS

For just war theory, the application of the principle of right intentions necessitates a differentiated analysis of the motives behind a decision to wage war. The various motives have to be weighed against each other, and assessed to see to what extent the objective of achieving the just cause—preventing and remedying severe injustices—was decisive in the decision-making process. This approach is also valid for a moral analysis of the decision to declare unilateral independence.

Little is said in this volume about the heterogeneous nature of the motives for secession. The authors assess the moral validity of the cause defended by secessionist leaderships, but do not complement this analysis with an assessment of the extent to which their motives may have other sources. This lack of interest in the subjective aspect of decision-making on secession contrasts with the close attention authors working in the field of just war theory have paid to the principle of right intentions. The question of how far the 1990–1 Gulf War was primarily motivated by aims other than the restoration of Kuwait's sovereignty was central to debates on its moral legitimacy. In principle, it would likewise be possible to examine to what extent secessionist leaderships strive for international sovereignty in order to protect personal or particular group interests. This may include the attempt to secure increased protection for political leaders from criminal prosecution for war crimes or other types of crime.

When their state attains sovereign status, political leaders may also enjoy substantial political or economic advantages which are not of a criminal nature but which have nothing to do with the satisfaction of the just cause—the remedying or prevention of serious injustice. Under the Soviet federal system, the local leadership of subordinated federal entities enjoyed substantial political and material privileges. These were consolidated by the international recognition of their state in the difficult process of adaptation to democracy and a market economy. Easier access to international funding is a further advantage. None of the authors in this volume claims that such motives should be taken as being the driving force behind secessionist policies. This approach—which contrasts with the accusations often put forward by governments attempting to prevent secession—is not due to any lack of understanding of the motivational structure of secessionist movements. It seems that most authors would not deny the existence of such motives, but tend to regard them as secondary in an analysis of the legitimacy of the secessionist cause. This means that none of the authors explicitly claims that the principle of right intentions is not respected in the case they examine.

LEGITIMATE AUTHORITY

As a rule, the just war principle of legitimate authority prescribes that, in order to be legitimate, the choice of using military force has to be taken exclusively by those who have the authority to do so. Its concrete meaning has changed over the centuries, being given different interpretations in the Roman Empire and again in the Middle Ages. Religious and secular authorities have also developed a variety of discourses on this principle. In modern times it has gradually come to be associated with the authority of officials representing sovereign states. Just war theory has drawn up a number of criteria for qualifying the use of force as emanating from a legitimate authority. The capacity to wage war by establishing a monopoly of the use of force on a state's territory is one of them. According to Anthony Coates, the legitimate authority of a modern state derives from its commitment, as part of the international community, to the common good and the rule of law.[13] These goals may be further specified as the defence of human rights, democracy, justice, and international peace and security.

After World War II, governments saw their exclusive right to wage war challenged at the international level by the authority of the UN Security Council and at the domestic level by revolutionary, anti-colonial, and secessionist movements. In the following, we will focus on the normative meaning this concept of a legitimate authority holds for secessionist movements. There is a need to develop criteria that may help to determine the legitimacy of decisions to declare unilateral independence. Some of the secessionist movements analysed in this volume have gained control of a territory and a population as a consequence of war. In the case of the non-recognized entities of Chechnya, Abkhazia, the Turkish Republic of Northern Cyprus, and Taiwan, the legal concept of a *de facto* state[14] and its defining characteristics of a well-defined territory, a permanent population, government, and the capacity to enter into relations with other countries, are relevant.[15] According to the 'declaratory school' in international law, recognition is a political act which does not confer sovereign statehood but takes the factual existence of statehood into account. The way in which the discussion on the

---

[13] See Anthony J. Coates, *The Ethics of War* (Manchester, Manchester University Press, 1997), 126–8.

[14] See Ian Brownlie, *Principles of Public International Law*, 4th edn. (Oxford, Clarendon Press, 1990), 71–2; Oppenheim's *International Law*, vol. i: *Peace*, Introduction and Part 1, ed. Robert Jennings and Arthur Watts (Harlow, Longman, 1992), 127–203; Scott Pegg, *International Society and the De Facto State* (Aldershot, Ashgate, 1998), 26–7.

[15] See James Crawford, *The Creation of States in International Law* (Oxford, Clarendon Press, 1979), 36–76.

'factual' reality of states is dealt with in a legal approach to the question of international recognition can be contrasted with the way this reality is interpreted from the perspectives of history and political science.

When the legal definition of statehood is applied to the four cases mentioned above it may well be concluded that they would all qualify as *de facto* states, with the exception of Chechnya after the marginalization of the Maskhadov government in the 1999 war with Russia. But this kind of qualification is in itself quite inadequate for informing us about the need to recognize such a *de facto* state as a state. The People's Republic of China refuses to establish 'state-to-state' relations with Taiwan, despite its factual statehood, and Georgia has a similar attitude towards Abkhazia. For the international community the act of recognition is a political deed, where the acknowledgement of factual statehood is only one criterion among others. This question is not strictly governed by law but remains largely an issue of policy.[16] Nor is the concept of a *de facto* state a sufficient guide for responding to the many questions raised in a normative theory of secession. It has to be combined with other theories, which make it possible to raise questions about issues such as domestic legitimacy and the capacity to deliver public goods. Such approaches can be found in political science.

The concept of a 'failed state' is particularly important in this context. Failed states share a number of characteristics. According to Robert I. Rotberg, they are 'deeply conflicted, and bitterly contested by warring factions'.[17] The loss of authority over large tracts of territory and the transfer of allegiance by the local population to warlords explain the enduring character of internal violence. Such states are unable to deliver public goods such as education, health services, economic infrastructure and a legal framework. Their executive structures may be functioning, but their legislatures and judicial systems are weakly developed, if they exist at all. Rotberg describes the economic opportunities provided by such states as favouring only a small élite. Other indicators include massive corruption.

A state's failure may be judged by the degree to which it fulfils these various criteria, on a continuum ranging from weak states to total collapse, a point characterized by a total vacuum of authority. Among the states that may be regarded as *de facto* states, a differentiation then has to be made between those that have consolidated and the others, which have more or

---

[16] See Roland Rich, 'Recognition of States: The Collapse of Yugoslavia and the Soviet Union', in *European Journal of International Law*, 4:1 (1993), 36–65; on the internet on http://www.ejil.org/journal/Vol4/No1/art4.html

[17] Robert I. Rotberg, 'The New Nature of Nation-State Failure', *The Washington Quarterly*, 25:3 (Autumn 2002), 85. On the following, see 85–96.

less failed to establish their statehood. For all the cases mentioned in the book, a precise investigation is needed in order to determine their degree of statehood.

When using the concept of a *de facto* state, all four criteria mentioned above have to be examined one by one. In the case of Abkhazia the first criterion is not in doubt. The territory under its control is relatively well defined, with the exception of the Kodori Gorge. Agreements between the two warring parties are based on delimitations of the territories under their control. The second criterion is fulfilled to a lesser degree. The majority of the pre-war population has left Abkhazia. Some of the country's rural Georgian population return periodically to their farms to work on the land, but cannot do so on a permanent basis, owing to the lack of security and acceptable living conditions. The emigration flows among the various national communities that have remained in Abkhazia—including the Abkhazians themselves—make it difficult to estimate the present size of the population.[18] But the definition of a *de facto* state would still apply as regards the criterion of a permanent population. Where the third and the fourth criteria are concerned, the *de facto* existence of the Abkhaz authorities is acknowledged by the international community, and the agreements between Abkhaz and Georgian authorities are based on the assumption that the Abkhaz side has the effective authority to implement them.

If we then complement such an analysis with the criteria mentioned for establishing the degree of state failure, the legitimate authority of the Abkhaz authorities to proclaim unilateral independence may be questioned. As in many other breakaway states, the large number of inhabitants who have been prevented by war and state policy from returning to their homes makes it difficult to speak of a permanent population. Such a common-sense perspective contrasts with doctrine in international law, which lays down only minimal standards for this criterion of statehood. The Abkhaz authorities have established a measure of administration, but the provision of public services does not meet minimal needs. Georgian guerrillas have been operating on large areas of Abkhaz territory. The country is greatly (although not entirely) dependent on the Russian Federation in its military, social, and economic policies. A large part of the remaining population in Abkhazia has acquired Russian citizenship and Russian passports. The collapse of the economy, the scale of economic inequality and the degree of corruption are other indicators of the extent of Abkhazia's failure. But the

[18] According to a UN report, in 1998 the population of Abkhazia was between 180,000 and 220,000, as compared to 525,000 in 1989. United Nations Development Programme (UNDP), *United Nations Needs Assessment Mission to Abkhazia*, Georgia, March 1998, on the internet on http://www.abkhazia.org/pindex.html

government still manages to uphold a minimum of state order, which differentiates it from Chechnya.

If we analyse the four secessionist states mentioned above in terms of the degree to which they meet these four criteria, Taiwan would rank first, followed by the Turkish Republic of Northern Cyprus and Abkhazia, while Chechnya would definitely be considered the most wanting. Chechnya's failure to establish statehood or to achieve domestic and international legitimacy through the implementation of democratic institutions and the rule of law was followed by its eventual collapse. This collapse included loss of control over population and territory, as a result of its military defeat at the hands of the Russian forces.

In an analysis of legitimate authority, historical traditions of statehood also play a role. As a result of Soviet policies, the Autonomous Republic of Abkhazia was a constitutionally recognized political unit; the titular nation at its core, however, sought not only to dominate that unit but also to reconquer history. Abkhaz historians have referred to twelve centuries of statehood. Such an outlook strengthens national pride and reinforces the right to proclaim sovereignty. Historical traditions of statehood and experience in government are used not only by breakaway states but also by secessionist movements in federated states that are striving for independence. Montenegrin nationalists assert that their state acquired internationally recognized statehood as early as the Berlin Congress of 1878, and that the creation of Yugoslavia did not abolish this statehood.[19] Tatar statehood goes back to the Golden Horde and the Kazan Khanate. It was interrupted by the Tatars' incorporation into the Russian Empire but restored with the Soviet creation of an autonomous republic. In this particular case, such traditions strengthen the argument in favour of domestic sovereignty. In Quebec and Taiwan, advocates of independence see the exercise of governmental power as strengthening the claims for international sovereignty. From this perspective, shared and *de facto* sovereignty are seen as paving the way for full sovereignty.

Positive experiences in governance and statehood must not be neglected in an analysis of the legitimate authority of a state or an independence movement, as the counter-example of Chechnya demonstrates. Before the creation of the Soviet Union, it had never acquired traditions of statehood or centralized self-government. After it was made an Autonomous Republic under Soviet rule, its new élites were severely repressed by Stalin's regime. When World War II started, it had already lost its educated officials and intellectuals. After their genocidal deportation to Central Asia in February 1944, the Chechens were rehabilitated under Khrushchev, but the leadership

---

[19] Mijat Sukovic, 'Independence of the Montenegro State—an Efficient Option for the Future', paper presented at the conference 'The Future of Montenegro', Centre for European Policy Studies, Brussels, 26 Feb. 2001.

of the republic was largely Chechenized only in the very last years of Soviet power. This tragic history goes a good way towards explaining why the attempt to create an independent state was doomed to failure.

A further aspect to be taken into account in applying the principle of legitimate authority is the presence of a sizeable self-defined community that supports secession. This condition means that the way in which secessionist states and movements address the problem of ethnic differentiation has to be investigated. The distinction between 'civic' and 'ethnic' policies of nationhood is important in this context. When this normative distinction is used for a moral assessment, it is generally accepted that civic policies may increase the legitimacy of states and movements to represent the values and interests of the whole population of the seceding territory. When this distinction is used for a descriptive analysis, however, it should not be done unequivocally in terms of either/or. A differentiated analysis of particular movements may, for instance, lead to the conclusion that one type of policy or another tends to predominate at different times in secessionist movements or leaderships. Ronald Rudin has examined this thesis in the light of the discourses of the Parti Québécois leaders.

An exclusivist view is abundantly clear in the xenophobic policies of the Lega Nord, which has tried to create a match between people and polity in Northern Italy by referring to an aggregate of regional identities. Here, identity is defined in territorial terms (the North) and united by a common Celtic ancestry. The 'European' origins of the Celts and their historic settlement in northern Italy allow southern Italians and non-European immigrants to be excluded. The fear of the minorization of its own community in the event of a massive return to Abkhazia of the Georgian refugee population has led the state's leadership to stress the exclusive character of the right to self-determination of the Abkhaz 'titular nation'. But the need to gather minimal political support among the other non-Georgian nationalities (e.g., Armenians and Russians) has also made it necessary to develop an inclusive discourse on popular sovereignty. The Tatar leadership has favoured 'parity nationalism' for 'the multinational people of Tatarstan'. Some Tatar nationalist leaders, however—not being free from xenophobia or anti-Semitism—reject mixed marriages. In Taiwan, the independence movement has popularized the notion of 'new Taiwanese', to overcome the ethnic fault lines between 'Taiwanese' and 'mainlanders'. But political debates on these fault lines between those who mostly originated from mainland China generations ago and those who took refuge on the island after World War II re-emerges periodically, as during the campaign for the parliamentary and local elections of December 2001.[20] This shows that

[20] See *Financial Times*, 25 Oct. 2001.

Taiwanese society does not constitute a clearly self-defined community, but that its ethnic composition and political regime are primarily a historical result of the Chinese civil war.

In the former Soviet Union, the federalization of the state through the setting up of union and autonomous republics and autonomous regions gave 'titular nations' the right to varying degrees of self-determination. Although this system did not allow for a fair distribution of political privileges among the various nationalities, it indicated quite clearly which nationality could claim such privileges. In the Soviet constitutional tradition, the sovereignty of federated states (the so-called 'Union Republics') included a formal right to secession. Already in the Soviet period, the leaderships of the 'titular nations' of Tatarstan, Chechnya, and Abkhazia were clamouring for the status of their autonomous republics to be upgraded to sovereign statehood. In the former Yugoslavia a different constitutional arrangement—acknowledging the right to secession of nations but not nationalities or states—led to complex questions in any attempt to define who had the right to exercise self-determination: Serbia or Serbs? Just Serbs in Serbia, or also Serbs in Croatia and Bosnia? Croatia or Croats? Just Croats in Croatia, or also Croats in Bosnia? Kosovo Albanians or Kosovo Serbs? These questions are immediately linked to the ethnic/civic distinction and to the question of sovereignty: who are the people? Who has legitimacy to rule? Once the authority of the Communist Party had waned, neither of the two federal constitutions managed to solve conflicts between the various levels of power or to determine with sufficient precision who had the legitimate authority to declare sovereignty or independence.

All the cases in this volume describe conflicts between people living, intermingled, on the same territory, who are unable either to devise strategies for sharing power or to agree on procedures for secession. The answer to the question of what gives a breakaway state or secessionist movement legitimate authority to declare independence lies in the area of democratic legitimacy, procedural accountability, and individual rights. These criteria were used by the international community when it was confronted with the dissolution of the Yugoslav federation. The Chechen case for independence was vitiated by the violent revolutionary manner in which power was seized in 1991, and then retained through harsh repression against those opposing Dudayev. A gradual approach, respectful of the principles of democratic legitimacy, procedural accountability and individual rights, was adopted by the secessionist movement in Quebec. This could prove to be of crucial importance if ever Quebec unilaterally declares its independence after a referendum victory by the pro-sovereignty vote and a failure of negotiations on Quebec's exit from the Canadian federation. It would then be easier for the Quebec government to claim that, in declaring independence, it has legitimate authority to represent the sovereign will of the people of Quebec.

In none of the cases of unilateral attempts at secession depicted in this volume has there been a clear majority in support of it among the population of the seceding territory, with the sole exception of Kosovo (and those states in the former Republic of Yugoslavia whose independence has been recognized by the international community). This means that the international practice of recognition is broadly in line with this particular criterion of a legitimate authority. No referendum on independence has ever taken place in Chechnya and, according to opinion polls, only a minority would support secession in Corsica, northern Italy or Taiwan. Tatarstan is a special case: in the 1992 referendum a majority of the electorate of the entire republic, local Russians included, voted in favour of sovereignty. In the particular political context of that time, however, this did not mean independence. In October 1999 a referendum was held to ascertain the attitude of the Abkhaz population to its constitution, which was supported by an overwhelming majority of votes. The Abkhaz authorities then declared the state's independence. This referendum was held in the absence of a large section of the pre-war population. Between 26 and 30 September 1991 a referendum was conducted in Kosovo on sovereignty and independence, and although not recognized by the Yugoslav authorities as legally valid the vast majority of the population of the region expressed a wish for Kosovo to become sovereign and independent. Kosovo is thus—significantly—the only case in this book where this particular criterion—a clear majority in a referendum on independence—applies, but where independence has not been recognized by the international community. It is also the case in which the just cause criterion is most applicable. But this does not mean that the Kosovar authorities have had, or have now, the legitimate authority to declare independence unilaterally: Kosovar state structures are still defective in the areas of democratic legitimacy, procedural accountability and minority rights, particularly with regard to the mass expulsion of the non-Albanian population in the wake of NATO's intervention in 1999.

The organization of a referendum in a seceding territory is not necessarily acknowledged as a legitimate means of measuring the degree of popular support for independence. It may find no acceptance at all in the international community when the results of a referendum have been predetermined by a policy of ethnic cleansing. But even when it is respectful of the individual rights of all the inhabitants of a territory, a referendum remains problematic. It is based on the assumption that one section of the population of a state may, as a well-defined community, express a particular point of view concerning the future of that state. A referendum may even be construed as the expression of an inherent right to unilateral secession. For this reason, it has been argued that the question of sovereignty or independence for a seceding unit should be put not only to the population in the seceding territory, but also to that of the state as a whole. A referendum also ceases to be the expression of an inherent right to unilateral secession when it is seen as part of a complex legal procedure which will eventually involve political negotiations between the seceding entity and the institutions of the central state.

Opinions on this issue vary, depending on the historical context in which the debate is taking place. The Taiwan Independence Movement argues that a referendum on the future of Taiwan should be organized on the island. This would be totally unacceptable to the People's Republic of China. The international community considered the holding of such a referendum in Abkhazia in 1999 to be illegitimate, as it had been organized without the consent of the Georgian government and without the participation of the large number of refugees. In Corsica, some autonomists argue that there should be a referendum on the status of the island involving the participation of all French citizens of Corsican descent. Where northern Italy is concerned, the absence of an unequivocal definition of 'Padania' is certainly a major impediment to organizing such a referendum. In the case of Northern Ireland, the Good Friday Agreement provides for the possibility of a reunification of the island, if the population of the region should express a wish for this. Insofar as procedures on this issue have been mutually agreed, the secession of Northern Ireland from the United Kingdom ceases to be a case of unilateral secession.

But there are two hypothetical cases in which a unilateral declaration of independence would accord with the principle of legitimate authority. The first is that of Quebec, where the supreme court has ruled that the Canadian and Quebec governments must negotiate on sovereignty if a clear majority of the population gives its support to such a cause. If the Quebec government were to apply these legal prescriptions in good faith and garner the support of a majority of the electorate, without subsequently reaching a political agreement with the Canadian government on the conditions of secession, it would have legitimate authority to declare unilateral independence. This does not necessarily mean, however, that it would have respected the principles of just cause, right intentions, likelihood of success, proportionality, or last resort. Issues such as the intransigence of one of the parties would also have to be examined. Under these circumstances, the international community would be confronted with the difficult question of whether, and under what conditions, to recognize Quebec as a newly independent state.

The second case is that of Montenegro, where the option of either unilateral or mutually agreed secession is possible. According to an agreement between Serbia and Montenegro, mediated by the European Union in March 2002, they are to restructure their relations within a 'state union' in which, on the expiry of a three-year period, both members will have the right 'to institute proceedings for a change in the status of the state, that is, withdrawal from the state union'.[21] The agreement provides for a referendum in both member states and for succession proceedings. Increased powers for Serbia under the new agreement and falling expectations concerning the viability of this union also open up the possibility that a majority in both federated entities would support independence.

The Introduction to this volume argued in favour of the need for a broad definition of secessionist processes, one that includes state reforms such as federalization or other steps taken to deal with secessionist crises. The term 'secessionist process' is justified to the extent that it is impossible to predict the final outcome of democratic state reform in the circumstances of a severe ethnic conflict. Such an approach is fully adequate for the cases addressed in this volume. The political consequences for nationality conflicts of the functioning of the Canadian federal institutions may only become apparent in the long run. Confronted with the impossibility of predicting the long-term consequences of arrangements such as the 1998 agreement on Northern Ireland or the 2002 agreement on Serbia and Montenegro, it is necessary to develop a long-term time frame that encompasses different stages in a process that may lead to secession.

LIKELIHOOD OF SUCCESS

In just war theory, the analysis of a decision to use force in terms of the principle of legitimate authority is far removed from its analysis in terms of the principle of the likelihood of success. The question of whether injustices can be remedied or prevented through the use of military means is indeed very different from the question of the extent to which those who take such a decision have legitimate authority to do so. Both principles take on a different meaning in the context of the ethics of secession, where they are closely linked. The concept of a legitimate authority has been reinterpreted above. The likelihood of success principle means, in this context, that a unilateral declaration of independence can be made only if it has a reasonable chance of being recognized by the international community. This principle is a prudential one. It says that no authority has the right to engage the population it claims to represent in a desperate cause. Regardless of all other ethical considerations, a population should not be expected to bear the heavy costs of an attempt to achieve unilateral secession unless it has a reasonable chance of being reintegrated into international society.

---

[21] 'Proceedings Points for the Restructuring of Relations between Serbia and Montenegro (Belgrade, 14 March 2002)', on the internet on http://www.yuembusa.org/agreement.htm (15 August 2002). See also International Crisis Group, 'Still Buying Time: Montenegro, Serbia and the European Union', 7 May 2002, on the internet on http://www.crisisweb.org/projects/showreport.cfm?reportid=638

An application of this principle to Chechnya and Abkhazia would indicate that their declarations of independence were illegitimate. Exceptional cases are the unilateral declarations of secession by Slovenia and Croatia. These two successful unilateral attempts—the first since the secession of Bangladesh from Pakistan in 1971—are due to particular circumstances that are not to be found in any other case described in this volume. The likelihood of success principle appears to constrain the actions of at least some secessionist movements. The Montenegrin government's acknowledgement of this principle led it to accept the proposal for a Union State with Serbia arising out of EU mediation in March 2002. The Parti Québécois holds the view that in principle Quebec has the right to unilateral secession, but few believe it would exercise that right in present circumstances. Since his victory in the Taiwan presidential elections of 2000, Chen Shui-pian of the pro-independence DPP has adopted a far more moderate stance on the right to secession than the one set out in his party's charter. A unilateral declaration of independence, or even the holding of a referendum on this issue, would indeed entail formidable risks to the security and economy of Taiwan, and such risks are unacceptable to the vast majority of the population. In political debates in Taiwan on the establishment of special 'state-to-state' relations across the Taiwan Strait, arguments based on the likelihood of success principle figure prominently. A large section of the political establishment feels that such a view of the status of Taiwan is unlikely ever to be acceptable to Beijing.

PROPORTIONALITY

The principle of proportionality is likewise a prudential moral principle that is central to normative discussions on both war and secession.[22] War and secession have high moral costs, which have to be weighed against the benefits of remedying or preventing injustices. This calculation cannot be made exclusively from the perspective of one's own nation. An ethical approach to war and secession would, on the contrary, also include the resulting damage and benefits to the international community, including the enemy nation and/or the nation one wishes to secede from. In the case of secession, it is indeed legitimate to ask how far Chechnya, Abkhazia, or Quebec bear responsibility for the fate of the country of which they have been a part.

Just war theory has dealt extensively with the difficulty of knowing when the costs of war outweigh its benefits. The principle is relatively easy to use in cases where a clear disproportionality exists between the merits and demerits of the use of force, and it is also applicable in borderline cases where

---

[22] Viva Ona Bartkus devotes a substantial part of her analysis to the costs and benefits of membership of a community. Viva Ona Bartkus, *The Dynamics of Secession* (Cambridge, Cambridge University Press, 1999).

the probable outcome is uncertain. As a prudential principle, it says that the nature of war makes it generally difficult to assess all its moral consequences, particularly in the long term. It is precisely because of this difficulty that decision-makers are obliged to exercise moral restraint. This argument is also valid for decisions concerning secession.

There is an important difference between applying the proportionality principle in the ethics of war and the ethics of secession. Wars are waged for a limited period. Sovereignty, on the other hand, is not limited in duration. For this reason, the consequences have to be measured differently. From the perspective of the international community, there is a fear that the institution of sovereignty as the cornerstone of international order may be devalued through a multiplication of sovereign states. Secessionist crises may also threaten international peace and security in other ways. Regarding the status of Taiwan, considerations to do with regional instability following breakaway would dictate respect for the 'One China' principle. But particular security considerations may also lead the international community to recognize unilateral declarations of independence outside the non-colonial context: for example, acknowledgement of the sovereign status of a secessionist party may facilitate international intervention in an escalating conflict. In January 1992, such an assessment led to the recognition by the European Community of the unilateral proclamations of independence by Slovenia and Croatia.[23] In 1999, international diplomacy debated whether recognition of the independence of Kosovo would make increased international involvement possible. But the prevailing opinion was that the recognition of Kosovo as an independent state would have a severely destabilizing effect on Bosnia and Herzegovina, and on Macedonia. The particular conditions in each individual situation have to be assessed on a case-by-case basis.

Concerning the costs and benefits for the seceding nation and the rump state, some general considerations also need to be taken into account. In international politics, one of the main issues when it comes to secession is minority rights. Movements striving to overcome their minority status by achieving state sovereignty invoke the principle of national self-determination, while refusals to acknowledge their claims are based on the argument that redrawing international boundaries means creating new conflicts with new national minorities. Such debates on minority rights and the right to national self-determination are prominent in violent conflicts (for instance in the wars of secession in Croatia, Bosnia-Herzegovina, Abkhazia and Chechnya) and in peaceful areas (such as Quebec and Tatarstan) that are striving for sovereign status.

---

[23] International support for a two-state solution to resolve the Israeli–Palestinian conflict emerges out of a very particular set of circumstances.

Just cause theories shift the emphasis from an absolute right to national self-determination to relative legal amelioration and the means used to achieve remedies. They are firmly located within the evolving international practices of universalism and the increasing number of conventions dealing with human rights principles. In keeping with this, procedural aspects come to the fore: a right to secede can be conceded only if the new human rights position of the seceding community will be a clear improvement over the status quo.[24] Deliverance from one set of unpleasant rulers to another, even if they are now 'your own', hardly constitutes much of an improvement. The relevance of this to the Chechen case hardly needs to pointed out. Putin's defence of renewed intervention in Chechnya in 1999 broadened the argument by insisting that secession should be opposed in order to protect peace and the rights of individuals not so much in Chechnya as in Russia as a whole. But there were also deep fears among the Russian public that the resumption of the war would, on the contrary, come to threaten the democratization project in Russia itself.

Less prominent but no less crucial in debates on secession is the argument made by Buchanan, based on Hirschmann's *Exit, Voice and Loyalty*, that a relatively easy right to secession (exit) reduces loyalty to existing democratic institutions and undermines their ability to reform. In the Russian case, these institutions were only *in statu nascendi* in 1991, and in claiming the right to exit the Chechens were threatening to break the state structure within which democracy could grow. The same argument could be made against the independence of Kosovo and Montenegro after Yugoslav President Slobodan Milosevic was overthrown in October 2000.

LAST RESORT

In just war theory, the principle of last resort is one of the most important. In the context of the ethics of war it means that, before the use of force can be justified, all means to remedy or prevent a severe injustice have to be exhausted. In the context of an ethics of secession, a unilateral declaration of secession may only be justified where remedying or preventing severe injustices by any other means seems impossible. Most contributions to this volume have explored such alternatives in depth.

Comparing the choices open to the Tatar and Chechen leaderships may clarify the issues at stake in applying the normative principle of a last resort. Under the leadership of Mintimer Shaimiev, Tatarstan obtained considerable economic and political powers from Moscow. At the heart of the

---

[24] This issue is explored by Wayne Norman, 'The Ethics of Secession as the Regulation of Secessionist Politics', in Moore, *National Self-Determination and Secession*, 34–61.

Tatarstan model—so argues Alexei Zverev—was the attempt to increase 'the republic's constitutional prerogatives inside Russia' through negotiations; the 'model' thus denotes the peaceful resolution of issues relating to the republic's status.[25] The circle was squared in the case of Tatarstan by the development of a particular type of domestic sovereignty. Could such a solution have made it possible to square the Chechen circle? Tatarstan and Chechnya's membership of the Russian Federation is involuntary, but in 1991 the opportunity existed to restructure that relationship in legal form. In the context of Russia's asymmetrical domestic federalism, there was considerable scope at the time for institutional innovation. In a federation, sovereignty is an attribute of both federal government and regional units. Federalism, it must be stressed, is all about shared sovereignty in the internal affairs of a state, with at least two levels of government sharing supremacy within a given territory. Russia as we know is a multinational state, but to a degree under Yeltsin it had become a multi-state state.[26] Although the first war in Chechnya (1994–6) had been a struggle between competing sovereignty claims, one side made absolute demands while Russia, under Yeltsin, was willing to accept flexible definitions of sovereignty—as long as the country's territorial integrity was not explicitly challenged.

The very different historical contexts of Tatar and Chechen political attitudes should be stressed. In the previous section, on legitimate authority, we mentioned the relevance of traditions of statehood. We must also take into account the weight of past injustices. Tatar and Chechen attitudes are derived from different interpretations of history but also from the different types of oppression they have experienced in the past, and in particular the scale of this oppression. In 1944, the Soviet authorities responded to the alleged threat posed by Chechen resistance to Moscow rule by deporting the entire population of Chechnya to Central Asia (other small nations of the Northern Caucasus were also deported at that time). There was continuity between the harsh repression endured under the Tsarist and Soviet regimes, and the deportation could be construed as one of several dramatic events in the long history of Russian domination over Chechnya. Stalinist terror in Tatarstan was extremely harsh, but it did not lead to a genocidal deportation as in the case of Chechnya. There are also other differences between the two forms of repression. As described by Zverev in this volume, unlike in Chechnya, the Stalinist terror that Tatarstan endured in the Soviet

---

[25] Alexei Zverev, 'Qualified Sovereignty: The Tatarstan Model for Resolving Conflicting Loyalties', in Michael Waller, Bruno Coppieters, and Alexei Malashenko (eds.), *Conflicting Loyalties and the State in Post-Soviet Eurasia* (London, Frank Cass, 1998), 119.
[26] See Richard Sakwa, 'The Republicanization of Russia: Federalism and Democratization in Transition', in Chris Pierson and Simon Tormey (eds.), *Politics at the Edge: The PSA Yearbook 1999* (London, Macmillan in association with the Political Studies Association, 2000), 215–26.

era had no counterpart in the Tsarist era, and in addition there were many Tatars among the early Bolsheviks and in the Stalinist *nomenklatura* and secret services. For the Tatars, de-Stalinization and democratization—and not secession—were readily perceived as a reasonable alternative. But the Chechen leadership was not forced to take a unilateral decision on independence, even though the massive scale of the oppression of their nation made it difficult to perceive past oppression as calling for anything less than full sovereignty. There was widespread opposition in Chechnya itself to the Dudayev regime, in favour of a federal arrangement with the Russian authorities. The cause of Chechen independence gained increased popularity thanks to the fateful and ill-conceived military intervention by Russian troops in 1994, but the subsequent failure of the Maskhadov regime to re-establish statehood after 1996 strengthened the position of those forces in Chechnya who did not believe in the option of full independence.

It is generally acknowledged that civic policies of state- and nation-building, forging states into a multinational polity, increase the legitimate authority of secessionist movements and states to declare independence. But in some cases civic policies may also be unable to respond to a possible secessionist challenge. The Soviet and Yugoslav policies of state building had a clear civic dimension, and the same is true of the British case as it is described in this book. In all three cases, civic policies failed to integrate claims for national self-determination. Civic policies may even favour secessionism. The French constitutional principles, rooted in civic (if not Jacobin) republicanism, prescribed the creation of a homogeneous legal space throughout the country, territorial integrity and universal citizenship. In Corsica, for years these principles impeded even moderate forms of self-government, which could have facilitated a mutual agreement on autonomy. In the Soviet Union, Yugoslavia, the United Kingdom, and France, the central government has accused nationalist forces of basing their conception on an exclusive, non-civic view of a national community. Such accusations were not helpful in the search for alternatives to secession.

The history of Irish–British relations, as described in this volume by Richard Kearney, clarifies the origin of exclusive identities. In a long process of 'mirror-imaging', British and Irish forms of self-identification have been differentiating themselves from one another. In a desperate struggle, both parties have tried to retain a sense of pure, uncontaminated identity. But this process did not stop the emergence of dual identities in Northern Ireland. British–Irish relations are not alone in featuring an ambiguous insider–outsider relationship: Tatar–Russian relations can be described in a similar way, as demonstrated by Alexei Zverev in this book. In this case too, dual national identities have been strengthened. In theory, such multiple identities may underpin federal or other institutions permitting the sharing of sovereignty. In the cases of Cyprus, Kosovo, and Abkhazia, however, there has been little room for nested identities. There appears to be no direct relationship between such processes of national self-differentiation and the degree of violence that marks secessionist conflicts. Identity-building is also only partly a direct result of conscious political design by a central government. In Yugoslavia and the Soviet Union, for instance, dual identities developed more strongly among some nationalities than others.

In Italy, the Lega's identity-building is largely centred around the North–South question, which not only weakens national solidarity but also reduces possibilities for reform. According to Huysseune, alternatives to the secession of northern Italy can only be effective when the grievances voiced by the secessionist Lega Nord, such as the inefficiency of the Italian state and the high degree of corruption, are taken seriously. But addressing these problems without questioning the interpretative framework provided by the Lega Nord, which is based on a reified juxtaposition of Northern and Southern identities, entails the risk of discrimination against the South, which would further undermine national unity.

The time perspective is crucial in a decision to recognize unilateral forms of independence, as already demonstrated in the context of the proportionality principle. According to just war theory, the use of force may be justified if the postponement of such a decision would disproportionately magnify a manifest injustice. On the basis of such an interpretation of the last resort principle, it is necessary to postpone a declaration and recognition of independence to the maximum extent possible. As explained above, for the international community the recognition of a state's sovereignty represents a point of no return. Moreover, the range of alternatives to secession is relatively wide. At the internal level, these alternatives include federal and other institutional arrangements providing for minority rights and the realization of the right to national self-determination. At the international level, they include international guarantees for an internal constitutional arrangement up to the creation of a provisional international protectorate.

State- and nation-building are not the affair of a single generation. From such a historical perspective, options short of independence are in principle open to any nation confronted with unjust rule. The Irish republican case for the independence of a unified Ireland has been strengthened by the long-term failure of the United Kingdom to reform until the late 1990s, despite the controversies on necessary concessions that have racked British politics since the late nineteenth century.[27] With the onset of devolution for Scotland,

---

[27] See Vernon Bogdanor, *Devolution in the United Kingdom* (Oxford, Oxford University Press, 1999).

Wales, and Northern Ireland, even such an archetypally centralized and unitary state as the United Kingdom can now be called quasi-federal.

Secessionist leaderships can postpone a declaration of independence or take steps short of secession. It is possible, for instance, to have a unilateral declaration of sovereignty without necessarily having a declaration of independence: the Tatar parliament declared its sovereignty in August 1990 and reaffirmed it in 1991,[28] without ever declaring independence. Even where there are severe forms of injustice, negotiations generally remain possible. In the case of Cyprus, the invasion by Turkish military forces and the partition of the island appeared to be a last resort solution when the government in Cyprus fell victim to a military coup in July 1974. Shortly afterwards, with the ensuing collapse of the Greek military regime, the option of partition and secession was shown not to have been the 'last resort' after all. In the case of Abkhazia, the authorities had already declared the sovereignty of their Autonomous Republic before the 1992–3 war, but were still prepared to negotiate a confederal arrangement with Georgia after the Georgian military intervention. The Abkhaz leadership only took the decision to declare independence in 1999. In the case of Kosovo, international guarantees on self-government and on the security of the Albanian Kosovars have been provided since NATO's military intervention in 1999. There was no lack of alternatives in any of the situations described in this book. Even in the case of the Yugoslav federation, when it became clear at the beginning of the 1990s that all possibilities of reform had been exhausted, confederal alternatives to secession could have been found. At the time, talks on this issue did not achieve any compromise solution, although a confederation may well have promoted the gradual emergence of mutually acceptable rules for coexistence and regional integration or—at worst—for separation. But even this latter option is an alternative preferable to any unilateral form of secession. Seen from this perspective, the mediation efforts by the European Union to enable Serbia and Montenegro to create a loose federation is to be seen as a valid choice.

A discussion on federal alternatives to secession has to take into account the fact that it is far easier to design political institutions based on the principle of shared sovereignty in the field of domestic policy than in foreign policy. Regionalism likewise permits a certain division of competencies in the domestic field. Where the foreign affairs of a federation are concerned, we have to bear in mind that the institution of sovereignty severely restricts the possibility of overcoming relations of subordination between federal government and federated states. The external aspect of sovereignty is less amenable to a division of power than the internal. There are even stronger links of subordination between levels of government in the foreign relations

[28] See Zverev, 'Qualified Sovereignty', 124–5.

of regions, which generally do not have constitutional powers in this respect. The exclusion of non-sovereign entities from international security organizations also makes it difficult to design international security guarantees of the autonomous status of regions and federated states. But multilevel bargaining, as made possible by the European Union, has increased the ability of federated states, and even regions, to overcome unilateral forms of dependence on the federal or central government, particularly at the informal level. The chapters in this volume on Northern Ireland and Cyprus demonstrate that multilevel governance in a European framework may be seen as a credible alternative to classic remedies for secessionist crises, where federal or consociational agreements are backed up by international security guarantees.

The case of Cyprus also demonstrates that the question of how to apply the last resort solution may be answered differently depending on the time perspective chosen. According to Alan Buchanan, the religious and cultural differences between two nationalities may be so profound that all attempts to reintegrate them in a single state are bound to fail. This may be because 'it is simply not possible for them to cooperate in the practices of deliberative democracy'. If this happens, it may make sense to 'redraw political boundaries to reflect the fact that there are two political communities, not one'.[29] In her chapter on Cyprus, Nathalie Tocci states that the differences between the Greek and Turkish communities created by the partition of the island over several decades have now reached a stage where it has become impossible to imagine classic federal solutions working. But European integration may provide new background conditions which will allow for joint decision-making in a democratic federation.

The particular consequences of European integration for intra-state relations have to be assessed on a case-by-case basis. The case of Cyprus also indicates that European Union policies may lead to increased difficulty in solving particular secessionist conflicts: the prospect of the Republic of Cyprus acceding to the European Union significantly increased the bargaining power of the Greek Cypriot community in discussions about the possibility of a bicommunal federal state for Cyprus, something that has not encouraged the communities to make feasible compromises.[30] The European Union's reluctance to offer Turkey a starting date for talks on accession to the European Union was another factor determining the attitude of the Turkish Cypriot side in 2002.

---

[29] Buchanan, 'Democracy and Secession', in Moore, *National Self-Determination and Secession*, 23.

[30] See also Tozun Bahcheli, 'The Lure of Economic Prosperity versus Ethno-Nationalism: Turkish Cypriots, the European Union Option, and the Resolution of Ethnic Conflict in Cyprus', in Michael Keating and John McGarry (eds.), *Minority Nationalism and the Changing International Order* (Oxford, Oxford University Press, 2001), 203–45.

OUTLOOK

One of the main conclusions to be drawn from this volume is that the application of the various *jus ad bellum* principles to cases of unilateral secession allows for a differentiated normative analysis. The choice of secession may be in accordance with some of the principles and not with others. At the end of the 1990s Kosovo had a just cause for secession in order to remedy severe injustices currently being inflicted, and to prevent future ones, but other principles, particularly those of proportionality and last resort, did not apply. The second main conclusion that may be drawn from this book is that in applying the last resort principle it has to be borne in mind that international recognition of independence is a political decision which cannot be undone. It therefore involves a time perspective that is different in principle from the one implied in a decision to use military force. War is legitimately waged where it paves the way for the restoration of a just peace. In secessionist crises, the last resort principle prescribes tireless efforts for alternatives to unilateral secession which—if political reform of the existing state is for some reason not a viable option—may even include a jointly agreed legal framework that makes the dissolution of the common state acceptable to both parties.

These conclusions have focused on the moral legitimacy of a political decision to secede unilaterally. The comparative analysis has also considered the moral legitimacy of possible responses to secessionist crises. A comprehensive normative theory of secession would require a new ethics of unionism: what are the normative bases for keeping a state intact? The question of the bonds—including moral bonds—that keep a multinational state together is greatly under-theorized in the literature, and is usually reduced to issues of *realpolitik* and economic functionality. The lack of understanding of these themes in the ethics of secession may have serious practical consequences. As mentioned by Alexei Zverev in his chapter on Tatarstan, the unravelling of the Soviet Union and the Yugoslav Federation came as a rude awakening to those who had heard innumerable professions of the friendship between peoples and believed in the potential of economic and political transformation to overcome ethnic strife in multinational states.

Ties of friendship and mutual need do keep states and peoples together, and any study of secession has to be balanced ultimately by an understanding of the factors that allow states to cohere or that inspire the creation of new political unions. Secession raises the question of when and how a community has the right to dissociate itself from another political entity, but also how to render unity appealing. The forces that sometimes drive states apart have been the focus of this book, and by providing a contextualized account of a number of cases we hope that this collaborative study has not only contributed to debates about state disintegration but has also provided a deeper understanding of the processes of state-building.

Index